ANIMATE ILLUSIONS

ANIMATE ILLUSIONS
Explorations of Narrative Structure

by
Harold Toliver

UNIVERSITY OF NEBRASKA PRESS • LINCOLN

Permissions for the use of copyrighted material are listed in the Acknowledgments section, starting on p. 403, which constitutes an extension of the copyright page.

Publishers on the Plains

UNP

The publication of this book was assisted by a grant from
The Andrew W. Mellon Foundation.

C O N T E N T S

PREFACE

If the theory of fictions has preoccupied us in the past few years, it is partly because, as inheritors of old disputes between the sciences and the arts, we have come more and more to realize the extent to which we create what we see. We would be lost without the "as if" constructions with which we anatomize reality and sometimes render it poetic or entertaining. Hence despite a continuing faith in facts and scholarly objectivity in some quarters, a good many modern historians, philosophers, and poets now assign to imagination what were once supposed to be more or less direct and truthful representations of reality. Drawing upon a "Central Bank of Symbolic Forms" (as Sol Yurick has recently labeled our cultural heritage), they concede real value only to organic systems or gestalts that perceivers create in putting together their compositions. Thus when we measure the impact of narrative forms on social and psychological phenomena and ponder the logical "sets" inherent in a narrative way of thought and expression, we realize that forms of expression are experience — and that new forms are new experience.

Under pressure from several directions, however, formalists are no longer at ease with so simple an equation: it is obvious that experience is also form, and that new experience is met by the creation of new forms that react to it. Or to put it less starkly, experience has its own patterns that artists respond to strategically and dialectically. Some of these may be formal predispositions of a Kantian kind, and others may derive from literary conventions; but many of them are not directly attributable to either our intellectual mechanisms or our verbal universes: they are closely tied to nature itself and to the dynamic processes of social interchange. They come from a marketplace where one person's verbal currency traffics constantly with another's in an always evolving historical process. Hence like other artists, the narrator works not with some absolute chaos that he is totally free to shape as his individual imagination suggests but with partly coordinated materials, any response to which is prodded by social realities extended to him by a given time and place. The work he ultimately hands to us is the product of an assembly line that begins in a culture and an economy, proceeds through his imagination, and ends in a perceiver. Both ends of that process are molded by such things as manners and natural settings in their historical dynamics.

Yet the formalists of some years ago were surely not entirely wrong to insist that the referential meanings and preshaped materials of art are nonetheless recast in each work and that in their routing through the imagination, they are shaped into a symbolic enactment that does not exist in nature, preverbal experience, or even those recurrent categories and modes of literature that Northrop Frye labels so well and finds so universal. In honoring both the incipient forms of reality and the artist's creation of relatively self-contained new worlds in words, paint, or musical notes, the critic in his turn must learn to read as sensitively as he can the ways in which form and experience constantly respond to one another. Neither is static or fixed: a way of saying creates a way of seeing; a vision creates a way of saying. Fine art and practice thus alter upon contact with each other. This is as true of the ways in which narrators take their withdrawals from the Peoples' Symbolic Bank as it is of any other art. As David Levin suggests in *In Defense of Historical Literature*, it is nearly as true of the art of historians as it is of the art of novelists. The concern of this book is the craft of that art and the experience it reflects and creates.

In the large tanglewood of narrative theory that such a concern plunges into, one would quickly be lost were it not for those who have erected signposts along the way. Among those who at one stage or another have treated more than peripherally the formal aspects of fictions are Paul Goodman in *The Structure of Literature*, Robert Kellogg and Robert Scholes in *The Nature of Narrative*, Frank Kermode in *The Sense of an Ending*, Erich Auerbach in *Mimesis*, and Edwin Muir in *The Structure of the Novel*. Philip Stevick's *The Chapter in Fiction* would have been of greater moment to me had it appeared sooner, as would the interdisciplinary journal *Clio*, the contributors to which have looked frequently into the matters I've taken in hand. Equally helpful critics have explored the social and psychological aspects of fictional theory, among them Georg Lukács, Ian Watt, Lucien Goldmann, and Raymond Williams. By doing their work well, they have enabled me to concentrate on the business of linear logic more exclusively than I could have otherwise. John Dewey's *Art as Experience* has also proved to be of timely use.

I am indebted to the Regents of the University of California for a Humanities Institute award that helped a summer's work to go more smoothly. Several undergraduate and graduate classes at Irvine have contributed their skepticism to the gradual shaping of the text over the past four or five years. Nor have I lacked stimulation from colleagues. These I'll not incriminate individually, but as they realize, proximity breeds awareness, and awareness brings qualifying clauses — not enough of them, perhaps, but more than would have sprung from an un-challenging workshop.

Harold Toliver

University of California, Irvine

I. LINEAR LOGIC

CHAPTER ONE

Consequential Narrative

The figure a poem makes. ... It assumes direction with the first line laid
down, it runs a course of lucky events, and ends in a clarification of life —
not necessarily a great clarification, such as sects and cults are founded on,
but a momentary stay against confusion. It has denouement. It has an outcome that though unforeseen was predestined from the first image of the
original mood.
> Robert Frost, "The Figure a Poem Makes"

It is posed and it is posed.
But in nature it merely grows.
> Wallace Stevens, "Add This to Rhetoric"

It is probably true that even in a period such as ours that values sensations and unconnected highs no one would wish the world any less co-
herently sequential and logical than it is. A liking for continuous plots is
unquenchable and leads us to invent them where we do not find them —
which is nearly everywhere. No doubt many of the conspiracies we find
in history, for instance, owe something to a love of secret connections
and the social groups that formed around them — even though, were the
truth known, the conspirators have only casual and accidental links.
"Well-systematized delusions" and the outcomes they promise seem
better than indefiniteness to any lover of enclosed and logical form; fiction and history alike capitalize on our entrancement with them — with
the "lowest and simplest of literary organisms," as E. M. Forster calls a
story. Suffice it to say, fondness for storied connection and outcome, not
reality itself, is responsible for many of our most intriguing moments —
and probably has been, as Forster suggests, since Neanderthal men first
gathered around campfires. The distinction between what really happens and what anecdotes say happens is lost in the exhilaration of our

pursuit of chronological events under the spell of narration. It is lost
partly because, considered structurally, historiography and fiction share
many of the same problems and raise many of the same questions; their
bonds hold in forms of fiction other than those dominated by what Mary
McCarthy calls the fetishism of fact[1] and for types of history writing
other than those embellished with narrative art. They are both purposeful in linear, anecdotal ways that derive from the same impulse that
makes an incident out of an encounter at the market.

I want to begin with some unabashedly broad and perhaps obvious
distinctions between fiction and history and between linear art and art
comparatively more susceptible to synchronic or static organization.
The somewhat finer and (I hope) more useful distinctions that will
follow in due course will depend upon some basic premises that had
best be explicit — that narrative form is a way of seeing, transforming,
and to some extent reexperiencing reality; that basic as it is, narrative is
quite extraordinary in its construction of integral worlds; that when we
back away from these worlds and think of them by contrast to the worlds
of the lyric or the essay or the picture show we can see how vulnerable we
are to the silent epistemological principles of our fictions. This vul-
nerability and the perspective we get on it by taking a panoramic view of
the narrative mode are justification for posing some basic questions: Do
fictional narratives such as myth and legend establish their beginnings,
consequential developments, and conclusions in different ways from
other arts, and from historiography and biography? What kinds of liberties do imagination and invention take in reconstituting the realities that
narratives pretend to offer? What is the relationship in different narrative kinds between general laws and particulars, types and individuals?

1. Mary McCarthy, "The Fact in Fiction," *Partisan Review* 27 (1960): 438–58. As
Thomas R. Preston points out in "Historiography as an Art in Eighteenth-Century
England," *Texas Studies in Language and Literature* 11 (1969): 1209–21, historiography
as early as the eighteenth century was defended both as a nonimaginative mode of writing
(dealing in part with records of exemplary conduct) and as an art. The function of facts in
fiction and of artful narrative in history writing began to be problematic when modes like
the documentary novel made a point of verisimilitude. See also Morton White, "The Logic
of Historical Narration," in *Philosophy and History: A Symposium*, ed. Sidney Hook
(New York: New York University Press, 1963), pp. 3–31, and the discussion of White's
position by Lee Benson, "On 'The Logic of Historical Narration,' " ibid., pp. 32–42; Ernest
van den Haag, "History as Factualized Fiction," ibid., pp. 212–26; Raziel Abelson, "Cause
and Reason in History," ibid., pp. 167–73; David Levin, *In Defense of Historical
Literature* (New York: Hill and Wang, 1967); Avrom Fleishman, *The English Historical
Novel: Walter Scott to Virginia Woolf* (Baltimore: Johns Hopkins Press, 1971), pp. 3–15.

How do various goal-oriented systems such as Christian and Marxist thought affect narrative development and denouement? What happens to the sequential logic of anecdotes when hidden strands emerge into visibility and join open or acknowledged plots? When gaps are left for inference and details are omitted in foreshortening and inexplicitness, how does a work "represent" what is absent? What is the place in anecdotal logic of Logia, essays, intruding authorial perspectives, scenic representation, and other "types of narrative situation" such as Franz Stanzel categorizes in *Die typischen Erzählsituationem im Roman*?[2]

In the distinction between factual and fictional narrative, to single it out for a moment, we discover that even provisional answers to such questions run into confusions that are not easily disentangled. Sometimes we can scarcely tell isolated segments of one from segments of the other. It is not beyond the fictionalist, as part of the game he plays with the reader, to insist that he is really a historian in disguise — that the conspiracies he has uncovered in society really exist — though to avoid libel he has had to change names and places. For many eighteenth-century novelists eager to distinguish themselves from romancers, the association between the novel and history seemed much stronger than the association between the novel and other kinds of imaginative literature. Even for Conrad the roles of fiction and history were almost interchangeable — except that writers of fiction are likely to be more accurate in some respects than those who find their materials largely in documents:

> Mr. Henry James claims for the novelist the standing of the historian as the only adequate one. . . . I think that the claim cannot be contested, and that the position is unassailable. Fiction is history, human history, or it is nothing. But it is also more than that; it stands on firmer ground, being based on the reality of forms and the observation of social phenomena, whereas history is based on documents and the reading of print and handwriting — on second-hand impression. Thus fiction is nearer truth. But let that pass. A historian may be an artist too, and a novelist is a historian, the preserver, the keeper, the expounder, of human experience.[3]

---

2. Franz Stanzel, *Narrative Situations in the Novel: Tom Jones, Moby-Dick, The Ambassadors, Ulysses,* trans. James P. Pusack (Bloomington: Indiana University Press, 1971).

3. Joseph Conrad, "Henry James: An Appreciation," in *Notes on Life and Letters* (London: J. M. Dent & Sons, 1905), p. 20. Cf. Leo Braudy, *Narrative Form in History and Fiction: Hume, Fielding and Gibbon* (Princeton: Princeton University Press, 1970). See also Philip Stevick, "Fielding and the Meaning of History," *PMLA* 79 (1964): 561-68;

That Conrad has a point and that the logic of fiction takes off frequently from what we assume to be a logic in history itself will be obvious to anyone who examines a solidly convincing documentary realism, or even a work that mixes fantasy and realism, like *Gulliver's Travels*. The motives of those who decide Gulliver's fate in Lilliput, for instance — once we accept the oddity of sizes and shapes — are entirely credible on historical grounds. They are versions of the same motives that govern normal societies. Gulliver could at times be describing a European court of the eighteenth century:

> In the mean time, the Emperor held frequent councils to debate what course should be taken with me; and I was afterwards assured by a particular friend, a person of great quality, who was as much in the secret as any, that the court was under many difficulties concerning me. They apprehended my breaking loose, that my diet would be very expensive, and might cause a famine. Sometimes they determined to starve me, or at least to shoot me in the face and hands with poisoned arrows, which would soon dispatch me: but again they considered, that the stench of so large a carcase might produce a plague in the metropolis, and probably spread through the whole kingdom. In the midst of these consultations, several officers of the army went to the door of the great council-chamber; and two of them being admitted, gave an account of my behaviour to the six criminals above-mentioned, which made so favourable an im-

---

Frank Kermode, "Novel, History and Type," *Novel* 1 (1968): 231–38; Russel B. Nye, "History and Literature: Branches of the Same Tree," in *Essays on History and Literature*, ed. Robert H. Bremner (Columbus: Ohio State University Press, 1966), pp. 123–59. Other critics who link narrative modes and forms across the fluid boundary that separates history and fiction include Northrop Frye in *Anatomy of Criticism* (Princeton: Princeton University Press, 1957), pp. 303–14, and Kenneth Burke in a number of places (to be discussed later). "Cultural studies" have frequently joined the two as aspects of total cultures, usually with a focal interest not in the works themselves but in regional and national institutions, as for instance both Faulkner and a regional historian might be said to mirror the same Mississippi culture. The interest of the critics listed above is by and large quite different from that. It lies in the transformative nature of individual works and kinds of works whose remaking of an assumed reality is sufficiently radical to justify a formalist look at narrative reconstruction itself. Cultural totalities are "rendered" in special ways by records — documents, architecture, music, fictions, movies, plays, histories, biographies.

By "consequential" I do not mean simply the opposite of "inconsequential," though insignificance accompanies a lack of connection. I mean primarily the successiveness of meaning from one phase of a plot or one event to another as it enlivens each in turn. Consequential narrative goes beyond the chronicle in linking events in plots so that one thing follows not merely *after* but *from* another. The distinction is basically the same as E. M. Forster's familiar distinction between "story" and "plot" in *Aspects of the Novel*.

pression in the breast of his Majesty and the whole board in my behalf, that an imperial commission was issued out, obliging all the villages nine hundred yards around the city to deliver in every morning six beeves, forty sheep, and other victuals for my sustenance; together with a proportionable quantity of bread, and wine, and other liquors.[4]

The consequences that the emperor and his counselors consider are moral and physical. They are embedded in the realities of society and nature and complicated by problematic entanglements, as such things normally are. And the information is presented to us as though it came not from an author who has invented it but from a narrator of rather limited intellectual means who has several concurrent threads to keep going (as "in the mean time" indicates). Reality is assumed to be going on in villages, armies, and nature on the periphery of his field of vision whether or not his words are at the moment actually summoning them to consciousness. (These external places continue to supply timely agents when the story requires them.) Though characters usually get what they deserve in fiction more often than in history and though the Lilliputians are fantastic in many respects, Gulliver thus keeps us entranced in his story as though it presented a tangible world of precise quantities, numbered objects, determinable shapes and places, real politics, and recognizable psychology, each of these heightened by the exaggeration.

Whereas fiction moves toward history in presenting an assumed historical reality, history writing moves toward fiction in its storied coherence and embellishments. It can do so without focusing on the bedchamber of Charles II or the exploits of Richard the Lion-Hearted. It can do so even with the dry material of cabinets and parliaments, because by comparison to normal events, historiography is obviously relatively organized and bounded and is subject to the always forming wholeness of a sequence of a certain kind. Its excitement lies not in the mistresses of kings or battles or attempted assassinations but in its progressive sense. Even when the "conclusions" of history writing are primarily logical or descriptive rather than anecdotal (as in the ending that Karl Marx imagines for the state), they are nonetheless arrived at by the dramatic movements of individuals and societies, or may be treated as though they were. The

4. Jonathan Swift, *Gulliver's Travels and Other Writings*, ed. Louis A. Landa (Boston: Houghton Mifflin, 1960), p. 26.

reader is set on the trail of an outcome word after word; and caught up in that chain, he looks ahead for a boundary, a termination, that will prevent his getting lost in unending twists and turns. His psychology is controlled, in other words, as it is controlled in fiction, by ever re-forming prospects and retrospects, by the rhythm of re-sisted and satisfied understanding, and by the segmentation of linear units — chapter and verse, event and episode. Hence a theory of linear form assumes that wherever the anecdotal method holds sway, the art of presentation remakes according to the rules of "con-spiracy" the apparent reality it conjures. If narrative "bristles with questions," as James remarks in *The Art of the Novel*, it bristles pre-cisely as a linear art.[5]

It bristles all the more for the special relationships it fosters be-tween the analytic, the documentary, the descriptive, the historical, the dramatic, the lyric, and the scenic or pictorial. We must pause a moment in seeking distinctions between the logic of historiography and the logic of fiction — long enough to notice that they both take remarkable liberties in bringing allies to the task of making stories be-lievable: because if narrative creates its own way of perceiving and experiencing for the reader, it does so not in some purity of anecdotal conventions but in conjunction with complex resources of language — with reflective, descriptive, logical, and other ancillary orders that partake of the synchronic. It adds abstraction, thematic statement, image clusters, paradigmatic patterns, and the device of foreshorten-ing to its basic chronicles. Lying is never more convincing than when it is buttressed by apt observation, philosophic aplomb, and circum-stantial evidence.

But the reader is as culpable in helping conspiracies fall together as the artist is in dressing them up so beautifully. Because narrative art consists largely in evoking a movement of intelligence through words and because the reader's movement backward and forward is a rationalized, reflective experience, a theory of narrative logic must pay special attention to the reader's contributions to the manifold "connections" all narratives presuppose. To use J. Hillis Miller's apt word, narratives are polyrhythmic:[6] they concern not merely the

5. Henry James, *The Art of the Novel* (New York: Charles Scribner's Sons, 1934), p. 3.
6. J. Hillis Miller, *The Form of Victorian Fiction* (Notre Dame: University of Notre Dame Press, 1968), p. 11.

movements of actions but the movements of readers through revelatory symbols, guided by authorial signposts and short cuts. In Gulliver's account of the Lilliputians, for instance, we are constantly pleased to share with Swift the job of forming judgments and reflecting satirically on men who refrain from murder only because extraordinarily large carcasses spread extraordinarily large smells. We gladly cooperate in joining his coterie of men-among-men, whose perceptiveness has so amusingly laid bare the secret levers of power. Thus our perspective overleaps merely sequential matters and forms judicious conclusions even when the final proof is still far in the offing. The end, in other words, is implicit in every detail along the way, and as quick detectives we rejoice in guessing it almost before Swift drops his clues. The whole bears constantly on its phases in this delightfully coherent world that flatters our intelligence; the real world by comparison makes us feel always a little obtuse in our incapacity to see where anything is truly headed. If the materials of a sustained narration flicker into interest and create a charmed lifelike movement, then, they do so only because the logic of an outcome hovers teasingly over events in progress.

At the same time, the end and its final demonstrations of judgment are often less explicitly anticipated in fiction than in expository writing and must be earned by dramatic ordeal. The various rhythms of narrative art include the creation and relaxing of dramatic tensions in episodic form. The emperor's treatment of Gulliver falls into place as merely one stage in the Lilliputian introduction to him and in our introduction to the satiric method and program of the work. In the overall rhythm of the book, it provides a single unit in the loose mixture (*satura*) that Swift's satiric medley comprises. Though another method might bind such a unit more tightly to adjacent units and make it less episodic, most fictional methods insist upon that linear *ordeal* — which after all is part of the game of intrigues that the reader expects.

We can see the effects of both analytic overviews and decisive temporal boundaries more clearly, perhaps, if we entertain the possibility of an illogical or endless narrative chain, in a type of narrative, for instance, that drives to no clear consummation or leaves us lost in bottomless speculations about whys and wherefores. Here dramatic ordeal replaces logic. In "The Far Field," for instance, Roethke writes of a typical modern journey in which the end is a kind of fizzle:

I dream of journeys repeatedly:
Of flying like a bat deep into a narrowing tunnel,
Of driving alone, without luggage, out a long peninsula,
The road lined with snow-laden second growth,
A fine dry snow ticking the windshield,
Alternate snow and sleet, no on-coming traffic,
And no lights behind, in the blurred side-mirror,
The road changing from glazed tarface to a rubble of stone,
Ending at last in a hopeless sand-rut,
Where the car stalls,
Churning in a snowdrift
Until the headlights darken.[7]

The journey toward this grinding down has its logic, but Roethke's point is that nothing particularly revealing is likely to happen in this landscape, where civilization breaks down and yields to nature. Movement stops before the will to move is finished; the wheels spin hopelessly; and then the lights simply go out.

That is the narrative fate of many moderns, to arrive at an end before or after the intelligence wishes, or at an end in no way a consummation of the drive that set it going. The reader is thus put in the position of the swimmer in John Barth's "Night-Sea Journey," who thrashes about in an indefinite sea without ship or shore in view. In this more striking case of purposeless movement, a shore, as Barth's swimmer indicates, even if there were one, might turn out to be essentially a nothing, an eternity of inaction — a paradise to some but merely death to others. But even such a meaningless boundary would at least be a "somewhere," a point toward which all historical process could be said to move. Safely cast ashore, one could view the process that leads to it as a whole and think, "No more night, no more sea, no more journeying." One could drive toward it if only to find there a blank page and a moment of silence — an ambiguous vacancy devoid of further complications and expenditures of energy. At the point where the field of perception closes, one could turn the work's references back upon themselves reflexively and in some satisfying way define the existential journey.

In all of these things, the god Terminus, the patron of boundaries and defined properties, demonstrates his worth. If the narrator allows anyone to enter his fictional world who is not qualified by a signified

7. Theodore Roethke, "The Far Field," *Collected Poems* (New York: Doubleday, 1965), p. 199.

intent and a badge of authorial permission, the confusion of his art will resemble the confusion of life — which Barth's lost swimmer remembers only too vividly in his own ungoverned plunge: "The carnage at our setting out; our decimation by whirlpool, poisoned cataract, sea-convulsion; the panic stampedes, mutinies, slaughters, mass suicides; the mounting evidence that no one will survive the journey — add to these anguish and fatigue; it were a miracle if sanity stayed afloat."[8] Lacking an adequate authorial purpose, beginning and middle possess no inherent principle of rhythm, movement, or segmentation.

The special functioning of temporal limits in agonistic, linear structures is equally clear when we approach them from the opposite direction, from the kind of firm boundaries that the fixed arts have. (Later we will have occasion to consider the issue of pictorial presentation in James and others who have thought of the poetics of narrative in the context of nontemporal arts.)[9] Whereas still photographs, paintings,

8. John Barth, *Lost in the Funhouse* (New York: Bantam Books, 1969), p. 9.

9. Much that has been written about the spatialization of modern fiction argues against an emphasis on the linearity of narrative. It is sometimes guilty, however, of misconceiving the relationship between synchronic and unfolding form. While it is true that chronology has been greatly complicated in fiction since Joyce and Proust, the temporal foundations of narrative remain unquestionable even in radical experiments with the calendar in Donald Bartholme, Alain Robbe-Grillet, Julio Cortazar, and others. Parts of a verbal composition are never merely juxtaposed — even in paratactic constructions or tabled columns — partly because words depend upon syntactical order and rhythm at the basic sentence level. Verbal coherence is profoundly temporal; the psychology of reading and listening is based on successiveness and rhythm. Moreover, the arrangement of sentences in paragraphs, vignettes, and episodes, however brief and fragmentary these larger units may be, is also rhythmic and sequential. All *re*arrangements of narrative chronology depend upon chronology for their effects.

Hence we find in radical experiments in fictional technique not the complete abandoning of linear form but what we might call a two-system chronology. They establish a tension between a sequence of supposed events and a sequence of presentation. Each of these is linear, but each may be comparatively liberated from the other. One might go even further and say that we cannot understand the function of pictorial, analytic, or other nontemporal elements unless we see them as part of a psychology of irreversible movement, in which what is past is past and must be retrieved. We can then add to that linear psychology complications that stem from cross-references, pictorial metaphors, and radical juxtapositions.

For useful discussions of spatial and linear form, see Joseph Frank, "Spatial Form in Modern Literature," in *The Widening Gyre: Crisis and Mastery in Modern Literature* (New Brunswick, N.J.: Rutgers University Press, 1963), pp. 3–62; Murray Krieger, "*Ekphrasis* and the Still Movement of Poetry; or, *Laokoon* Revisited," reprinted in *Perspectives on Poetry*, ed. James Calderwood and Harold Toliver (New York: Oxford

sculpture, and architecture impress us with an aesthetics of fixed postures and inexpressive, nonverbal composition, the controlled before and after of narration operates by another kind of logic and fosters another kind of experience in the reader. It can be sustained and rounded out only as motive and act, and cause and effect — with attendant psychological expectations, organic changes, gradual knowledge, turns and climaxes, catharsis and denouement. Whereas confusion and decomposition in static arts are primarily matters of disarranged or disproportioned relationships, in narrative they stem from inconsequence and disconnection, faulty rhythm and inappropriate segmentation.

Also, whereas in visual arts relationships are established by the nonabstracting techniques of color, shape, and more or less defined objects, in language they can be made by nonrepresentational means.

University Press, 1968); J. A. Ward, "Picture and Action," in *The Search for Form: Studies in the Structure of James's Fiction* (Chapel Hill: University of North Carolina Press, 1967), pp. 29–59; Joseph Wiesenfarth, *Henry James and the Dramatic Analogy* (New York: Fordham University Press, 1963), pp. 30–42; statements by recent writers such as Charles Aukema and Donald Barthelme in *Cutting Edges*, ed. Jack Hicks (New York: Holt, Rinehart and Winston, 1973).

Nearer to the emphasis I place on linear form are the following: Miller, *The Form of Victorian Fiction*; Melvin Friedman, *Stream of Consciousness: A Study in Literary Method* (New Haven: Yale University Press, 1955); E. K. Brown, *Rhythm in the Novel* (Toronto: University of Toronto Press, 1950), pp. 63ff.; John Henry Raleigh, "The English Novel and the Three Kinds of Time," in *Perspectives in Contemporary Criticism*, ed. Sheldon Norman Grebstein (New York: Harper and Row, 1968), pp. 42–49; Frank Kermode, *The Sense of an Ending: Studies in the Theory of Fiction* (New York: Oxford University Press, 1967); Edwin Muir, *The Structure of the Novel* (London: Hogarth Press, 1967); Paul Goodman, *The Structure of Literature* (Chicago: University of Chicago Press, 1954); Giorgio Melchiori, "The Moment as a Time Unit in Fiction," in *The Tightrope Walkers: Studies of Mannerism in Modern English Literature* (London: Routledge and Kegan Paul, 1956), pp. 175–87; David Paul, "Time and the Novelist," *Partisan Review* 21 (1954): 636–49; Nathan A. Scott, Jr., "Mimesis and Time in Modern Literature," in *The Broken Center: Studies in the Theological Horizon of Modern Literature* (New Haven: Yale University Press, 1966), pp. 25–76; see also Robert Scholes and Robert Kellogg, *The Nature of Narrative* (New York: Oxford University Press, 1966); Cleanth Brooks and William K. Wimsatt, Jr., *Literary Criticism: A Short History* (New York: Vintage Books, 1957), pp. 681–86. Finally, John Dewey's discussion of temporal movement in painting and of spatiality in literature suggests a proper balance and reciprocity between them. See *Art as Experience* (New York: G. P. Putnam's Sons, 1958), pp. 162–213. In one chapter, "The Common Substance of the Arts," Dewey's emphasis falls upon the likeness of literature, painting, architecture, and music, but with many necessary distinctions among them.

As even Barth's floundering philosopher illustrates, "arrival" can consist not merely of a terminal shore but also of interior generalizations. Every form of narration has its own way of making interim pauses — lyric, expository, philosophical, meditational, proverbial, or descriptive — and in these it combines the logic of linear progression with frameworks of conceptualizations, feelings, rational categories, psychological attitudes, or typical social postures. Far from insisting upon the uniqueness of successive events and waiting for the finality of its temporal enclosures, consequential logic welcomes interim visits from the philosopher and marriages between particular events and universals. When it dwells with historians, it is used to enduring the suspension of the story for large amounts of analysis and sociological or geographical fact. In its more tolerant moments it abides patiently the musings of archeology, psychology, economics, and other deliberative partners in the march of evidence and conclusions. It shows no great intolerance for an author who stops to address his listeners or makes a story serve an ethical point and capture a universal. (Biblical narrators, for instance, frequently stop for "wisdom passages," as in the proverbs and in the elegiac lamentations of the preacher when he concludes broadly, "To everything there is a season, and a time to every purpose under heaven.") It is true that narrative interest flags before masses of mere information and is dispersed by endless ramifications — once the historian or novelist looks beyond the walled area of his particular topics, actions, or careers. Though capable of overleaping lacunae and detouring around bracketed interruptions, narrative logic cannot legitimately encompass an aggregate or a miscellany. But it will gladly enter any construction that avoids discontinuity; it hungers merely for consistent views and whole worlds capable of drawing us "on and on." It is at home as equally with didactic allegory as with realism, with the *roman à thèse* as with romance and fantasy.

But of course the art of truth-saying and the art of lying are never quite identical even though both may practice similar techniques; nor do fictional and historical narration make the same proportionate use of generalized conclusions. Fiction is obviously more dramatically artful in entangling the reader's course in the psychological moments of characters; history writing is more likely to provide us with rational platforms and perspectives that transcend the march of events and liberate us from the rhythms of those who caused things to happen. Moreover, the historian may be ironic, but he is seldom playful when it comes to vouching for the events he describes, whereas the *fictor*, or inventor, as soon as he makes shoes speak or badgers meditate, openly confesses a playful intention. And in varying ways, nearly every fiction implicitly acknowledges its freedom to play with materials. The consequences that the Lilliputians debate with so much verisimilitude, for instance, are radically altered by the diminutive size of the race. The entire world of Gulliver, believable as it may seem in local places, is knocked askew by devices of perspective through which the work gains its satiric leverage and much of its fictive interest. Swift seeks a method that will magnify and distort common behavior in order to shake us loose from custom and make us judge physical and moral deformities afresh.

This freedom to nest an edifying, corrective, or entertaining view of things in a dramatic action is uniquely the fictionalist's. Like other aspects of narrative art, it depends upon his absolute control over the framing of the story, its drawing to a conclusion. "The prime effect of so sustained a system, so prepared a surface," as fiction presents to us, as James observes in *The Art of the Novel*, "is to lead on and on; while fascination of following resides, by the same token, in the presumability *somewhere* of a convenient, of a visibly-appointed stopping-place" (p. 6). On the basis of both the playfulness and the control, we may drive most of our wedges between fiction and normal experience and between fiction and historiography. Each of these has its version of linearity, but because it is not a closed field, normal experience seldom consummates what it begins, and history, in its commitment to the openness of that experience, is relatively less sustained than fiction. It is more vulnerable to contingencies, accidents, and intrusions from beyond the realm of pure anecdotal logic. No method of investigation or linear presentation will allow the historian to impose a calculated logic on his materials as Swift does on Gulliver's apparent autobiography.

If the logic of a given history is strong, it is because its perspective is very high and it has swept aside a quantity of details. The opening paragraphs of Bernard DeVoto's *The Course of Empire*, for instance, conceives of the course of westward expansion as an explainable series of events preceded by governing preformations of character and opportunity:

Seven centuries of hardly intermitted war created the Spanish people and they, the most medieval people in western Europe, created the Kingdom of Spain. The seven centuries forged the Spanish soul of valor, honor, and chivalry, and tempered it in fanaticism, cruelty, and treachery. In 1492 the army of Ferdinand of Aragon and Isabella of Castile broke the last remnant of Moorish power in Spain and the conquest was complete. But there would still be a use of conquistadores: in the same year a navigator in the employ of Isabella discovered the New World.[10]

Thus when the conquest of the New World begins, it has already been shaped, in DeVoto's view, by seven centuries of influence on a national "soul." The form of the conquest will stamp that character on all ensuing opportunities. The lucky coincidence that ends one phase the same year as the next begins provides a logical transition from the preforming period to the subsequent narrative — all of which gives the narrative some of the continuity we expect of fiction. But of course DeVoto is not free to invent paradigmatic heroes or model actions in illustration of a thesis. He can characterize, select, compress, and arrange what the relevant documents place in his hands; but he cannot render poetic justice, create six-inch Lilliputians or giants, or marry Spanish heroes to beautiful Aztec maidens, as the imagination might prefer. Nor can he intertwine plots and subplots and play freely upon the psychology of the reader: his work is governed by the dominant rhythm of expository statement. It is when Shakespeare does these things with Holinshed's chronicles, already somewhat mythologized, that we know we are in the presence of history plays and not history proper.

The structure of historiography, then, differs in essentials from the structure of fiction. Conrad's insistence on the historical truths of the novelist ignores the fact that consequential logic teases out its revelations with more design and foresight in the novelist than it does in Gibbon or Hume, that the revelations of fiction are more fully entangled in the psychological form of the reader's suspenseful anticipation. For all his reliance on abstract statements, Barth's Progresser interests us finally because his "Logia" are after all concretely embedded in the evolving metaphor of the fictional journey. Barth has written not an essay or a true biography but a psychologically effec-

10. Bernard DeVoto, *The Course of Empire* (Boston: Houghton Mifflin, 1952), p. 3.

tive, rhythmic monologue dependent upon sequential entrancement, not upon a continuous authored judgment of what happens. Likewise, whatever general judgments Swift wishes to make on human grossness and moral obtuseness attend upon Gulliver's capacity to tell a story in which he has been personally involved.

Hence if we are to entertain Conrad's position, we must insist on balancing it with a position something like Oscar Wilde's, that "Art takes life as part of her rough material, recreates it, and refashions it in fresh forms, is absolutely indifferent to fact, invents, imagines, dreams, and keeps between herself and reality the impenetrable barrier of beautiful style, of decorative or ideal treatment."[11] In reaction against the misuse of art as truth, fiction lovers like Wilde's Vivian (in "The Decay of Lying") insist that the logic of art is of a more dramatic kind than ordinary experience (or history writing) affords: "Two touches of nature will destroy a work of art," Vivian insists, because "art finds her own perfection within, not outside of, herself. She is not to be judged by an external standard of resemblance. She is a veil, rather than a mirror .... She makes and unmakes many worlds, and can draw the moon from heaven with a scarlet thread" (p. 921). Any order an artist offers is in large part his own creation. Any order that he offers in narrative is a systematized chronological illusion, woven out of the stuff of heroes, bright turns of plot, inspirations that delight the liar, and a love of masquerading that wins every tumble with hapless fact.

THE MIMETIC TRADITION

The tension between the positions suggested by Conrad and Wilde, between artfulness and imitative or historical accuracy, has always in some form occupied the theory of narrative — one presumes since the first storyteller strung together the first "and then . . . and then," blending observation and experience with the happy inventions of his own fertile wit. Both in the critical tradition and in practice the imitation of actual events and invention are often confused. Yet the attempt to distinguish them has sometimes been made and brought with it a clearer realization of the essentials of narrative form. Hence I want to turn next to the critical tradition in order to prepare for an

11. Oscar Wilde, "The Decay of Lying," in *The Works* (London and Glasgow: Collins, 1948), p. 917.

examination of modern theories of historiography and fiction. Though the Enlightenment attempted to drive these apart and insisted that poets are poets, scientists scientists, even in modern criticism the boundary remains sufficiently liquid to be problematic and admonishes us not to take distinctions for granted that have never been well-founded. And of course if we wish to understand the nature of fictions in earlier periods, we must recognize the reasons for their historical and mimetic underpinnings.

In looking at the early tradition, we discover — as we might expect— that the interior organization of narrative works is often felt to be a reflection of a preexistent order, usually established by a superior creator possessed of the same love of temporal progress, organic unity, and intelligible endings as poets and historians are. Real events are assumed to have an inherent linear logic, so that art may verify nature: the superior coherence of the written record — often a sacred record — extracts a design from what has already happened or will happen. Art's penetration to essences and verities is assisted by "bundles of relations"[12] and timely Logia, which are not so much the property of a shaping authorial intelligence as the collective wisdom of a culture centered in its priesthood or prophetic caste. This fundamental mimetic premise does not prevent either Greek or Hebraic traditions from proposing more than one logic of linear development or in some cases looking skeptically on generally accepted world chronologies.[13] Consequential movement in Genesis, for instance, is quite different from what it is in the prophetic books or again in Exodus

12. The phrase is Claude Lévi-Strauss's from "The Structural Study of Myth," *Journal of American Folklore* 68 (1955): 428–44.

13. In his discussion of "fictions of the end," Frank Kermode finds a "clerkly scepticism" about the Apocalypse, for instance, as far back as the tenth century. See *The Sense of an Ending*. Harry Levin's interesting book *The Myth of the Golden Age in the Renaissance* (Bloomington: Indiana University Press, 1969) has several chapters that bear upon the influence of eschatological fictions and the structure of narrative, especially "Fictions" (pp. 84–113) and "Historiography" (pp. 139–67).

For an account of Judaeo-Christian historiography, see C. A. Patrides, *Milton and the Christian Tradition* (New York: Oxford University Press, 1966), "Ascending by Degrees Magnificent: The Christian View of History," pp. 220–63, and *The Phoenix and the Ladder: The Rise and Decline of the Christian View of History* (Berkeley and Los Angeles: University of California Press, 1964). See also Nancy S. Struever, *The Language of History in the Renaissance* (Princeton: Princeton University Press, 1970), and F. J. Levy, *Tudor Historical Thought* (San Marino, Calif.: Huntington Library, 1967).

and the historical chronicles, with their noncyclical periodicity and ever new epochs.

Still more radically different is Christ's reconception of Old Testament narrative and historical logic, which focus not upon national or tribal goals and their irregular epochs but upon a single world destiny. Christ's Logia, too, are more encompassing than those of previous figures. As James Barr suggests, Old Testament narrative is historical in the sense that "it is cumulative in character, so that what is done and written is placed on relation to what has already been done and written. Most, though not all, of the non-narrative literature is 'placed' by its reference to the cumulative progression." And the wisdom passages reflect that comprehensiveness. But New Testament narrative reinterprets this much looser view of historicism and the "multiplex" nature of God's relationship with the prophets under the unitary revelation of Christ.[14] The result is a historical logic that redefines both outcome and progressive consequence. Christ alters the concepts of an evolving kingdom and of individual careers; he gives to individual cases the status of exemplars and connects them with the central paradigm of salvation. The story that reaches backward to Genesis and forward to the extremity of time is thus given a definite calendric center, to be reckoned eventually (as Oscar Cullman points out) as B.C. and A.D. sequences. "Fables" in Christ's version are fictional only on the surface; though they appear to be hypothetical models or imaginary paradigms, they are thinly veiled history making reference to that new chronology. The lives of Christ's listeners are thus brought forcefully into the pattern of the supposed fiction as the creative power of the Word makes history its instrument and fashions a perfectly enclosed story of history's raw materials.

Despite a similar confidence in the mimetic nature of fictions, Greek narrative is distinct from either Old or New Testament narrative in several vital respects. Some of the differences will be evident if we juxtapose typical narratives like the Parable of the Talents (Matt. 25) and the Allegory of the Cave (*The Republic* 7). For Plato, the

14. See James Barr, *Old and New in Interpretation: A Study of the Two Testaments* (New York: Harper and Row, 1966), pp. 21, 27, 24; Duncan Black McDonald, *The Hebrew Literary Genius* (New York: Russell and Russell, 1968), pp. 93–144; T. R. Henn, *The Bible as Literature* (New York: Oxford University Press, 1970); Oscar Cullman, *Christ and Time: The Primitive Christian Conception of Time and History*, trans. Floyd V. Filson (Philadelphia: Westminster Press, 1964).

question of a general historical purpose is muted by fixed, essential classifications, which are not subject to a world chronology working purposefully to an end through the episodes of a political and social history. What moves from point to point in Plato's parables is primarily the minds of philosophers engaged in capturing the Ideas behind temporal forms and shadows. Stories for Socrates are subordinate to the dialectic of question and answer; they are useful to illustrate argumentative points. Though the typical men of the cave may eventually be liberated and may come to see the full reality of the "sun," Socrates does not pretend to offer a model for historical revolution, nor does he purpose a millennial program for his listeners. He merely practices on Glaucon the educational processes that citizens of the Republic should follow. Stories are propaedeutic devices, fictions of convenience. They illustrate the general plight of men in their given epistemological situations; through the questions and answers that arise in the relationship between teacher and pupil, they enable pupils to rise above the conditions of the cave, to escape from ignorance and discover "the universal author of things beautiful and right."[15]

Presumably, then, no collective order seizes upon that vision to shape its own history or evolve a terminal kingdom, though in keeping with the ideal citizenry that Socrates proposes for the Republic, the education of a people should have for its continued goal the unfolding of truths, as "the best minds . . . attain that knowledge which we have already shown to be the greatest of all," that is, knowledge of the good (7.519D). Each mind, plunged at birth into the darkness of the earthly cave, must undergo that education on its own; every generation must renew it. As for historians of unique events, the battles and civil struggles that a Heroditus or Thucydides narrates can have little bearing upon the education of philosophers except for the moral and philosophical precepts they may yield. A parable in Socrates' handling thus renders essences in the special teleology that abstract thought has, in which trains of thought are brought to flower and concluded in comprehensive abstractions. Realization of the value of words like *the intelligible, the beautiful, being,* and *the good* constitutes the goal of narration. The logic of the story condenses the

15. Plato, *The Dialogues*, trans. B. Jowett (New York: Random House, 1937), from *The Republic* 7.517C.

logic of intellectual exploration and discovery. As the eye of the cave dweller is "unable to turn from darkness to light without the whole body," so the instrument of knowledge, the parable itself, can only, by the movement of the whole soul, "be turned from the world of becoming into that of being." In both places, true philosophers "learn by degrees to endure the sight of being, and of the brightest and best of being, or in other words, of the good" (7.518 C–D).

The repercussions of this conceptual outcome are worth looking into, especially with a view to understanding the use of authorial judgments in modern fictions, but for the moment it is sufficient to note that Socrates' use of parables requires that he become a fabler of a quite different kind from the poets that he seeks to banish from the Republic (on the grounds that, absorbed as they are in appearances, they never manage to disclose true being — or perhaps do not wish to). Where Socrates offers Glaucon a concrete poetic fiction precisely as a way of approaching, by degrees, the "sight" of unconcrete being, presumably others might also do so: the structure of fictions might become the structure of thought — the model of the mind's movement toward a cathartic illumination in which all passion-arousing confusions are resolved. Thus through linear fictions poets might promote psychological and intellectual growth, just as musicians in the *Timaeus*, by the exact intervals and concent of their music, help attune the discordant soul to the harmony of the spheres.

For Christ, narrative is obviously not subordinate to argument in this way nor do "conclusions" consist of universals and abstractions in Plato's sense. The Parable of the Talents is representative in its construction of a case that, though apparently theoretical, nonetheless applies directly to a particular historical situation:

> For the kingdom of heaven is as a man travelling into a far country, who called his own servants, and delivered unto them his goods. And unto one he gave five talents, to another two, and to another one; to every man according to his several ability; and straightway took his journey. [Two servants plant and gain returns, one hides his money and gains nothing.] After a long time the lord of those servants cometh, and reckoneth with them. And so he that had received five talents came and brought other five talents, saying, Lord, thou deliveredst unto me five talents: behold, I have gained beside them five talents more. His lord said unto him, Well done, thou good and faithful servant: thou hast been faithful over a few things, I will make thee ruler over many things: enter thou unto the joy of thy lord. [The same is said to the second ser-

vant.] Then he which had received the one talent came and said, Lord,
I knew thee that thou art an hard man, reaping where thou hast not
sown, and gathering where thou hast not strawed: And I was afraid,
and went and hid thy talent in the earth: lo, there thou hast that is
thine. His lord answered and said unto him, Thou wicked and slothful
servant, thou knewest that I reap where I sowed not, and gather
where I have not strawed: Thou oughtest therefore to have put my
money to the exchangers. . . . Take therefore the talent from him, and
give it unto him which hath ten talents. For unto everyone that hath
shall be given, and he shall have abundance: but from him that hath
not shall be taken away even that which he hath. And cast ye the
unprofitable servant unto outer darkness: there shall be weeping and
gnashing of teeth. When the Son of man shall come in his glory, and all
the holy angels with him, then shall he sit upon the throne of his glory.
[Matt. 25:14-31]

The basic analogy that the parable builds upon is obviously not between narrative images and static essences such as "ignorance" and
"illumination," as in Socrates' parable; it is between the kingdom of
heaven and a representative or ambassador, presumably Christ himself among his apostles. Where Socrates' cave dwellers are a generalized representation of all men dwelling in their relative darkness,
Christ's figures "refer to" particular people. These may themselves be
types and representatives with a kind of power of attorney for others
(Christ for God, the servants for mankind); and their actions may
therefore establish a model for all times and periods, which will practice ritual reenactments of the pattern. But on the primary level, the
figures in the fiction have historical uniqueness and belong to a
particular linear continuity. The visitation of the lord is a turning
point in an organic plot enacted within a historical context. The
talents that the lord dispenses are messages to the apostles, as in other
parables the "seed" that Christ sows and the "light" that he brings are
figures for sacred truth, which in the very telling he offers at this one
historical time only. Again the literal historicity of the parables does
not prevent the talents or the seeds from representing everyman's capacity to receive the gift, in whatever times and places it may be
offered. And the gift will in fact be made again and again. But it will
be made as a retelling of the parables embedded in a scriptural context that claims documentary accuracy as history: that is, the *telling*
of the parables will also be told. Indeed, telling the circumstances of
their original narration is precisely the assigned task of the apostles,

who, like the servants of the Parable of the Talents, are to invest the Word, to spread it into the nooks and crannies of history. Their visitations, then, to the Christian, become effective promulgations of gospel in imitation of the traveling lord, as the Word breeds their words. Quite literally to the Christian, Christ has traveled into a far country, has left, and will return to pronounce judgment, exactly as he describes in the parable.

At the same time that the parable respects literalness and sweeps particular figures (John, Matthew, James) into its story, it also takes a radical leap beyond normal expectancy. As a king may invite wedding guests off the street and then have one of them suddenly seized and cast into outer darkness for wearing the wrong attire, so Christ at the judgment will call many but choose few (Matt. 22:1–14). Where the master-servant relationship suggests a model of prudent management and the wedding suggests the logic of social occasions, Christ's postscripts to this effect assert that time, place, and character are relatively indifferent *ultimately*. The end redefines the "midst," and the surface of the parables is misleading despite its degree of literalness. One party is no less than the right hand of God, and the other is not really composed of servants and guests but men who in their eternal aspect are something quite different. Thus the eschatology that rises out of the historical model breaks with it; the denouement breaks with deliberate reason. There can be no mediation between the finite and the infinite, or between the historical case and the anagogic reality toward which it points. Though everything retains its usual aspect and its uniqueness as event, from the end it also assumes terrible or wonderful aspects as a prefiguration (with traumatic results that can perhaps best be gauged in Kierkegaard and Berdyaev).[16]

At least one kind of Christian fictive narration thus has the peculiar effect of involving its figures in an exorable logic of historical cause and effect and yet eventually in unpredictable crises and a basic discontinuity between now and then. The parables offer abundant materials for the "crisis theology" of Protestant theologians like Calvin and Karl Barth, in which the worthy may sometimes be struck down as readily as the wicked, and for reasons that lie beyond visible logic.

16. See Nicholas Berdyaev, *The Meaning of History* (Cleveland and New York: World Publishing Company, 1962), chaps. 1–4.

Whereas the dispensations of the Old Testament — inscrutable enough in their own right — work through covenants that commit Yahweh to history and to a chosen tribe, the new dispensation of pre-emptive grace destroys sequential logic in the old sense. The apocalyptic imagination is no respecter of right process and normal sequence. As Calvin remarks, "Each moment of faith becomes the foundation of all existence. I see myself continually flowing away; no moment passes without my seeing myself at the point of being engulfed." Revelation is "a *mysterium tremendum*," without a "human medium in which or by which it can be comprehended. Faith is a pure gift,' ineffable and untranslatable."[17]

However, the leap in logic required of those who seek to understand the parable is itself part of the message of the parables. In this respect the figures inside and the listeners outside the story are in the same dilemma. As Matthew indicates, some are chosen to understand, others are not:

> It is given unto you to know the mysteries of the kingdom of heaven, but to them it is not given. For whosoever hath, to him shall be given, and he shall have more abundance: but whosoever hath not, from him shall be taken away even that he hath. Therefore speak I to them in parables; because they seeing see not; and hearing they hear not, neither do they understand. [Matt. 12:11-13]

He adds:

> All these things spake Jesus unto the multitude in parables; and without a parable spake he not unto them: That it might be fulfilled which was spoken by the prophet, saying, I will open my mouth in parables; I will utter things which have been kept secret from the foundation of the world. [Matt. 12:34-35]

The parables condition their audience to accept a presumed reality, however far it may stretch beyond normal expectancy. It is evident from them, in fact, that Christ has confidence in the effectiveness of the Word to make the "fiction" come true. And as Erich Auerbach

17. See M. C. D'Arcy, S.J., *The Meaning and Matter of History* (New York: Farrar, Straus and Cudahy, 1959), pp. 200, 169. The first quotation is from Calvin, the second a summary of Barth. For a succinct treatment of the Christian view of history and time, see J. L. Russell, "Time in Christian Thought," in *The Voices of Time: A Cooperative Survey of Man's Views of Time as Expressed by the Sciences and by the Humanities*, ed. J. T. Fraser (New York: George Braziller, 1966), pp. 59-76.

suggests, biblical narrators in general, not merely Christ, maintain an exacting belief in what they narrate. What they write is not "oriented toward 'realism,' " it is "oriented toward truth":

> The Bible's claim to truth is not only far more urgent than Homer's, it is tyrannical — it excludes all other claims. The world of the Scripture stories is not satisfied with claiming to be a historically true reality — it insists that it is the only real world, is destined for autocracy. All other scenes, issues, and ordinances have no right to appear independently of it, and it is promised that all of them, the history of all mankind, will be given their due place within its frame, will be subordinated to it.[18]

The problem of unresolved strands and open-ended realism does not arise in such a mode because the "real" is precisely what the story deals with and finds answerable to the will of the storyteller. The Word is so effective that any given moment, object, or person is capable of joining the perfection of the Logos. By suppressing the difference between history and fiction, biblical narration thus avoids Plato's distrust of poets and in fact finds poets and prophets often virtually the same, since both repeat in their ways the power of the Word. To Plato, of course, poetic imitation can offer no perpetuity, beauty, coherence, radiance, or truth because "the imitator or maker of the image knows nothing of true existence; he knows appearance only." Since a poet "awakens and nourishes and strengthens the feelings and impairs the reason," he may be justly refused a place in a well-ordered kingdom (*The Republic* 10.598, 605). But to the New Testament narrator, truth, perpetuity, and coherence are the special domain of an illustrative "fiction": they exist foremost in the Word itself.

Unfortunately, neither view, Plato's or Christ's, encourages us to consider the significance of fictive design and organic plot as something apart from normal experience. It is left to Aristotle to defend fictions on more far-reaching aesthetic principles. He does so partly by proposing that what a poet makes is not essentially images of objects but unified actions or organic intrigues. These may or may not be plots of things that have happened; their literalness is not at issue

18. Erich Auerbach, *Mimesis: The Representation of Reality in Western Literature* (New York: Doubleday, 1957), pp. 11–12.

as it is in Judaeo-Christian versions of fictional logic. Teleologically oriented as he is, yet not committed to a messianic view of history, Aristotle is free to regard fictions as self-contained systems whose denouement is established by a series of clarifications made within the work itself. Because he looks to dramatists as examples, it is clear to him that what a poet does is arrange series of events in meaningful unities. Though the concept of organically related parts is bound up in the concept of a well-ordered universe, a fiction is merely analogous to such a world, not its direct representation. Indeed, whereas events in the real world are composed of many strands and unplotted elements (*Poetics* 10.9), a play has *only* related events; and it may limit itself to these precisely because the poet is free to establish his own temporal boundaries. These are set not by a real edenic beginning or an apocalyptic conclusion but by a verbal maker exercising his linguistic prerogatives.

Aristotle views fictions, then, as Christ looks upon history, as single concatenations unfolding as illumination, leading to sufficient revelations beyond which one has no desire to proceed. But a fiction has human in place of divine intent, and art in place of literal history. What is historical "epiphany" to Christ is managed "anagnorisis," or recognition, to Aristotle. With respect to the latter difference, implicitly answering Plato's charges against the poet, Aristotle suggests that if in fact what poets imitate are teleological actions rather than objects such as "beds," they link objects together in such a way as to render them mutually, serially intelligible. By formulating designed plots, the poet controls those passions that Plato accused him of merely arousing: because of its structural movement toward a denouement, literature can be cathartic and moral as well as pleasurable. Whereas the end that Christ will envision purges all anxieties and sorrows (as one's fate is settled once and for all), the "end" that Aristotle proposes for a fiction is the clarification of riddles raised by the fiction itself and settled by defined identities emerging from behind the masks and confused exchanges of the work. Where Christ's parabolic models present to their believers a relief for real doubt and suffering, then, Aristotle's models dramatize a fictional relief, to be experienced vicariously by those who recognize the fiction as a fiction. For Christ, the parable is not superior to history writing or philosophy, because in a basic sense it *is* history writing, and it contains all the philosophy one needs. For Aristotle poetry is higher than history because it possesses a superior connectedness and expresses universals.

As this distinction between nature and fictions suggests, it is to Aristotle that we must look for an account of the linear psychology of fictions and for a rudimentary distinction between the spectator's course in the presence of the work and the course of his normal experience. Both recognition and catharsis, for instance, are terms that look to the intellective and emotional continuities of someone vicariously implicated in the development of a plot. They depend upon the animate life and logic of a design and upon our identification with figures whose discoveries we follow and whose recognitions we share, though with different intensities and different timing. The internal development of the work is always enough like the sequences of life to enable us to participate in it, and yet the work has its own coherence; we participate in it with an intelligibility denied to life.

Effective as it is in interpreting poems as self-sufficient structures, however, Aristotle's view of literary structure is only half to the point. It does not strike at the weakest point of the Socratic argument — the failure to see the lack of organic connectedness among objects, episodes, and careers in real experience. Though Aristotle acknowledges the imperfection of nature, like Plato he assumes that in essential ways the world is basically coherent. He implies in the concept of imitative actions that poets may in some way reproduce the logic of events even while improving artfully upon them. Had he pursued his notion that in its total proliferation of events and processes nature is anything but a coherent whole, he might have argued more forcefully that a poetic structure is a reordering of nature's elements in the interests of beauty and harmony. More particularly, he might have argued that the making of plots directs us psychologically and intellectually to outcomes absent from the temporal boundlessness of nature, or at least quite different from nature. He could also have mentioned that plot-making resembles the philosopher's discovery of first principles in deliberative discourse — even though, as Sidney later points out, the poet represents his universals in concrete instances and much more "sweetly."

Aristotle pursues the subject of nature's comparative shapelessness only briefly, however, and despite the dominating importance of the *Poetics* to a structural consideration of fictions, several key elements are missing from it. The Aristotelian concept of fictive structure is not prepared to juxtapose meaningfully the order of fictions and the progressions of an as yet unformulated world. Neither the Greek nor the Hebraic-Christian tradition examines the constitutive order of language or questions the real existence of such conclusive abstractions as "the beautiful" or "the good." Neither attributes to the word *fiction* the formative dimensions that it will eventually encompass.

However, when the two traditions encounter each other subsequently, as they do in Saint Augustine and Christian-Platonist theorists in the Renaissance, their very collision as systems brings to the forefront the problematic relationship of fictions and history writing. (That they do collide seems indisputable. It is not true as Huntington Brown suggests that "the Hebrew mythology," unsurpassed in its kind, "supplies no model for the occidental kind of historiography or fiction," that "the Greek historians and orators and their Roman imitators are the models to whom the modern storyteller — historian or novelist, reasoner, organizer, and moralist that he is — turns as by instinct."[19] Theories of narrative would be less vagrant and confused if the models were uniform and consistent in this way.) The amalgamations are troubling, but often in fruitful ways. Though we cannot examine a great number of specific examples, it is well to have their main implications in mind if we are to understand later views of fiction and the eventual emergence of theories of fiction and historical writing that attempt to exclude one from the other.

Some of these implications are evident in Dante's amalgamation of Platonist and Hebraic-Christian fictions, which patterns the inventions of poets on the truths of theologians, which are based in turn on literal history. Though the poet's fictions are beautiful lies whose primary events have never actually occurred, the poet's view of reality should nonetheless be unquestionable. It should concern the same matters that concern theologians. If poets play with literal events more freely than theologians, then, they do so only in order to make similar truths available to the reader. In some regards, the poet may also make use of the Platonist view of fictions. As Plato's cave dwellers turn from becoming to being, Dante's pilgrim in *Paradiso* passes from an unclear provisional world to a realm of essences and realized potentials. This realm is both the heaven of Platonic cosmology and the end envisioned by apocalyptic thought: his pilgrim's

19. Huntington Brown, *Prose Styles: Five Primary Types* (Minneapolis: University of Minnesota Press, 1966), p. 33.

progress is a structured movement toward a profound realization of his and mankind's destiny and of the creator's qualities as summed up by the philosopher's abstractions. Unlike Platonic allegory, however, the poet's surface fable cannot be too readily dismissed as a deceiving appearance.[20] Whereas Socrates undermines the fiction he uses in pointing toward a basically imageless and nonnarrative set of truths, Dante's ultimately realized vision is to his pilgrim's initial stages more as childhood to adulthood. The germ of being is present all along in the processes of becoming, as it presumably is in the Old Testament's prefiguration of the New, adumbrating in a "figural realism" what can only be clear in time. Thus in his amalgamation of Platonist and Christian narrative, Dante insists upon both a realistic, mimetic surface and upon the poet's freedom to make all parts of a plot contribute to the clarification of its ends.

Other Renaissance narratives conceive of the blend somewhat differently. Spenser, for instance, suggests several variations of it. The schematic allegory outlined in the letter to Raleigh establishes for *The Faerie Queene* a primary continuity of philosophical and ethical argument. Though a fashioning of a gentleman in private and public virtues suggests largely philosophical ends and fictions of convenient, general illustrations, however, Spenser obviously insists not merely on the ideality of these but also on their religious and historical dimensions. Una and Red Cross represent together a search both for enlightenment, as Platonist abstraction conceives of it, and for Christian holiness in a militant, historical church. Other outcomes complicate that marriage and suggest the difficulties a fiction has in making its heroes arrive at final things when their field of operation is a world of natural and social processes. Beyond the fairy court stands a New Jerusalem that rises utterly above history, while the city of Cleopolis itself remains a national institution and points toward the always un-

20. As Joseph Mazzeo remarks, if Dante confused the allegory of theologians and poets, he did so because his poem is based on autobiographical experience in part and is not a fiction embellishing arbitrarily a truth on another plane. "It is on the one hand fiction because the journey never happened; it is on the other hand truth because the elements of the poem, cosmological, ethical, and personal, are true" (*Structure and Thought in the Paradiso* [Ithaca, N.Y.: Cornell University Press, 1958], p. 34). Cf. Erich Auerbach, "Figura," *Archivum Romanicum* 22 (1938): 436–89; Charles S. Singleton, "Dante's Allegory," *Speculum* 25 (1950): 78–83; Richard Hamilton Green, "Dante's 'Allegory of Poets' and the Mediaeval Theory of Poetic Fiction," *Comparative Literature* 9 (1957): 118–28. See also Brooks and Wimsatt, *Literary Criticism*, pp. 149–54.

finished work of the chivalric war on evil — hindered by recurrent
duplicity, falsehood, and always renewable vices. Red Cross's
eventual illumination is to be beyond time, like that which Love fosters in the Hymns:

> Faire is the heaven where happy soules have place,
> In full enjoyment of felicitie,
> Whence they doe still behold the glorious face
> Of the Divine Eternall Majestie;
> More faire is that where those Idees on hie
> Enraunged be, which Plato so admyred,
> And pure Intelligences from God inspyred.
> ["An Hymne of Heavenly Beautie," lines 78–84]

But his hindrances come from an impressive and lasting underworld
of confusion. They include not only Roman Catholicism but also
Mutability in general, which can never be defeated by temporal institutions. They belong to a world of progressive change and structureless flux that constantly threatens to sidetrack and destroy intellectual and moral "careers."

The difficulty is that once the poet commits himself to a literal level
of allegory that includes the contemporary kingdom, he finds that he
has thrown out of focus the world calendar that looks to beginning
and ending. Given to the events of time and place, he may himself
hunger for "false Beauties" and "vaine deceitful shadows," as Plato
had warned, since it is after all the special way of poetic inventions to
value sensuous images and a tangible worldliness. It is revealing in
this regard that Red Cross's foes are hindrances not only to a discovery of holiness but also to a proper narrative-argumentative
method, to a programmatic set of educational phases: as false beauty
and arch image-makers, Duessa and Archimago have affinities with
poetic lying and invention — in a world in which fictions can be both
a strategy of illumination and a detour through the erotic imagination and its tantalizing illusions. What they propose in effect are alternative paths for the consciousness to follow and alternative conclusions: if as the Hymns suggest, Platonic love guides one to ultimate
truth and beauty, the love of beautiful illusions leads back to the cave
and the underworld, the caves of error and despair, for instance, the
dungeon of Orgoglio, and the Queen of Night's underworld confusion. Less clearly evil but just as dangerous are the gardens of delight, pastoral bowers, ornamental and glittery castles, and the cos-

tumes of the shapely world of appearances, all of which give *The Faerie Queene* its chivalric brightness and its application to the fairy queen's splendid courtly establishment.

On one level, then, Book I is a study of narrative progress in which the reader and Red Cross must both learn to distinguish bright fictions from authentic truth. The programmatic discipline of the ideal knight wants to take two directions, the path to the New Jerusalem and the path back to court. Though in one way the proper end of Red Cross's search is the unveiling of Una and the unmasking of those multiple faces and deformed shapes that have been mistaken for her throughout, in another way he can achieve no end while he serves the court. The founding of an effective church to manifest Christ's image is itself nationalized, of course. The crown and the church are the secular and religious arms of a militant historical vision that goes on indefinitely. Red Cross is after all an English hero, and his goal is to free not merely Una's parents, the originals of mankind, but also their ever renewed English progeny. The implication is that whatever Plato's One may be and whatever Christian holiness may be can best be seen in the continuity of the political world; it can be seen in recurrent types like Saint George, whose renewed presentation of the well-dented Christian shield helps carry the oneness of truth into a succession of temporal conditions.

When combined in this way, the plots of Book I — the biography of the hero, the fruition of a church, the illustrative stages of a programmatic, spiritual growth, and the overall chart of history from Adam to the holy city — obviously make for a very complex sense of consequential logic and culmination. Though Spenser seems to look forward to a final end with some confidence, at no level is an ending quite realizable within the bounds established for Red Cross. Instead of a philosophical, religious, personal, and national completion, the poem actually presents a vision of several postponed goals and continuing plots. Both Red Cross's reception into New Jerusalem and his marriage to Una are delayed; the city of Cleopolis, though it is the best of earthly courts and will become better, is not to be confused with the ultimate place of which it is a laboring type; the unveiled Una is described only briefly and then set aside; the church is presumably well founded by Red Cross as Saint George but must continue to battle its enemies. The endings that seem so simple and paradigmatic in Plato and Christ's parables have thus ballooned into an epic of proliferating, unfinished actions. A subtle indefiniteness has crept into both the progress of single plots and the relations of all the plots together. (The effects are especially pronounced in a fairy tale, which presumably offers all the advantages of authorial arbitrariness and high fictional enclosure.)

Some of Spenser's tentativeness in the marriage of historical process and final things is evident in other Renaissance poets as well. Milton's Adam and Eve, for instance, finish in *Paradise Lost* by descending into the wilderness to begin new lives; Bunyan's Christian, having arrived at the celestial city himself, feels compelled to return and start over again with his family. Even so, the Christian and the Platonist poet guard more zealously than others the right to impose on fictions the sense of a designed scheme of things. In this respect, he remains a shaper of fictional actions such as Aristotle describes and adds to that office the imagining of a perfection outside the text, a perfection whose self-contained logic reflects unfavorably on the un-shaped materials of history. In Renaissance parlance, he imagines a golden age capable of quieting all proddings to action, an age by which one measures the immediate world. Indeed, the idea of a com-plete fiction and the idea of paradise are virtually inseparable in the Renaissance.[21]

If this twofold perspective of an unfinished, fallen world and a paradisal place of timeless beauty provides part of the tension of Red Cross's quest, Christian's fate, and Adam and Eve's future, it also figures prominently in the most important theory of poetry between Aristotle's *Poetics* and the romantics, Sidney's *Apology for Poetry*. Sidney proposes what we might call an ideational mimesis: he makes poems the models of things-as-they-ought-to-be rather than of what nature in her imperfect way offers. Sidney's most frequently noticed statement in this regard is that poets imitate not merely the objects and actions that accident and circumstance provide but a second na-ture: "Only the poet, disdaining to be tied to any . . . subjection [to Nature], lifted up with the vigour of his own invention, doth grow in effect, another nature, in making things either better than Nature bringeth forth, or quite anew, forms such as never were in Nature, as

21. Cf. Harry Berger, Jr., "The Renaissance Imagination: Second World and Green World," *Centennial Review* 9 (1965): 36–78: "The second world is the playground, laboratory, theater or battlefield of the mind, a model or construction which the mind creates, a time or place which it clears, in order to withdraw from the actual environment. It may be the world of play or poem or treatise, the world inside a picture frame, the world of pastoral simplification, the controlled conditions of scientific experiment. Its essential quality is that it is an explicitly fictional, artificial or hypothetical world" (p. 46).

the Heroes, Demigods, Cyclops, Chimeras, Furies, and such like."[22]
Where ordinary nature is "brasen," the poet's re-creation is golden.
And thus by inventing heroes and imagining ideals that nature neglected to produce, he projects a future in the manner of the *vates* or
prophet — not necessarily because he foresees the actual shape of
things inevitably to come but because he suggests what could be.
Rather than merely reporting or imitating history, then, the poet
intervenes in it and helps the figments of his imagination, his beautiful lies, come true; failing that, he nonetheless influences the reader's
concept of the ideal. It is in this creative capacity that men are most
clearly godlike, in Sidney's view, and reflect the pure reason that was
man's blessing before the fall. If the creator originally set man above
nature, poets may even now recapture that sovereignty and in poetry
reveal "the force of a divine breath." It follows that the best species of
imitation are those that most clearly reveal divine favor, as for instance, David's psalms, the Song of Solomon, and the hymns of
Moses. The Word that in the beginning initiated the forms of paradise is therefore repeatable in the poet's words as he "bringeth things
forth far surpassing" nature's regular "doings" (p. 101). Erect reason
and divine inspiration are his means of grasping beginning and end
things even in the midst of a distorting historical process. But reaching back to a former golden time, the imagination does not create *ex
nihilo* its own second nature; it is still in some sense imitative. It
reconstitutes a real order that once existed.

If fictions are imitative to Sidney, however, they are not so precisely in Aristotle's sense. They are imitative in such a way as to provide a firmer answer to the conclusion of *The Republic*, and of course
more immediately to Sidney's contemporary Puritan critics. By
leading us out of the confusions of nature, poetry purifies the wit, as
Sidney remarks, enriching the memory, "enabling" the judgment, enlarging "conceit," and taking for its final end the task of drawing us
on "to as high a perfection as our degenerate souls, made worse by
their clayey lodgings, can be capable of" (p. 104).[23] The effective

---

22. Sidney, *An Apology for Poetry*, ed. Geoffrey Shepherd (London: Thomas Nelson, 1965), p. 100.

23. In this respect, Sidney and Jonson assume similar positions. In *Discoveries*, Jonson remarks, "Now, the Poesy is the habit, or the art: nay, rather the Queen of Arts: which had her original from heaven, received thence from the Hebrews, and had in prime estimation with the Greeks, transmitted to the Latins, and all nations, that professed civility. The study of it (if we will trust Aristotle) offers to mankind a certain rule, and pattern of living

difference between poetry and philosophy in this regard is not poetry's invention of an order that exists only within its own rules but in its greater clarity and proficiency in enticing people to love wisdom. Where philosophy is crabbed and obscure, poetry is "food for the tenderest stomachs." The "poet is indeed the right popular philosopher" (p. 109).

Despite the increased scope that Sidney allows the imagination in re-creating a golden age and applying it as a corrective to present realities and degenerate souls, he appears at times not actually much closer to a distinction between fictive design and preexisting realities than Plato and Aristotle were. He does not take particular notice of the differences between the structure of events and the structure of imaginative works, or again between the reader's psychological progress in the text and the progress of normal experience. Nor does he resolve the tension between outcome as the intellectual definition of essences and outcome as the end of a linear, aesthetic structure or history. He assumes that nature is not itself incurably and permanently debased, even in its brass state. Though it requires perfecting and the poet requires imagination, it is nothing like a chaos.

These versions of narrative structure and fictive models that Dante, Spenser, Sidney, and other Renaissance poets illustrate are of some importance both as stages that the theory of fictions has passed through and as perspectives on later concepts of narrative structure. It should not go unnoticed that a good many Elizabethan fictions — romances, picaresque narratives, and dramatic plots — have little or no relationship to either Christian or Platonist concepts of outcome, just as a good many Greek and Roman historians, dramatists, and writers of romance paid little attention to Platonism in developing their own versions of historical logic.[24] However, it is no distortion to

---

well, and happily; disposing us to all civil offices of society" (*Ben Jonson*, ed. C. H. Hereford Percy and Evelyn Simpson, vol. 8, *The Poems, the Prose Works* [London: Oxford University Press, 1954], p. 636).

24. Benedetto Croce observes that the ancients "were entirely occupied with the joy of the effort of passing from myth to science and thus to the collection and classification of the facts of reality." They supplied naturalism "with the instruments which it still employs: formal logic, grammar, the doctrine of virtues," and while doing so neglected to conceive of progress beyond a few sketches of advancing civilization ("History of Historiography," in *History: Its Theory and Practice*, trans. Douglas Ainslie [New York: Russell and Russell, 1960], pp. 190–92).

consider Platonist and Christian teleology and their combinations major parts of the theory of fictions until well into the rise of the novel. Even in the eighteenth century they are by no means entirely set aside for other narrative logics. *The Dunciad*, for instance, gains its concluding effectiveness from a contrast between the doomsday reign of Dulness and the usual end of the great story to which Pope's readers were accustomed. As the ultimate in duncery, Pope's "Goddess of the city" yawns a conclusive yawn — the outcome of her progress toward intellectual stupor: "More she had spoke, but yawn'd — All nature nods: / What Mortal can resist the Yawn of Gods?" (4.605-6). The types of dullness are abundant, but they are also strictly obedient to her patterns as the typological tradition suggests that they should be; and when she ends the arts and sciences, she ends them apocalyptically. They become as though a prolific Logos had never summoned them forth:

> Thus at her felt approach, and secret might,
> *Art* after *Art* goes out, and all is Night.
> See skulking *Truth* to her old Cavern fled,
> Mountains of Casuistry heap'd o'er her head!
> *Philosophy*, that lean'd on Heav'n before,
> Shrinks to her second cause, and is no more.
> *Physic* of *Metaphysic* begs defence,
> And *Metaphysic* calls for aid on *Sense*!
> See *Mystery* to *Mathematics* fly!
> In vain! they gaze, turn giddy, rave, and die.
> *Religion* blushing veils her sacred fires,
> And unawares *Morality* expires.
> Nor *public* Flame, nor *private*, dares to shine;
> Nor *human* Spark is left, nor Glimpse *divine*!
> Lo! thy dread Empire, *Chaos*! is restor'd;
> Light dies before thy uncreating word:
> Thy hand, great Anarch! let's the curtain fall;
> And Universal Darkness buries All.
>
> [4.639-56]

All means of arrival — logical definition, moral law, chronological doomsday, escape from the Socratic cave of shadows, the unveiling of religious mysteries — are here negated by a power so strong as to make even metaphysics call on sense.

Among Augustans generally, fictions of the end fare better than other fictions, which are assigned only problematic value in the theory of fictions between Dryden and Coleridge. The skeptical attitude of Dr. Johnson toward works of the imagination, to take a salient example, is directed toward classical myths, the fabled deities, and fictions of the golden age. "Poets, indeed, profess fiction," Johnson reluctantly concedes, but "the legitimate end of fiction is the conveyance of truth." One form of mythology is as repugnant as another; time has tarnished the splendors of classical figures and literary modes that depend upon them: "A fiction, not only detected but despised, can never afford a solid basis to any position," Johnson remarks about pastoral. Johnson's wielding of the word *truth* is even more telling. In the Realist tradition in which he so often writes, such a word requires only tautological reaffirmation: "Truth indeed is always truth, and reason is always reason; they have an intrinsic and unalterable value."[25] Given that certainty, the mind arrives at its rational goals with every discovery of recurrent form and law. The only tangible advantages left to fictions are moral and rhetorical ones: "Their authors are at liberty, though not to invent, yet to select objects, and to cull from the mass of mankind, those individuals upon which the attention ought most to be employed. ... It is justly considered as the greatest excellency of art, to imitate nature; but it is necessary to distinguish those parts of nature, which are most proper for imitation."[26] The poet does not create a second world of hypothetical speculation and play apart from his daily experience; he arranges what is representative and universal in an intelligible order for the reader's moral inspection.

However, while Milton's *Lycidas* can be accused of tampering with fictions when it should be attending to sincere grief (*Lives*, 1:295), the greater myth of Lycidas's apotheosis is not, for the moment, the kind that Johnson is disposed to question. He can be scornful of Neptune, Jove, Orpheus, or Proteus partly because he holds so confidently to the logic of the old cosmology and the Platonist abstractions that reinforce it. Similarly, Edmund Waller, Abraham Cowley, and Joseph Addison condemn poetry's reliance on miracles, supernatural machinery, fairies and nymphs, and other patently outmoded fic-

25. Samuel Johnson, *Lives of the English Poets*, ed. George Birkbeck Hill (Oxford: Oxford University Press, 1905), 1:271, 59.

26. Samuel Johnson, *Works*, ed. John Hawkins (London, 1787), 5:20-26, quoted from *The Critical Opinions of Samuel Johnson*, ed. Joseph Epes Brown (New York: Russell and Russell, 1961; originally published by Princeton University Press, 1926), p. 110.

tions; but they assume the validity of abstractions, universal laws of nature, and the traditional chronology of the world's story.

In all likelihood no very adequate theory of fiction could have evolved until some attempt similar to Johnson's had been made to separate historiography and the natural sciences from "myth," which involved eventually a more distinct separation of poetry from science. Johnson's common-sense division of "truth" from "fabrication" was a basic step in the same direction that philosophers, members of the Royal Society, and historians had taken and were to take more and more firmly, first in challenging the Greek and Roman pantheons and discrediting literal belief in satyrs, unicorns, medieval legends, and then in undermining the traditional chronology and logic of world history. There were other elements in their emergence, to be sure, but the replacement of the logic of providential consequence with the creative contributions of poets was clearly crucial to nineteenth-century theories of both fiction and historiography and eventually to their modern outgrowths.

It is not of course like poets to be overly precise about the nature of any comprehensive calendar. To the myth-maker, the Hindu, Hebrew, Roman, and Gregorian calendars are all useful reckonings of time: each provides names for the seasons and points from which the tabulation begins and perhaps toward which it heads. However, every mythopoeic vision requires not only calibrations of time and segments for the days, months, and years, but also a bounded orientation, a sense of climax and proportion, due season, propriety, and teleology. And once the old chronology is seriously questioned, not all the newer calendars prove to have equal poetic potential. The anthropological invention of ever less refined steps backward into an abyss, for instance, gives to the modern sense of history an indefiniteness that destroys the association between reality and storied consequence. Stages of human development and the progress of societies may be marked with increasing exactness, but the initiating causes and goals disappear — and with them all adjustments of Spenser's and Dante's kind between the moment and the end. The historian then discovers that he must look into the nature of his own method, into the implicit logic of historical chronicle, for the keys to a humanized organization of time. His partnership with the poet is broken in ways that Spenser and Milton, confident of the general B.C.-A.D. reckoning, never imagined that it could be. The finer calibrations of social movement that the novel illustrates, by comparison to the symbolic and programmatic courses of Renaissance fictional types, are one indication of the imaginative power released by this liberation from the old calendar. But at the same time the difficulty of linking the day-by-day diaries of a Moll Flanders or Tom Jones to a governing providence or a coherent universe are the reverse side of that liberation: on one hand, a storyteller was now free to trace meticulously the course of a multitude of social negotiations and economic stages; but on the other hand he found little opportunity to suggest plausibly that his characters' lives could be charted as spiritual paradigms, or that the anecdotes of one time and place are the symbolic epitomes of everyman, in all times and places.

In the eighteenth century, then, a plurality of possible narrative logics was opening to the historian and the novelist, and an initial separation of myth and science was accompanied by the founding of several relatively new methods of investigation — sociology, anthropology, biology (as evidence for evolution), and a more thoroughly documented social history. Each of these possessed its own concept of logical progress and to some extent its own kinds of narrative presentation. That opening up sets the stage for the modern theory of fictions and theory of historiography.

VAIHINGER, BURKE, AND STEVENS: PRAGMATIC VIEWS OF "AS IF"

The treatment of ideational forms of the whole conceptual world as mere products of the imaginative faculty was originally accomplished by Hume and Kant, and continued by Schopenhauer and Herbart. But to treat them as fictions in our sense is to include the idea that these constructions are, from a logical point of view, identical with scientific fictions, i.e. with constructs that, from a practical point of view, are useful and necessary, though theoretically they are false.

Hans Vaihinger, *The Philosophy of "As If,"* p. 63

Though we cannot regard Ernst Cassirer as to any great extent a pragmatist, his emphasis on the functions of structures and forms suggests that forms are not merely aids to cognition but aspects of all man's symbol usage: the pragmatic life depends upon them. It is accordingly in pragmatists and in the pragmatic asides of neo-Kantians like Cassirer and Hans Vaihinger that we find the most fruitful cultivation of the common ground between supposedly truthful representations of reality and fictions. (An extended footnote to

that opinion will be found in the appendix.) In the strange blending
of Benthamite and Kantian traditions, this common ground touches
upon not merely literary but epistemological problems and scientific
methods. As Cassirer suggests, for instance,

> Not only science, but language, myth, art and religion as well, pro-
> vide the building stones from which the world of "reality" is con-
> structed for us, as well as that of the human spirit, in sum the World-
> of-the-I. Like scientific cognition, they are not simple *structures* which
> we can insert into a given world, we must understand them as *func-
> tions* by means of which a particular form is given to reality and in
> each of which specific distinctions are effected.[27]

"Cognition, language, myth and art," then, are in the same boat as
history: "None of them is a mere mirror, simply reflecting images of
inward or outward data; they are not indifferent media, but rather the
true sources of light, the prerequisite of vision, and the wellsprings of
all formation" (p. 93).

The study of cultural forms proceeds best when we remember that
common ground in molding differentiated materials under the imprint of symbolic modes. It is perhaps inevitable that the truth of fictions and the fictional dimensions of truthful formulations would be
more obvious to those whose concern is the *applicability* of symbolic
representation in all cultural forms. Whereas the older mimetic tradition confused history and myth, however, the leading premise of
modern views of "as if," in reuniting them, is that the two have in fact
already been well distinguished. More important, there intervenes between the romantic view of fictions and modern theorists as widespread as Henry James, Kenneth Burke, and Wallace Stevens a
branch of utilitarianism much less hostile to fictions than the Royal
Society, Jeremy Bentham, Dr. Johnson, Thomas Love Peacock, and
others had been, and therefore much readier to concede certain values
to the imagination. More sophisticated in the analysis of propositional statements and language generally than their predecessors, the
pragmatists find the epistemological powers that Coleridge, Wordsworth, Keats, and Shelley attribute to the imagination present in
scientific formulations as well and indeed defend "scientific fictions"

27. Ernst Cassirer, *The Philosophy of Symbolic Form*, 2 vols. (New Haven: Yale
University Press, 1953), 1:91. Cassirer's concept of symbolic forms amplifies Kantian
categories and extends them to a variety of cultural expressions from myth to history and
from the arts to the sciences.

with some of the same arguments that Shelley proposed for the defense of poetry.

In pursuing a combination of Kantian thought and pragmatism, for instance, Vaihinger finds all systems basically fictional, or "as if," constructions. Whether or not there are actually "dryads in Hyde-park" or "naiads in the Regent's canal," as Peacock enjoyed imagining that poets believe, there are unquestionably nonexistent zeros and infinities in the mathematical park and artificial boundaries and properties in the gardens of physics. Vaihinger's contemporary theorists of fiction corroborate that opinion in different ways. Guy de Maupassant, for example, speaks for a number of fictionalists (including Henry James) when he considers not merely literary statements in themselves but "our receptive vessel," the "furniture of our little plot of universal consciousness" (in James's paraphrase) as part of the illusion-creating mechanism. James pounces upon that assumption as a way to defend the artist's pragmatic social and psychological functions:

> How childish . . . to believe in reality, since we each carry our own in our thought and in our organs. Our eyes, our ears, our sense of smell, of taste, differing from one person to another, create as many truths as there are men upon earth. . . .Each one of us, therefore, forms for himself an illusion of the world, which is the illusion poetic, or sentimental, or joyous, or melancholy, or unclean, or dismal, according to his nature. And the writer has no other mission than to reproduce faithfully this illusion, with all the contrivances of art that he has learned and has at his command. The illusion of beauty, which is a human convention! The illusion of ugliness, which is a changing opinion! The illusion of truth, which is never immutable! . . . The great artists are those who make humanity accept their particular illusion.[28]

All social games and inward psychological structures are composed of orders projected by habit and imagination into what we are pleased to think we see.

As these and other defenses of the usefulness of fictions suggest, Vaihinger is by no means as isolated in his corner of late nineteenth-century philosophy as he may appear. Though the combination of pragmatic and structural approaches to fictions that he began to assemble in 1871 (apparently with only slight knowledge of Bentham

---

28. Quoted from Henry James's essay "Guy de Maupassant," in *The Future of the Novel*, ed. Leon Edel (New York: Random House, 1956), p. 196.

or Mill)[29] has never had much direct influence, the four decades that he worked on his theory saw William and Henry James, many of the modern theorists of history, Wallace Stevens, Frost, Wilde, Eliot, Conrad, Yeats, and Joyce enter their formative or productive years. Many of the functions of the imagination that those decades advanced were not really new, nor was Vaihinger's pragmatic critique of scientific and philosophic language, which borrowed many of its basic tenets from a well-traveled nominalism. But the philosophy of "as if" stressed afresh the ways in which "facts" are necessarily reconstituted by systematic arrangement, under the influence of given methodologies. It analyzed the problem of structure with increased precision and sophistication. Indeed, partly through Vaihinger, the end of the century discovered the organization of fictions as the romantics discovered epistemology — the juxtapositions of fictions, their boundary-making, their chaptering and segmentation, their framing orders, their resemblances and contrasts to reality, and the writer himself producing his illusions "with all the contrivances of art that he has learned and has at his command."

Vaihinger's initial steps in outlining a theory of "as if" are necessarily structural, because he defines fictions at the outset as the organization of basic sensations, which are the only nonfictional givens of experience. Because "we have only sensations," he suggests, "our ideas both of movement and nerves, that is to say, of matter, are constructs of our productive phantasy, of fiction. The whole conceptual world is, in other words, inserted between *sensations*; these alone are ultimately given to us. The conceptual world is thus a structure made up of elementary sensations and their residue."[30] What are these

29. C. K. Ogden suggests that Vaihinger was influenced by Bentham through Mill. See *Bentham's Theory of Fictions* (London: Kegan Paul, 1932), pp. xxxi–xxxii. Bentham's treatment of fictions is more linguistic than structural; that is, his main concern is with substantives, fictitious and real objects, and certain aspects of the nominalist controversy. Consequently, he contributes very little to a theory of fictional design or to the possible uses of poetic fictions, which he distrusted as profoundly as Dr. Johnson and in somewhat the same terms: "Between poetry and truth there is a natural opposition: false morals, fictitious nature. The poet always stands in need of something false. When he pretends to lay his foundations in truth, the ornaments of his superstructure are fictions .... Truth, exactitude of every kind, is fatal to poetry .... If poetry and music deserve to be preferred before a game of push-pin, it must be because they are calculated to gratify those individuals who are most difficult to be pleased" (p. xciii).

30. Hans Vaihinger, *The Philosophy of "As If": A System of Theoretical, Practical and Religious Fictions of Mankind*, trans. C. K. Ogden (London: Routledge and Kegan Paul,

sensations and what kinds of sequences do they have either before or after we get through with them? For Vaihinger, unlike William James and the gestaltists, they are initially undifferentiated stimuli having proximity in time but no necessary or inherent arrangement. They are timeless and unconscious, possessed of no history, culture, or psychological orientation until a "differentiated perception" emerges from them. In sensations themselves "no concept of a particular thing is as yet discernible . . . for the vast, vague, nebulous mass of sensations only gradually takes on a rotary movement and only gradually do the individual elements that belong together combine to form perceptual objects and intuitions of the particular" (p. 157).

James and other contemporary psychologists will later argue that perception itself is so organized at base that there is nothing gradual about our intuitions of the particular, except perhaps the learning process by which perceptual patterns are initially acquired. But even in such passages in Vaihinger as those quoted above — where Vaihinger begs the question of connections among sensations themselves in their daily and yearly repetitions[31] — the main point is emphatic enough: everything that comes between sensation and what we ultimately render in verbal systems is created by the perceiver. It does not "exist." "Understanding," Vaihinger remarks, "is the well-known feeling of pleasure due to the empirical transformation of sensations into categories" (p. 171); and categories of course are all "fictions."[32] Abstractions, personifications, juristic conveniences, ethical principles, and various disciplines such as mathematics, the sciences, art, and religion are aspects of the same general power of linguistic and perceptual arrangement that people practice on their environment in

---

1935), p. 67. The first version of Vaihinger's study was a dissertation (1876), which he expanded in a second part between 1877 and 1879. The entire work was reviewed and expanded further after 1906 and published in 1911 (see pp. xl and xli).

31. Paul Fraisse, in *The Psychology of Time*, trans. Jennifer Leith (New York: Harper and Row, 1963), cites several kinds of periodic order, for instance, that are inherent in the organism and its immediate environment: the pulse, respiratory cycle, rhythm of the digestive organs and sleep, menstruation, seasonal rhythms of vegetable life, sexual activity, migrations, etc. (p. 17).

32. The root of *fiction, fig*, justifies most of the uses to which Vaihinger puts the word. *Fingere* means "arrange," "conceive," and "form" as well as "fabricate," and *figura* of course encompasses "form" and "shape," "kind, nature, and species," "figure of speech," and thus all separable classification and integral units as well as the "arrangements" of various branches of inquiry.

every waking moment. If in positivism the terms of the mind's meetings with reality are dictated entirely by the way-things-inherently-are, then, in Vaihinger's epistemology the meeting is a dramatic exchange, a collision, the result of which is always a systematic "as if" construction. The make-up of a particular system is determined by a number of contingencies, mental, linguistic, and physical. At one time all the disciplines of human investigation recognized a common affinity: though scientific fictions are now distinguishable from aesthetic and religious fictions, myth once served as the common mother of them all. Indeed, "the psychological genesis of fictions is the same in all fields of inquiry" (p. 81).[33] Vaihinger thus anticipates Cassirer in suggesting that all forms of spiritual and intellectual action share a single impulse, since as Cassirer remarks, "Every authentic function of the human spirit has this decisive characteristic in common with cognition: it does not merely copy but rather embodies an original, formative power .... This is as true of art as it is of cognition; it is as true of myth as of religion. ... Each of these functions creates its own symbolic forms" (*Philosophy of Symbolic Forms*, 1:78). It could also easily have been Vaihinger who said, "If we approach spiritual life, not as the static contemplation of being, but as functions and energies of formation, we shall find certain common and typical principles of formation, diverse and dissimilar as the forms may be. ... The diversity of the *products* of the human spirit does not impair the unity of its productive process, but rather sustains and confirms it" (Cassirer, *Philosophy of Symbolic Form*, 1:114).

More important to Vaihinger than the branches of fictive statement, however, are the uses to which fictions are put. These uses extend beyond anything that Sidney or the romantics envisioned for the utility of poetry and mark a potential but largely unexploited turning point in the modern defense of poetry. "The duty of a logical theory of fictions," as Vaihinger conceives of it, is "to discover the mechanism by means of which [fictions] perform their service" (p. 67). Both the concept of mechanism and the concept of service are typical and significant: they point to the inevitability of fictive arrangements and

---

33. It has become common to concede as much and to trace the origins of philosophy and history to religion. See, for instance, Clement J. J. Webb, "Religion, Philosophy, and History," in *Philosophy and History*, ed. Raymond Klibansky and H. J. Paton (New York: Harper and Row, 1963; originally published by Oxford University Press, 1936).

the necessity of our turning to them in any attempt to control reality. The importance of a philosophy of "as if" is that only by becoming conscious of our habitual fictionalizing may we use it for ethical ends — as William James, Kenneth Burke, and Wallace Stevens each insists that we do. In this respect, illusions are much like paper money, in one of Vaihinger's luckier metaphors: " 'Fictional value' is the name given in political economy to paper-money and such ideas as, for instance, the pound sterling, etc. The paper is regarded *as if* it had the value of metal; the computation is made as if we were really dealing with 'pounds sterling' " (p. 160). Just as money, when we believe in it, passes muster, so any given fiction, in being treated as if it were true, makes possible certain intellectual transactions that could not be carried on otherwise. And just as our economic system would crumble without money, our perceptual and intellectual life would collapse without fictions. "Highly differentiated transactions are only possible by this means, even if we are forced to admit that there has been many a 'swindle' in the realm of thought, where people have given up valuable material goods for valueless paper, for valueless thoughts" (p. 161). "All higher speculation and the whole of our intricate system of exchange are only possible by this expedient and by these fictional values" (p. 160). The case could not be put more strongly, and back of it one glimpses in Vaihinger, as in Shelley, the marvelous poetic act that once went into conceiving of new metaphoric "transfers," when metals were stamped with symbolic marks, ciphers were recorded on paper currency, or human attributes were compared imaginatively to those of animals and plants in the mythologizing process. In the humdrum regularities of business we lose sight of the inventive foundation of our pragmatic transactions, whose linguistic expression was initially a poetic creation.

If transactions in thought are comparable to transactions in goods, and systems of terminology are comparable to currency systems, their pragmatic value is indisputable. As we can create marvelous structures in blueprints or recipes — without touching a plank or a pinch of salt — so in words we prepare for the handling of material reality, creating both what we see and the actions we will perform. If in our social accord we then wish to convert recipes into apple pies or revolutions, we may do so with a knowledge of at least some of the consequences that lie before us. Fictions may or may not "legislate" in precisely the way Shelley assumed, but as the tools of social intercourse and analytic processes, they clearly make legislation possible. Even to "behave" and to "think" are impossible for Vaihinger without fiction-making. "Thought undertakes ingenious operations, invents brilliant expedients, is able to introduce highly complicated processes. The material of sensation is re-modelled, re-coined, compressed, it is purged of dross and mixed with alloys from the fund of the psyche itself, in order to render possible a more and more certain, rapid, and refined solution to the problem of the logical function" (p. 6).

The implications of these "ingenious operations" reach into all disciplines in Vaihinger's sweeping panorama of fictions, just as they do in William James's application of psychology to philosophy and again in Kenneth Burke's philosophy of literary and social forms. In mathematics, for instance, our "apperceptive constructs" reduce events to known measure and control the numberless sensations that swarm around us. In juristic fictions, we classify one thing as if it were another in order to handle it more conveniently under an existing social contract — as when we consider a son-in-law as if he were a son in order to apply to him a son's categories of legal rights. If the law had to interpret every event as unique, as "in fact" it is, there would be no common law. Likewise, only when we "fictionalize" historical persons and occasions and associate them with preexistent categories and generalities can we control them socially and make them truly available for historiography. The rhetoric and the logic that historians use are parallel to the law in that any definition, classification, metaphor, or analogy gathers unique events into acknowledged frameworks and kinships. Once we have classified "Socrates" among "mortals," for instance, we can systematize our view of him under the laws of that particular kind, or construe the individual case under a universal grammar. Associating "love" with red, red roses, we fictionalize it, "re-model, re-coin, and compress" it.

In sum — reading between the lines of Vaihinger's comments on language — we find that linguistic and legal fictions do not merely arrest "the vanishing apparitions which haunt the interlunations of life," as Shelley ethereally puts it in the *Defence of Poetry*: they create all *groupings* of gross sensation. Love is not love or anything beyond mute affection until we fasten it to a linguistic structure, and then, in Vaihinger's terms, it becomes a fabricated or fictional love.

In proposing this pragmatic operation of fictions, Vaihinger departs from the acknowledged influence of Kant and from empiricism and logical positivism as well.[34] As he takes pains to make clear in the statement quoted as an epigraph to this section, his fictional kinds are quite different from Kant's a priori categories. Unfortunately, he is less careful to distinguish relatively capricious and odd fictions from those that make a convincing and logical organization of sensations. Some categories, Kant's among them, strike us as basically empirical or necessary, whereas others are obviously fantastic. Nor does Vaihinger distinguish primary, personal sensations from attested and recorded facts communicated to us by others — as though saying that "a son-in-law is a mule" before the law would be as normally service-

34. Vaihinger distinguishes his critical positivism from skepticism and nominalism. Finding a skeptical disbelief in the reality named by generalized nouns to be paralyzing, Vaihinger insists upon the usefulness of verbal artifice, including abstraction. In the opposite direction, however, he also distinguishes critical positivism from conceptual realism, which mistakes what is merely logical and invented for what is actual. For Vaihinger, even the *ding an sich* does not actually exist: it is a convenience, like the concept of adjectival qualities that attach to the "thing." He gains support in this from recent philosophers of language. Alfred Korzybski, for instance, suggests that acts of perception contain much that might be called mythic in view of the fact that objects outside us are really a "mad dance of 'electrons,' . . . different every instant, which never repeats itself, which is known to consist of extremely complex dynamic processes of very fine structure, acted upon by, and reacting upon, the rest of the universe, inextricably connected with everything else and dependent on everything else." "What we see," Korzybski maintains, is structurally only a "specific statistical mass-effect of happenings on a much finer grained level." Our neurological systems present to us a relatively coarse or generalized set of perceptions in no way accurate in reproducing that "mad dance." They are assisted by language from the early age at which we learn names for things and create fictitious borders, textures, stabilities of mass, and defined shapes.
One could maintain with Max Black that even the supposedly "real" characteristics of the objects with which Korzybski begins are really abstractions: one cannot name even a "mad dance of electrons" without using fictional abstractions. A "label is not the object nor the event, but a still further abstraction," and "once it is admitted that the characteristics of the scientific object . . . are themselves abstractions, there is no longer any basis for the sharp distinction between the alleged external reality and the supposed subjectively manufactured abstractions." Korzybski is quoted from Max Black, *Language and Philosophy: Studies in Method* (Ithaca, N.Y.: Cornell University Press, 1949), pp. 235 ff. See also *The Labyrinth of Language* (New York: Frederick A. Praeger, 1968), pp. 85–89 on "fictions."
Like Bentham and modern semanticists, William James also takes a primarily linguistic view of fictions. See *Pragmatism and Four Essays from the Meaning of Truth* (Cleveland and New York: Meridian Books, 1955).
An extensive bibliography of works on the philosophy of language may be found in *The Linguistic Turn: Recent Essays in Philosophical Methods*, ed. Richard Rorty (Chicago: University of Chicago Press, 1967).

able in human discourse as more ordinary statements. If "the true and final purpose of thought is action and the facilitation of action" (p. 66) as he suggests, all fictions are reduced to mere instrumentality; one is tempted too readily to set aside thorny questions of validity, relative truth, and the nature of the poetic imagination, not to mention the historian's difficult task of probing into correspondences between documents and reality.

These are reasonably serious omissions in Vaihinger's theory of "as if," and they are accompanied by others. The fictions that interest him most are scientific, legal, logical, and mathematical rather than aesthetic. Though he anticipates Cassirer in a good deal, he does not ask such important modal questions as the following, which are central to Cassirer's inquiry:

> Is there a natural or only a mediate and conventional connection between the form of language and the form of reality, between the essence of words and that of things? Is the inner structure of reality itself expressed in words, or do they reveal no law other than that imprinted on them by the caprice of the first coiners of speech? [*Philosophy of Symbolic Forms*, 1:122]

Moreover, because he never describes very fully the "definite laws" by which sensations are converted into systematic fictions, the ways and means of fictive creation appear much too simple to him. The goal of aesthetic fictions, for instance, is vaguely to awaken in us "certain uplifting or otherwise important feelings" (p. 82), which does little to explain comic, satiric, or novelistic modes, among other things. Indeed, even with these grander products of spirit, we never discover what sensations they arise from, how they are transformed, what feelings are aroused, or how particular aesthetic models manage them. For all his emphasis upon the structure of fictional statements, Vaihinger says remarkably little about the psychological movement of particular kinds of fiction — scientific, religious, or aesthetic. He does not consider history writing as such, or the central myths of his or any other culture, and hence avoids in this area, too, the relative truthfulness and inventiveness of the orders he assumes that people live by. (What are the pragmatic and ethical functions of the myth of progress, for instance? Or the myth of sacrificial heroes and resurrected gods? Or the myths of Marxism?) Without a depth psychology at his command and with apparently little interest in cathartic functions of

symbolic structures, he does not attempt to discover how an audience participates in art's "uplifting or otherwise important feelings,"
though the ethical and pragmatic functions of a fiction obviously vary
according to how audiences react to it. And finally, he pays very little
explicit attention to problems of language, the "sets" of grammar, the
implications of style, or the conventions of everyday usage.

Despite these gaps, Vaihinger's insistence on a wide variety of fictive systems and cultural forms opened up new possibilities for a
theory of fictions at a stage between Bentham and the modern revaluation of fictions that needed something like a serious philosophy
of "as if." Though he did not finish what he began, others quickly
added to it, and luckily those aspects of fictions that he most ignored
are the very ones that more recent philosophers, critics, and poets
have taken most seriously. Perhaps most notable among his
successors (besides Cassirer) are Kenneth Burke and Wallace Stevens,
both of whom, without directly following him or referring to him,
follow a similar pragmatic bent and a similarly broadened sense of
symbolic formulations.

Like Vaihinger, Burke treats symbolic formulations as primarily reactive or "dramatistic" instruments. He does not assume that the "sole
reality" is a set of "actual sensations" or that any act of formulation
or conceptualization constitutes a fiction-making act; but in effect he
treats all verbal constructions as fictive systems, or "terminologies."
At the same time, he makes broad distinctions between relatively fictional and relatively factual modes of formulation, the latter being
less emotional and psychological than the forensic or fictive arts. And
he is much more specific than Vaihinger about the properties of given
modes such as the dramatic, lyric, and narrative. In recognizing the
transactional values of different kinds of symbol systems, some of
them poetic and some of them primarily factual, he is led to stress the
influence of symbols in themselves. Thus if we were to extend Vaihinger's financial metaphor, the substitution of paper currency for
real goods and real gold would alter for Burke the nature of the exchange itself. We grow attached to a symbolic mode for its own sake;
we learn to love rhymes, dramatic forms, and narratives — not to
mention paper money — for the intrinsic pleasure they afford, and we
are seriously changed by them as we learn to perceive new realities

through them. A society may become a "monied" culture, for instance, with all the strata, jobs, and bureaucracy that depend upon its particular "currency."

Both Vaihinger and Burke naturally wish our fictive inventions to be used to humane and ethical ends, then, but whereas Vaihinger is content to point out the dangers of naive falsifications of reality, Burke explores the ins and outs of structured human "play" and the influence on it of the symbolic materials of finance, poetry, myth, or science. To that end, like philosophers of language such as Cassirer, he becomes a careful observer of the psychic world between Vaihinger's entering gateway of sensation and exiting gateway of thoughtful action. His habitual emphasis, like John Dewey's also in *Art as Experience*, falls upon ways in which psychology and the progression of fictive works are entangled in one another, and his most characteristic view of fictive structure makes it preeminently a cathartic, ritual enactment, a movement of intellectual and emotional states in the reader. In fictions as opposed to real life, an author strategically stages an experience that the audience shares, undergoing as it does so a vicarious passage toward an outcome.

Perhaps Burke's clearest and most emphatic statement of those psychological stages in the audience remains the early essay "Psychology and Form" in *Counter-statement* (1931), in which he argues that since we cannot take pleasure in what is entirely new — only in recurrent form — "information" is subordinate in dramatic literature to formal structure. As music illustrates, for repeated performances the less information the better: "Music, . . . fitted less than any other art for imparting information, deals minutely in frustrations and fulfillments of desire, and for that reason more often gives us those curves of emotion which, because they are natural, can bear repetition without loss." What strikes us as "true" at a given moment in a work of art is not what imitates reality but what falls into place in the satisfaction of a program: "Truth in art is not the discovery of facts, not an addition to human knowledge in the scientific sense of the word. It is, rather, the exercise of human propriety, the formulation of symbols which rigidify our sense of poise and rhythm."[35] Thus if Shakespeare has led us to expect the arrival of King Hamlet's ghost and has teased us with a contrasting merriment

35. Kenneth Burke, *Counter-statement* (Los Altos, Calif.: Hermes Publications, 1931), pp. 36, 42.

in the court's carousal while we wait, the particular pattern of desire and fulfillment he has aroused can be completed only when the ghost appears. At that point, the play holds true as a transaction between playwright and audience, not to a world that does or does not contain ghosts but to its own self-sustaining form. The information of the work is of whatever variety its own patterns sanction. Hamlet's delay, too, is not a problem for psychoanalysis, at least not centrally, but a necessary complication in the audience's linear pattern of confirmations, which are teased into complexity by Hamlet's reluctance to complete the pattern laid out for him by the revenge plot. Thus the sequence of events in any storied enactment carries an audience through a linear journey or *mythos* toward an anticipated but delayed outcome.

A given work promotes a social transaction between author and audience on the basis of this shared psychology of linear form, which is the reality conveyed by the fictive currency we undertake to believe in momentarily. However, unlike Vaihinger's "as if" constructions, Burke's fictions work primarily because they suggest something *like* reality; they are both formal rituals and imitations. We expect to find in them as in true statements a fund of common beliefs. Some of these beliefs are already structured for us by nature. In his account of "the poetic process," for instance, Burke discovers, again like Dewey in *Art as Experience*, that some aspects of coherent psychic actions such as a gradual rise to a crisis or a crescendo are like sequences in nature itself. "The accelerated motion of a falling body, the cycle of a storm, the procedure of the sexual act, the ripening of crops — growth here is not merely linear progression, but a fruition. Indeed, natural processes are, inevitably, 'formally' correct, and by merely recording the symptoms of some physical development we can obtain an artistic development" (*Counter-statement*, p. 45). Hence in some respects we proceed full circle back to Aristotle's mimetic theory: the roots of literary form are nourished in nature and in the audience's delight in realistic recognition.

Despite the verifiable content of linear works, however, the co-presence of patterns in everyday experience and in literary works does not mean that the work is a simple extension of reality. The work establishes a sense of proportion, pace, timing, and heights and depths of organized feeling that exist nowhere outside it. The psychology of linear form depends upon common experience not so much as something to *recognize* in the work as something to establish *conditions of appeal* in the transaction between author and audience: "There need not be a 'divine contrast' in heaven for me to appreciate a contrast; but there *must be* in my mind the sense of contrast. The researches of anthropologists indicate that man has 'progressed' in cultural cycles which repeat themselves in essence (in form) despite the limitless variety of specific details to embody such essences" (p. 48). Though shades of Comte are perhaps evident in this concept of universal form by which patterns in experience prepare for the reception of patterns in works of art, rather than insisting on the scientific value of universals Burke suggests merely that they have a place in a theory of literary archetypes and recurrent kinds. Like Cassirer, he touches upon the concept of cultural forms in which the products of every culture are expressions of like aspects in the productive human spirit. But human creations are also answerable to individual motives and dispositions. Under provocative stress, when an artist is led to seek symbolic relief, he usually does so in strategic echoes of bodily, psychological, and sociological patterns to which he gives his own stylistic twist. In the best of art, we therefore find recurrent forms and a special talent for innovation in the artist, though this talent, too, must find something answerable in the audience if it is to arouse a response:

> If we are enmeshed in some nodus of events and the nodus of emotions surrounding those events, and someone meets us with a diagnosis (simplification) of our partially conscious, partially unconscious situation, we are charmed by the sudden illumination which this formula throws upon our own lives. Mute Byrons (potential Byrons) were waiting in more or less avowed discomfiture for the formulation of Byronism, and when it came they were enchanted. [P. 58]

The crucial points in these positions on the structure of fictions thus appear to be two, our being initially enmeshed in some mutual complex of real, historical preconditions of art, and our liberation from these relatively disorganized preconditions by appropriate symbolic enactments. Accurate appraisals of reality are secondary in art to organization, to the success that fictive structures have in arousing, hindering, and fulfilling desires in a programmatic way. A good symbolic structure affects us "like the magic formula of the savage, like the medicine for an ill" (p. 61). As it is for James in *Principles of Psychology*, the question of reality for Burke is thus also secondary to what men believe and find useful. Art is pragmatic, but it may not move mountains or build cities as the fictions of engineering, law, and science presumably might. Its pragmatism depends directly upon its formal order and its echo of inchoate structures in the culture and the individual psyche. When it is answerable to these, it works.

The special importance of linear consequence in this cathartic realization of artistic formulas is evident in two similar passages from works twenty years apart in Burke's exploration of symbolic fictions, *The Philosophy of Literary Form* (1941) and *The Rhetoric of Religion* (1961). In "Principles of Governance Stated Narratively" in the latter, Burke considers what happens when a fixed scheme or principle of governance is converted into linear sequence, or logical into temporal arrangement. Thus rather than saying that "the first six primary classes would be such-and-such," Genesis assigns the first class to a first day, marking the division of the days and classes by a ritual break in the creation, a temporal rhythm. By the inherent logic of narrative, classification thereby becomes history or story. Besides its temporal succession, the same narrative logic also brings to the stages of its unfolding a sense of outcome or purpose: after each of the days, an accordance between the creative event and the original intent is announced. Thus each day fulfills an intentional form and is absorbed into a realm of complete and acknowledged intelligibility; temporal acts prove the image of the creator. They unfold (to augment Burke's comments slightly) an animate logic. Since an outcome demands a more personal creator than the notion of an orderly, classified world, the commands "let there be" and the benedictions at the end of each calendar period extend a spirit world from a humanized source and point toward a total outcome, a calendric goal. Thus in Burke's logological reading of the narrative, man himself emerges as the first visible "principle of personality [already] implicit in the idea of the . . . creative fiats," as their cumulative purpose and the creator's most complete image.[36]

Other logological implications also stem from the narrative form of the exposition in Genesis. Because each created thing is separated from all others as a distinct division, it is opposed to them, and one can say that the logic of narrative requires concealment, hindrance, and plot complication. From the word *good*, as Burke suggests, we

36. Kenneth Burke, *The Rhetoric of Religion: Studies in Logology* (Boston: Beacon Press, 1961), pp. 201ff.

lean forward to the discovery of evil; the fall is inherent in the very terminology of the six days' creation. Narrative, as opposed to expository explanation, depends upon this method of hinting-and-withholding that brings evil forward only at the proper moment. Treated logically rather than narratively, evil would result in a fixed Manichaean polarity without narrative concealment, turning points, or rhythm. As in music certain notes which, when taken together, produce a chord or discord produce a melody when taken as linear movement, so in Hebraic and Christian thought the linear treatment of evil makes it a momentary unease on the road to healing perfection; it has no chordal permanence.

Burke's analysis of the creation myth in Genesis 1–3 suggests several aspects of the modern theory of fiction that go beyond the traditional concepts of organic action in the Aristotelian tradition and Vaihinger's rudimentary psychology of form. It indicates clearly that what might in other quarters be acceptable as historical truth or theological articles of faith can be treated by a theory of fictions as an illustration of the organizing power of linear myth. The structure of narrative is clearly not in any exact way the structure of reality; it is the structure of a particular mode of thought and rendered expression. The inherent stresses of narrative form, some of which we will examine later — the retardation of design, the anxiety that accompanies knowledge, the reversals brought about by the unburying of inexplicit strands — are projected as an organization of reality; but we are not obliged to believe literally in the "history" displayed before us. Dr. Johnson's precept that "a fiction, not only detected but despised, can never afford a solid basis to any position" is virtually reversed: only the discovery of the fictive root of any mode of analysis enables us to believe in the mode in our modern, provisional way. If men are to propose to themselves a fulfillment, as Stevens suggests, they must do so in fictions recognized as fictions.

Though historiography is one of the few fields that Burke has not extensively tilled, a concept of historical narration is also implied by this analysis. Many of the obstacles to gathering and formulating "facts" are removed by it or sufficiently reinterpreted to make them less perplexing. Though it makes use of things that have actually happened rather than inventions, history writing is merely another way of satisfying the rage for formal satisfaction. As Ortega y Gasset remarks in an essay, "History as a System," in terms that Burke could be imagined to sanction, man invents for himself a programme of life, a static form of being, that gives a satisfactory answer to the difficulties posed for him by circumstance. He essays this form of life, attempts to realize this imaginary character he has resolved to be. He embarks on the essay full of illusions and prosecutes the experiment with thoroughness. . . . he comes to *believe* deeply that this character is his real being.

If in all symbol systems we create identities, in history we create identities based on historical continuity. In going on to a second or third program, we hold to what we have been to some extent, until an "authentic 'being' " stretches the "whole length of [the] past." In Burke's view of our talent for creating structures, as in Ortega y Gasset's, man has thus no necessary nature of his own beyond that prescribed by his habitual symbol usage: "What he has is . . . history. Expressed differently: what nature is to things, history, *res gestae*, is to man." We progress constantly on to new forms of symbolic action, carrying with us an awareness of the past that we recapitulate in the logic of narrative:

What was it that made us understand, *conceive*, our being? Simply the telling, the narrating that *formerly* I was the lover of this and that woman, that *formerly* I was a Christian, that the reader in himself or through others he has heard of was an absolutist, a Caesarist, a democrat, etc. In short, the reasoning, the *reason* that throws light here consists in a narration. Alongside pure physico-mathematical reason there is, then, a narrative reason. To comprehend anything human, be it personal or collective, one must tell its history. ... Life only takes on a measure of transparency in the light of *historical reason*.[37]

Given such a retrieval of the past entirely through symbolic systems, it is not surprising to find Burke treating literary genres in a book on history and suggesting, as he does in the essay "Poetic Categories" in *Attitudes toward History* (1937), that each of the great poetic forms stresses its own peculiar way of building the mental equipment (meanings, attitudes, character) by which "one handles the significant factors of his time."[38] One's categorical attitudes — resignation, warning, magnification, mourning, debunking, complaint, etc. — lead to characteristic forms of expression like epic, tragedy, elegy, lyric, comedy, satire, burlesque, and the grotesque. Some of these are more imaginative and less truthful than others, but

37. José Ortega y Gasset, *History as a System and Other Essays toward a Philosophy of History* (New York: Norton, 1961), pp. 214ff. Reprinted in *Philosophy and History*, ed. Klibansky and Paton, pp. 311–13.

38. Kenneth Burke, *Attitudes toward History* (Boston: Beacon Press, 1961), p. 34.

all of them are strategies in response to the circumstances we are enmeshed in. All of them express attitudes toward history and grow out of a need to take its measure. They are not necessarily historiography as we usually think of it, but they can be understood only by a variety of historical reasoning, as moves in a continuing and complex chess game against history's raw materials. These materials create the stresses and strains that goad both the artist and the historian into the creation of their linear orders and cathartic outcomes.

What we frequently realize in reading Burke's accounts of such symbolic categories — especially if we come to him from nineteenth- and early twentieth-century debates over the nature of fictions and historiography — is that we live in a world created and sustained by systematic books. In one of his more panoramic moments, Burke attributes to fictions nearly the whole of instituted social and intellectual life:

> Can we bring ourselves to realize just . . . how overwhelmingly much of what we mean by "reality" has been built up for us through nothing but our symbol systems? Take away our books, and what little do we know about history, biography, even something so "down to earth" as the relative position of seas and continents? What is our "reality" for today (beyond the paper-thin line of our own particular lives) but all this clutter of symbols about the past combined with whatever things we know mainly through maps, magazines, newspapers, and the like about the present? In school, as they go from class to class, students turn from one idiom to another. The various courses in the curriculum are in effect but so many different terminologies. And however important to us is the tiny sliver of reality each of us has experienced first-hand, the whole overall "picture" is but a construct of our symbol systems. To meditate on this fact until one sees its full implications is much like peering over the edge of things into an ultimate abyss.[39]

Whereas previous times and theories of fiction locate form in inherent laws of nature or Ideas, then, a modern theory of structure in Burke's view must locate it in the terminologies of various disciplines, in philosophies of "as if."

In some respects, Burke's pragmatism and his desire to read the creation of symbol systems as a response to common experience lead to a somewhat limited view of the origins of given poems. They discount too readily the poet's need to publish for fame or money, his

39. Kenneth Burke, *Language as Symbolic Action* (Berkeley and Los Angeles: University of California Press, 1966), p. 5.

inspiration from other literary texts, his special moments of joy or illumination, his emotions recollected in tranquillity; they lead momentarily in "Literature as Equipment for Living" (in *The Philosophy of Literary Form*) to a reduction of the basic strategies of literature to those of the proverb. But seeing narrative and dramatic fictions as in some way always an order-making response to complex and usually disorderly realities is no longer an uncommon first step in explanations of linear structures and the overlapping concerns of fiction and historiography. Outcome is not merely the finish of a logical system but the closure of a pyschological field; it brings into equilibrium the dramatic tensions and animate powers at work in the moving of actions. It prevents the intrusion of still other exuberant forces and the breakdown of logic and dispersal of psychic energies.

Burke's comparative indifference to the distinction between primarily true and primarily fictional statements, like Vaihinger's more obvious indifference, prevents him at times from expanding on exactly how the combination of imitation and form works in fictive enactments. We are never quite sure in many of his analyses just how the work actually releases us from its enclosed system to the exterior world or how we get into the world of fictions in the first place — what its climate changes are, what its references to reality accomplish, or how long its therapeutic value lasts. How does the organization of psychic energies in art actually apply to the threatened and disarranged environment of its making? What does the structure of expectations in *Hamlet* have to do with anything *except* the work and the audience's presence before it?

We have somewhat less difficulty with such questions when we look at factual narrative because there the author's editorial opinions and evaluative estimates are usually a forward part of the mode. No one pretends about history writing that it is aesthetically sealed off from life, that it is a "fine" or useless art, an end in itself. The librarian's and reader's impulse to classify fictional and truthful works separately in this regard is not entirely misleading, nor are the only grounds for such a classification those outlined in "Semantic and Poetic Meaning" (*The Philosophy of Literary Form*). We cannot abolish the distinction between imagination and reality — as Vaihinger and other pragmatists tend to do — merely by observing that all forms of symbolicity are partly false. Some apply directly to acknowledged situations and others are hypothetical, inactive, or intransitive. But we are still too far from answering too many basic questions about the psychology of perception, the nature of the mind's contributions to reality, and the functions of imagination to offer firm views of the distinction here. We should not presume to say too quickly what really exists, what we contribute to it in the act of seeing and formulating, how we pass from enclosed fictions back to the world (and how we pass differently from historical systems to the present world), how we glance up from the work to reality and return to the work again, how the reader's vicarious course through a work differs from the hero's. Having turned away the stronger thrusts of empiricism and positivism, the pragmatic theories of fictive structure that we have pursued leave nearly all of these questions in a problematic state.[40]

For the moment our own path does not lead further into them, though we will return to some of them in due course. It leads instead toward another line of inquiry left untouched by Vaihinger — the relationship between imagination and perception. Over this area of modern fictional theory Wallace Stevens presides with sufficient authority and comprehensiveness to make him an important milestone in any theory of fictional structure and linear systems.

Stevens's view of fictions, too, is deeply pragmatic, more so than has generally been acknowledged. He writes of his own poems, "The author's work suggests the possibility of a supreme fiction, recognized as a fiction, in which men could propose to themselves a fulfilment. In the creation of any such fictions, poetry would have a vital significance."[41] As a pragmatist, he recognizes, like John Dewey,

40. Psychologies of perception and imagination have not been very immediately helpful in relating the two, but see R. W. Gerard's suggestion that "imagination may be the word for that all-important no man's land between the end of the receptive process and the start of the expressive one" ("The Biological Basis of Imagination," pp. 226–51 of *The Creative Process: A Symposium*, ed. Brewster Ghiselin [New York: Mentor, 1955; published originally by the University of California Press, 1952]). Gerard remarks that even before anything crosses that mysterious "arch" between receptive and active sectors of the brain, the sensory messages that we receive "are not merely relayed and regrouped, they are also reorganized and reworked" (p. 240).

Cf. W. Russell, *Brain, Mind, Perception and Science* (Oxford: Blackwell, 1951); D. W. Hamlyn, *The Psychology of Perception: A Philosophical Examination of Gestalt Theory and Derivative Theories of Perception* (London: Routledge and Kegan Paul, 1957); R. J. Hirst, *The Problems of Perception* (London: George Allen and Unwin, 1959); K. Koffka, *Principles of Gestalt Psychology* (New York: Harcourt, Brace and Co., 1935).

41. *Letters of Wallace Stevens*, ed. Holly Stevens (New York: Knopf, 1966), p. 830.

that there are also many nonfictional fulfillments, achievable without the benefits or the handicaps of poets and the imagination. Indeed, whatever has a semblance of structure and moves toward a conclusion is in some sense fulfilling, whether it is the making of a house, a graduation, a chess game, or the scoring of a touchdown. As Dewey writes of *an* experience (as opposed to experience in general),

> A piece of work is finished in such a way that is satisfactory; a problem receives its solution; a game is played through; a situation, whether that of eating a meal, playing a game of chess, carrying on a conversation, writing a book, or taking part in a political campaign, is so rounded out that its close is a consummation and not a cessation. Such an experience is a whole and carries with it its own individual quality and self-sufficiency.[42]

In such experiences, "every successive part flows freely, without seam and without unfilled blanks, into what ensues" (p. 36). A climaxing moment converts each step on the way toward it into a meaningful part of an organized field.

As Burke suggests and as Stevens frequently assumes, the poet takes advantage of these natural "careers." In twanging on his wiry string, the man with the blue guitar renders in his own style,

> Sounds passing through sudden rightnesses, wholly
> Containing the mind, below which it cannot descend,
> Beyond which it has no will to rise.
>
>   It must
> Be the finding of a satisfaction, and may
> Be of a man skating, a woman dancing, a woman
> Combing. The poem of the act of the mind.[43]

However, the kinds of fulfillment that are available in the real world in acts of skating, dancing, and combing, before the poet sounds them on his strings, are limited. Poets can easily imagine others, more grandly conclusive, nobler, funnier, more tragic — or if nothing else, more perfectly representative of human ordinariness. He can imagine these only in fictions, in which not merely some but all in-process moments and strands of action come to fruition. A supreme fiction would presumably propose a fulfillment that leaves nothing hanging,

42. Dewey, *Art as Experience*, p. 35.
43. Wallace Stevens, "Of Modern Poetry," *The Collected Poems* (London: Faber and Faber; New York: Random House, 1945), p. 240.

nothing incoherent, nothing to be resumed. Its calendar would be not only well segmented and rhythmic but bounded at both ends. It would indeed be an act of mind.

The phrase "recognized as a fiction" is critical to Stevens's proposing of such a fiction, and it would probably not have occurred to preromantics, whose supreme fictions were accepted as legitimate, mimetic images of essential realities. It is also critical to the usefulness Stevens imagines for poetry, which after all gives us only very tentative and hypothetical enclosures of reality. In fact, in the course of his works a modern poet proposes not one supreme fiction but many fictions, all of them entertainments possessed of a degree of irony and playfulness. As Stevens imagines it, then, poetry is both responsible to a pragmatic life and free of excessive daily commonplaces. It celebrates the oddity and colorfulness of the opportunities presented to it by nature and by words. It values both enclosed form and the world of unending process. As James Baird points out, poetry to Stevens is a matter of rejoicing, partly over its own gaudiness. Where the imagination flourishes in its fictions, the poet is free to chant his version of the liturgy, "I praise thee, O free imagination."[44]

In the poetry of the thirties, especially in *Ideas of Order* and *The Man with the Blue Guitar*, Stevens is concerned with bringing together the playful, the extraordinary, and the ordinary. He is concerned with how a tentative fictional construction can influence a downcast and hungry people who may not be overly receptive to imagination. Devoted as he is to "things as they are," the man with the blue guitar seeks, in playing on his instrument, to heighten bare, flat earth with the perceptions native to myth. For one thing, he offers men a fresh return to basic, noneconomic blessings of the kind that poetry has always celebrated. His audience tells him that poetry

> Exceeding music must take the place
> Of empty heaven and its hymns,
>
> Ourselves in poetry must take their place,
> Even in the chattering of your guitar.
> [*Collected Poems*, p. 167]

Above all, the tune that replaces the older hymns of a fictive heaven is

44. James Baird, *The Dome and the Rock: Structure in the Poetry of Wallace Stevens* (Baltimore: Johns Hopkins Press, 1968), p. xix.

A tune beyond us as we are,
Yet nothing changed by the blue guitar;

Ourselves in the tune as if in space,
Yet nothing changed, except the place

Of things as they are and only the place
As you play them, on the blue guitar,

Placed, so, beyond the compass of change,
Perceived in a final atmosphere;

For a moment final, in the way
The thinking of art seems final when

The thinking of god is smoky dew.
The tune is space. The blue guitar

Becomes the place of things as they are,
A composing of senses of the guitar.
[*Collected Poems*, pp. 167–68]

If the poet's fictions are in a sense supreme, it is only because "for a moment," paradoxically, they seem "final": for the privileged occasion of the poem the mind and emotions take their pleasure from ordering things "beyond the compass of change," in the poem itself, which replaces the normal landscape of things and becomes their transfiguring place. Older fictions of heaven such as Herbert's and Milton's also enabled men to perceive things in a final atmosphere, but they were not recognized as fictions; one participated in their hymns as in a holy and sacred reality without the intervention of the imagination — without assuming that the way of expressing them had become itself the composing "place of things as they are."

Because earth is "flat and bare," then, the poet is called upon to invent new tunes and give us perceptions as though they were final. He is also in need of his own historical continuity to condition the moments of poetry with an awareness of where men have come from and may be supposed to be headed. In "Notes toward a Supreme Fiction," Stevens finds it part of poetry's function (especially as "abstraction") to propose its own radical beginning and ending. The fledgling poet is admonished to begin

by perceiving the idea
Of this invention, this invented world,
The inconceivable idea of the sun.
[*Collected Poems*, p. 380]

If the world is an invention primarily, an idea is its source; all other origins are inconceivable. The world springs anew in the poet's imagination *ex nihilo*; it is impossible, but it exists. It is real; but in our attempts to conceive of it, it is also an emanation of an idea, an invention. The best exercise in escaping the distortions that men have accumulated in their fictions of Apollo and other gods is therefore an exercise in radical annihilation, out of which the true *guadium* of poetry comes:

> The poem refreshes life so that we share,
> For a moment, the first idea . . . It satisfies
> Belief in an immaculate beginning.
>   [*Collected Poems*, p. 382]

By the logic of narrative consequence that governs some poetic celebrations, the beginning from nothing sends us "winged by an unconscious will, / To an immaculate end" (*Collected Poems*, p. 382). Before Adam and Eve, the earth itself existed:

> The clouds preceded us
>
> There was a muddy centre before we breathed.
> There was a myth before the myth began,
> Venerable and articulate and complete.
>
> From this the poem springs.
>   [*Collected Poems*, p. 383]

By following thought back to the "candid kind" of everything before it grew stale, Stevens's fledgling poet finds a myth comparable to the old chronology of the world, comparable to the myths of Eden, for instance — but of course devoid of the single creator and his ministering angels. The poet conducts a new ceremony for every occasion. He does not repeat the old chants; his own enchantment is ongoing and continuous. He sees mankind beginning in the mire of organic earth, not as the scientist poses such a beginning but as the beginning of a responsiveness between mind and earth that presupposes a planet neither totally accommodating to men's wishes nor totally hostile. He also imagines man's return to dust in apocalyptic terms, as the same kind of exercise in "ideal" or immaculate clarification. Establishing these calendric bounds, he can imagine, even now, definition by reference to ultimates. He sees neither the true procession of time nor its final directions until he conditions each occasion (in the midst of ever changing perceptions) with an awareness of the whole world thus enclosed.

Paradoxically, it is because the poet in this and other myths lies, distorts, and misconceives that he is able to rediscover reality "as it is." Though the function of ultimate fictions is to set off the realities within which men live, fictions are exercises in elevated and encompassing thought; they condition the acceptance of the world both in its wintery nothingness and its summer fulfillment. "To be at the end of fact is not to be at the beginning of imagination but . . . to be at the end of both."[45] All phenomena are perceivable only in a season. When the season fails to generate its proper celebrations, its moments of dead calm render the poet inoperative: he becomes "A most inappropriate man / In a most unpropitious place" (*Collected Poems*, p. 120). When the poet and reality are mismatched, his present moments wash out. Moreover, in each new season, past fictions die:

> The truth is that there comes a time
> When we can mourn no more over music
> That is so much motionless sound.
>
> There comes a time when the waltz
> Is no longer a mode of desire, a mode
> Of revealing desire and is empty of shadows.
>
> Too many waltzes have ended.
> [*Collected Poems*, p. 121]

The ultimate fictions of today will be no more enduring than those of the past. But the poet in Stevens is often the opposite of the historian in his attitude toward that fact. He rejoices in his liberation from the dead past and his perception in the present of ever renewed life. Every fresh perception, by definition, dispenses with the past: "Metaphor creates a new reality from which the original appears to be unreal," as one of the *Adagia* says; or as "An Ordinary Evening in New Haven" puts it, "Alpha continues to begin / Omega is refreshed at every end" (*Collected Poems*, p. 469).

Because the world is re-created with every perception of it, each poem is its own new world and must run its own inevitable course. But its career is verbal rather than eventful in a primary sense; the

45. Wallace Stevens, *Opus Posthumous* (London: Faber and Faber; New York: Random House, 1957), p. 175.

poet has an absolute control over it that he does not have over daily life. In his exuberance he holds a world upon his nose and twirls it confidently (*The Man with the Blue Guitar*, xxv): he treats it like his bauble, playing with it in an outrageous flamboyance. However, when he returns from these excesses of imagination and remembers the gulf between words and things, he may also find his highest dreams inaccessible. The "Mountainous music" of his imagination seems then "to be passing away" (xxvi). In any mood, he is recurrently aware that the subject of his song is always in some respect poetry itself and that life and poetry are as distinct as truth and fiction. Thus if "the theory of poetry" is "the theory of life," or if "a theory of fiction is a theory of reality," as Stevens insists in *Adagia* (*Opus Posthumous*, p. 178), it is so only in the special sense that one knows each by contrast to the other, just as a theory of infinity may be at one and the same time a theory of the finite because they are incompatible. Stevens understandably tends to speak in paradoxes when he unites the two:

> The final belief is to believe in a fiction, which you know to be a fiction, there being nothing else. The exquisite truth is to know that it is a fiction and that you believe in it willingly.
>
> [*Opus Posthumous*, p. 163]

The poet's privileged moments must always be self-appraising and ironic in this way. "The poet represents the mind in the act of defending us against itself," defining its own exercises in abstraction and withdrawal and thus defining simultaneously what is not mind, what is "reality."

When we have come from a survey of theories of fiction, especially from Vaihinger, such a precept has its appeal as a much needed complexity. Certainly it offers a defense against attacks of empiricism on myth and against preferences for a neutral perception of reality uncolored by metaphor or poetic distortion. And it offers in turn a defense against an art-for-art's-sake formalism. If science ignores the associating and organizing that the mind does in perception, the pure aesthetician ignores the form-giving value of the exterior world. In their naive assumptions about pure art and pure science, both sacrifice the fruitful interactions of mind and phenomena. To combine fact and fiction in such a productive interaction, as Stevens does, is to make poetry and poetic perception profoundly pragmatic. Not only is art experience and experience the raw material of art, but to be aware of both, and simultaneously, of the gulf between them, is to suggest a way to interpret such realities as the industrial suburbs of New Haven. They can be seen as poetic without destroying them as real places and things. As the man with the blue guitar insists, for instance, Oxidia, the banal suburb supreme, becomes Olympia in our minds. Yet it remains Oxidia also. Stevens's description of it convinces us both that it is and that it is not Olympia. He does so by discovering a lambent beauty playing across the surface of its crusty stacks and machines but forcing us also to be aware of the game of his pretense. As is so frequently the case in Stevens, it is an excess of poetic language that points up the poet's exuberant fictionalizing, as in those "Dew-dapper clapper traps" that blaze "From crusty stacks," or in "Ecce, Oxidia is the seed / Dropped out of this amber-ember pod, / Oxidia is the soot of fire" (*Collected Poems*, p. 182). These descriptions are purposely outrageous, but they contain a grain of truth. Or we may wish to reverse the emphasis: they have a grain of truth, but they are outrageous. Either way, the poet exercises his inherited license to render things freshly, ironically aware of the lie of metaphor.

But Stevens is also puzzled by the potential usefulness of such acts of fictive thought. What of those who struggle to work each Monday, caught in a society whose myths are mainly drab or shabby: can they rejoice in Oxidia? Is it Olympia even to them? As the final poem of *The Man with the Blue Guitar* suggests,

> That generation's dream, aviled
> In the mud, in Monday's dirty light,
>
> That's it, the only dream they knew,
> Time in its final block, not time
>
> To come, a wrangling of two dreams.
> Here is the bread of time to come,
>
> Here is its actual stone. The bread
> Will be our bread, the stone will be
>
> Our bed and we shall sleep by night.
> We shall forget by day, except
>
> The moments when we choose to play
> The imagined pine, the imagined jay.
>
> [*Collected Poems*, pp. 183–84]

The best answer is perhaps that poetry is after all occasional, and occasionalism is the guitarist's most far-reaching anecdotal principle. If the fictions of the last generation are no longer valid in our present, even what we dream at night we may have to forget the next morning. But in like moments, when we elect to sit again at the guitar, we may reconstitute Monday's unfavorable light on the strings, "replacing" it there in its final light.

In any case, if "poetry creates a fictitious existence on an exquisite plane," it does so always incipiently, in the way the mind awakens in "Not Ideas about the Thing but the Thing Itself" to a "new knowledge of reality." Or it does so in the way a landscape puts itself together differently from each altitude of a mountain climb, which suggests again the supreme importance of narrative consequence and outcome — reinterpreted as the rendering of a new calendar of ever changing perceptions:

> We live in a constellation
> Of patches and of pitches,
> Not a single world,
> In things said well in music,
> On the piano, and in speech,
> As in a page of poetry —
> Thinkers without final thoughts
> In an always incipient cosmos,
> The way, when we climb a mountain,
> Vermont throws itself together.
> ["July Mountain," *Opus Posthumous*, p. 114]

These "patches and pitches" are by no means to be despised merely because they are occasional and exist hazardously in a pluralistic world. Though as thinkers we never "arrive" intellectually, the intellect shares in the arrivals of emotion when it believes in the fictions by which things are "said well." Vermont *will* be thrown together despite itself, because we need it to be and because the points of view we take on it leave us no alternative. Vermont is continuously mythologized before the viewer's constellating eyes.

Whatever the limitations of a given point of view, then, chosen moments of reality do stand reconstituted in the poet's expression of them. Stevens reaffirms his faith in that principle in a number of statements that bring up to date the age-old questions of fiction's impact on experience, and the impact of experience in turn on fictions:

The exquisite environment of fact. The final poem will be the poem of fact in the language of fact. But it will be the poem of fact not realized before.

The relation of art to life is of the first importance especially in a skeptical age since, in the absence of a belief in God, the mind turns to its own creations and examines them, not alone from the aesthetic point of view, but for what they reveal, for what they validate and invalidate, for the support that they give.

Perhaps there is a degree of perception at which what is real and what is imagined are one: a state of clairvoyant observation, accessible or possibly accessible to the poet or, say, the acutest poet.

Poetry is a purging of the world's poverty and change and evil and death. It is a present perfecting, a satisfaction in the irremediable poverty of life.

To study and to understand the fictive world is the function of the poet.

God is a symbol for something that can as well take other forms, as for example, the form of high poetry.

Poetry is a means of redemption.

[*Opus Posthumous*, pp. 164, 159, 166, 167, 167, 167, 160]

If, as other *Adagia* also suggest, God *is* a symbol for the conversion of noble dreams into realities through the operation of the word-maker, the poet can be seen as his reduced modern equivalent, making word-structures from "things as they are." Life is "a composite of propositions about it," as Stevens remarks; it cannot be "free from its forms." The best of those forms and the most pleasing of its propositions for Stevens are obviously the poet's.

Other axioms of similar import demonstrate Stevens's continuing preoccupation with the functions of poetry. Their presiding idea is that by itself the world is poverty-stricken — both literally, in not providing enough basic sustenance for human economy, and in an equally serious way, in not providing fulfillment for the imaginable nobility of men. But the second poverty is mainly within and may be alleviated when a given landscape is transformed and raised to "an exquisite plane." Though modern culture (with its sixty-second commercial fictions) may pass ironic comment on Stevens's high hopes for the widespread usefulness of fictions, the explosion of fictions in an impressive multiplicity of new forms in modern poetry bears testimony to his insistence that whether our fictions are good or bad, we cannot escape them: they give shape and significance to everything they gather into their organic structures. Though Stevens's own concept of occasional moments is tailored to the lyric, all kinds of fiction, even extended realism, share the imaginative perceptions that he finds central to a modern theory of poetry. Because the fictionalist is himself solely responsible for his enclosed world, he can twang his wiry string in such a way that intellect and emotion find sudden rightness in the dramatic unfolding of experience. He is never assaulted by characters who enter unannounced, possessed of motives he does not understand, nor is he overwhelmed by floods, famines, madmen, or unlovely masses. None of these may enter his verbal domain unless he chooses to admit them.

This is no less true of the naturalist or existentialist who relishes the absurd or the incoherent: the obligation of a fiction to its audience is precisely to frame and bracket interruptions of logic in such a way as to make them contributions to a more complicated kind of rightness. Indeed, no phenomenon testifies more to fiction's paradoxical accountability to fact, and yet liberation from it, than this structuring of whatever it includes, even if the fictionalist wishes to insist upon general chaos. Chaos is inimitable; one cannot even make a statement about it without violating its nature. Hence, wherever the modernist begins in a theory of fictions, he is brought back sooner or later to the basic principle of the philosophy of "as if": fictions cannot avoid either mirroring or remaking reality according to their own predispositions. Whether the problem of fictions is located in mathematical, scientific, and legal methods, where Vaihinger finds it chiefly; in history and sociology, where theorists in historiography find it; or in a theory of literary kinds, where criticism tends to find it, it concerns consequential logic and the arrangement of successive parts. These are vital to the formulation that the nerves, the mind, and the imagination impose on experience.

Outside of Stevens, perhaps no poet has been more persistently aware of the struggle between the "environment of fact" and the poet's artifacts than Robert Frost. And his works have perhaps no more fitting portrait of the fictionalist with which to conclude than the brief narrative poem "For Once, Then, Something." In the poem, Frost suggests that the poet may have to acknowledge those fortuitous, unrevealing accidents that so often shatter one's expectations.

But all makers of fictions like to play at omniscience, and Frost's speaker peers into his reflection as though from a heaven framed by fern and backed by clouds. Focusing on the thing at hand, the imagination penetrates as far as it can; the speaker sees through the opaqueness of matter almost to the bottom of the well.

As a realist, however, the speaker also realizes that he is at the mercy of circumstances. A drop of water from the edge of the framework spoils the composition and shakes its contents into dense, unreadable stuff. Nature refuses to render *vestigia dei* or allegories from an oracle; both the continuity of the story and its outcome are frustrated because nature does not entirely "make" into language or human meaning. Hence in place of revelations of the kind that might please a mythic poet, the speaker is left largely with questions. But the poem, as opposed to the episode it purports to narrate, is after all a closed field, a narrative decisively begun, developed, and finished. Paradoxically, even as the drop of water spoils the picture, the poem defines and masters the altered picture itself. Merely by naming such an intrusion, the poem lifts it out of the realm of random accident into the order of syntax and imagery, into poetic statement. After a series of questions comes a relative closure delivered as a typical Frostian deliberative summary. Like Barth's antistory of the shoreless swimmer, the poem thus gives us a definitive view if not of great depths at least of limits and possible attitudes toward them when they disappear. It defines the provisional and circumscribes the bombardment of chance. It is sufficient that a word like *something*, by its encompassing abstraction, can lay the inquiry to rest and free the poet to be charmed by the mystery of the well, even if it is not Plato's "The Good" or "The True." He is also free to cherish certain words — *truth, quartz, something* — which despite their mutual friction give body and voice to a well-designed emotional course. Even the blurring and the blotting are transformed: frustrating to the presumed victim of the past, they are a source of satisfaction in the form of the poem.

Frost's attitude toward inconclusive vision in "For Once, Then, Something" is typical of modern fictionalists and theories of fiction, which are characterized by an awareness of the arbitrary enclosures of stories, of half illuminations, and renewed battles with the random and the absurd. No fictive narrator who values his prerogatives wishes to do less than Frost's narrator accomplishes with this paradoxically tentative finality; and yet very few modern fictionalists claim to do more. As Frost writes elsewhere, "There is at least so much good in the world that it admits of form and the making of form. And not only admits of it, but calls for it." The catch lies in the last phrase: we cannot ignore the call because we inherently respond to the need for form; yet it is formlessness that makes the call and dictates the terms. Perhaps more confidently than others who have answered its summons, Frost adds, "I thank the Lord for crudity which is rawness ... which is the part of life not yet worked up into form. ... A real artist delights in the roughness for what he can do to it. ... Get a few words alone in a study and with plenty of time on your hands you can make them say anything you please."[46] But those privileged moments when the artist does so stand apart from the flow of normal existence. They do not predict or recapitulate or carry shades of final reality, as the privileged moments of Plato's and Christ's fictions do; they come capriciously framed by matters irrelevant to them. Yet they remain nonetheless consoling; and beyond that, the fictions that express them are necessary and unavoidable. The reasons for our return to them are in part, as Frank Kermode suggests, that

> we have our vital interest in the structure of time, in the concords books arrange between beginning, middle, and end. . . . Our geometries, in James's word, are required to measure change, since it is on change, between remote or imaginary origins and ends, that our interests are fixed. In our perpetual crisis we have, at the proper seasons, under the pressure perhaps of our own end, dizzying perspectives upon the past and future. ... Merely to give order to these perspectives is to provide consolation. [*The Sense of an Ending*, pp. 178–79]

Fictions that are too escapist, however — that fail to "make discoveries of the hard truth here and now, in the middest" — eventually go on "the dump with the other empty bottles" (p. 179), and we are reminded by the act of discarding how easily an artful product that once aimed to seal off its own formful world is reclaimed by the greater world surrounding it.

Which brings us to a closer look at the mechanisms of that inter-

---

46. *Selected Letters of Robert Frost*, ed. Lawrence Thompson (New York: Holt, Rinehart and Winston, 1964), pp. 418, 465.

change of art and experience. I want to turn to an extended example, Wallace Stegner's *Wolf Willow*, in order to explore historiographic and fictional methods in particular before taking up the nature of anecdotal time and the theory of modes. *Wolf Willow* suggests itself because its combination of biography, journalism, history, and fiction (Hemingway's *Green Hills of Africa*, Doris Lessing's *The Golden Notebook*, Kurt Vonnegut's *Slaughter-House Five*, Norman Mailer's *The Armies of the Night*, Truman Capote's *In Cold Blood* come to mind as other examples) provides a serviceable spectrum of kinds and leads us some distance toward an appreciation of the art that has gone into them. From this excursion into Stegner's Northwest culture, we will return to theoretical matters, putting aside, however, the history of their treatment and the nature of historiography for more limited topics in linear movement that reveal the methods by which varieties of anecdote arrange their "concords."

CHAPTER TWO

Retrieving Wolf Willow:

The Collaborations of History, Story, and Memory

James's Ralph Pendrel in *The Sense of the Past* is not alone among lovers of framed order and art in preferring the past to the present, at least as a subject of meditation, nor is he unique in desiring to make the past part of the now in which he lives:

> His interest was all in the spent and the displaced, in what had been determined and composed roundabout him, what had been presented as a subject and a picture, by ceasing — so far as things ever cease — to bustle or even to be. It was when life was framed in death that the picture was really hung up. If his idea in fine was to recover the lost moment, to feel the stopped pulse, it was to do so as experience, in order to be again consciously the creature that *had* been. . . . What he wanted himself was the very smell of that simpler mixture of things that had so long served; he wanted the very tick of old stopped clocks.[1]

For a sense of an ordered, framed, "hung up" life, one likes, as James remarks, a just-past, not an extremity of the past beyond anecdotal connection to the present. What has recently gone by is qualitatively different; it carries with it still the "slant on the walls of the light of afternoons that had been," the tones, articulation, and associative reactions that interest us most: "With the times beyond, intrinsically more 'strange,' the tender grace, for the backward vision, has faded, the afternoon darkened; for any time nearer to us the special effect hasn't begun" (*The Art of the Novel*, p. 165). Hence, James remarks,

> I delight in a palpable imaginable *visitable* past — in the nearer distances and the clearer mysteries, the marks and signs of a world we

---

1. Henry James, *The Sense of the Past* (New York: Scribner, 1917), pp. 48–49. For a brief but suggestive treatment of the past in James, see George Poulet, *Studies in Human Time*, trans. Elliott Coleman (New York: Harper, 1959), pp. 350–54.

may reach over to as by making a long arm we grasp an object at the other end of our own table. The table is the one, the common expanse, and where we lean, so stretching, we find it firm and continuous. That, to my imagination, is the past fragrant of all, or of almost all, the poetry of the thing outlived and lost and gone, and yet in which the precious element of closeness, telling so of connexions but tasting so of differences, remains appreciable. With more moves back the element of the appreciable shrinks — just as the charm of looking over a garden-wall into another garden breaks down when successions of walls appear .... We are divided of course between liking to feel the past strange and liking to feel it familiar; the difficulty is, for intensity, to catch it at the moment when the scales of the balance hang with the right evenness. [*The Art of the Novel*, p. 164]

One's altars for the dead are erected for people illuminated by that special light or fixed at that balanced moment, as for instance, in James's own visitation of his sister Alice's grave:

Everything was there, everything *came*; the recognition, stillness, the strangeness, the pity and the sanctity and the terror, the breath-catching passion and the divine relief of tears. William's inspired transcript, on the exquisite little Florentine urn of Alice's ashes, William's divine gift to us, and to *her*, of the Dantean lines —
> *Dopo lungo exilio e martiro*
> *Viene a questa pace* —
took me so at the throat by its penetrating *rightness*, that it was as if one sank down on one's knees in a kind of anguish of gratitude before something for which one had waited with a long, deep *ache*.[2]

In some respects the past may show more clearly in retrieval than it does in even the freshest of unassisted memories. In Ralph Pendrel's recovery of "the lost moment," the frame of death, like the frame around a picture, makes the portrait available for decisive contemplation, organizes its spaces, stations its shades and tones in relation to each other, and detaches the whole from the world of indefinite process and extension. And because what lies within that framework is finished, one's attitudes and moral judgments about it can be settled: one knows whether to take an ironic tone or to celebrate, whether a given line of consequences has borne fruit or not. Yet the surface of such a portrait fails to embody directly all that it portends. It gestures toward a totality that escapes; and in this again

2. Henry James, *The Notebooks*, ed. F. O. Matthiessen and Kenneth B. Murdock (New York: Oxford University Press, 1961), p. 321.

it is like a visitation to altars of the dead. The triumph of recaptured, fictionalized and idealized life is conditioned always by the ache of a missing, actual possession. As Pendrel discovers, the act of framing the past makes the border line between it and the present assert its absoluteness: one cannot actually live in both at the same time. If one imaginatively moves into the framed picture, like a poet dwelling among the figures on a Grecian urn, one must leave behind his own circumstantial, ever advancing present. What exists within the frame either of the historian's recapitulation or the artist's creation belongs entirely to the realm of representation — to the icons of memory, the words and images of the poet, the discursive generalizations of the essayist, the musings of the philosopher, the social calibrations of the novelist, the celluloid imprints of the photographer.

In Wallace Stegner's collection of pieces in *Wolf Willow* we find a splendid showcase of ways of dealing with the relatively near past and the problem of the retreat, especially the historian's and fictionalist's reconstructions of it. The volume as a whole marks certain distinctions among autobiography, essay, and fiction; it presents a series of revisits and explorations of the past, a taking up of old ties, and an inquiry into their reverberations in the present. As such it ponders the nature of its own retrievals and the disappearance of once meaningful events that now scarcely touch the present except as one still sees them passing over the horizon. Like all sensitive historians, Stegner realizes that the "death" which frames a subject and offers it up to recollection also consigns much of what once was to oblivion and challenges all methods of retrieval. He remarks with respect to one scene of his childhood, for instance,

> I don't want our shack to be gone, as I know it is; I would not enjoy hunting the ground around it for broken crockery and rusty nails and bits of glass. I don't want to know that our protective pasture fence has been pulled down to let the prairie in, or that our field, which stopped at the Line and so defined a sort of identity and difference, now flows southward into Montana without a break as restored grass and burnouts. Once, standing alone under the bell-jar sky gave me the strongest feeling of personal singularity I shall ever have. That was because it was all new, we were taking hold of it to make it ours. But to return hunting relics, to go down there armed only with memory and find every trace of our passage wiped away — that would be to reduce my family, myself, the hard effort of years, to solipsism, to make us as fictive as a dream.[3]

3. Wallace Stegner, *Wolf Willow* (New York: Viking Press, 1955), p. 9.

Wolf Willow is seriously conditioned by this oblivion because it is committed to recollecting details, shades, tones, and specific objects, and all gaps are felt as personal losses; foreshortening is truncated identity. Narrative is fretted by these losses like a moth-chewed tapestry.

Among the tools available to excavate the past, Stegner implicitly asks, which are most capable of handling the kind of past that his family and the town of Whitemud have had? What narrative method is most true to the material? Are several required, each making up for the deficiencies of the others? Is a general description of lasting social and natural conditions necessary to a national history? Or is a fictional narration of exemplary events as effective in its own way? What can fictional reconstruction do that a memoir or an analytic history cannot?

As soon as we pose such questions we notice the drawbacks of two extremes of narrative method — a narrow focus on personal lives and their unique happenings (in the realm of anecdote) and a panoramic focus on general social and natural conditions.[4] In taking events and actions to be mere illustrations of general conditions, an analytic history loses the complexity and solidity that experiences of the just-past tell us all the past once possessed. From the perspective of analytic thought, unrepeatable, singular realities fade into a generality

4. See note 13, appendix; also Maurice Mandelbaum, "A Note on History as Narrative," *History and Theory* 6 (1967): 413–19; Richard G. Ely, Rolf Gruner, and William H. Dray, "Mandelbaum on Historical Narrative: A Discussion," *History and Theory* 8 (1969): 275–94; and A. R. Louch, "History as Narrative," *History and Theory* 8 (1969): 54–70. Mandelbaum and Gruner build extreme cases against history as narrative without exploring fully either the differences between static, descriptive analysis and narrative, or the contributions each makes to the other as joint enterprises in nearly every historian's work.

Once we assume that historical explanations are governed by their focus and that they concern temporal movement, the difficulties in weighing the restrictive contribution of analysis and narrative are partly alleviated. To explain the course of Roman empire requires a focus sufficiently large to include all the internal forces, many of which can surely be described sociologically; but it also has to register the impinging influence of barbarians, the Far East, and Africa, whose contributions to the course of empire come as partly "hidden causes," on specific occasions. If one were to write a history of the planet, these causes would no longer be hidden because the focus would include them; but then extraterrestrial matters would come from outside as events. And so forth. The point is that whatever impinges from outside at a specific time and place presumably requires narrative treatment even if one is otherwise fully satisfied with a static description of institutions and general laws.

of forces at work in a culture — or into the abstract laws that historians substitute for them — just as the marks and signs of Stegner's homestead have faded into the unbroken expanse of the prairie.

Missing in a basically nonnarrative summary of sociological history are all the collisions that give twists and turns to individual linear careers. From analytic hindsight, everything is describable and the impact of colliding individuals is merely part of a composed tableau. Thus when the social analyst treats "trends," he does so in an Olympian manner, not as felt change. As soon as his perspective rises high enough to frame his subject and treat its elements as more or less static — like the make-up of the entire body of voters over forty or the mores of postadolescents — he may put aside the unpredictable, singular course. From the opposite direction, from the lesser perspectives of everyday anecdotes it is the broader subjects of historical inquiry that become invisible. When the historian's focus narrows to the course of a single topic or career, as in the chronicle, the diary, or the personal memoir, those forces that are the subject of analytic study lie outside his framework and he is unable to explain them: they emerge and combine with the narration at unpredictable junctures — producing stoppage, reversals, accelerations, climaxes, and diversions as part of a dramatized movement. What happens is then no longer attributable to abiding laws; a given career in its uniqueness merely begins, progresses, and ends, its movement influenced throughout by hidden causes and colliding "accidents" that come from outside its bracketed singularity. A historian who wishes to make such a private or unique career intelligible must find ways to transcend its contingencies and consign it to the already-finished.[5]

The implicit question for Stegner is, How much of the uniqueness of the past can be included in a memoir without endangering intelligibility, and in turn how much sociology can be ventured without one's encumbering what is after all chiefly a "memory" of the last plains frontier? As a sociological analyst and a writer of personal memoirs alternatively, Stegner works near both extremes on occasion; but the strength of *Wolf Willow* lies in their interlacing. The narrative of individual careers is enhanced by a sense of

5. See the treatment of substitution, replicas, categorical representation, legal representation, mimesis, and other aspects of representation in Richard Bernheimer, *The Nature of Representation: A Phenomenological Inquiry* (New York: New York University Press, 1961).

permanent and general conditions; and the turns and impassioned anecdotes of individuals are rendered more meaningful by social and natural settings.

But let us descend to particulars. As the first memoir indicates, the landscape of *Wolf Willow* — the province of Saskatchewan and the plains of Canada and upper Montana — is a constant force in the midst of historical change. As such, it assists the recollection of the past and recurrently impinges upon the careers of individuals, as the smell of the willows comes to the adult revisiter and brings, intact, the sense of a self that has existed continuously for decades but has been lost in the twists and turns of the anecdotal past. The scene touches upon myth as well as upon sociological and geographical laws (the myth of Eden and paradise, for instance); upon the general chart of progress toward a perfectable society that liberal philosophy since Condorcet looks for in all "undeveloped" places; and upon the personal self-reliance that accompanies the early stages of that progress and urges a heroic mastery of hardship. Stegner initially attempts to define the relationship between men and terrain and in the process to separate fact and imagination. He wishes to reconstruct what actually happened, both its particulars and its basic, situational conditions. What is it that the plains inevitably are, have been, and will be? What is merely fictive or collective dream? Where does reality end and myth begin?

Stegner finds in "The Question Mark in the Circle" that in answering these questions memory itself is incurably mythic and unreliable, yet obviously indispensable to autobiography. It reorganizes old relationships, enlarges some things and shrinks others; it contributes to the creation of gun-toting heroes out of ordinary men and mere criminals: it allows illusions to run rampant. In short, "memory, though vivid, is imprecise, without sure dimensions, and it is as much to test memory against adult observation as for any other reason that I return" (p. 6). As the autobiographer searches for solider truths among the records that Whitemud affords, the gradual corroboration of memory in present observation gives the running structure of the memoir. The just-past is not framed, isolated, and panoramic but alternately clear and vague, and intermittently penetrated by an ongoing present. The separation of present and past can be overcome only when the narrator finds a continuous reality shaped by them.

Eventually, the chain he reconstructs extends into the past of

Western Europe and the impact of its institutions upon the plains. It reaches to dramatists, philosophers, and novelists who, though not part of the immediate scene, are nonetheless part of the "field" of an educated mind. In this respect, autobiography in Stegner's handling shows perhaps more clearly than *Wolf Willow*'s other forms of narration how influences that come from discontinuous and nonadjacent times and places actually feel in the development of a sensitive intelligence. A single work by Homer may have no great impact on a general culture, which absorbs it along with a multitude of other influences, but it may have a significant impact on the interior life of a single man. Stegner's point is that even in Saskatchewan one is the product of a considerable history and that the impact of an inherited culture is often painfully odd in new circumstances. As the periphery of his autobiography expands to include selective parts of that history, the puzzlement of the question mark at the center of the circle increases. If the plains are continuous, stable, and unmoved, the searching historical intelligence within them is enmeshed in extensive influences beyond them; and even in the act of writing, it is itself still changing and moving. Hence the just-past that the historian seeks to recover retreats into greater and greater vistas. It insists upon its sociological elements.

Among these perplexities, however, there are several relative certainties, one of which, recurrently, is simply the surface and texture of the physical environment. The plains are the preconditions of the fictions and the human institutions that pass impermanently across them. Whatever stability history has stems from them and from the impact they have upon the psychology and the social institutions of the settlers:

> Whatever the sky may do, however the earth is shaken or darkened, the Euclidean perfection abides. The very scale, the hugeness of simple forms, emphasizes stability. It is not hills and mountains which we should call eternal. Nature abhors an elevation as much as it abhors a vacuum; a hill is no sooner elevated than the forces of erosion begin tearing it down. These prairies are quiescent, close to static; looked at for any length of time, they begin to impose their awful perfection on the observer's mind. Eternity is a peneplain. [P.7]

By comparison, men are unstable, enigmatic, fleeting, prone to error, and hostile to horizontal quiet: if geography gives us forms of geometric composition, men are movement, sequences of unrepeatable events, and suffering.

The plains of course *can* be altered, and they become an antagonist in the specific turns of historical dramas when settlers seek to incorporate topography into the logic of progress — to plow, raise cattle, and build towns. Their "occasional" impact makes them the source of historical eventfulness. However, the chief instability of the first memoir is Stegner's particular past, and the central movement of the chapter is the retrieving of a topography as it once was for him. After several tantalizing false leads and errant memories, the narrator in the present arrives at Wolf Willow as though returning home, and his semi-Proustian recollection, anchored to the solidity of place which "represents" or symbolizes him to himself, overleaps strict chronology in making two spots of time continuous:

> The perspective is what it used to be, the dimensions are restored, the senses are as clear as if they had not been battered with sensation for forty alien years. And the queer adult compulsion to return to one's beginnings is assuaged. A contact has been made, a mystery touched. For the moment, reality is made exactly equivalent with memory, and a hunger is satisfied. The sensuous little savage that I once was is still intact inside me. [P. 19]

Up to this point, the narrative maintains a double focus: Whitemud and the memories do not coincide; the river, the buildings, and the streets are not as they should be. But the climax of the memoir realigns geography, which is abiding and stable, and the internal form of the self, which dwells both apart from place and in place:

> The sensuous little savage, at any rate, has not been rubbed away or dissolved; he is as solid a part of me as my skeleton.
> And he has a fixed and suitably arrogant relationship with his universe, a relationship geometrical and symbolic. From his center of sensation and question and memory and challenge, the circle of the world is measured. [P. 19]

The certainty of this recognition is convincing, and it contains those elements of historical explanation that we require of a satisfying return to the past. It makes use of the attested record of what remains in the geography of the plains, before an eyewitness whose account is founded on the logic of what normally happens to towns and regions in their usual courses. The episode could serve as a model of historical retrieval of a limited and personal sort.

Yet as the periphery of the historical investigation expands to include the social roots of what Whitemud has become, questions about the nature of historical explanation begin to qualify significantly the triumph of the first essay — which resembles fiction perhaps too closely in taking shape as hindrance, unveiling, anticipated climax, and a final recognition that clarifies mysteries. Succeeding essays view Whitemud as part of the broader story of the westward expansion — as they must, because a personal memoir cannot after all claim the advantages of fictional closure or scientific experiment. History is not staged in a laboratory and is not an entirely invented system. As James suggests, even the fictionalist has difficulty in drawing the circle of his narration tight:

> Where, for the complete expression of one's subject, does a particular relation stop — giving way to some other not concerned in that expression?
> Really, universally, relations stop nowhere, and the exquisite problem of the artist is eternally but to draw, by a geometry of his own, the circle within which they shall happily *appear* to do so. [*The Art of the Novel*, p. 5]

And the difficulty of the fictionalist in this regard is compounded by the historical essayist, who finds every chain of events endless. Stegner is reminded of the complex components of his young savage's family and its town, which concentrate much of the history of the plains. "The successive stages of the Plains frontier flowed like a pageant through these hills . . . . My disjunct, uprooted, cellular family was more typical than otherwise on the frontier. More than we knew, we had our place in a human movement" (p. 20). To deal effectively with these ever extending avenues, the historian resorts to the notion of the typical, the epitome, and the relationship between smaller and larger units of the historical continuum — all of which, as a cultural historian, he handles somewhat differently from either the writer of fiction or the autobiographer, singling out his "representatives" from the choices that history provides rather than inventing ideal or illustrative types. To some extent, however, individuals must always be ambassadors or representatives of their times to him. They drop some of their historical singularity to become specimens.[6]

In the essay "History as a Pontoon Bridge" they also join a linked succession of stages, though each generation adds its span in a some-

---

6. See Roy Pascal, *Design and Truth in Autobiography* (Cambridge, Mass.: Harvard University Press, 1960), pp. 1–20, and Wayne Shumaker, *English Autobiography: Its Emergence, Materials, and Form* (Berkeley: University of California Press, 1954).

what haphazard way. Unfortunately, the metaphor of the bridge fails to acknowledge the dead ends and the randomness of all the possible directions that individuals and the collective history have taken. The collision between European culture and the plains that so affects the young boy, for instance, spins different people off in different directions, not all of them memorable. Obviously, not everyone becomes an ambassador to the present, or material for the historian's bridge. Even with respect to the boy now being recorded by the man, rather than imposing controls on his growth, the books that represent his inherited culture tend to pull him in different directions. ("Books didn't enlarge me; they dispersed me.") More generally, the past, carried into the plains partly between the covers of books, does not impose its direction as a particular blueprint or even an intelligible framework on the plains; and only such a framework, applied continuously to the present, would create a single bridge. If in fact the European inheritance and the new life do not fuse, or if in some cases they operate as friction to wear away those caught between them, we can expect the citizens of Whitemud to go in unpredictable directions; and we learn eventually of a number of them who did, or who in effect went nowhere at all. Yet they are part of Whitemud's history as a total field, played upon by a diversity of influences.

What the pontoon bridge ignores in this regard Stegner suggests in another image, the dump ground, which is both a real place on the fringes of Whitemud and a symbol of those aspects of its history that have failed to make it into history's continuous bridge. The books of some households surely ended up there, if not literally, at least in effect, as they lay neglected on some shelf. But much else turned up there as well, since a dump is after all a place where communities discard items that no longer mean anything to them. It includes everything that falls outside the framework of the picture — even though, paradoxically, merely by mentioning them the historian rescues them. For the most part, individual items of a trash heap have no lasting effects; their charms, their usefulness, and their chains of cause and effect decay with them. We are never more conscious than in the presence of them of the gulf between "now" and "then" — and of our dependence upon records to salvage the past. A graveyard, with its compression of lives in dates and inscriptions, arranges what it salvages as a special message, a kind of anecdote for the future to remember. But the dump tells us clearly that we are severed from the memorable and the unmemorable alike.

Not only towns but households have their localized discard area filled with items in transition to rubbish. A particular wastebasket at a particular desk contains old tax records, correspondence, pages of a manuscript — all once useful in coordinating a small unit and a social milieu but now of no more value than the minerals they return to the soil. We can carry the notion of the dump further, because individual brains, too, are stored with information and partially recollected sensory experience growing ever less lifelike. Like the minerals of a rich soil, they may condition us, but they do so no longer as structured parts of whole and continuous experiences, only as the general tendencies of a constituted character. And as with households, towns, and individuals, so with those larger corporate institutions, armies, civil governments, and the like: each throws off in time's vortex a steady stream of expendable materials. Thus by extending Stegner's metaphor, the historian can discover in the dump of Whitemud the fate of nearly all achievements except that small portion of enduring artifacts, ideas, and residue of pragmatic life that is deposited in records: nearly everything that once existed lies dispersed outside the organized compositions of the historian's symbol systems. The pontoon bridge that remains is constructed out of fragments salvaged in the amber of signs and effigies by the present looking backward and collecting what it wants — just as an account of a battle (written most likely by the winners) extracts from a multitude of events a thread of continuity leading to a known outcome. As George Kubler remarks, "The replication that fills history actually prolongs the stability of any past moments, allowing sense and pattern to emerge for us wherever we look." On the other hand, to discard is to reverse the values that underlie that stability. It is a decision against one kind of stability on behalf of another kind.[7] It is part of a systematization, a measurement of cultural evolution.

If tombs, histories, and memorials represent society's desire to retain where nature discards, then trash heaps represent the opposite. Both are meaningful only as decisions in a particular chronology of a particular culture, as the abandoning of the internal combustion engine in 1980 would indicate a different set of priorities than its abandonment in Detroit in 1935. But the past that is readable in the dump is not meaningful in the same way that the past of salvaged records is,

7. George Kubler, *The Shape of Time: Remarks on the History of Things* (New Haven: Yale University Press, 1962), p. 77.

because the act of discarding is perpetrated precisely against continuous meaning and historical connection. Whitemud's dump is a miscellany of articles broken out of syntax and explanation. Whereas a culture is a synchronized, self-perpetuating set of institutions managing some sort of forward movement against the resistance of its members, a dump has no arrangement, movement, or true culture. All its items are "one"; they are not parts of a subordinated whole. They implicitly rebuke anyone who would found science and history on mere facts because mere facts are what they have become — freed of symbolic systems, representation, and relic value. In dropping out of the range of intelligibility, they are preparing to be recycled into new structures — once they have fulfilled a penitential period as shards and dust.

Thus in the dump we see the past on the brink of oblivion and transformation and feel the complex doubleness of historical time in which memory cannot salvage a great deal. To bring forth a few items from the dump as Stegner does is to liberate them from that miscellany before they have completely disintegrated, to rearrange and polish them, and establish them once more as part of a continuum. In a saving web of narrative re-collection, a few items enter a new collage of potential symbols. But unlike the connection and syntax of their original usefulness they are now a special class of objects, like poetic emblems, the occasions of nostalgia permeated with a sense of what has dropped away from them. As one side is illuminated by a new framework that draws them forward and makes them stand forth as solid objects, the other side turns toward oblivion. The inadequacy of analytic overviews is especially poignant from the perspective such items give, because they insist on their particularity and their lost personal associations. They may be typical; they may "represent" and "signify" after we have rescued them; but at the same time we know that they have had a personal, anecdotal history that we cannot recite; and we know that most of the present will join them in that obscurity. No book, artifact, idea, institution, invention, or species carries an inherent warranty against the defect that may cause it to be consigned with them. When new civilizations are built on the dust of earlier ones, the imprint of a foot crunches into a completely disintegrated past; the jab of a surveyor's stick penetrates to the heart of lost Babylons.

It is possible, however, as Richard Wilbur points out, to see that

universal metamorphosis of shapes and forms as also a marvelous re-
claiming of the world's junk:

> The sun shall glory
>   in the glitter of glass-chips,
> Foreseeing the salvage
>   of the prisoned sand,
> And the blistering paint
>   peel off in patches,
> That the good grain
>   be discovered again.
> Then burnt, bulldozed,
>   They shall all be buried
> To the depths of diamonds,
>   in the making dark
> Where halt Hephaestus
>   keeps his hammer
> And Wayland's work
>   is worn away.[8]

To this Ortega y Gasset might be called forth to add that only by
discarding its trash can a civilization manage to grow; change is not
merely the privilege but the necessity of a culture: "There is no . . .
cause for weeping overmuch concerning the mutability of everything
human. This is only possible to one who is not linked to-day to what
he was yesterday, who is not caught for ever in that being which is already, but can migrate from it into another."[9]

Not all refuse becomes diamonds, of course, and even diamonds,
beautiful as they are, remain silent about what has been compressed
into their glittering emptiness. But like Wilbur and Ortega, Stegner
does not dwell unduly on the morbidity of his symbol. Though the
brief presence of the dump in the first section of the volume, close by
the retrieval of Wolf Willow, haunts the remainder of the essays and
reinforces the initial premise that only the clean-swept abstraction of
the plains has real permanence, subsequent essays stress the means by
which men establish enduring milestones in their personal and
collective histories. In the cultural and sociological essays of the
volume, Stegner offers three further symbols — the forty-ninth

8. Richard Wilbur, "Junk," *The Poems* (New York: Harcourt, Brace and World, 1963),
p. 9.
9. Ortega y Gasset, "History as a System," in *Philosophy and History*, ed. Klibansky
and Paton, p. 314.

parallel (the "medicine line"), the garden of the world, and the making of paths — that comment usefully on the making and recording of history. They also raise a number of further difficulties in matching narrative forms to the just-past; and in a sense each remembers the dump in its own way, especially the making of paths. More important for our immediate purpose, they suggest methods by which the historian and the fiction writer come to settlements with the past, transferring as much as they find salvageable into the record of words, as Stegner has in fact done in the volume *Wolf Willow* — which is neither a bridge nor a trash heap but a "history, a story, and a memory."

It is evident with respect to the medicine line that planned coherence contributes to the future intelligibility of the written record: the historian does not deal with merely a chaos; he deals with partly cohesive materials. Like most boundaries between countries, the medicine line was the product of an arbitrary social agreement and therefore in the historian's reordered record may share with all acts of definition the fictive nature of symbolic transactions. In dividing where nature failed to divide, the invisible line across the continent between the United States and Canada creates quite different cultures north and south of the border. Stegner realizes both the fictional nature of the line ("the 49th parallel was an agreement, a rule, a limitation, a fiction . . . and the coming of law, even such limited law as this, was the beginning of civilization in what had been a lawless wilderness" [p. 85]) and the difficulty of imposing such a fiction on a geography so little inclined to receive it. The drawing of the line is a surprise or hidden cause to the plains insofar as their geometric monotony seems beyond change and culture of any kind is an unpredictable intrusion. The agreement that there will be a border is a twist from which the plains will never recover. History is therefore to some extent created out of the imagination of individuals looking forward and amalgamating selected experiences of the past with future prospects. The social planner, the dreamer, the prophet, and the legislator are all creators of enclosure and intelligibility; they plan systems and seek outcomes. Indeed, no greater evidence of the limitation of geographical determinism could be offered than the cultural disparity that Stegner describes between Canada and the United States: the *res gestae* of each are shaped by citizens in pursuit of their own anecdotes.

The interesting aspect of the forty-ninth parallel is not so much this cultural variability, however, as the collision between preconception and fact. In Stegner's account, it fell to the surveyors of the line to put themselves into the discipline of the preconception, to deviate not so much as a yard to the right or left whatever the provocation, to be totally unresponsive to weather, hills, and bogs. They were to make a fiction come true, to inscribe history in their straight line of markers. As it turned out, their success was virtually the only part of the plan to reach fulfillment. After the survey, the line of course remained established and arbitrary, but its by-products became progressively much less predictable in the march of distinct cultures. What had been shadowy unreality as a dream became nationality, law, custom, and a thousand daily cultural differences. Bureaucracies, divisions and subdivisions, character types, material goods, and individual deeds followed from it.

How this individuation worked in detail can be seen in the sectional divisions that made a further articulation of "plots" down to the boundaries and small stories of the homesteader. Within these socially defined and accepted enclosures, the individual took his stand and declared his personal existence. The history of the settler and his heirs was thereafter conditioned by the ground they stood upon and what they did to it. And therein lay one's personal jurisdiction over history. One's particular *res gestae* were definable within the constitutional powers guaranteed by the national group, but they were enacted in many collisions of individual will with elements, neighbors, and lawmaking agencies at large.

In this light the original surveyor was a type of the subcreator, operating in the mythic garden of the West to lay out a grid within which the dream of private, self-sustaining paradises could be worked out. The private paths of the homesteaders branched off from the main social arteries and thoroughfares to their holding in the collective dream. At the sensitive nerve ends of this communications network, where the homesteader tried to make his particular fictions come true, came the severest trials and the most painful clashes of the myth of progress and daily attempts to articulate it, to give it enactment and body.

In "The Making of Paths," Stegner describes those collisions as he traces individual paths to their ends and returns from the sociological breadth of general history to personal memoir. As the narrative mode grows less public, less "historical," it is more endangered by the principle of discards and the shocks of change: it is at the end of the public way, in fact, that true oblivion lies, where, to speak linguistically, particles drop out of saving, permanent generalization. There it is especially clear that all that is unique perishes, that historical retrieval subjects all that it rescues to transformation, in the chemistry of language, into the terms we have in common. For a good many settlers the prefiguring dream and the practical reality are simply too far apart; the act of making dreams into realities fails, and lacking the continuity of fulfilled plans, everything they own and do drops out of the collective "bridge." Nearly everything about the homesteader makes a contribution to the dump that lies "out back." Concerning the difference between the surviving and the perishing record, the public, continuous life and the private life, Stegner notes that whereas a townsman like Martin may leave something behind him — "A town, a cemetery" ("even a dump ground is an institution of permanence"), what they accomplished at the homestead "was written in wind. It began as it ended — empty space, grass and sky" (p. 268). A normal homesteader could defeat undifferentiated space only for a moment: "We printed an earth that seemed creation-new with the marks of our identity. And then the earth wiped them out again" (p. 273).

Momentarily, however, the paths that they make declare their existence and give them hope, and it seems to them that they enact history in a personal way:

> And that was why I loved so the trails and paths we made. They were ceremonial, an insistence not only that we had a right to be in sight on the prairie but that we owned and controlled a piece of it. ... It was our own trail, lightly worn, its ruts a slightly fresher green where old cured grass had been rubbed away, that lifted my heart. It took off across the prairie like an extension of myself. [P. 271]

Such paths are what make autobiographical narrative possible, but they do so of course in the retrieving symbolic system of the narrative, not as an abiding part of literal homesteads. They do so in a new "trail" of words, where they die as reality in order to live as symbols. The making of paths, the realization of phantom dreams, and the mistaken belief that one is doing something enduring explain the "root-cause of the American cult of Progress, the satisfaction that *Homo fabricans* feels in altering to his own purposes the virgin earth." But that original making becomes as nothing without the historian's remaking in the preservative of communication, the book of common language. "Those tracks demonstrated our existence as triumphantly as an Indian is demonstrated by his handprint in ochre on a cliff wall" (p. 272), Stegner remarks. And he is correct in the essential matter: nothing else the Indian did in his cave is remembered; only the sign embedded in stone still speaks to us. And it does so as art, not as salvaged reality.

There are good reasons why more is not salvageable than the handprint of the Indian and the word-marks of the historian — faint images of the flesh-and-blood originals that they are. The difficulty with the articulation of the original dream lay from the beginning, in Stegner's view, in a mismatching of preconception and reality. In passing from the mind into fact, the imagined reality changed. It is only natural in return that in becoming intelligible word-systems, facts are again translated. Ideas and realities never coincide; if they did, all plans might be fulfilled and all items salvaged from the dump. As it is, the civilization that existed on the plains marked a compromise between what was planned and what the prairie allowed — between the inherent resistance of nature to human planning and what determination and technology managed to build. And the historian's method works a compromise between what existed and what he can say about it, what he can *re*conceive. The idyllic garden that the homesteaders sought existed only in the mind and could only be ephemeral. They were victimized by the "folklore of hope" (pp. 280–81). And from the other end of the bridge, even if the dream of a new Eden had not perished in precisely the way it did, it would have perished in some other. It might, for instance, have been "improved" out of existence like most dreams of land development: "Anyone who has lived on a frontier knows the inescapable ambivalence of the old-fashioned American conscience, for he has first renewed himself in Eden and then set about converting it into the lamentable modern world. And that is true even if the Eden is, as mine was, almost unmitigated discomfort and deprivation" (p. 282). Thus one system and one plan incessantly replace another. The historian can only trace the records and the discards.

The abandoning of dreams and illusions in the face of realities is the subject also of the story "Genesis." By placing it among pieces of basically factual writing, Stegner gives it the appearance of historical and sociological fiction. But as a story it stresses, more than historiography can, the shape of a single action and the interior record of the protagonist Rusty. At one stroke the fictionalist is relieved of the burden of literal retrieval. But he is obviously not liberated from a desire to represent "truth." Rusty is representative, for instance, and he has his own discards and severances from the past. The difference is that unlike the discards of history that Stegner's homesteaders suffer, Rusty's changes are an organic part of a planned story, no part of which is discardable for the reader. Whatever he does in his supposed personal history, the work as a whole makes use of. Nothing that he leaves behind is without meaning, because a story is continuous and programmatic, from a beginning before which nothing happens to an ending after which nothing happens. In this difference, we can see clearly the major structural distinction between fiction and historiography that I shall insist upon in the next chapter: both Stegner in the autobiographical sections of *Wolf Willow* and Rusty in the story seek to be memorialized; they wish to be known, to commit themselves to paper, and thereby to become truly historical. But in fiction nothing exists except what the record causes to exist; everything is presumably organic, memorable, and aesthetically functional. Where the undifferentiated space of the prairies and the backward recession of time are annihilating to the historical self, they are a defining "antagonism" to the hero of a fiction. Thus the author supplies a framework for his characters that history does not supply for the self-reconstructions of real people.

Rusty himself accounts for some of the changes he undergoes and practices a rudimentary form of history writing. He comes to Saskatchewan as to a mythic landscape and sends reports back to civilization, recording each day's events in a journal and in letters home. As in so many stories of new beginnings, his initial impetus as a new Adam in innocence is checked by a fall or reversal that brings unexpected complications and a loss of an initial self-conception. Before he has gone very far into his ordeal he sees that the journal entries he has written are "very windy," falsely enthusiastic, and "very, very young" (pp. 170–71). In this respect, his difficulty resembles that of the plains settlers in establishing a historical continuum: the plains do not tolerate landmarks, patterns, or enclosures; they are not hospitable to human distinction. Rather than incorporating the outside world into man-made systems, the men are

themselves encircled by the unmarked prairies, absorbed into the vast
blankness of general nature.

The struggle between them is evident in several recurrent images,
most notably in the contrast between the inside of the crew's tent in
the warm, humanly controlled environment of their comraderie (but
with increasing tensions), and the raging storm outside, which at one
point unpins the tent, collapses it about their ears, and closes down
upon them with a cold flurry of snow. With the collapse of the tent,
certain man-made orders and agreements are scattered, and so fragile
are the standards of conduct that even the toughest of westerners become forgetful of the human contract. It becomes evident that to
break with sociality is to be scattered beyond history, to be broken
loose from the continuum that exists by the grace of human agreement. The wolfer and those who have resorted to cannibalism, for instance, are in danger of returning to unhistorical animalism; and
some such disintegration appears for a time to be a possible outcome
of Rusty's own ordeal. He considers it very likely at least that he will
be separated from the world of heroic legends, journals, and memorable deeds and thereby rendered nameless. The hindrance of the
plains pushes the men in any direction it chooses. It forces them off
their task and loses them in a wilderness of blind, undifferentiated
matter. The myth of the garden, the fictions of romance, and even the
simple pragmatic goal of rounding up cattle are undermined by an
unprecedented series of absurdities.

As Rusty's original pageantry is thus dispersed and routed, his concept of the West transposes from something appropriate to heroic romance to a realism in keeping with a hazardous and capricious nature. This movement coincides with the drift of *Wolf Willow* as a
whole. Stegner typically passes from misconceptions of one kind or
another to attested fact. But unlike the more complex strands of
Whitemud's history, Rusty's story finds a solid principle of
accomplishment and closure, not perhaps of the specific kind that
Rusty expects but of a typical initiation variety. The storms bring not
a disintegration of the social unit but a new solidarity based on other
principles. The little world of the fragile tent is replaced with the
stronger protection of a shack, where Rusty finds himself no longer
an outcast, though not a celebrity either: "The mystic smells of
brotherhood were strong in the shack. The stove lids puffed out
worms of smoke once more, and once more sucked them inward. The

wind went over and around them, the ancient implacable wind, and tore away balked and shrill" (p. 219). It is the privilege of fiction to come to such conclusions in theme, image, and plot, and to look no further, except to note the continuing storm that still defines the periphery of the human circle. The story is not obliged to reopen to the uncontrolled and raging fury outside; it has paid its dues to ancient implacable enemies, steered its course through potential pathlessness, and arrived at a destination summed up in the welcoming of the successful initiate to the tribe.

Stationed as it is in the context of more extensive views of Saskatchewan, the disorganized dump, and the trackless prairie, however, the fictional enclosure of "Genesis" is less complete than it might seem in isolation, as pure fiction. We have been shown some of what it dismisses. The impact of the winter is more far-reaching in Stegner's sociological analysis than it is in the story, where its influence is limited to its impact on Rusty's circle and their initiatory rites. The vistas of the historian, as opposed to the plotted limits of the short-story writer, stretch beyond the definite genesis of an adventure and the concluding recuperation of the men in a harbored place. *Wolf Willow* itself concludes as a whole:

> Unless North American tourists discover the beauty of the geometric earth and the enormous sky brimming with weather, and learn the passion of loneliness and the mystery of a prairie wind, Whitemud is going to have too little to work with; it will remain marginal or submarginal in its community and cultural life.
>
> Nevertheless, with its occasional impulse to the humane. Nevertheless, with its occasional Corky Jones. And therefore not hopeful. Give it a thousand years. [P. 306]

As opposed to the personal self recalled by the smell of the willows on its outskirts, Whitemud cannot be fully retrieved or accounted for. Its roots lie beyond speculation and its future is as yet unimaginable; and neither its more immediate past nor its present can exist apart from the full career of all the forces joined in its making. Or to put it another way, our view of Whitemud cannot be assimilated into the historical mainstream because the mainstream is itself indefinite. None of the archetypal fictions that Stegner touches upon — the myth of progress or the myth of the garden, for instance — is quite appropriate to it. None gives us an indication of where Whitemud's particular pontoon bridge is headed. That bridge will merely get longer. It may not in fact arrive anywhere; it may be abandoned entirely, like the paths of the homesteaders.

If Whitemud is a fair test, most of the schemes or blueprints, mythic eschatologies, moral absolutes, and doctrines of the historian and the fictional realist are likely to wear out against the prairies or any of those greater times and spaces that extend beyond one's pitifully inadequate modes of formulation. The narrative most answerable to the plains is a miscellany that lends itself to tentative conclusions. Even so, the prospect is not unhopeful in Stegner's eyes. What has managed to survive so far will probably continue to survive for some time, pursuing its fragile thread of historicity. If its just-past were not reachable to some extent even in the transforming generality of language, we would be forced to concede also the meaninglessness of the present, and we are reluctant to do that. As it is, all significance is in the eye of the beholder, and the narrative fixes there with admirable clarity and relative permanence some of the things we are determined not to discard too soon. Anecdotes of time, place, and character, whether literally true or fictionally symbolic and representative, are ways of salvaging parts of the just-past, ways of making them for the writer and the reader a richer still-present. If the abstractions of analytic history are inadequate to them, we have anecdotes to flesh them out, and if anecdotes grow tiresome or meaningless, we have the underpinning of philosophic and generalized statement to fall back on. If in the long run all systems of retrieval fail, in the short run we nonetheless keep to our bridges, which are not merely means of transportation from one point to another but life rafts.

II. MODES AND METHODS

CHAPTER THREE

Narrative Kinds

As James's concept of the novelist's use of the just-past and Stegner's various narrative experiments with it in *Wolf Willow* illustrate, the boundary between fictional and truthful narration is sometimes very fluid. However, Stegner's mixtures of narrative and expository methods also reveal crucial differences between them, some of which I want to isolate more clearly before turning to basic kinds of fictional narration.

Since we are not often tempted to apply the word *plot* to the course of true events, it is perhaps primarily what that term implies about the sequent movement of fictional events that most distinguishes the creative contributions of the imagination to the making of fictions. Certainly it is through plot design that a story gathers, redistributes, and renders intelligible the materials that history and experience have provided the writer. A plot causes us to focus on those spirited "motions" or motives that lead a protagonist and a society into their complications and toward certain ends, arranging the forwarding and arresting elements in a paced movement. Where in daily experience, information comes to us by chance, burdened with irrelevancies and contingencies, in the novelist's art it is teased out as impassioned, timed discovery. And where history writing seeks to lay bare the event and the cause as distinctly as possible, the novel renders the process of discovery itself and suggests that it is not merely the reader's but is inherent in the enigmas the work seeks to clarify. Perhaps no novelist has explained this advantageous organicism more clearly than Henry James. The Jamesian investigator, summed up so well in the narrator of *The Sacred Fount*, is, as Philip Weinstein suggests, a "version of the artist himself at work." Like the artist, "he is obsessed with the way things compose, with the figure in the carpet, with the latent story buried in phenomena that, to the untrained eye or passive imagination, seem blankly innocent. He exaggerates in the interest of form; his deepest allegiance is to 'story,' an imputed pattern of human relationships, richer, more throbbing and intense than appearances may actually justify."[1] Like that investigator, James explores a society often through dialectical cross-examination and the close readings that one intelligent and involved observer makes of the signs, gestures, and actions of another — which means that the plotted structure of the work is in part a chain reaction of onlookers extending outward to the reader at the periphery.

Thus when we consider the plotted course of stories, we mean not merely the logic of what happens but an "agonized" or dramatic discovery of that logic in which intelligence matches presumed happenings step by step. The cerebral processes of minds working in collaboration to uncover mysteries are of as much concern as the happenings themselves. As Austin Warren remarks about James in particular, the collaborators "piece together their evidence, or like attorneys for the defense and the prosecution they proceed alternately. . . . There are examinations and cross-examinations. There are mutual misunderstandings, false clues, shifts of position."[2]

More broadly conceived, this concern with the reactive witness is the social branch of a recurrent concern with what Tony Tanner describes as "wonderful," where again James figures prominently:

> Henry James was the first, and [is] still by far the greatest, writer to inquire into the fate of wonder when it is introduced into the clotted complexities of society . . . . For James is quite as interested in the naive wondering vision as any American writer. But rather than allow it the passive meditation prescribed by Emerson, James forced it — condemned it, even — to work on exclusively human, social material. None of his characters can withdraw to Walden Pond; none of them can flee "down river"; none of them [is] even allowed that saving reimmersion into nature which Nick Adams enjoys by his "river."[3]

1. Philip M. Weinstein, "The Exploitative and Protective Imagination: Unreliable Narration in *The Sacred Fount*," in *The Interpretation of Narrative: Theory and Practice*, ed. Morton W. Bloomfield (Cambridge, Mass.: Harvard University Press, 1970), p. 193.

2. Austin Warren, "Henry James: Symbolic Imagery in the Later Novels," reprinted from *Rage for Order* in *Henry James: A Collection of Critical Essays*, ed. Leon Edel (Englewood Cliffs, N.J.: Prentice-Hall, 1963), p. 125.

3. Tony Tanner, *The Reign of Wonder: Naivety and Reality in American Literature* (London: Cambridge University Press, 1965), p. 261.

The transformation of materials when imbued with questioning, wondering intelligence is distinctly accomplished in *What Maisie Knew*, for instance, where James sets for himself the task of binding his and the reader's processional intelligence to Maisie's own perceptions:

> I should have to stretch the matter to what my wondering witness materially and inevitably *saw*; a great deal of which quantity she either wouldn't understand at all or would quite misunderstand — and on those lines, only on those, my task would be prettily cut out. To that then I settled — to the question of giving it *all*, the whole situation surrounding her, but of giving it only through the occasions and connexions of her proximity and her attention; only as it might pass before her and appeal to her, as it might touch her and affect her, for better or worse, for perceptive gain or perceptive loss: so that we fellow witnesses, we not more invited but only more expert critics, should feel in strong possession of it. [*The Art of the Novel*, p. 145]

To master the perceptions of the novel is, paradoxically, for the reader, both to benefit from Maisie's wonder, despite all the poisons fed into it by her warring parents, and to work independently of her limited articulation of moral problems. Because what we see is only what passes before her eyes in the "phantasmagoric theatre" of her various households, it is transformed by the processes of her observation until it is no longer the sordid doings of her guardians but the embalmed wonder of her way of seeing:

> She is not only the extraordinary "ironic centre" I have already noted; she has the wonderful importance of shedding a light far beyond any reach of her comprehension; of lending to poorer persons and things, by the mere fact of their being involved with her and by the special scale she creates for them, a precious element of dignity. I lose myself, truly, in appreciation of my theme on noting what she does by her "freshness" for appearances in themselves vulgar and empty enough. They become, as she deals with them, the stuff of poetry and tragedy and art; she has simply to wonder, . . . about them, and they begin to have meanings, aspects, solidities, connexions — connexions with the "universal"! — that they could scarce have hoped for. [*The Art of the Novel*, p. 147]

Maisie thus makes her surroundings "portentous" and beautiful. In doing so, she also makes them both typically Jamesian in some respects and distinctly novelistic as opposed to biographical or historical, because her evolving acts of seeing are basic fictional transformations; she "brings them together" in the unity of her wonder. Actually, her coordination of events is assisted by her only half seeing, half comprehending, so that the beauty she casts over things lies in the shading of tones and shadows, glimpsed depths, intuited charms that excite the mind in the probing. It is only because she is *not* explicit or fully articulate that she can promote the teased-out structure of perceptions. The relationships of her family are awkward and painful at best and hysterical at worst, until Maisie enters into them and by the dynamism of her projected wonder redeems them. The end of that process of redeeming discovery is also the end of her freshness and of her capacity to rescue Sir Claude and Mrs. Beale, who in each other find only mutual weaknesses. It is when a new kind of perception is in order for Maisie at the end of her childhood — not when a certain course of action has been run — that James finds a natural conclusion: what matters all along has been what Maisie knows and how, in the knowing, she reorganizes and illuminates. In the final pages, the ironic distance between her intellectual grasp and the reader's closes; she moves into the same, sad world of adult complexity to which the novel returns us and from which it has rescued us for the duration of Maisie's innocence.

Whether or not the reactive witness is explicitly present within the work like this, the dramatic coherence of fiction assumes the presence somewhere of a knowing center before which the material of the story is placed in a certain sequence and timing that gives it the coloration of dramatic discovery. Whereas historical narration seeks for coherence largely in the subject itself, or in general statements about it, and is forced to acknowledge frequently its partial success, fiction locates it in a controlled epistemological, dramatic process over which the art work has absolute control. The intelligence may have to be flogged into alertness, corrected, and turned about, like Sterne's hypothetical reader; it may be courted and teased as in *Tom Jones*; or it may be enshrined in the narrator or a reliable interior character. But at some level in, or on the periphery of, the text, a discovering, wondering intelligence is a vital part of fictional design. It is no less so in drama as well; but in fiction the reader is assumed to be capable of putting together more disparate materials — direct representation, foreshortened summary, expository comment, description, and streams of consciousness. He is assumed to be adaptable to various modes and mixed rules of the game without confusion. In James, for instance, what the reader knows and how he discovers it are linked to the working processes of the author himself: as the author develops the full expression of an initial, inarticulate potential, an expandable idea, the growth of the organic seed in him is akin to the growth of the reader's awareness.

The creative process and the reading process are much less alike in most other art forms deprived of the analytic, the expository, and the interior witnessing by which the points of view of the author and reader are joined. Paintings, for instance, are put together brush stroke by brush stroke, no doubt often as Matisse suggests:

> I put on the canvas the particular red that satisfies me. A relation is now established between this red and the paleness of the canvas. When I put on besides a green, and also a yellow to represent the floor, between this green and the yellow and the color of the canvas there will be still further relations. ... The relationships between tones must be instituted in such a way that they are built up instead of being knocked down. A new *combination* of colors will succeed to the first one and will give the wholeness of my conception.[4]

But a finished painting retains few if any of these aspects of its serial construction. The viewer replaces them with a perceptual rather than a compositional sequence as he notices first this and then that detail. Though it is also true in narrative that the process of creation and the process of reading are unlike each other in crucial respects, a story does have a built-in temporal guidance. The courses of the writer, the hero, and the reader are closely identified. A recurrent complaint concerning James, in fact, is that we are sometimes too close to the author's working intelligence — that he does not sufficiently conceal it or make his characters independent enough. They rationalize, analyze, and forward the story as though James were in them. (James himself was aware that "the artist is present in every page of every book from which he sought so assiduously to eliminate himself.") The difficulty is that unlike the historian, the fictionalist begins with only the slightest piece of external incident, and the rest is of his personal making:

> One's subject is the merest grain, the speck of truth, of beauty, of reality, scarce visible to the common eye — since, I firmly hold, a good eye for a subject is anything but usual. Strange and attaching, certainly, the consistency with which the first thing to be done for the

4. Quoted from Dewey, *Art as Experience*, p. 136.

communicated and seized idea is to reduce almost to nought the form, the air as of a mere disjoined and lacerated lump of life, in which we may have happened to meet it. Life being all inclusion and confusion, and art being all discrimination and selection, the latter, in search of the hard latent *value* with which alone it is concerned, sniffs round the mass as instinctively and unerringly as a dog suspicious of some buried bone . . . . Hence the opportunity for the sublime economy of art, which rescues, which saves, and hoards and "banks," investing and reinvesting those fruits of toil in wondrous useful "works." [*The Art of the Novel*, pp. 119–20]

The interest of the artist "resides in the strong consciousness of his seeing all for himself. He has to borrow his motive . . . . But after that he only lends and gives. . . . He alone has the *secret* of that particular case, he alone can measure the truth of the direction to be taken by his developed data" (*The Art of the Novel*, pp. 122–23).

The artist runs other dangers in this as well. In the organicism of enclosed fictional systems lies a potential solipsism in which he may after all merely conduct conversations with himself, making characters the puppets of his intelligence system.

James is not alone in running this risk, of course. The setting of boundaries, the processes of anticipation and recollection in a consequential logic, the subordination and coordination of actions, and the timed or phased linking of events as vehicles of impassioned knowing are key elements of all fictional narrative, and they cannot help but suggest an identity between the creator's desire for form, the world he projects, and the reader's pursuit of a linear logic. All characters must be puppets to some extent if they are to function as parts of a fictive design. Whereas any "career" outside fiction may be out of phase with contiguous and intersecting careers and may proceed at a different rate and in a different direction from its neighboring actions, every fictional career is presumably phased with every other within the work. And the operations of the synchronizing intelligence are evident everywhere when we choose to look for them, though the disguises are more elaborate in some modes than in others.

The distinction among kinds of fictional narration and between factual and fictional narration in general cannot be entirely clear in this respect until we retreat a step and imagine the generation of basic narrative forms. Certain events have inherent boundaries, coordinated participants, and a consequential logic of their own, as an episode at the supermarket, the cycle of a day, a runner threading his way to the goal line. The "career" of the latter, for instance, has a beginning, ending, and cause-and-effect progression; impinging forces from this and that quarter give it the twists and turns that every narrative trajectory has as dramatic fiction. We can even say that diverting forces come from within an enclosed field and are explainable with reference to a single action. And to some extent this kind of coherence is typical of everyday life, including social games, institutions, even biological courses from birth to death, all of which operate within partially enclosed spheres. These seem provisionally storylike, inherently linear, sometimes crudely dramatic in their climaxes, and exciting in their focal heroes. Like the blueprint of Stegner's medicine line, such an event as the halfback run is thus obviously not merely the "series of messes" that history is sometimes assumed to be — where things are mostly unrehearsed and executed haphazardly. As a single "episode" (we are tempted to grant it the benefit of fictional terminology) it may even be public and well-witnessed and hence subject to standards of acceptable judgment, reaction and applause, and attested proof, so that there are limits to the ambiguities and doubts it may raise.

But the closer a true phenomenon comes to fictive shape the more one is impressed finally by the gulf between anything "out there" in normal experience and anything enclosed within the totally systematic movement of invented and artful worlds. The fact is that no historical event follows a preordained and intended script entirely. It is always open to some contingenices and changes of plan that even in the wisest retrospect cannot be accounted for, and there are always uncontrollable perspectives on the event. The course of the halfback has abundant loose ends, frustrated motives, and irrelevancies much in evidence up and down the sidelines: like Whitemud and its dump, it leaves debris scattered in its wake.

The more important question for a theory of narrative forms, however, is whether in their raw state even the "used" and organic elements of any real event actually have in them what James might recognize as meaning — whether they in fact make any sort of revelation to implicated witnesses. Is "organization" sufficient to make them "organic" to the intelligence? We quickly notice about so-called natural careers from historical fields of action (and of course battles, biographical careers, the rise and fall of empires, the coming and going of floods and droughts, and the development of institutions are all representable to some degree as analogous "fields of play") that the closer to complete intelligibility the historian brings a narration of them the more "fictive" his account begins to seem and the further the order of words detaches itself from the rush of events. The quandary of a would-be truthful narrator lies in his inability to verbalize a subject without transforming it. In "The Question Mark in the Circle," for instance — for all its appearance of true autobiography — Stegner stretches credibility by offering glimpses and anticipations of what is to come and especially by his climaxing recognition of a past identity. We cannot quite shake the suspicion planted by the "essay" itself that too many years of fiction writing have conditioned the autobiographer to remake the sequence and structure the impact of facts according to the psychology of fictive form. The smell of the willows is Proustian not only because Stegner has revisited a boyhood haunt and finds it as it was but also because, like Proust, he knows how to position the climax of an intellective process. To be "organic," word systems, as intellectual phenomena, must break from the contingent world and answer not to a living course of events but to a phantom course, an illusion of life transposable only in the vehicles of thought. They cannot remain mired in "unspiritual" phenomena. What Cassirer suggests with regard to significance in language in general, therefore, applies doubly to fictional signification:

> Not in proximity to the immediately given but in progressive *removal* from it lie the value and the specific character of linguistic as of artistic formation. This *distance* from immediate reality and immediate experience is the condition of their being perceived, of our spiritual awareness of them. Language, too, *begins* only where our immediate relation to sensory impression and sensory affectivity *ceases*. The uttered sound is not yet speech as long as it purports to be mere repetition; as long as the specific factor of signification and the will to "signification" are lacking. The aim of repetition lies in identity — the aim of linguistic designation lies in difference. . . . The more the sound resembles what it expresses; the more it continues to "be" the other, the less it can "signify" that other.[5]

That order, rules, and boundaries constitute much of the difference between the controlled games of art and the comparative chaos of

5. Cassirer, *The Philosophy of Symbolic Forms*, 1:189.

open historical situations is evident also in the fact that if a historian were true to even a majority of elements in a simple career, he would have to render all the points of view of all the spectators on each of the parts. There are as many careers in a historical field as there are potential observers, which presumably includes everyone within proximity or reachable by any sort of replay. To say this is merely to affirm that events have the fatal weakness, as non-art, of carrying no necessary or intended significance. As Wallace Stevens observes,

> Twenty men crossing a bridge,
> Into a village,
> Are twenty men crossing twenty bridges,
> Into twenty villages.[6]

Even if a certain number of spectators do happen to be locked into a particular point of view and infected with a group spirit that makes them "one man / Crossing a single bridge into a village," other observers are not obliged to accept it, any more than in watching old documentaries we are obliged to rise and cheer with Hitler's crowds.

To be permeated with genuine knowledge as a phased, significant revelation, then, a narration must first narrow to an intelligible perspective or controlled group of perspectives from which all aspects of the plot assume proportion, coordination, subordination, or other alignment. Virtually the first device of fiction is the establishing of mirrors or mediating intelligences in which act is no longer merely act but a symbolic vehicle of impassioned understanding.

In using James as a touchstone of fictional "organicism" in this matter, one is perhaps in danger of overestimating cerebral processes in the movement of fictional systems. But the same principles are equally clear when we juxtapose any model historical career with any work of fiction. Though we discover in the halfback's course the crude, inarticulate shape of dramatic development — crescendo, salient focus, and resolution — we have been implicitly qualifying somewhat the notion of Kenneth Burke and Dewey that we glanced at earlier, that certain forms of literary action are modeled upon natural phenomena (storms, the shape of social, psychological, and biological experience) as the conditions of appeal. In a sense the concept of imitation is perfectly appropriate here, and I will want to defend it in a moment on the grounds that real events do in a sense provide

6. Stevens, "Metaphors of a Magnifico," *Collected Poems*, p. 19.

models for fictional events. But the difference between the crescendo of events and the hinges and climaxes of *The Sense of the Past* or *The Brothers Karamazov* are too dramatic to be overlooked. The manifestation of concealed elements in raw events does not by itself explain either the "swerve" of the participant or the motives of what intrudes. What comes suddenly "on stage," unlike apparent contingencies in fiction, is truly unknown and unknowable even when it is finally manifest. It is unknowable because tracing its career backward would involve us in those retreating chains of consequence and endless ramification that lead some theorists of history to despair of narrative altogether. To explain anything as absolutely as it can usually be explained in the invented and controlled world of art we require a definite teleological principle, a closed boundary. Nor do we find much correspondence finally between the excitement and vicarious participation we experience in narrative or dramatic works and the excitement of historical events. Though any swerve or dramatic turn is intrinsically interesting, a climax or change of direction outside of art is not necessarily pleasurable, where threats are real and pleasures are consumed on the spot. Whereas people in real life can be married, wounded, or promoted totally without logic, in fictions, crises are governed by a figure's place in the plot, which will supposedly not leave either him or us ultimately stranded or bewildered. Hence the quality of anticipation and the quality of recollection are altered by their enshrinement in a symbol system where images are "representative," where phenomena are paradigms, and where men are protagonists and antagonists.

The ability to hold to boundaries is rendered difficult even in art by the tendency of words to sprawl in all directions. As Jorge Louis Borges remarks in *Labyrinths*, no proposition can stop short of involving the entire universe unless we arbitrarily cut off spatial, temporal, and numerical possibilities. For instance, to say "the tiger"

> is to say the tigers that begot it, the deer and turtles devoured by it, the grass on which the deer fed, the earth that was mother to the grass, the heaven that gave birth to the earth .... In the language of a god every word would enunciate that infinite concatenation of facts, and not in an implicit but in an explicit manner, and not progressively but instantaneously. . . . No word uttered by him can be inferior to the universe or less than the sum total of time.[7]

7. Jorge Louis Borges, "The God's Script," from *Labyrinths*, ed. Donald A. Yates and James E. Irby (New York: New Directions, 1962), p. 171.

This puts the quandary of the would-be truth-sayer — the literalist — in strong but essentially accurate terms. And because it fears above all that plurality and extent, even the most ambitious piece of fictional realism refuses to approach the complexity of the thinnest slice of reality. As Georg Lukács observes: "The novel's closeness to life differs from the mere copying of empirical reality; naturalism is not the innate style of the novel. The span of the hugest novel is limited. If one were to take the *Comédie Humaine* as a single novel, it would give only an infinitesimal fraction, even in breadth, of the incommensurable reality of its time. An adequate quantitative, artistic reflection of the infinity of life is quite out of the question."[8] Fictional time imitates historical time only insofar as its moments contain echoes and presentiments. It cannot duplicate the number of successive careers taking place at a given moment or their indefinite extensions forward and backward from the present.

The psychological form and coherence we think we discover in events may partly be there, then, as mimetic theories insist; but to a great extent they are also put there by modes of formulation, which are the despair of a naive mimesis or a naive sociological criticism.

One of the initial points that we must make with respect to those modes is that all kinds transform their materials "ideally," according to conventions and intrinsic predispositions. We can perhaps get a sense of the remaking that basic modes perform on reality if we consider them progressively, according to their degrees of departure from normal experience. Even an immediate replay of an event selects salient moments of what was just a moment before part of a continuous and complex action. In film versions, it may exercise the prerogative of slowing down or stopping action for closer observation, or adding verbal accompaniment or imposing other shaping and stylistic increments. And these primitive translations of history into legend already begin to reveal some of the structural qualities of fiction. They create a contemplative distance that the "now" originally lacked. Perhaps the first step toward organic formulation in fact is the stationing of the event in the past as a potential "episode," in which duration and focus, guided by technique and knowledgeable commentary, begin to define a perspective.

With greater reshaping, we can make the same raw event into an

8. Georg Lukács, *The Historical Novel,* trans. Hannah and Stanley Mitchell (London: Merlin Press, 1962), pp. 138–39.

epitome or typical pattern, such as everyman moving toward a goal against hostile forces, or the fruits of teamwork, or some form of social cooperation in parable form. To satisfy the taste of the social scientist, we can also abstract and quantify an event such as the half-back run, thereby placing it in a mathematical framework, remembering as we do so that every social phenomenon contributes to someone's "seasonal totals" and has a comparable length, size, or number. Such generalizations and epitomes may or may not strike us as highly significant in themselves, but even when they do, they do not yet compose what would normally be called a fiction because what really happened and is discoverable from other sources remains foremost in the intent of the narrator and central to the literal happening of his narration. The mode is still basically historical. A moralizing of stark events that makes use of a narrative case as a paradigm — though it stands for analogous situations and helps us organize a broader field — also subordinates its phased action to true discursive statements. The fictional attributes of the model, if there are any, are subordinate to discursive logic, whereas even in a highly didactic, foreshortened mode such as an Aesop fable, a fictionalist does not make the course of literal past events the sole foundation of his inductive reasoning. (In fictional uses of illustrative anecdote, general precepts are resident in the animation of a design, whereas in true records, information, to borrow Burke's distinction, presides over rhythm and form.)

Hence we must imagine a further step in the transcription of events before we arrive at truly fictional modes in the common distinction. We cross the line at the point at which the narrator's commitment to organic plot-making and form causes him to put aside his commitment to literal events knowable in ways beyond the story. At that stage, he is free to juxtapose the career of a representative hero with other kinds of careers in such a way as to create multiple or parallel plots; he can then devote all the ironic or concordant commentary that juxtaposition makes possible to the logic of the parallels. Such a logic transcends each plot line separately and transcends the implications of a literal replay. The fictionalist is now committed to the assimilation of an action into the realm of symbolic significance or poetics. He is entirely free to *play* with events or *work* them. They belong to him and not to history; they exist and are knowable only in his witnessing of them, and he need not release them until he has infused them point by point with the preservative of a systematic meaning. At that decisive step he also plunges the witnessing intelligence into the "pathos" of animate illusions. With something like a continuous aesthetic satisfaction, a witness now finds before him a fusion of concrete materials and artistic form and sees in the very texture of the linear movement elements of style and beauty not expressly functional to pragmatic ends.[9]

As we progress toward these fuller implications of fiction, we notice in its transformations a law of diminishing returns: the further the narrator brings events into the domain of continuous aesthetic form and structured feeling and intelligence, the less historical the subject seems. The more the material is made to yield, the less its harvest belongs to the realm of the actual. (Even when a commentator first adds analysis to an instant replay, he has already begun to dissolve the literal event into analogous events, comparing, evaluating, lifting it piece by piece out of the arena of unique actions and setting it into a museum of preserving documents and mosaics.) This is not to say that no variety of history writing manages to remain relatively close to "what actually happened" without sacrificing interest and intelligibility; it is merely to reaffirm a few obvious principles: that art tends to live long and reality a short time, and the former lives only by its relative liberation from the latter; that nonetheless both are inseparable; that symbolicity and human significance belong in a category quite distinct from life; that the psychology of aesthetic perception is governed by principles quite different from those of daily processes; and that the flow of time in plots is distinct from what it is in the uncoordinated pluralism of historical careers.

All of these are truisms, but even so some further distinctions are needed before we can confidently ask what the main modes of fiction are and how they transform experience. Some kinds of fiction obviously emerge more directly from facts than others. Documentary novelists frequently develop out of reporters and capitalize on their journalistic experience, as Defoe and Dickens illustrate. The characters of Balzac and Stendhal are partly historical and partly invented, and they move through history's real "broken fields" in Paris

---

9. To the argument that a potential aesthetic texture is buried in nature's raw materials and needs only polishing to emerge, like the grain of finished wood, one may reply that we can never know about a potential poetic element until the craftsman has been at work, and then the "frame is fitted, the picture made." Works of art are made, not found.

and elsewhere — against an opposition that readers easily recognize as factual circumstance. Even in romance, myth, and epic, the dividing line between fictional and factual narration is sometimes far from distinct. Homer's heroes, some of them at least, pursued historical careers that Homer subjected to a not-so-instant replay as well as to mythologizing. Indeed, whatever radical transformations fictions work upon life, we persist in reading them as though they had some bearing upon our experience. We do so partly because in all thinking moments — as opposed to Vaihinger's unthinking flux of sensations — we constantly organize experience along the lines of literary formulation. Without questioning the essential correctness of Borges's and James's observations or seriously qualifying Lukács's observation, we notice that we seldom let the pluralities and endless ramifications of mere truth interfere with our daily single-mindedness. Paradoxically, we sometimes grasp things of indisputable reality best in the enclosures of artifice and get at truth more handily through lies: as metaphor sometimes gives us a revealing distortion, so in art we warp, edit, and simplify events in order to hold them steady for observation.

A fond mother looking at a snapshot of her son, for instance, knows, if she pauses to think, that a thin piece of paper, a two-dimensional picture, has almost none of the attributes of flesh-and-blood about it; yet it nonetheless gives her a sense of time and reality recaptured. Even in its frozen, framed image it defines its subject in such a way as to possess reality on its own terms. The images and actions of art are reorganized much as memory and inherent legendizing tendencies reorganize our perceptions, even without help from illusionists. The world of process and fleeting forms, and the fictional world of fixed and named objects — so opposite in duration, pace, surface, texture, and cohesiveness — meet not only in fables, then, but in the mind's habitual operations. They meet in our shuttling back and forth, with such dexterity and so little embarrassment, between dream and fact, illusion and reality. What art might be said to imitate, then, is not so much reality in itself as our selective impressions of it, our habitual amalgamating, associating, and rearranging in the interests of associative plots and designs.

These grounds for a qualified defense of mimesis deserve emphasis here because once we have sufficiently guarded against the confusion of art and experience and realized the significance of fictive structures in reconstituting a world of its own, we are forced to relocate certain aspects of fictive design in the bent and disposition of memory and the psychology of perception, especially in the reader's amalgamation of his own experience and the guided discoveries of the work. That is, fictional worlds with their synchronized and phased careers play upon our habits of perception and on abiding categories and generalizations. If even a snapshot that makes no attempt to keep pace with what it records may suggest storied careers and three-dimensional realities to someone who fills in the gaps, how much more may a fiction give us a sense of historical realities, with its fondness for dramatic collisions and its artfully controlled anxieties about the future. Hence we must be as sensitive to the likeness between art and life as we are to their difference if we are to realize the impact of their union on each other and define the modifications of temporal sequence that various fictional modes characteristically make.

THE PROBLEM OF MODES

Assuming that fictional and nonfictional narration are distinguished broadly by structural matters, especially by differences in consequential logic, juxtaposition, gaps and concealments, outcomes, and the linear psychology of readers, we can perhaps locate some distinctions within the family of fictional kinds along similar structural lines. (Though only limited modal distinctions can be made from the evidence provided by kinds of linear careers alone, I prefer to stick to structural matters for the moment, leaving fuller modal considerations for later, when we turn to fictive symbols and signs and particular works and allow matters of style and content to assert themselves more forcefully. In any case, structural aspects of a work — the timing of information, periodicity, the retrieval of the past at certain junctures, prediction, adventure, and impact on the reader's searching out of continuous meaning and eventful clarification — are vital enough to justify close attention to them.)

One of the first functions of an overall action or design is to give each detail of a work as it appears an augmented interest, to lend to it the heightened excitement of a meaningful associativity; the manner of that connection is the first principal of any concern with structure. What James describes as the author's "complete expression," worked out gradually from the germ of stories, entails the articulation of an

invisible potential in a stylized, paced turning of each revelation. For
reasons intrinsic to narrative materials and to the audience's exposure to them, different modes proceed by distinct rates of discovery and principles of association.

When we consider the linear program of heroes, for instance, certain distinctions in timing and juxtaposition become evident among
modes. In myths, as Charles O'Hare suggests, the hero is more
directly goal-oriented than in other forms. He arrives at important
stages in the life cycle such as death, rebirth, or some period of
initiation. Joseph Campbell puts it more strongly: "Creation myths
are pervaded with a sense of the doom that is continually recalling all
created shapes to the imperishable out of which they first emerged."[10]
As opposed to the *Bildungsroman* and other basic development
stories, myths also veil the hero's stages of growth, so that events unfold ahead of his interior assimilation or the reader's share in his
revelations. To put it another way: whereas the conversation and the
interior focus of a Jamesian novel allows very little to pass until the
intelligence has seized it, declared it portentous, and taken up the
next complexity, in myth and romance intelligence is out of step with
action. The hero is exposed to instructions whose import is not clear
— to obscure messages, dark hints, and intrusions from beyond —
and these cast over his progress the suggestion of inexpressive sacred
or demonic powers, often of the "imperishable" that Campbell mentions.

In fairness to the complexity of generic distinctions, we should also note that mythic and demonic powers and a certain wonder and
awesomeness are present also even in realistic fiction, as James's
ghost stories and the hovering, abiding wonder of certain of his
heroines indicate. But the "romance" of astonishment and enigma is
ordinarily a very subordinate dimension of the hero's or the reader's

10. Joseph Campbell, *The Hero with a Thousand Faces* (New York: Meridian Books,
1956), p. 269. See Charles Bernard O'Hare, "Myth or Plot?: A Study in Ways of Ordering
Narrative," *Arizona Quarterly* 8 (1957): 238–50; FitzRoy R. S. Raglan, *The Hero: A
Study in Tradition, Myth, and Drama* (London: Methuen, 1936); Thomas A. Sebeok, ed.,
Myth: A Symposium (Bloomington: Indiana University Press, 1958); John Middleton,
ed., *Myth and Cosmos: Readings in Mythology and Symbolism* (Garden City, N.Y.:
Natural History Press, 1967); Claire Rosenfeld, "From Myth to Literature, from Sacred to
Profane," in *Paradise of Snakes: An Archetypal Analysis of Conrad's Political Novels*
(Chicago: University of Chicago Press, 1967), pp. 11–42; Northrop Frye, "Literature and
Myth," in *Relations of Literary Study*, ed. James Thorpe (New York: Modern Language
Association, 1967), pp. 27–56.

progress through the social novel's materials; and it is primary in myth and romance, where sequent elements are juxtaposed without self-evident bridges for the reader to cross over. Indeed, one form that myth takes in creating the leaps and the swerves of the hero's course is the intersection of forces of quite different magnitude whose joining defies ready understanding. Here the matter of tempo and sequential logic is especially important. The powers that move the action and govern our response are difficult for the hero to assimilate precisely because they encompass longer durations than he is used to considering and involve highly discrepant principles of enclosure and period. Mythic design is often difficult to grasp until we see, for instance, that natural growth on the human scale is linked to an encompassing sacred or cosmic time — that the hero's particular life cycle is keyed to basic powers of sun, moon, thunder, or sea, or to their embodiment in immortal figures like Apollo, Diana, Zeus, or Neptune.

Though even these gods have human experiences and cannot be imagined entirely apart from human or animal shapes, they are also different in radical ways. The god or goddess tends to stand for recurrent powers or abiding abstractions that transcend the particular and unique career of the single hero, who is allowed only momentary exposure to them. In the typical cycle plot of the monomyth that Campbell describes, the hero thus abandons the logic of wakeful sequences and normal human careers, descends into another kind of connectedness like that of dreams, and returns to a wakeful state enriched by the shadows and apparitions that still cling to his experience. When the gods prevail and infiltrate human existence, history from their mythic point of view expands in vistas of recurrence denied to the records of merely linear and unique events. Their perspective is confirmable for the audience through the extraordinary experience of the hero. Thus elements of the marvelous that in fairy tales are domesticated in the offering of timely help to lowly heroes are much more numinous in myth: the hero is charged with bringing hidden injunctions and energies into manifest action and making a cosmic chronology bear upon himself and his society. As Cassirer remarks, "Only when the world of the mythical begins . . . to flow, only when it becomes a world not of mere being but of action, can we distinguish individual independent figures in it."[11]

11. Cassirer, *The Philosophy of Symbolic Forms*, 2:105.

Actually, the performances of the gods both individuates them and generalizes the hero, who shares in their enduring powers. The hero's changes, crises, and resolutions require an adjustment of perspectives whenever he is open to this expansion of vistas. His plight is similar to that of figures whose fate is to come to grips with a foreign system — social, psychological, biological, cosmic — from which they are initially insulated. But the mythic hero, unlike the ordinary protagonist of a social novel, confronts a multileveled puzzle: his guides are not Kate Croys, Mrs. Beales, or Edward Causabons but shamans, seers, and emissaries from the unknown. Hence he cannot put his career entirely under the control of foresight and accumulated experience. Like Hercules undergoing mythic labors, he takes the shield of Jupiter, the sword of Mercury, or the bow and arrows of Apollo as his arms.

Romances that touch upon myth illustrate perhaps even more clearly that several rates of development may follow their own distinct courses in forming a complex and tangled pattern and that the more discrepant the temporal sweep of these courses, the further we move from mimetic principles. Malory's Sangreal quests are typical in this regard; I want to dwell upon them a moment as combinations of myth and romance at some remove from normal experience.

The introduction of the grail in Malory comes at a time when the story of the round table is already well advanced and the separate tales of the knights have been linked to the central group of Arthurian fellowship. As an intersection of differently phased careers, the collision of the social and the sacred kingdoms thereafter forms a more complex narrative than either does separately. Specifically, the grail reinterprets both the concept of the table and what constitutes a fellowship at it. It reinterprets also the duration of one's worship or fame. If Malory's tales of King Arthur (as Vinaver arranges them)[12]

12. See Eugene Vinaver, *The Works of Malory* (London: Oxford University Press, 1959). Quotations from Malory are from this edition. Vinaver believes that the tales are largely separate, but see also D. S. Brewer, "Form in the Morte Darthur," *Medium Aevum* 21 (1952): 14–24; Robert H. Wilson, "How Many Books Did Malory Write?" *University of Texas Studies in English* 30 (1951): 1–23; Viva D. Scudder, *Le Morte Darthur of Sir Thomas Malory and Its Sources* (New York: Haskell House, 1965), pp. 280–315, passim; E. K. Chambers, "Some Points in the Grail Legend" and "Sir Thomas Malory," in *Sir Thomas Wyatt and Some Collected Studies* (New York: Russell and Russell, 1965), pp. 1–24; Mary E. Dichmann, "Characterization in Malory's *Tale of Arthur and Lucius*," *PMLA* 65 (1950): 877–95; R. M. Lumiansky, "Malory's 'Tale of Lancelot and Guenevere' as Suspense," *Mediaeval Studies* 19 (1957): 108–22.

have a central strategy in the later parts, in fact, it would seem to consist of a search for ways to unite these disparate planes of time. The early tales concern the rise of Arthur as a central power in a world otherwise fragmented among factions and competing chivalric figures whose exploits are narrated in a loosely episodic way. The various knights who eventually join the fellowship are in partial conflict with the extended career of the collective group, but each assumes an added social purpose when he joins it. The table, as a fellowship reinforced by a superior magic and predictions of a fated rise, creates a sufficient centrality among episodes to suggest an integrated set of adventures. This collective principle enables Malory to explore the dynamics of social aggregates. As each knight gathers a name from his exploits, he brings it as tribute to the group. Worship and fellowship are keyed to public as well as personal fame and spread both to the periphery of the society and to the durational limits of the kingship.

The grail shatters these limits in a spiral of expanding discoveries. It enters as an intangible, floating, spiritual center and by its awesome power disperses Arthur's hard-won order, usurping the bonds already established by that order. At the same time, it collects many of the motives and principles of narrative succession that have been organized for other purposes: henceforth it is the grail that is favored by doom, and it is the secrets of sacred allegory that occupy the interpreter of concealments and revelations. As the interest of fate shifts from Arthur's career to Christ's, the kingship passes out of temporal reach. Thereafter individual careers have two centralizing orders to answer to, the social union of the table, as secular fame, and the communion of the grail. Each of the knights feels the rival power of a new fealty in his own way, and some of them never return to the old order.

Like the all-encompassing doom of Tolkien's ring quest, this expansiveness of the grail plot, which has the impact of a foreign power on the mythic hero, is answerable to an inner need of the knights for greater worship, a need that can be described in part in terms of the duration and extent of their public identity. Unlike the hero of the novel, the hero of myth, epic, or romance is often doomed to an exposure beyond those immediate generations implicated in a transfer of property, position, or individual fame. For instance, Tolkien's Frodo at critical moments is led to take the harder path because only it leads into the "whole story" of the ring, with its control

over vast epochs. In a similar way, the periphery of individual fame in
Malory expands. Nine generations have existed between Christ's first
bishop (Joseph) and Galahad, the most perfect of contemporary
knights. It is true that the cultic possessors of the grail and of
Christian wisdom have not publicized their exploits in any ordinary
quest for worship. They have wished to be known only to Christ and
to the cult itself. But the ultimate fame they seek lies thereby not beneath but beyond social memorialization. The new fame requires the
suppression of the social-minded ego in order to be magnified as
another variety of worship. Lancelot's relationship to the round table
and to Guenevere is surpassed by Galahad's relationship to the King
of Love; *courtship* and *chivalry* are translated as divine petition and
divine love. To abdicate — to remain on the social plane and seek
merely to unhorse more knights in more tournaments for more ladies
— would be to reject the most conclusive self-fulfillment and high
perspective by which a knight joins the longer vista.

The progress of the knights from Arthurian fellowship to visions of
the grail, then, carries the various knights through what amounts to
stages of a spiritual dialectic and shifts of temporal gears to bring
them within reach of new planes, the narrative method appropriate to
which translates the surface of events into the veiled expression of
spiritual allegory. Their antagonists, for instance, cease to be merely
rivals for fame and become largely hindrances to a religious consciousness or reminders of their failures. The narrative mode, in other
words, adds to the devices of chivalric romance some of the qualities
of religious parables. It grafts onto older tales another kind of "enchantment" and "magic," another kind of timely revelation. It becomes evident to Lancelot, for instance, that a quite different
coordinating principle underlies his exploits and subordinates lesser
mysteries to itself. Where it was once safe to survey a tournament,
enter the side of the weaker party, and carry off new worship, knights
in white now prove to be virginal servants of the Lord and knights in
black agents of the fiend. One's guesses tend to fall short.

The new doubts and obscurities that plague Lancelot can be resolved only by a vision of considerable extent given to him by cultic
members of the new fellowship versed in esoteric signs and symbols.
The reader shares both his bewilderment and his enlightenment. An
armed body lying in a tomb, the reader discovers, betokens "the duras
of the worlde, and the grete synne that our Lorde founde in the

world" (p. 643). When a knight comes upon two roads parting left and right, one can be certain that his alternatives will not be, as in earlier books, different paths to Orkeney or to Gaul; they are now, according to an interpreting priest or hermit, "higheways" of "oure Lorde Jesu Cryst . . . [for] synnars and . . . myssbelevers" (p. 646). The new status of heroes is gauged by their readings and misreadings of these allegorical signs, which usurp an immediate sequence of events and, by typological expansion, figure in it some of the age-old paradigms of everyman's spiritual struggle.

The various time cycles of romance often coexist without resolving their differences, and so it is with Malory's multiple plots. By inserting the grail stories between the completed rise of the table and the ultimate death of Arthur, Malory complicates the elegiac mood of the final books and makes the fall of the round table as much a product of a dissociation of the order of church and the order of the state as it is of tensions between the public standards of the kingship and the private or "sentimental" intrigues of chivalric love. The coordinated grail stories together offer a graduated series of heroes whose careers collide or fuse with the paradigm of the Christian pilgrim. As a comparatively limited hero on a sacred quest, Lancelot never manages to lose himself in the archetype of the Christian knight. His contributions to the fall of the round table in loving Guenevere are thus twofold, his betrayal of Arthur's fellowship and his betrayal of the grail fellowship, one a violation of social codes and manners, the other a violation of the spiritual vision Galahad achieves. After the grail quests, it is obviously impossible for him to mediate among chivalric love, fealty to the king, and religious vistas; despite promises to the contrary, he resumes his adulterous love for Guenevere and follows its schedule of appointments and crises. Yet one part of him continues to cling to the old loyalties of Arthurian fellowship — courtesy, respect for chivalric status, and the championing of the weak by force of arms — as another part remains committed to the values of the grail quest.

The tension among the time schemes and concepts of careers in Malory represents a typical dynamics of narrative movement and expectation in myth and romance and a typical disparity in principles of connectedness between one kind of career and another

within the general organicism of fictions. We discover similar
principles of timing, periodicity, and plot connection in other modes,
but with significant differences which point up the importance of
scheduled discovery and temporal association in all fictive narrative
design. We have seen that in Christ's parables, for instance, ordinary
motives and sequential logic are displaced by an eschatological outcome of another order, as they are again in the stories of Abraham
and Isaac and the tragedy of Job. Essentially what happens in these
narratives, as in Malory's grail quests, is that new perspectives based
on an extension of temporal vistas are imposed on what have been
largely social and naturalistic careers — among people who marry,
have children, accumulate property or fame, and build dynasties. As a
branch of chronicle history, scriptural narrative frequently concerns
the continuity of the generations and the record of tribes; but as
sacred myth it also emphasizes the intrusions of providence at certain
crystallizing junctures and the expanded perspectives of the tribes and
their patriarchs. What biblical narrative does in the relatively condensed form of the parable and the narrative of Abraham and Isaac
the grail quests extend and particularize in uniting the loosely
episodic form of romance to the multileveled grail plot. Each episode
of Lancelot's mature career tends to be parabolic and to contain
the same mechanism of surprise and forced revaluation of evidence as
biblical narrative, as Lancelot misreads surfaces, realizes painfully the
shortsightedness of his errors, and stretches to encompass the fuller
significance of the grail. His need for reeducation in so many episodes testifies to the stubbornness of the chivalric codes and the natural rhythms of affairs of love and war.

Whereas all fictional narratives assemble a line of events as a cognitive series, then, the sudden expansions of vista that myth, romance,
and sacred literature introduce devour the logic initially established,
break the apparent limits of one temporal system, and supplant them
with a logic of different scope and value. Both the characters within
the story and the reader are required to revise previously apparent
theories. James finds the essence of romance in precisely that liberation from the pursuit of the ordinary:

> The only *general* attribute of projected romance that I can see, the only
> one that fits all its cases, is the fact of the kind of experience with
> which it deals — experience liberated, so to speak; experience dis-
> engaged, disembroiled, disencumbered, exempt from the conditions

that we usually know to attach to it and . . . drag upon it, and operating in a medium which relieves it . . . of the inconvenience of a *related*, a measurable state, a state subject to all our vulgar communities. [*The Art of the Novel*, p. 33]

James's definition of romance, however, is essentially negative and modern in seeing the dissociation of romance plot from social realism without acknowledging the values that traditionally replace shattered limits. Modern romance tends to replace the expanded vista of the tradition with a sense of not transcendent beings but non-being. The gap between levels becomes an abyss. Greater duration becomes an extension of silence or oblivion; one logic is replaced not with another but with an awareness of the absurd.

The modern modes closest to traditional myth, romance, and sacred parable, and religious epics in this regard are antiromances like Hawthorne's, Conrad's, Barth's, and Kafka's, which are capable of equally great displacements of social and personal continuities. The "interfering power" in a modern work of this type is not likely to be either a namable divine force of Malory's type or a definable force of realism such as we might find in Hemingway, Wright Morris, Edith Wharton, William Styron, or Norman Mailer.

Consider, for instance, the interception of an established temporal logic in the following radical parable from Kafka's *The Great Wall of China*. Though short enough to be quoted in full, it is also disjunctive enough to suggest the clashing of levels and the difficult adjustment of investigative procedures that both the protagonist and the reader must attempt:

> I was stiff and cold, I was a bridge, I lay over a ravine. My toes on one side, my fingers clutching the other, I had clamped myself fast into the crumbling clay, the tails of my coat fluttered at my sides. Far below brawled the icy trout stream. No tourist strayed to this impassable height, the bridge was not yet traced on any map. So I lay and waited; I could only wait. Without falling no bridge, once spanned, can cease to be a bridge.
>
> It was towards evening one day — was it the first, was it the thousandth? I cannot tell — my thoughts were always in confusion and perpetually moving in a circle. It was towards evening in summer, the roar of the stream had grown deeper, when I heard the sound of a human step! To me, to me. Straighten yourself, bridge, make ready, railless beams, to hold up the passenger entrusted to you. If his steps are uncertain steady them unobtrusively, but if he stumbles show what you

are made of and like a mountain god hurl him across to land.

He came, he tapped me with the iron point of his stick, then he lifted my coat-tails with it and put them in order upon me. He plunged the point of his stick into my bushy hair and let it lie there for a long time, forgetting me no doubt while he wildly gazed round him. But then — I was just following him in thought over mountain and valley — he jumped with both feet on the middle of my body. I shuddered with wild pain, not knowing what was happening. Who was it? A child? A dream? A wayfarer? A suicide? A tempter? A destroyer? And I turned round so as to see him. A bridge to turn round! I had not yet turned quite round when I already began to fall. I fell and in a moment I was torn and transpierced by the sharp rocks which had always gazed up at me so peacefully from the rushing water.[13]

Despite our implicit preparation for nearly anything once we have acknowledged a talking bridge (that has already been destroyed), the parable nonetheless startles us with the turn it takes. The bridge seems initially to have been fixed in a firm world of reasonable actions, and the accomplishments it projects prepare us for a crisis that will somehow fulfill its promise — a crisis supposedly in accord with its situational logic. The imperatives that occur to the bridge — extend, prepare, hold — are thus perfectly understandable, considering what it has observed of itself. Is it not already extended and does not the gulf beneath it argue forcefully to "hold"? What reason does a bridge have to exist if not to help creatures cross chasms? Even its stiffness points toward a static essence, a permanence amidst whatever change or trial may come to the mountains. And so it reads its circumstances as a mandate to give safe passage in responsiveness to whatever contingencies may arise. If the step of its entrusted visitor is uncertain, it will compensate; better still, if someone should fall, it will save him dramatically, like a god. In so responding, as we fill in its logic, it will become known in actuality, in narrative deeds, for the bridge that is initially only unhistorical potential — which is to say that plot will stem from character, motive, and circumstance, as it should.

Unlike the shock of parables like Christ's, the bridge's reversal, rather than leading to another logic of equal validity but greatly expanded vista, defies logic altogether and points toward indefinite

13. Franz Kafka, *Description of a Struggle* and *The Great Wall of China*, trans. Willa and Edwin Muir, Tanya and James Stern (New York: Schocken Books; London: Secker and Warburg, 1960), pp. 116–17.

chains of reasoning. Whatever rival system of values the intruder represents, he makes no explicable contact with a bridge that bores, clamps, flutters its coattails, and waits for the moment. That a catalyst should come from outside an initial sphere of awareness and contribute unexpectedly to a new concatenation is not at all unusual in any form of narrative, of course, but for it to come altogether from outside the explicable, without sanctions granted in the name of some authorizing power, is an assault upon the logical process itself. The assailant therefore forces a rethinking of the nature of attested evidence and fictive logic. Is he a creature in a dream? (The entire experience is dreamlike, but even dreams must make sense if they are to be narrated.) Is he a demon or a tester of bridges sent to see how well they concentrate on their tasks? Has he merely chanced upon this particular bridge in his wanderings and acted upon an inspired sadism or a habitual cruelty? Or was he assigned a role by some script that he understands no better than we? Perhaps he originates his own plots and travels from some far country to execute long-range aims in defiance of paltry human logic.

Whatever his purpose, or lack of purpose, it lies buried in his silence and renders the existence of the bridge and its surroundings absurd. At the end of a series of bewildered questions that shatter the imperatives it has reasoned out, the bridge is led to do what no bridge can do, turn around in wonder, thus destroying its very identity. It tries to bear witness, to see its assailant, to explain, but it cannot: no act of witnessing is possible, either for it or for the reader. And this surely is the "meaning" of such a break with consistent sequence: its collapse renders fruitless all speculation about possible relationships between character and destiny, or between logic and actual existence.

Actually, the trauma of most radical narrative forms contains a hint of what Kafka here makes the governing mystery of the story. The progress of a romance hero toward the knowledge he is destined to have is always an anxious progress, whether it occurs in the realm of the wonderful or the realm of the awful. The self-destruction demanded of Lancelot by the grail quest and the terrible relocation of values in Abraham's near sacrifice of Isaac need only a slight turn to suggest Kafka's intuition of abysmal self-destruction and to plunge the reader into endless speculation.

A notable modern example of greater force and compass is Conrad's "Heart of Darkness," in which the central intelligence, Marlow, discovers not a grail fellowship (obviously) but a demonic equivalent. For Kurtz — Marlow's messenger from "beyond" — the Word and Light emanate from a source of terror, as though divine being and omniscience had become inversions of Milton's invisible light or Galahad's bright illumination. Like the voyages of Malory's knights away from the logic of the Arthurian kingdom and its chivalric order, Marlow's journey takes him beyond the accustomed order of modern bureaus and the capitalist empire in Africa. The absolute negation that he is led to see shatters these several illusions of modern causal logic and economic growth, including, in retrospect, not only the progress of empire but the entire surface life of Western European cities, further undermined in *The Secret Agent.* Even the growing course of Marlow's own illumination is ironically inverted, as the heart of darkness has previously reversed Kurtz's expectations. Marlow's way stations to the abyss lead downward as abruptly as Galahad's stages of illumination lead upward; and as the Arthurian feast can only approximate the grail supper, debased colonial capitalism can only approximate the total darkness of Kurtz's vision. Indeed, since the heart is total darkness, any "view" that Marlow might have of it is contradictory. It is ineffable. The reader is invited to share "illusions," not "knowledge" in the ordinary sense. Where the mystic plunges through a period of annihilating darkness to reach an indescribable, unintelligible joy, Marlow plunges through stages of illusory vision to an unspeakable anguish and an epistemological negation. All that can be narrated or talked about in either case ultimately is the visible surface, the periphery, before the light has disappeared: "the meaning of an episode was not inside like a kernel, but outside, enveloping the tale which brought it out only as a glow brings out a haze, in the likeness of one of those misty halos that sometimes are made visible by the spectral illuminations of moonshine."[14] The words of Kurtz — the most gifted of word-makers — at the end of Marlow's search are both exalted and contemptible. They form a "pulsating stream of light, or the deceitful flow from the heart of an impenetrable darkness."

Unlike Galahad, who disappears into his vision, and unlike the bridge that plunges into Kafka's abyss, Marlow comes back to the living and presumably returns the reader, too, to his workaday world,

14. Joseph Conrad, "Heart of Darkness," *The Works* (London: J. M. Dent, 1946), p. 48.

his job aboard ship. In doing so, he makes a telling commentary on the dilemma of the antiromanticist who wishes to describe, in a literary form that depends upon sequential order and illuminated outcome, a realm of "logic" that is indescribable, timeless, eventless, and motiveless, like eternity. Having looked into the impenetrable and indescribable, Marlow should be reduced to silence about it. His strategy in lieu of silence is to tell the story in all its contradictions once as a lie to Kurtz's Intended and again to his fellow seamen as an exposure of the lie. Neither narration resolves the contradiction between the halo-exterior of his episode and the inner, eventless void. But from the outside, Conrad points up the dilemma by manipulating the circumstances of the telling and our witnessing, keeping us at one remove from the ever darkening ship that is the scene of the narration. As Marlow lets Kurtz's Intended believe in her Victorian-style romance, darkness creeps gradually over her in the drawing room; the last gleams of light shine in her eyes and on her forehead and are finally consumed. And darkness falls, too, over Marlow's second telling and seems to lead across the water to the nonverbal nothingness that ends the story. Yet despite the story's own plunge into silence eventually, Conrad continues to name shapes and describe actions; even "nothing" has a name, and we must continue to push ever forward in the stream of acts and words as if they had meaning. As the Intended walks blindly on in Kurtz's painting of her, "draped and blindfolded, carrying a lighted torch" (p. 79), so others who would walk toward some imagined destination must persist in holding up an instrument of predictive seeing.

In a later section on narrative stress systems we will examine at greater length two other texts, *Sir Gawain and the Green Knight* and *Paradise Lost*, to consider their competing schedules of discovery and rival narrative logics — neither of them as disjunctive as Kafka's and Conrad's. Since our purpose here is merely to test a few modal distinctions that structural matters enable us to make, I want now to turn to modes somewhat closer to the norms of realism and look there for other kinds of linear design. We also need to look further into the assumption that serial events in fiction are elements in cognitive and emotional series. Before considering specific cases, however, we need to add to the critical tools thus far brought to bear. Having distinguished between narrative plots and comparatively incoherent sequences in experience and concentrated on ways in which careers in plotted works follow their own directions, tempos, and durations while clashing with other careers at the hinges or turns of the plot, I have purposely not raised many of the complicating questions that the work's reception by an audience involves. For instance, if fictions are indeed distinguished by consequential logic or clashing logics — which remain sequential despite all the reversals and blows they may contain — how do they keep before the reader the always fading significance of former episodes and the never clear or manifest things yet to come? How does the not-present influence the tangible texture and immediacy of the sentences we are reading, especially if they belong to different orders, like Arthurian and Christian fellowships? How is the just-past of a symbolic order related to the visitable past of experience?

If fiction could be as spatial or "architectural" as some critics maintain, we would not be pressed to ask such questions, but the fact seems to be that however single and spatial an author's original grasp of his subject, the effect of fiction lies too much in the many articulations of phrase, spoken word, gesture, and act — too much in the multitudinousness of finely textured expression brought recurrently to bear upon a web of connections — to pretend that one is ever satisfied with anything so skeletonal as a geometric, pictorial, or architectural concept of design. Hence in terms of technique we are led to ask what in fact a fiction writer does to delineate plots in lieu of the painter's simultaneous stationing of pictorial elements, or the expository writer's express transitions, repetitions, and abstract summaries. What *especially* does he do in long works like the novel or works of such discordant and unparallel planes as Malory's tales?

Some of the tools we require to approach these questions are suggested in our earlier sense of the differences between fiction's replays of a real or pretended just-past and the biographer's or true chronicler's replays. "Significance" in artful narrative is obviously augmented by formal periodicity and redundancy more often and more tangibly than it normally is in expository discourse or true narration. It emphasizes repeated symbolic patterns, formal returns to beginnings, and echoes of various sorts. Another way of saying basically the same thing is that the difference between fiction's use of these and their presence in factual writing amounts to an emphasis on form rather than information. I use these terms in part as gestalt psychology and information theory have, assuming that *form* means primarily repeatable elements of perception and experience, *information* whatever is original and as yet unrepeated. (Independently of these sources, Kenneth Burke suggested some time before information theory developed that the high coherence we expect of invented lies and cognitive systems depends upon the predominance of form over information.) Abraham Moles remarks, for instance, that a human receptor can absorb only a limited amount of information into habitual, formal constructions without finding the message garbled: "Forms are abstractions, elementary stages of intelligibility." They are structures equivalent to mental forms: "The more structured a message is, the more intelligible it is, the more redundant it is, and the less originality it has."[15] In a sense, daily experience, even when it seems monotonously routine, is without a truly intelligible form because the total context surrounding our habits and routines changes moment by moment, and nothing can be fully accounted for when recurrence is swallowed by ever new turns of coincidence, combinations of sensory experience, and a quantity of unintelligible "information." In any case, only on the basis of repeatability can we wager about the future and retrieve the past, thus making continuums of experience or careers: total originality would be total formlessness.

In any symbol system as opposed to raw experience, the use of familiar words, recognizable grammars, and recurrent forms of image, thought, and expression creates an enclosed system of values on the basis of which the past is reconstituted and the future predicated. The high coherence of fictions is due in part to their exploitation of this inherent formality of symbols and governed repetition of signs and symbols within the work and its plot systems. Even so, however, several structural questions are raised by the distinction between information and form. If prediction and retrieval are significantly different in literature from what they are in daily prospect and retrospect, in what way can fictions be considered

15. Abraham Moles, *Information Theory and Esthetic Perception*, trans. Joel E. Cohen (Urbana: University of Illinois Press, 1966), pp. 74–75. Cf. G. Spencer Brown, "Chance and Control: Some Implications of Randomization," in *Information Theory: Papers Read at a Symposium*, ed. Colin Cherry (London: Butterworths Scientific Publications, 1956), pp. 8–17, and D. M. MacKay, "The Place of 'Meaning' in the Theory of Information," pp. 215–25 in the same collection; Leonard B. Meyer, *Music, the Arts and Ideas: Patterns and Predictions in Twentieth-Century Culture* (Chicago: University of Chicago Press, 1967).

temporally mimetic? How does that meeting ground of the actual and the invented — the reader's mind — predict the form of a work either from the information offered at a certain point by the work or from what the mind brings to the text? What aspects of tone, style, character, theme, and point of view reinforce "significant" or reduplicated form, and how do they do so differently in realism, say, than in forms of romance, allegory, or myth? With more specific reference to particular critics and narrative works, what does "probability" mean to a realist like Defoe that it might not have meant to Aristotle in the *Poetics* — looking primarily as he did at examples from classical tragedy? Is the form of Milton's assumed real universe equatable in any way to the narrative form of the work with respect to its surprises, predictions, and recollections? How does the separation of plots on distinct planes (as in Malory) affect the processes of reduplication and readers' predictions?

As several of these questions suggest, not all aspects of the problem of literary modes can be approached purely in terms of the work itself; they have to do also with the reader's previous experience and his capacity to follow the text. The reader's *reconstructed* form and the *inherent* form of the work (ideally or hypothetically posited) obviously overlap and depend upon each other; we constantly make assumptions about one when talking of the other. But unfortunately, unlike listening to music, reading a book does not carry with it even minimal controls of the kind necessary to experiment with and discover principles of psychological form. This is especially true with respect to duration and timing, which have so much influence on the cognitive series of a fiction's transformed world. Readers can vary the act of "reception" almost at will, for instance. Besides coming to the work with different backgrounds in reading and experience, readers may unpredictably look ahead to the ending, skip passages entirely, skim some quickly while dwelling fondly on others, repeat passages at will, and in general commit any venial sin permitted by the privacy of reading. Even with the purest of intentions all readers of longer works break the reading for varying lengths of time and at different places while they pursue other activities — forgetting in the interim some of the threads the author in his naive expectation of a close reading entrusted to them, and altering thereby the tempo of the work, its elements of repeatability, and its dramatic or psychological form. In a normal reading, a book does not control the quality of a reader's attention, the frame of mind he brings to it on a given day, or his capacity to interpret clues and make predictions. Combined with these variables, the inherent ambiguities of language (as opposed to the relative certainty of other kinds of signals such as sequences of tones in a melody) make it unlikely that any two readers will receive the same work of art from the text, even if one reads it out loud to the other. We have only to administer a few quizzes on novels — or delve into criticism on any work — to realize how prevalent and serious differing responses can be. Wherever a work of art "really" exists, it is clearly not in the common agreement of its readers.

In self-preservation, criticism quickly turns from that line of inquiry and trusts that the general principles of periodicity, redundancy, foreseeability, and significant form in general remain firm in crucial respects and can be based on plot systems. Luckily, they depend not merely upon the reader's errant progress but also upon the hero's acknowledged and explicit memory and predictive capacities, upon his own idea of plotted continuity. They are subject to authorial anchors and appeals to evidence. Nearly all aspects of linear structure reverberate in the echo chamber of the reader's mind; but even though they may reverberate differently in individual cases, the structural principles by which they work are not automatically rendered invalid. Hence for some purposes we may safely beg many of the questions I just raised. Every practical critic must assume something like an ideal or normal reading of the text, governed by the script and not subject to nodding attention, overly personal responses, greater than normal obtuseness to repetition or to plots, motives, and characters. He must assume an acceptable degree of correspondence between the form of the work, in print or narration, and the form of the work in the psychology of perception, where all retrieval, sensation, and prediction ultimately have their impact.

To return to realistic fiction thus forewarned: it is evident at the outset in our reading of it that hidden strands are less mysterious and the discrepancies among temporal careers less pronounced than they are in romance and myth. The reader obviously pursues in realism chains of relatively self-explanatory clues. The progression of the work is a disclosure of information of a comparatively uniform kind, tangible in quality, and substantial in quantity. The difficulty is paradoxically that, self-evident as all the facts of Moll Flanders's life may be, fact and information are not in themselves highly significant or conducive to a coherent psychological sequence. As the novels of Doris Lessing indicate, the ponderous weight of too much detail bogs down the progress of dramatic interest and curiosity. Our vicarious participation in a realistic novel is often a considerable distance from the intensity of our participation in dramatic ritual. The obviousness of facts and the absence of mystery is a barrier to our identification with the hero's internal world because he scarcely has any; or if he does, his psychic life is not heightened by the excitement of intuitive leaps and the *need* to know. Even when realism makes use of parallel plots, what remains hidden to the hero at a given juncture is of a level and quality that manifest elements have already put before him.

For a number of reasons *Robinson Crusoe* suggests itself as an appropriate example to set beside the disjunctive plots of romance and confirm our sense of the kind of plotted continuity realism has. Defoe's method is typical of realism in assigning a certain importance to goods and property as the objective measurement of the hero's progress, but his concept of fictional boundaries and intrusions from beyond also reflects such preceding works as *Pilgrim's Progress* and *Paradise Lost.*

The problem of form in realism as *Robinson Crusoe* illustrates it is related to the burying of clues, not in mysteries and hidden powers from another time schedule or in some alien logic, but in much that seems inconsequential, dull, repetitious, and ramshackle — or scarcely enlivened by an animate plot at all. If fiction is distinguished by the preeminence of intelligibility and form over unique information, a high-information mode as journalistic as Defoe's provides an interesting challenge. Apparently sensing the pressure of this formlessness, Defoe has Crusoe offer frequent foreshadowings of what is to come and recapitulations of what has happened. These elements of form are roughly equivalent to the habits that the tending of property engenders in the hero and in the bourgeois sensibility of Defoe's audience. (Few modern realists would tip their hands so obviously, but even in doing so Defoe prepares his readers and future novelists for subtler methods.) Crusoe's father, for instance, predicts that if Crusoe leaves home he will be miserable and have no one to relieve him in time of distress, and Crusoe has frequent occasion to look back upon that "prophetic discourse." His father lectures him also on the principles of household management, the middle estate beneath the temptations of the wealthy and above the vicissitudes of the poor, the sure retribution that providence exacts for willful and needless risks, and the desirable long-term prospect of gradual, safe increase, all of them recurrent topics in the novel. Since "peace and plenty" are the handmaids of that middle fortune — especially when reinforced by "temperance, moderation, quietness, health, society" — we can expect these to be form-giving goals for Crusoe under the duress of adventure, which is definable mostly by their lack. They enable men to go "silently and smoothly through the world, and comfortably out of it,"[16] thus providing a value system for both an ideal narrative progress and an ideal ending.

The pattern of broken security and lost contentment is reiterated whenever Crusoe is about to do something foolish, and it is repeated again after he has finished doing it. Thus it forms the intelligible framework within which the unaccustomed and the contingent happen and are interpreted:

> I could not be content now but I must go and leave the happy view I had of being a rich and thriving man in my new plantation only to pursue a rash and immoderate desire of rising faster than the nature of the thing admitted; and thus I cast myself down again into the deepest gulf of human misery that ever man fell into, or perhaps would be consistent with life and a state of health in the world. [P. 42]

It is predictable from statements of this kind not only that Crusoe will be cast away but that a just punishment will be the gearing of his tempo of advancement toward prosperity to what "the thing admits," to the tempo of circumstances. Defoe's realism requires here and elsewhere that the protagonist continuously adjust his career to the intrusion of material accident, which imposes long delays indeed on the hero. "Circumstance" is the most obvious complicating factor in a Defoe plot — the not-so-hidden cause of swerves in a hero's course. It differs from sentient intrusion by its inherent inexplicability and factualness.

But if fiction is in fact committed to a high degree of coherence, the novelist cannot admit mere contingency into its course, and Defoe exercises a considerable narrative skill at times in assimilating real-seeming circumstances into a meaningful career. He has Crusoe ponder the kinds of questions that will interpret environment and adventurous fact as the elements of a proper story. Crusoe never

16. Daniel Defoe, *Robinson Crusoe* (New York: Random House, 1948), p. 5.

resembles Bunyan's Christian more than in his broadest meditations
on direction and purpose, as his startling encounters with danger
suggest them:

> What is this earth and sea, of which I have seen so much? Whence is
> it produced? And what am I and all the other creatures, wild and tame,
> human and brutal, whence are we?
>
> Sure we are all made by some secret Power who formed the earth
> and sea, the air and sky; and who is that?
>
> Then it followed most naturally, It is God that has made it all. Well,
> but then, it came on strangely, if God has made all these things, He
> guides and governs them all and all things that concern them; for the
> Power that could make all things must certainly have power to guide
> and direct them.
>
> If so, nothing can happen in the great circuit of His works either
> without His knowledge or appointment.
>
> And if nothing happens without His knowledge, He knows that I am
> here and am in this dreadful condition, and if nothing happens with-
> out His appointment, He has appointed all this to befall me. [P. 102]

Following this chain of reasoning, which embraces everything from
Genesis to Crusoe's present condition and connects his story to an
acceptable frame of reference, Crusoe discovers that all careers have
an appointed pattern no matter how chancy they seem. Whatever "befalls" is never really accidental. His main effort is to construct out of
a wilderness of apparent contingencies a chronology in which events
are the sequent measure of providence. He seeks to impose on the
daily doings of his own industry a regime not so rigorous as the re-
gimes of a monastery nor so ceremonial as rituals of penitent devotion but nonetheless carefully measured out in both business and
pleasure. As Lewis Mumford observes in *Technics and Civilization*
with respect to the new "masters of regimentation" that arose in the
seventeenth century, Robinson Crusoe is the ideal man of a new order that replaces image-making with invention, and contemplation
with experiment. True to his kind, he schedules every activity
rigorously; "Timed payments: timed contracts: timed work: timed
meals: from this period on nothing was quite free from the stamp of
the calendar or clock."[17]

We must qualify a previous comment about the lack of startling
intrusions from other planes in realism sufficiently to allow for linger-

17. Lewis Mumford, *Technics and Civilization* (New York: Harcourt, Brace, 1934), p.
42.

ing elements of devotion and these recurrent providential signs that Crusoe discovers. But the curious thing about Crusoe's meditating on these signs is that the wonderful is so often domesticated and scheduled and thereby made to accord with Defoe's basically nonfabulistic, nonmythic, unromantic method of detailed observation. Storms and shipwrecks aside, Crusoe's romantic influences are reduced largely to the activities of daily georgic labors, to the work of the seasons and the filling of the granary. Traumas of the kind that afflict Job and Abraham are but passing crises to him, not the abiding demands of a Lord who calls for permanent reversals of intention in view of a far-off eschatology. Crusoe's injunctions and mandates never come to him directly. He is left to his own speculation as to what his circumstances seem to argue about his duties, or he is left to the chance guidance that he finds in scripture when he alights upon a given passage.

Even if providence is in some mysterious way responsible for what befalls him, then, we have no way to predict what will come of its intrusions in a world of opportunities, surprises, and monotonous labor except to note that since it is a providence strongly influenced by double-entry bookkeeping, debits and credits will sooner or later balance: Crusoe will probably get what he deserves in this loosely rationalistic universe. And whatever he believes about the course that divinity rough-hews for him, it is finally his own bourgeois logic that prevails moment by moment.

Crusoe's successful reduction of the providential framework to habit and productive labor indicates that some principle of form other than a single unifying power must be summoned to bring his numerous adventures into significant form. Crusoe's continuity as a character will be threatened if he cannot establish his own thread of consistency, and this he does less with a rigorous religious consciousness or concept of the self as a moral being in the bosom of Abraham than with an application of pragmatic technology to whatever circumstances set before him. We would not be far off to say that it is chiefly habit as instituted by technology that constitutes form for him — as wit and cunning are form to the picaro in the midst of his adventurous wanderings. What he habitually seeks to impose upon random encounters and strange situations is the shape of what he long ago came to value in the process of middle-class acculteration: he seeks a regular periodicity of production and demand. He is a prudent foreseer, a maker and consumer, not a prophet; his plans extend mostly to the next crop and to the extension of his holdings through five-year plans. His rescue from slavery in Africa comes through the lucky stashing away of provisions in a small boat and the fortunate circumstances of his theft of it. All his contacts with wild beasts and natives down the African coast are explained by the need for food and water, and his rescue from the African waters is explained by the trade routes of European commerce. The present is always an investment, at a certain rate of interest. The periodicity of nature, cycles of hunger and satisfaction, the biological course of the organism, the increase of flocks, and the expenditure of stores govern his choices and provide perspectives on his circumstances.

Foreshadowing and prediction on the basis of habit and consistent characterization are nothing new to the novel or to Defoe. All narratives lead both the reader and the hero to expect certain things from the recognizable and accustomed habits of characters, since it is chiefly through consistent characterization that any periodicity of actions imposes its patterns on new experience. On a broader scale, societies and orders of various kinds apply their abiding constitutions to the details of renewed action, as the orders of chivalry and the grail in Malory apply habitual continuums to "systematize" a great number of adventures. In effect, then, any narrative pattern salvages potentially random, errant, and unique moments of unredeemed characters by incorporating them into a repeatable logic, a disciplining stamp of form that regiments their wildness — with more success in character types of romance than in the inventive grotesques and rogues of the fabliau or picaresque.

But periodicity and predictability in Defoe, as in documentary realism generally, are nonetheless of a distinct kind in their emphasis upon the economic animal and his producing and consuming habits. Crusoe's strongly pragmatic bent masters a variety of wildly improbable adventures, as wild leopards, slave traders, hungry wolves, storms, shipwrecks, and sudden sickness are overcome by discovered uses for them or techniques of handling them. For all of these things — indeed for everything — Crusoe has a pedestrian answer. Like money itself he is a great transformer and equalizer; grapes, barley, and servants circulate through his mechanism and come out stamped with a definite value. When the same "secret overruling decree that hurries us on to be the instruments of our own destruction" relents in timely deliverances, its relenting gives opportunity, after a brief thanksgiving, for the work of the shovel and the handmade pestle. Paradise is restored after the fall from his father's household not by a mechanism of repentance and spiritual journeying but by the crafts of husbandry.

The style of Crusoe's realism is of a piece with its plot. As each new day, whatever it may bring, is inventoried by a notch on Crusoe's calendar pole, so adventures are stored away in Crusoe's ready-made narrative containers. As simulated journalistic recollection, his story quite properly has an additive method: it combines the moving perspective of the day-to-day diary with the recapitulative perspective of the autobiography. As nature and random history march before him, Crusoe discards the waste and saves the seed. From the distant point of his final assembling of the story, everything makes a particular sense: time in all its dreadful delays and trials of patience has been as assembly line for both a finished household and moral observations.

Since so many episodes follow the same additive method, we can choose one to represent them and assume that it probably represents as well the typical adjustment of realism between information and form. The critical meeting between Crusoe and Friday, to take a prominent incident, contains many of the elements of periodicity and redundancy that a normal reader notices in the novel and indicates clearly Crusoe's special control over the island. Crusoe's careful system is given a stiff test, however, by the startling appearance of the cannibals and by the difficulties of his rescue of the man he will name, significantly, for a regular work day:

> I observed that the two who swam were yet more than twice as long swimming over the creek as the fellow was that fled from them. It came now very warmly upon my thoughts, and indeed irresistibly, that now was my time to get me a servant, and perhaps a companion, or assistant; and that I was called plainly by Providence to save this poor creature's life; I immediately run down the ladders with all possible expedition, fetched my two guns, for they were both but at the foot of the ladders, as I observed above; and getting up again, with the same haste, to the top of the hill, I crossed toward the sea; and having a very short cut, and all down hill, clapped myself in the way between the pursuers and the pursued; hallooing aloud to him that fled, who, looking back, was at first perhaps as much frighted at me as at them; but I beckoned with my hand to him to come back; and in the meantime, I slowly ad-

vanced towards the two that followed; then rushing at once upon the foremost, I knocked him down with the stock of my piece; I was loath to fire because I would not have the rest hear; though at that distance, it would not have been easily heard, and being out of sight of the smoke too, they would not have easily known what to make of it. Having knocked this fellow down, the other who pursued with him stopped, as if he had been frighted; and I advanced apace toward him; but as I came nearer, I perceived presently he had a bow and arrow and was fitting it to shoot at me; so I was then necessitated to shoot at him first, which I did, and killed him at the first shoot; the poor savage who fled, but had stopped, though he saw both his enemies fallen and killed, as he thought, yet was so frighted with the fire and noise of my piece, that he stood stock still and neither came forward or went backward, though he seemed rather inclined to fly still than to come on; I hallooed again to him, and made signs to come forward, which he easily understood and came a little way, then stopped again and then a little further and stopped again, and I could then perceive that he stood trembling, as if he had been taken prisoner, and had just been to be killed, as his two enemies were; I beckoned him again to come to me and gave him all the signs of encouragement that I could think of, and he came nearer and nearer, kneeling down every ten or twelve steps in token of acknowledgment for my saving his life. I smiled at him and looked pleasantly and beckoned to him to come still nearer; at length he came close to me, and then he kneeled down again, kissed the ground, and laid his head upon the ground, and, taking me by the foot, set my foot upon his head; this, it seems, was in token of swearing to be my slave forever. [P. 224–25]

The moments at which a foreign intrusion enters a protagonist's life are always interesting as tests of habit, in the same way that a herald from another world in romance establishes by contrast the boundaries of the hero's own world. The footprint of the cannibals in the sand has previously had a pronounced impact on Crusoe's twenty-some years of accumulated progress and forced him to rethink his relationship with the island. Before the arrival of Friday, however, he has had time to adjust to that intrusion and assimilate the idea of cannibals. He is now called upon to react more suddenly, as once again his world of habit is threatened. The exactness of his apparently rambling prose and the pauses the narration makes to stress distances and relative positions are part of his accustomed logistics, measurements, and procedures. The deliverance of Friday depends upon that mechanism, just as the journals depend upon the functional interpretation of all random circumstances. Converting Friday from a potential cannibal's meal to a household servant is the equivalent, to Crusoe, of imposing value and logic on a potentially absurd world.

The rescue begins with a relatively neutral observation of facts and finds a direction-giving motive in the short catalogue of Friday's possible uses. Beginning with "I immediately run down," Defoe inserts a parenthetical flashback to explain Crusoe's readiness to act and then a subordinate clause "getting ...." Only after another subordinate clause do we arrive at the decisive "clapped," the artful fulcrum of the action, following which the sentence continues loosely in a trailing series of clauses that suggest nature's own stringiness and circumstantiality. What Crusoe does with Friday is basically no different from what he does with most properties that come within his range. As in all aspects of his calendar — his agricultural works and days, the schedule of each day's affairs, the overall growth of his economy, and the minute mechanisms of his labor — his timing is exact. Even preparedness, expedition, common sense, and courage are "technological" virtues for Crusoe in the sense that they mediate between raw material and the final product he makes of it — between the randomness of nature and history and the system he builds from them. The motive and the means for interposing come warmly — indeed irresistibly — over him as he realizes that now is the time, in the schedule of things, for Friday to appear. He has dreamed of such a moment for some time, when a refugee from the cannibals would rush toward his musket-protected enclosure and appeal for help, and together they would fight off their enemies. Now dream emerges as reality; romance descends to documentary fact.

If out of shipwrecks Crusoe creates raftloads of equipment and supplies, out of the excitement of the cannibal chase he creates the ceremonies of master and servant, the immediate end toward which the episode moves. The manner of their greeting indicates an adjustment on both parts to the colonial roles Crusoe has foreseen: Friday kneels frequently, Crusoe smiles a lot to generate trust, and the greeting is concluded by the placing of the foot on the head. This act seals their social contract and gives a formal end to the sequence as well as a direction to their future. It makes a stylistic crescendo of a mild sort suitable to realism, as it stamps chance with a meaningful domestic form, which in turn mirrors a larger social form in the manners of empire.

Whatever lies in the back of Crusoe's mind normally finds an occasion for expressive action in this way; very little of his character is left over as a complexity unmanifest in action. The implications of this accord between inner motive and opportunity is that providence, prefiguring dream, and Crusoe's psychological consistency are indistinguishable finally from each other and from the novelist's arrangement of his materials in a pragmatic, serial system. What Crusoe imagines comes true; what parades before him fits into the domestic, economic system he has inherently in him. No realms of mythic consciousness fail to take shape and proportion in believable detail. Character, scene, motive, and act join in a single logic. Thus as Friday bows, one more wild, free-floating product and one more dream are seized in flight and affixed in their opportunistic place together — affixed "forever" in a muted epiphany that confirms a kind of typology of servant and master, apostle and savior. The climax of the passage is appropriately rendered in almost metrical regularity and repetitive syntactical units, which are to Defoe's prose what Crusoe's bins are to the contents he stores in them:

> I smiled at him and looked pleasantly and beckoned to him to come still nearer; at length he came close to me, and then he kneeled down again, kissed the ground, and laid his head upon the ground, and, taking me by the foot, set my foot upon his head; this, it seems, was in token of swearing to be my slave forever.

Defoe uses a suggestion of King James English to celebrate the moment and set it apart in a modulated biblical rhythm, and Crusoe subsequently becomes to Friday a surrogate providence worthy of that biblical style. Friday joins Crusoe's days of labor and his Sabbath under the auspices of a skilled "technician of the sacred" (to borrow a phrase from a recent anthology of myths).

Ceremonial and finished as the passage is, it does not pause long; Crusoe picks up and goes on his plodding way. But it is evident that in making Crusoe's adventures fall into shape even to this degree, Defoe must keep in check other kinds of recalcitrant factualness that might conceivably overturn Crusoe's careful order. If Sterne were handling similar materials, for instance, he would obviously see the ratio of circumstance to form quite differently. The rescue of Friday would not conclude in a definition of identities or reach such a plateau of ceremony and form. The narration would in all probability never get that far because between the initial sighting of Friday and the gesture of his eternal gratitude, Tristram-Crusoe would offer a number of digressions, chance associations, and unplottable complexities designed to knot the reader's movement beyond unraveling. Mention of the two guns would bring not a recollection that they have been cited before and stationed where they are but a long history of family weapons. We would probably not escape, in passing, an essay on cannibals by the narrator's eccentric uncle written in imitation of Montaigne and summarized for the reader in a footnote. Additive and loose as his method appears, Defoe does not encourage a questioning of narrative coherence in this way; in even the most repetitious of passages he suggests nothing of Sterne's parody of narrative form. Nor does he confuse circumstantial realism with journalistic coverage or the shapelessness of naturalism. Any comprehensive index of his devices of periodicity, repetition, and symbolic pattern would reveal the firmness with which he has imposed systematic meaning on a variety of materials.

The frequent task of realism outside of Defoe, in the youth of the novel, was to seek its form in the ceremonies, contracts, and customs of middle-class manners. The "end of the story" presumed that a settling of social imbalances and a discovery of cures for what threatens the family establishment was termination enough. The network of the fiction was the believable network of the economy, the family, and the psychology of relatively normal human discourse, all of which follow schedules of growth, courtship, and transfers of power from one generation to another. Among these schedules, circumstances weigh more heavily than facts and opinions in other modes. And in later forms as well, the novel sought its logic in the impression of circumstance on social types. If the hero was to have recognitions and epiphanies, these must be grounded in a multitude of details that register on him realistically.

Unlike the old romances and epics, which build upon the descriptive topoi, types, and archetypes of tradition, each novel develops its own characteristic sense of place, social interaction, and interior consciousness.[18] The palpable Dublin of Joyce's Bloom bears upon his movement as more than a peripheral contingency: it is a defining set of forces that dictates the quality and direction of his call. The surroundings of Nicholas Nickleby and his fellow victims of nineteenth-century industry speak all too eloquently of what can and cannot be done and what there is to know. The surface of reality pre-

18. See Albert Cook, *The Meaning of Fiction* (Detroit: Wayne State University Press, 1960), "The Spacializing Sensibility," pp. 113–33.

sents to the immediate eye a discouraging finality of ends and means. The surface portends nothing beyond the cycles of birth, growth, decay, and social relationships:

> "There," said the schoolmaster as they stepped in together; "this is our shop, Nickleby!"
>
> It was such a crowded scene, and there were so many objects to attract attention, that, at first, Nicholas stared about him, really without seeing anything at all. By degrees, however, the place resolved itself into a bare and dirty room, with a couple of windows, whereof a tenth part might be of glass, the remainder being stopped up with old copybooks and paper. There were a couple of long old rickety desks, cut and notched, and inked, and damaged, in every possible way; two or three forms; a detached desk for Squeers; and another for his assistant. The ceiling was supported, like that of a barn, by cross beams and rafters; and the walls were so stained and discoloured that it was impossible to tell whether they had ever been touched with paint or whitewash.
>
> But the pupils — the young noblemen! How the last faint traces of hope, the remotest glimmering of any good to be derived from his efforts in this den, faded from the mind of Nicholas as he looked in dismay around! Pale and haggard faces, lank and bony figures, children with the countenances of old men, deformities with irons upon their limbs, boys of stunted growth, and others whose long meagre legs would hardly bear their stooping bodies, all crowded on the view together; there were the bleared eye, the hare-lip, the crooked foot, and every ugliness or distortion that told of unnatural aversion conceived by parents for their offspring, or of young lives which, from the earliest dawn of infancy, had been one horrible endurance of cruelty and neglect.[19]

There are no ends evolving from other time cycles to impinge upon the daily and weekly cycles of Squeer's young suffering scholars, no destinies of a yet unimagined grandeur to stretch their imaginations and complicate the reader's view of them — though of course Nicholas himself has a number of surprises in store for him. Everything tells its own immediate story; the only delay in understanding is caused by the sheer multiplicity of objects that assault the senses.

As a chain of symbolic clues of a certain kind, then, documentary realism is almost of a single plane. Like Crusoe's mastery of technology, it imposes a mechanism of factual succession upon per-

19. Charles Dickens, *Nicholas Nickleby* (Oxford University Press, 1950), pp. 87–88.

ception, as the reader keeps abreast of what he has to know by seeing what he has to see, by letting his vision clear and looking carefully about.

This is a reasonably obvious generic distinction, and it would have to be pursued much further if we were to aim for a firm sense of all the relationships between narrative modes and linear design. My immediate purpose, however, is to suggest only in a minimal way the place of certain principles of sequent structure in whatever concepts of typical form one investigates and to suggest some of the implications of the reader's process of discovery in a structural theory of narrative kinds. We will take further notice of genre on other occasions. I want next to consider the problem of modes in the more strictly technical matters of presentation — on the assumption that, at least from the perspective of the signal-gathering reader, the surface of a book and its means of representation figure prominently in the posture of the work toward us. What effect, for instance, do segmentation and highly manipulated artifices have upon the emergence into cognizance of concealed narrative patterns? What differences in the psychology of form do cinematic, lyric, and dramatic representation impose?

Such questions are again sufficiently large to discourage treatment in all their potential scope, especially when we assume that modes of presentation include such things as discursive, first- and third-person narration, stream of consciousness, descriptive and pictorial sequences, and the like: each of these has its own impact on the kind of information and aesthetic form a given work creates for us. Consequently, we will concentrate on a limited sample. I select first one of the oddest kinds of presentation, epistolary fiction, because its peculiarity highlights the structural impact of the fictive device. We will then look into the mixing of presentational methods before reopening the general problem of fiction's conducted courses through cognitive, dramatic series.

With respect to the subject of the next chapter, the epistolary novel, we should observe that where the novel of manners often emphasizes the management of small appointments in a schedule of dinners, balls, walks in the garden, love letters, seductions, and achievements of social position generally, such appointments may be scheduled rigorously by a series of letters. The revelations that events make are pointed up intermittently by their timely transcription into messages. Considered as devices for forwarding knowledge or intelligence in a fictive system, then, letters are an effective way to exchange information and convert it into intelligible, social form. They are also, as Richardson uses them, part of the contractual nature of middle-class ceremony: they place before courting parties those individual opinions and matters of fact that must be contained in an evolving social contract. Thus the instrument of timely intelligence is also an instrument of social action, or *trans*action, a method of discourse that welds plots and consciousness in a set of enveloped and enclosed statements.

As in any form of narration, characters in a letter novel work against resistance and intrusions from other continuities, intrusions that upset their chosen courses. The unfolding of a given action takes place in the context of *competing* schedules. In *Les Liaisons dangereuses*, for instance, our central example, Valmont tries to seduce Tourvel before her husband returns, thus placing the conflict between the libertine and the marriage contract under the pressure of time. Cecile's love for Chevalier Danceny must mature before her appointed marriage with Gercourt. Merteuil, whose instruction is designed to speed Cecile's progress, is the novel's foremost expert in the rates of love and manipulation of cross-purposes, and she knows each stage of love's growth and its decay. The structural skeleton of the work is thus keyed to distinct linear actions proceeding at their different rates and colliding with each delivery of the mails. The rates of progress are programs in education and expanding consciousness. "Ah, let her surrender, but let her fight!" Valmont says of Mme de Tourvel, "Let her be too weak to prevail, but strong enough to resist; let her savour the knowledge of her weakness at her leisure, but let her be unwilling to admit defeat."[20] And so the outline of a particular plot is laid out — with its paced forward impulse and strong resistance, its benefits in the savoring of knowledge won therefrom. Our own expectations of form are firmly directed by the "lettering" of these spirited dances of forward and resisting force. The schemes of seduction and the structure of society unfold together in the mannered meetings of morning, noon, and evening, the places of in-

20. Choderlos de Laclos, *Les Liaisons dangereuses*, trans. P. W. K. Stone (Baltimore: Penguin Books, 1961), p. 63. All quotations are from this edition.

trigue, and in the byways of display presented in so calculated a fashion in letters. As part of the documentation and communications system of society and as parts of a story, letters have the responsibility of verifying facts through eyewitnesses and documenting the progress of a federation of characters who know each other through their epistolary styles as well as through more normal ways.

In all of these elements of plot, the letter has its apt uses, and our aim is to discover what effect the device has on serial logic, as the letter sets up expectations and appointments, defines their terms, declares passion, manifests styles and values (often with masked carefulness), and allows confidants to declare their inmost schemes. The influence of the letter on interlocked time schedules, narrative foreshortening, abstract or discursive summaries, point of view, predictions, retrievals of the past, and other elements of narrative form can clearly be extensive.

CHAPTER FOUR

Fictional Documents and Letter Liaisons

I

Among kinds of narrative testimony (pretended third-person, first-person confession, journals, and the like), epistolary narration normally offers the greatest variety of unmediated viewpoints in greatest collision. It is especially useful as a method of setting forth interior feelings as they emerge into action and rhetorical postures. Most of the conventional practices of letter writing were well established, of course, long before novelists thought of adopting them, and many of them have since become neglected. Some idea of the range of those rhetorical techniques and their usefulness in presenting the views of different parties can be gained from manuals on letter writing such as Angel Day's *The English Secretary; or, Methods of Writing Epistles* (1586), which presents to the would-be epistolary stylist examples of descriptory, laudatory, vituperatory, deliverative, reconciliatory, hortatory, dehortatory, suasory, desuasory, conciliatory, petitory, commendatory, consolatory, admonitory, amatory, judicial, accusatory, purgatory, expostulatory, and deprecatory. In keeping with his emphasis on these varieties of rhetoric, Day's manual offers advice on judging one's audience, especially the reputations and stations of each party to an exchange; the decorum of one's delivery; the necessary tactfulness of one's disposition; humor; and even the mechanics of presentation — salutation, superscription, farewells, and the like.[1] Employed as a presentational device in a formally structured fiction, the letter obliges the novelist not to for-

---

1. Angel Day, *The English Secretary; or, Methods of Writing Epistles*, ed. Robert O. Evans (Gainesville, Fla.: Scholars' Facsimiles and Reprints, 1967). See Godfrey Frank Singer, *The Epistolary Novel* (New York: Russell and Russell, 1953; first published 1933), p. 22.

138

get tactical strategies and the social stations they presuppose. Beyond those implications for the meeting of classes and negotiating parties, as a signed, sealed, and delivered document of a certain art and formality addressed by one specific party to another, the letter has an impact also on the assembling of cohesive plots and cognitive sequences. It influences the forming of inner societies through a highly selective intelligence, based on privately exchanged information.

Actually, the establishing of chosen societies, too, is a traditional function of letters, not as the manual writer conceives of them, perhaps, but as the messages of certain kinds of literary modes. The verse epistle, the sacred epistle, and even the love letter often do much more than convey messages with a rhetorical flair from one individual to another. The sacred epistle is an interesting and revealing if somewhat special example because of its inherent cultic functions. It is by letter that Paul seeks to spread and perpetuate a church, forecasting his coming to outlying groups, consolidating his teachings, laying down policies, explaining moral judgments and dogma, and exploiting the formality of the letter to institutionalize, encipher, and, in a sense, "incarnate" the early church. Through the epistle, he is able to seal a cultic contract across great distances and spans of time. The language of his letters is laced with vouchers for the validity of the gospel message thus "lettered": he aims to enrich the utterance of his audience, to offer testimony to them and confirm their knowledge; only when these things have been accomplished will they form a genuine brotherhood. The spirit of the group is thus trusted to the epistle as its visible body. At times Paul writes almost as though the words attested to by his personal signature carry a magical value in conveying the "ghost" across a gulf to those gifted to decode his words:

> Do we begin again to commend ourselves? or need we, as some others, epistles of commendation to you, or letters of commendation from you?
> Ye are our epistle written in our hearts, known and read of all men:
> Forasmuch as ye are manifestly declared to be the epistle of Christ ministered by us, written not with ink, but with the Spirit of the living God; not in tables of stone, but in fleshly tables of the heart. [2 Cor. 3:1–3]

We have only to remember the astonishment of unlettered societies over the power of written messages to realize the marvel of en-

veloping thought and feeling, delivering them miles hence, and having the packaged ciphers register almost as a personal presence
among the chosen recipients.

The difference between the sacred epistle and the normal messages
of a secular literature is perhaps not as great as it first appears in this
respect. Cults of love, business, and social class make a similar use of
attested vows, iron out "doctrinal" differences, and cement an inner
accord, which in a sense Day's rhetorical strategies seek to do in a
variety of sophisticated secular ways. Hence in even its most
pedestrian use the letter retains something of its enciphered magic.
Though its testimony is not scriptural, it is as necessary for social
foundations as Paul's epistles are to the Corinthians.

Certain nonepistolary messages perform similar functions in narratives that exploit the plot-turning introduction of timely discoveries.
Messages from the distance have the effect of inserting one sphere of
action into another, creating thereby a single complex "society" of
plots. From this standpoint, messages are obviously indispensable in
bringing into a cognitive series things that have happened off stage or
on the periphery of a manifest action. As part of a fiction's
concatenation of events, messages thus "spread the word" so that the
scattered segments of a potential community and the isolated interiors of characters are redeemed from their dispersal, incorporated
into a single design. For Paul that design embraces all human history
and requires the enciphering of a universal spirit, the detailing of a
cosmic story. For less ambitious message writers, "spirit" is translat-
able as a principle of accord among separated parties sufficient to
weld a society — to unite lovers or consummate business transactions.

Indeed if we may believe John Barth's anonymous inventor of
writing in the "Anonymiad," the first inspiration for fiction itself
came with the discovery of ink, goat parchment, seagull quills, and a
message delivery system — wine bottles stuffed with words and released to the sea from a private isle. In the creative process, the
"spirits" that Barth's narrator empties from the bottle circulate
through his brain, come out again in words, are rebottled, and are
sent forth to fire other imaginations. The message need not be true to
anything actual; it may be a set of illusions:

> For eight jugsworth of years . . . I gloried in my isolation and
> seeded the waters with its get, what I came to call *fiction*. That is, I

found that by pretending that things had happened which in fact had not, and that people existed who didn't, I could achieve a lovely truth which actuality obscures — especially when I learned to abandon myth and pattern my fabrications on actual people and events: Menelaus, Helen, the Trojan War. It was *as if* there were this minstrel and this milkmaid, et cetera; one could I believe draw a whole philosophy from that *as if*.[2]

For a solitary man in his apartness, only the technology of the letter seems capable of building a reality, albeit in fictions, and thus capable of releasing a "Deucalion-flood of literature." Barth's maker of artificial worlds thus practices in his letters to mankind all genres from pastoral to satire, realism to pure fantasy — all the "effusions of religious narrative, ribald tale-cycles, verse-dramas, comedies of manners, and what-all" (p. 187). Each of these is carefully crused and sent forth to unite one mind with others. Even the audience of his jugged missives can be more imagined than real if necessary (as any diary to no one in particular illustrates); but the fictions harbored and bred in the dreams of the withdrawn and slightly inebriated inventor are projected as an action in an assumed social context. They engage a world on the writer's terms, reshaping his relationship to it in ways he could not manage while he remained in direct contact with, say, the court of Menelaus. *His* events, Barth's narrator realizes, unlike those strategically shaped by *them*, are precious and beautiful: "I could soothe me with the thought that somewhere outside myself my enciphered spirit drifted, realer than the gods, its significance as objective and undecoded as the stars." So much the better if beyond that newly embodied self committed to those bobbing bottles other correspondents and "isled souls" lie strewn about the world "and the sea a-clink with [their] literature!" (p. 189).

Whether or not Barth's scribbler actually succeeds in letting be known in one quarter what he has wrought in another (as Crusoe does in his journals from an island of much solider realities), the odd private-public impulse of his missives lies close to the heart of his fictive impulse. Pen, paper, and a moment alone generate all the imaginative masks and proliferated characters and actions the imagination craves. These are ever the basic conditions of the letter writer in epistolary fiction, the length and complication of whose messages are dictated not so much by the inherent materials a world

2. Barth, "Anonymiad," from *Lost in the Funhouse*, p. 186.

presents as by the size of his parchment and the length of time he has to write.

Even when the formal message is a relatively subordinate part of a narrative convention, it has formalizing functions similar to those of Barth's goatskin scribe. Epic messages, for instance, usually join widely different spheres, as Raphael's and Michael's messages in *Paradise Lost* and Venus's visit to Aeneas connect earthly and celestial phases of a widespread action. Though technically not committed to writing, these messages from beyond have the status of officially commissioned proclamations. (And of course Michael's message *becomes* sacred script in due course in Milton's chronology, as Milton puts into it almost word for word at times what he knows to be the sacred matter of his selective brotherhood of fit readers.) In forms of narration less explicitly heroic, official messages sometimes provide the equivalent of the hero's birth and death certificates, his credentials, his legal agreements, his marriage articles, and the like. They certify for the public the standing of its central figures and stabilize the "worship" due them. Northland sagas like *The Saga of Grettir the Strong* and *The Saga of Burnt Njal* make much of the official assessment of feudal fees, remuneration for slayings, formal judgments, and the founding of households, documenting thereby the hero's name and tabulating his substance through transmitted challenges, summonses, and legal decisions.

In general, then, what the formal message achieves in these instances is the witnessing in one corner of a complex and scattered society — or in two branches of a plot — of what is already known and vouched for in another. And in the novel, too, this remains a central function of the epistle. The hero's career in *Robinson Crusoe, Moll Flanders, Humphrey Clinker*, and *Tom Jones* depends upon vouchers that lead to a sanctioned marriage, some proof of parentage, or a list of assets that will guarantee the hero's social standing. His spiritual standing is of relatively small importance; what requires a "letter of credit" in the largely bourgeois interests of the novel's audience is not one's relationship to worlds beyond or to chivalric codes but to those reliable virtues that will perpetuate family stability and consolidate holdings. The official letters and documents interspersed through *Robinson Crusoe*, for instance, certify Crusoe's inventory, command transfers of money and goods, and cement the small, private kingdom he has established while, like Barth's more imaginative scribbler, he is enisled alone. All the stages of Michael Henchard's remarkable career in *The Mayor of Casterbridge*, to choose a more striking case, are marked by documents — letters, bills of sale, wills, agreements, some of them intended to be private, but all of them bearing eventually Henchard's shrinking public image. As James's ironic "A Bundle of Letters" illustrates, the device of epistolary narration in modern fiction presents personal perspectives in which each correspondent's eccentricities and cultural leanings can be exposed in the light cast from opposing views and adjacent spheres. As James remarks with respect to that practice of ironic crossfire, "On the interest of *contrasted* things any painter of life and manners inevitably much depends, and contrast, fortunately for him, is easy to seek and to recognise." Hence his readers in the volume containing "An International Episode," "The Point of View," and "A Bundle of Letters" find such contrasts offered "in no form so frequent or so salient as that of the opposition of aspects from country to country" (*The Art of the Novel*, p. 198). The epistolary form proves functional once again in pointing up that "international problem" and sending fragments of it abroad, across the waters. It does so in another way in C. S. Lewis's *The Screwtape Letters*, which presents a devil's view of human weakness and sends abroad advice for their exploitation.

We should note one more thing about these written messages by which adjacent or dispersed societies are joined, namely, the imprint of the whole upon its representatives. What Paul seeks to accomplish in the sacred epistle by the transmission of the Christian spirit abroad is the stamping of a paradigm on the recipients. The archdevil Screwtape seeks much the same in opposition to the Enemy. Nearly all documents, in fact, seek to spread a general set of values or attested truths and procedures to the remoter corners of a kingdom. Messages regularize; they stamp foreign parts with a standard. Barth's first fictionalist seeks implicitly to impose on his audience an interpretation of the society that has expelled him. His imagination is fired with ideal types and typical evils. Raphael and Michael seek to indoctrinate Adam with the image of God, especially as God enters historical action, as in Michael's typological interpretation of what will become the Old Testament. On another plane, a license to practice medicine testifies that one's extraction of a particular appendix will have the generic attributes of a recurrent method as practiced, say, at Johns Hopkins. This means that the act of communication formally set to paper is likely to be, paradoxically, not only an act of individual soul-enciphering, as Barth's writer conceives of it — an act of sincere confession — but also an act of surrender to standards. Certainly a consideration of the audience by the letter writer and the generalities held in common by writer and recipient demand a smoothing of differences. The rhetoric of courtship that Angel Day describes in so many varieties of correspondence is the lubricant by which differences are ironed out. The epistles of lovers, societies, and bourgeois families alike depend upon a commitment to "manners" as embedded in epistolary conventions. But in compensation, through public certification in the acceptance of one's letter, one presumably transcends individual moments and social isolation and enters the life-stream of enduring types and institutions — or enters the society of Screwtape's devils — as a fully documented and acceptable initiate. Such institutions owe their existence to the acknowledged intelligibility of their lettered members, whose union becomes available to historical thought through their records. One is transmittable in documents not only from one geographic place to another but from one age to another.

The importance of a documented social standing is revealed just as clearly when the key documents are missing or are ineffectual, as they so often are in modern novels of uncoordinated and dispersed societies and unexpressed interiors. Indeed the difficulty with the societies of many twentieth-century novels is that though they possess many documents none of them is likely to prove definitive. Public documents are squeezed by bureaucracy, and private ones remain notes from some personal underground, journals from invisible men, or golden notebooks written in despair of a lasting social accord or meaningful communication. Between the meaningless public communiqué read to millions over television and the indecipherable private message of an obscure modern poet lies a desert of impersonal forms to be filled out in triplicate, certificates of one's merit, and framed licenses on the wall that link one to institutions that are no longer "spiritual" brotherhoods. Even bourgeois documents — the last will and testament, the promissory note, the marital agreement, the official alliance, and the financial tabulation — are by and large lacking in novels that treat these things; such novels thus almost literally pass beyond "documentary" realism because the real self, whatever it may be, cannot be enciphered for public acknowledgment, linked to a cultic or cultural brotherhood, or even boiled down to a family name or institutional affiliation.

But carded and filed as we frequently are (licensed, listed, taxed, customs-inspected, passported, drafted, graduated, married, and registered from birth to death certificates), we are still exposed to many of the functions of documents that Angel Day ascribes to letters. We still attempt, at least, to vouch in one quarter for what happens in another. Possession of the right documents enables us, supposedly, to draw upon resources certified elsewhere and thus to pass from one sphere to another without undue loss of standing — as though drawing upon one peoples' bank of symbols in order to deposit in another. Thus if Johns Hopkins thinks that one *is* a doctor and issues an official parchment saying so, others are likely to think so too, barring evidence to the contrary. Considered in this light, the document is still a liaison device, a form of communiqué bearing kinship to the letter.

II

Though not all of these aspects of messages are used with equal authority in epistolary fiction, many of them are found there, and if we keep them in mind when we approach Richardson, Fielding, Smollett, Rousseau, and Laclos in the main epistolary tradition, we are not likely to settle for the limited range of effects that critics have been willing to grant letter writers. The social novel itself, of course, quite apart from letter narration, is often concerned with the integration of private lives and public institutions. It is uniquely privileged to view individuals and groups both from within and from without and to trace the progression of thought and a mass of objective circumstances simultaneously. Epistolary fiction makes a special use of the letter to instrument exchanges between the private and the public lives and mold them into a single world where interiors are constantly being sent forth in social negotiation. Hence with its twofold focus on inner consciousness and on exterior settings, manners, and circumstances, the novel can make extensive use of those tangible, dated, signed, and enveloped pieces of correspondence in which Pamela and Clarissa, Matthew Bramble, and the Marquise Merteuil inscribe their thoughts for a selected public.

On the other hand, as an exclusive technique for presentation, letters are also quite special. Epistolary fiction depends so strikingly on a string of messages to keep pace with a succession of assumed events that other means of social intercourse are muted, and relationships are likely to become somewhat strained and artificial. To keep pace with and be answerable to events is an imposing task even for the nimble fingers of Pamela. Indeed, a concealed subject of letter fiction is sometimes the transformation that documents perform on events, emotions, and institutions — the capacity of written records to capture the movements of complex social and psychological life and make known what must be known if either characters or readers are to decipher what happens. We thus see unfolding in a letter novel both the events of the novel and the efforts of the intelligence system to grasp, at timely intervals, what the events portend; we see the impact of letters upon life, just as in examining an instant replay we see the inherent structure of the medium winning its way over the structural tendencies of the phenomena it supposedly represents. The interior narrators and audiences of the epistolary novel put the problem of testimony and truthfulness squarely before us: in their very scribblings we see the story being assembled and observe the effects of their verbal art. Having delved within to discover the truth of her feelings, for instance, even the well-intentioned and eminently sincere Pamela has before her only pen, ink, paper, and a letter format to talk about them. The collision of her style and her variations of the story with other styles and perspectives calls into question the nature of testimony and narrative revelation — indeed the quality of sincerity itself.[3] Hence we observe in such correspondents the creative act of seeing enmeshed in the delivery system; we see an action rising into the formal design of its documents. As B. L. Reid aptly remarks, "A letter is an editing of life, not life itself," and a collection of letters surrounds an incident "as it goes its echoic progress . . . the incident

3. Quite apart from the perspectives of individual writers, the letter itself tends to select a certain range of experience: obviously, no writer of epistles in an eighteenth-century novel will be assigned quite Michael's or Paul's subjects. Letter novels often concern the bourgeois household, its connections with other elements of society, its family liaisons and marriages, and its variations of amatory intrigue. For a panoramic view of the subjects of letter fiction later in the century, see Frank Gees Black, *The Epistolary Novel in the Late Eighteenth Century: A Descriptive and Bibliographical Study* (Eugene: University of Oregon Press, 1940). See also Charles E. Kany, *The Beginnings of the Epistolary Novel in France, Italy, and Spain* (Berkeley: University of California Press, 1937).

occurs, is reflected on, committed to paper, committed to a porter, spied upon, received, reflected on, responded to, and perhaps returned to the original actors. The whole complex repercussive effect grows much thicker than the printed page."[4]

Before pursuing this line further, however, we should pause to take note of a quite different and in some respects contradictory view of letter fiction. That this view has usually prevailed in comments on letter novels is due in part to the fact that Richardson was its first spokesman and remains by both precept and example a forceful proponent of it.

In Richardson's comments on letter fiction as he understands and practices it, letters are not principally formal conveyances of the kind I have described but the instruments of immediate, personal experience, the confessional expression of outpoured feeling, and therefore a way to suggest dramatic immediacy and excitement. The letters of his characters are designed not to *document* affairs but to register urgent feelings under stress:

> All the letters are written while the hearts of the writers must be supposed to be wholly engaged in their subjects . . . so that they abound not only with critical situations, but with what may be called instantaneous descriptions and reflections. ... Much more lively and affecting must be the style of those who write in the height of a present distress; the mind tortured by the pangs of uncertainty (the events then hidden in the womb of fate); than the dry, narrative, unanimated style of a person relating difficulties and dangers surmounted, can be.[5]

It is true that by comparison to the detached and ironic historian-narrator in Fielding or to a "journalist" like Crusoe who chronicles his life long after the fact, a promptly responding, first-person letter writer may achieve remarkable dramatic effects and psychological realism. Like the perspective of the diary, the letter is a moving imprint of thought in process rather than a retrospective view of a completed period. Because its writer does not know the outcome of the segment of the story that he transcribes, he presents it with all the

4. B. L. Reid, "Justice to *Pamela*," *Hudson Review* 9 (1956–57), reprinted in *Pamela: A Collection of Critical Essays*, ed. Rosemary Cowler (Englewood Cliffs, N.J.: Prentice-Hall, 1969), p. 36.

5. Samuel Richardson, Preface to *Sir Charles Grandison* (London: Wm. Heineman, 1902), p. xxxix. See *Selected Letters*, ed. John Carroll (London: Oxford University Press, 1964), "Epistolary Theory and Practice," pp. 31–35.

racy uncertainty of present experience. The contingencies of the plot may be bearing down upon him even as he writes, altering accordingly prospect and retrospect, prediction and retrieval. A letter thus squeezed hurriedly into a pause between episodes is less an official record than an instrument of contemporary discourse, like dramatic speech; and certainly in Richardson the letter writer is seldom aware of discrepancies between his feelings and the act of writing the letter, or between the events he describes and the narrative mode he practices. He does not regard himself as a fictional transformer, a stylizer, or a calculator.

We can grant the importance of this point without compromising seriously the argument that letters are also quite different from face-to-face discourse, in which each new perception is always "suffered" and responded to immediately. Though letters can, of course, quote dialogue as any narrative method can, they are normally much more detached and composed than everyday speech or dramatic exchange. Richardson himself, a tireless and careful letter writer, knew and practiced the rhetoric of various kinds of letters, as did most educated people in his letter-writing age. Of the kinds of letters listed by Angel Day for the edification of subsequent generations, some are obviously much less spontaneous than others. Each has its own calculated art, even a letter of apparent pell-mell confession; and certainly the typical Richardson letter is anything but higgledy-piggledy confusion or transparent sincerity. The intensity of the letter's dramatic transaction, whether it is an act of beseeching, advice-giving, commanding, praise-rendering, confession, or reconciliation, is cooled considerably by the act of writing what is after all a member of the document family. Letters flow from and are often delivered to private sanctuaries; but they are also semipublic postures. While Richardson talks of the novel's "peeping into hearts" and readers have found *Pamela* and *Clarissa* keyhole views of virtuous private chambers, even virtue, as David Daiches reminds us, "is not a matter between oneself and God; it must be publicly known and admired."[6] It is therefore fair to remark that while Richardson attended primarily to the overflowing passions of his heroines, his critics quickly spotted what they considered the calculating heart within. Though we should perhaps not attribute to either Clarissa or Pamela an excessive amount of conscious deviousness — certainly not the quantity

6. David Daiches, in *Pamela: A Collection of Critical Essays*, ed. Cowler, p. 20.

of Fielding's Shamela — they are nonetheless the victims of a form of transaction that, in Dr. Johnson's words, "offers stronger temptations to fallacy and sophistication" than any other form of social intercourse. As contemporary parodies of Richardson's ardent female scribblers suggest, the closer to a dramatic situation and to confession an act of writing comes, the more incredible it seems — the more irreconcilable the formal mode and the claims for spontaneity it implicitly makes. Certainly, we should not be surprised to find in the letter novel much more descriptive information and expository organization than any young girl in trouble (or otherwise) could be supposed to muster.

The difficulty derives from the stretching of a device to cover all the demands of a fictional system, the greatest need of which is for plotted coherence and substantial views of society. In any form of narration the novelist has basic narrative and analytic duties to attend to that are complicated by an attempt to be fully neutral and dramatic. He must situate the isolated dramatic moment of a particular letter or dialogue within the larger narrative units, and his overall devices of structure betray his organizing hand. He may keep himself out of the styles of the letters themselves, then, but he cannot keep himself out of their *arrangement*. Thus whatever Cécile may wish to say at a given moment in her heart of hearts (in *Liaisons dangereuses*), Laclos must have her cooperation as a fellow writer engaged in putting together a novel. Pamela, too, sacrifices "instantaneous descriptions and reflections" when called upon to elaborate those less "lively and affective" matters of the book of conduct that prompted Richardson to invent her. In Smollett, letters not only string a plot together but provide the massive descriptive materials of the social novel mixed with travelogue, thereby lengthening frequently into journals and personal essays. In nearly all letter novels, retrospective letters (equivalent to flashbacks) are required to knit the present and past together, and hints of prospects, too, must somehow be planted. Whereas in everyday life letters may concern miscellaneous and unrelated events from the writer's life and opinions — pieces of news about someone's aunt or failing business, rising taxes or travelogue observations — novel letters obviously have a quite different set of criteria for revelance and follow different principles of interrogation and response.

In delegating some of his novelistic responsibility to the characters, the novelist makes them to some extent special kinds of people. The very decision to write a letter at a given time forces an act of communication upon a correspondent and draws from him explanations, pleas, justifications, exhortations, and the like. He cannot retreat or refuse to write if the author requires him to. (We could not imagine most modern novel characters taking to the pen often enough or well enough to be functional in epistolary fiction.) The letter testaments of Pamela affect the characterization of Pamela as surely as the delivery of a certain kind of message affects the characterization of Raphael and Michael in *Paradise Lost*. Even Smollett, who is comparatively indifferent to the devicemanship of letters, must search for ways to make their writing deliberate and meaningful. It is helpful to this end for Smollett to give Matthew Bramble (in *Humphrey Clinker*) a warmly explosive sensibility that requires the pouring out of his humanitarian sentiments and satiric spleen to sympathetic listeners. Lydia writes equally cathartic though in her case girlish outpourings. Both of them are thus made into analysts of the story as well as participants. In other cases, letter writing divides the participant from the narrator so that in anticipating his narration a character may be led to change the enactment to satisfy the storytelling art he will soon practice. The temptation is especially strong if he is among the controlling schemers and manipulators of the plot, as Richardson's Lovelace and Laclos's Merteuil and Valmont are. Thus Valmont, relishing the confiding of his exploits, deliberately sets out to make them the kind of exploits that will make good confiding. His life becomes a game of intrigues planned as generic pieces, savored in the telling almost more than in the doing. Life imitates the episodic art unfolding from one's own finger tips.

If writing letters makes habitual scribblers of certain characters and converts them into movers and interpreters of stories, it also influences the society they form. A society of letter writers is after all very special; it has letter love affairs (the suspended interim between the exchanges of lovers both hinders action and regulates passion, for instance), letter business transactions, and even letter social classes, whose inequalities of manner and position are as pronounced in style and spelling as they would ordinarily be in speech and gesture. More basically, the social liaisons of the epistolary novel are the product of the letter's special means of documenting, anticipating, and remembering. Because a letter is a hovering, reflective present lodged between events past and events anticipated, it allows its writer to play with the action and with his antagonists in a calculating way. It brings them under his control. He has ample opportunity to think about the uses he might make of his writing talent and to mix his interior career with the materials of a developing intrigue in just the way he wants. He uses the letter as a special means of converging individual psychology and social manners. He may create an entire letter empire by these means, as Valmont and Merteuil do, so that the nature of written messages affects all his social relationships.

As a correspondent omits the interim and selects what is to be represented, he also selects certain people to whom to give his information. A letter society is formed around not a common revealed center but chosen points of contact. The effect is sometimes like that of a dozen or so people engaged in a phone conversation, each of whom hears only a fraction of the total exchange and pieces together the rest from fragments. Not until the end of the novel are all letters normally exposed to public view. By then, any exposure of the whole truth may require a radical revision of everyone's view of everyone else. Thus Clarissa's main impact on her family and friends comes after she is dead; and the revelations of the true Merteuil in *Liaisons* reverses the viewpoints of surviving characters and realigns their relationships.

If letters affect social orders and characterization, they affect even more profoundly the timing and segmentation of narrative units.[7] Rather than limiting himself to the structural devices of the book or chapter (for which the writer himself takes obvious responsibility, as he does for intervals, summaries, sequences of parts, conclusions, crescendos, and thematic statements), the epistolary novelist assigns the creation of narrative units to the characters themselves. They are responsible for deciding when to write, how long the letters will be, how they will be structured, and how one will approach other members of a closed group. Their letters are inserted into the intervals and cracks between happenings and thus become interposed events in their own right: between a segment of action already past and another still to come the letter comes as a mediating, causal event, an overt act.

But as a meditative or analytic moment aside it also rises above

---

7. See Philip Stevick's suggestive treatment of narrative segmentation in "The Theory of Fictional Chapters," *Western Humanities Review* 20 (1966): 231–41.

mere action and exists on another footing from what it describes. It interleaves segments of digesting analysis with segments of a more spontaneous life. As such, as a moment of withdrawal, it also mediates between the reader and the event, compressing into a complex act (as we noticed earlier) the participant's involvement and the storyteller's aesthetic distance. As Alan D. McKillop has remarked, "The writing of letters is only the beginning; they are copied, sent, received, shown about, discussed, answered, even perhaps hidden, intercepted, stolen, altered, or forged. The relation of the earlier letters in an epistolary novel to the later may thus be quite different from the relation of the earlier chapters of a novel to the later."[8] When the form of narration becomes part of the implicit substance of the story in this manner, it is likely to change our view of manners, action, states of feeling, and the succession of events generally. We can see the peculiar effects of its interplay with what happens when a letter falls into the wrong hand and a character usurps the privileged information of the reader. He becomes part of the audience of the novel, transcending his normal ignorance momentarily and reentering the action possessed of a perspective closer to ours. Thus Pamela's letters eventually help convince her intercepting pursuer of her worth, as they have already convinced the reader; they reveal to him both her sincerity and her interpretation of him.

Meanwhile, as characters become privileged in the way of authors and readers, the novelist himself is prevented from establishing his normal relationship with the reader. "Points" of view become almost literally that, brief dramatic moments that offer no single, explicit panorama of generalizations or infallible commentary, only moving instances, diarylike, stationed within the stream of events. In return, every event is qualified by the moment of retreat and contemplation that produces the letter, and the entire transaction among readers, characters, and author is shuffled around: characters are drawn out of the plot to write their comments, standing at the window of their own stories and looking on from where the author and reader usually stand; the reader is drawn in as though looking over their shoulders — while the writer is both in the room participating and at the window describing.

8. Alan D. McKillop, *Epistolary Technique in Richardson's Novels,* Rice Institute Pamphlet 38 (1951), p. 36.

Numerous opportunities for irony are created by this shift in points of view. The reader is led to judge one correspondent less by an explicit authorial posture than by another correspondent's bias. This crisscrossing is assisted by the accidents that letters are prone to, passing each other in the mails, overlapping narrations and renarrations, reversals from one letter to another, loss, interception, misinterpretation, erratic or untimely delivery — all of which depend upon the special ignorance and partial information inherent in letter testimony, the exigencies of delivery, and the specialties of addressed correspondence. Though similar limitations in knowledge and similar ironies are possible in other forms of narration (and on the stage as well), to these ordinary contingencies of character and action, letter novels add revelations unintended by the writer, as when two pieces of information come together accidentally or a recipient proves unexpectedly unreceptive because of another liaison. Like the moment of detachment that normally produces the letter, then, these accidents that messages are prone to are part of the palpable mediation that letters effect between the act and its "instant replay."

The special letter society that results, to return to it a moment, is influenced in part by this selective and fallible system of information and in part by the context of the writing. Letters often create liaisons between houses as well as individuals, for instance. As documents, they carry the imprint of an address, a permanent place to collect and centralize the scattered threads of a career. As such they influence the conflict between a Clarissa and a Lovelace, which stems from an enmity between the houses of Harlowe and Lovelace — one without title and therefore jealously protective of its honor, the other titled and ancient as well as wealthy. (As Ian Watt points out, the code of courtship and marriage is dictated in each household by the nature of its social position. For the Harlowes, family advancement requires the protection of the daughters' marriage choices; for Lovelace, with name and rank assured, the mark of achievement is not family gain but cleverness and the exercise of personal charm.)[9] No letter from Clarissa to Lovelace forgets for long Clarissa's obligations to her family or her concept of self-respect, and Lovelace is compelled to acknowledge these if only to circumvent them in the name of his own

9. Ian Watt, *The Rise of the Novel* (Berkeley and Los Angeles: University of California Press, 1957), pp. 220ff.

house. Indeed, every conceivable liaison between brother and sister, mother and daughter, father and daughter, confidants, superiors, uncles and aunts, servants and masters, rejected and ecstatic lovers, clever plotters and victims, has some form of letter appropriate to it that may bear a household imprint. By extending the household in these liaisons, the letter puts it "in circulation." It sends the household abroad into the bourgeois order and thus vouches for the "household cult" in foreign quarters. As Fielding's Shamela understands perfectly, one is constantly on guard for the best alliances and may use the confessional letter to let one's closest family know how things are progressing — while keeping others tantalizingly in the dark:

> Now, Mamma, what think you? — For my own part, I am convinced he will marry me, and faith so he shall. O! Bless me! I shall be Mrs. Booby, and be mistress of a great estate, and have a dozen coaches and six, and a fine house at London, and another at Bath, and servants, and jewels, and plate, and go to plays, and operas, and court; and do what I will, and spend what I will. But, poor Parson Williams! Well; and can't I see Parson Williams as well after marriage as before: for I shall never care a farthing for my husband. [*Shamela*, Letter X]

The style of the confessional and the open dream of splendor, with its inventorylike style of articles to the contract, suits very well a young lady of ambition, material imagination, and household ideas. Besides counting off her future assets in a compilation of coordinate phrases, she can also compress into a phrase the designs of many a night of scheming, putting in a nutshell her plan of action: "I thought once of making a little fortune by my person. I now intend to make a great one by my vartue" [Letter X] — which of course she does, in common with Pamela.

III

Since the content of the novel is so often precisely these matters of household standing, reputation, parentage, and property transfer — especially as these come to focus in the propriety of courtship and in the "virtue" of Pamelas or "vartue" of Shamelas — the letter's private honesty and controlled publicity of the self, as a document, have a natural contribution to make to novelistic technique. Given private

access to the mails, the reader discovers beyond dispute the discrepancy between fronts and interiors, confidential selves and public,
historic reputations. He sees how privacy is transformed in documents made public. Letters not only make admirable instruments to
harvest the ironies of that discrepancy, as Fielding understood, but
are equally serviceable in timing the releases of information along a
highly segmented series of revelations. Their impact is as great on
form as it is on substance. It is the matter of form that I now want to
concentrate in turning to a specific example.

Les Liaisons dangereuses makes an interesting test case for the
structural effects of letter narration partly because it comes late
enough in the epistolary tradition to make ironic use of the devices of
that tradition and yet early enough to take at least some of them seriously. Many of the tricks of his predecessors Laclos turns inside out,
especially what he takes from Richardson and Rousseau. The critical
turn he gives their artifices and the strained production of letters is of
the kind that one associates with mannerism, that self-conscious later
stage of a style when it becomes aware of its own methods. Laclos's
self-conscious reflections on the form are all the more valuable to us
for the negative conclusions they suggest and the reinforcement they
give to one's assumptions about the impact of the storytelling method
on characterization, theme, and structure. His undermining of the
confessional letter is typical. The spontaneous confidentiality of
Richardson's heroines and their close friends Laclos refuses to accept
at face value; only the stupid and the silly write letters as openly
honest as Pamela's.[10] By making Tourvel, the most sincere of people,
also one of the least wise and most self-deceived, Laclos plays down
the moral struggle with the confessing angel; and by making the
young, innocent Cecile vain, simple, and sensual, he implicitly undermines the incorruptible soul pouring out its instinctive morality.
(Fielding, of course, preceded him in thrusting at the same chink in

10. That Laclos overrules not only Richardson but also Rousseau in the matter of the
sincere and spontaneous letter seems likely when we recollect that Rousseau banished
nearly all falsity and scheming from *La Nouvelle Héloise* and presents us with a heroine
entirely transparent from the beginning. Julie's letters are beyond not only deliberate
deceit but also unintentional calculation, as the novel puts the hearts of the lovers openly
on display in all their frequent sublimity, delirium, inflammations, languishing, serenity,
immortal fires, and consternation. See *La Nouvelle Héloise: Julie; or, The New Eloise*,
trans. Judith H. McDowell (University Park and London: Pennsylvania State University
Press, 1968).

Richardson's armor.) It is Merteuil, not these two, who dominates the novel's dangerous intimacies and indicates the chief generic difference between *Liaisons* and the typical letter novel: whereas the latter grows out of the book of conduct and the sentimental romance, *Liaisons* stems from theatrical comedy and the novel of intrigue. It is therefore better prepared to see certain aspects of the separation of letters and life built into masked rhetoric.

Besides taking a jaundiced and amused view of innocent female scribblers, Laclos sets aside or devalues other major concerns of his predecessors, among them one of Richardson's richest themes, the class struggle and the power of the middle-class marital code, one almost entirely absent from *Liaisons* and the other reduced to the stubborn prudery of Tourvel. Like Richardson, Laclos is concerned with contractual agreements — with family names and the truth behind various forgeries and masks — but he explores different aspects of these and registers more dramatically the impact of letters upon them. The result of Merteuil's plots, for instance, is not the establishing of a bourgeois household or the indirect confirmation of monogamy but the education of innocence in the motives of intertwined, vicious parties, who use the art of writing for malignant ends. Hence Laclos explores a war of the sexes that can arrive at no articles of peace. Valmont and Merteuil use their letters ultimately as a means to document their own treachery and to destroy each other. Similarly, on the basis of the letters it eventually sees, the wider society outside the closed groups of correspondents renders a damning judgment of the central characters. Unlike Richardson's outsiders, they cannot gather in respect around the heroine. The little packet of letters that Laclos "edits" comes to seem self-enclosed and narrow, like the evidence of a closet intrigue that cries out to be laid bare by a more candid and less intrigue-ridden society.

Laclos's "mannerist" advance over Richardson and Rousseau, then, consists chiefly in his discovery within the spontaneous heart and the sanctity of names and households a set of very complex contrivances and a creative urge to manufacture plots, assign roles, and dictate outcomes in the manner of the fictionalist. To innocent people like Danceny and Cécile, tutored in the tradition of Pamela and Julie, the calculated despair or rapture of Laclos's schemers sounds exactly right and proper: after all, lovers in novels have performed in precisely these balanced phrases and serial repetitions for decades. But

groups form around very special agreements and dangerous con-
fessions rather than around sentimental attachments, finally, and each
of these special arrangements violates some other, momentarily se-
creted away in another line of correspondence. Though each mask
may well express a "true" segment of a complex heart, the heart as a
whole finds no way to emerge and enter the institutional life of the
household or society — or to survive the exposure of its duplicity.
The self can be documented only one piece at a time, and a heap of
letters complies a heap of contradictions.

With this in mind, we can gauge the letter's contribution to the
novel's scheme of dangerous intimacies and intriguing groups, the
partial exposure of one to another, and the guided progression of the
reader through their ironic crossfire. As I suggested earlier, each of
the epistolary successions or closed intelligence systems follows a
different rate of progress, first toward the successful consummation of
an intimacy and then, eventually, toward a public exposure of its
place in the intrigue. We watch Cécile, for instance, progress from a
very young, passive, bored girl to a budding courtesan, from the
gradual weakening of her girlhood intimacy with Sophie Carnay to
intimacies of a quite different kind with Danceny, Valmont, and Merteuil (who administers her advanced training). The main stages in
each of these evolving connections are well marked by explicit
comments from her tutors, in letters unavailable to her, and of course
by the events themselves. Her career is a lesson in the losing of
simple, openhearted, fluffy relationships and the gaining of in-
criminating secrets and dangerous connections. An underworld of
guilt and intentional evil opens beneath her feet — not all at once in
such a way as to frighten her into drawing back, but teasingly, bit by
bit. She progresses from innocent games, in which deceiving one's
mother is childlike sport, to serious calculations, upon which her
future depends. By juxtaposing her letters with letters of much greater
sophistication and inside knowledge, Laclos reinforces at given points
our sense of how far she has progressed into the corrupt heart of the
society and how much further she has to go. Whereas with Pamela
and Julie we witness a step-by-step strengthening of idealistic resolves with which we are meant to identify, with Cécile any potential
sympathy is blocked intermittently by contrasting perspectives. The
worldly intelligence of Valmont and Merteuil, which we share as
fellow conspirators from the beginning, is never in danger of being

impressed by her girlish scruples or monogamistic "virtues."

Valmont's rates of progress with Mme Tourvel, Cécile, Chevalier Danceny, and Mme Merteuil are more complex and more intricately intertwined with the segmented phases of the others. Like Merteuil, Valmont is a master of love's schedules, which he controls by letters, notes, and other devices. As a character of plans — meeting surprises with more complex plans — and as a mixture of scientific investigator and *calculateur* who tests the formulas of the libertine against specific cases, he conducts his affairs as though writing, directing, and acting in a play. His progress is marked by the crescendos and reversals of the seduction schemes he himself stages: the greater the hindrance, the more delightful and educational he finds the affairs. In this manipulated world, the most important talent one can cultivate is a capacity to read the flutters, blushes, and hesitations of one's victim and the messages between the lines of her cold epistolary style. Unfortunately, he has a dangerously hubristic and vainglorious faith both in his plans and in the capacity of his letters to advance them. Though his numerous setbacks compel him to reexamine feminine psychology frequently, he does not learn fast enough in the race against Merteuil, his unrecognized antagonist. In the vital area of self-knowledge he makes no progress at all. Hence, trapped by a fatal sympathy for Tourvel and by his blindness toward Merteuil, he is unable ultimately to establish a real confidence with anyone. His letters do not humanize or transcribe him; they provide him merely with masks and instruments that are his undoing.

Mme Merteuil's rates of love are still more closely geared to the controlled world of letters and intrigue. Her career, by far the most knowledgeable and encompassing of the novel, includes much more than the miscellaneous succession of affairs into which Valmont's profligate inclinations lead him. It entails a wider social vision and a lifelong dedication to revenge that subordinates various intimacies to a single, connected career. Whereas Clarissa's letters merely respond passively to situations forced upon their writer, Merteuil's are generating and moving letters; she spaces the episodes and pulls the strings. Perhaps the most important of her contributions in this line, however, are not her plots and schemes but her essays on manners and morals: these, too, are carefully adapted to the letter medium in its instructional and confessional departments. She knows especially well the psychobiological growth of women, beginning with the ingénue Cécile experiencing her first flirtations and progressing to the young married woman Tourvel, in a first (and last) infidelity, and ending with aging women like Volanges and Rosemonde, now safely removed from the traumas of love but still looking interestedly on from outside. Her letters on these subjects provide key thematic summaries and interpretive perspectives from which we learn to judge Valmont and lesser schemers and eventually Merteuil herself. As she understands perfectly, she herself follows the career of the cynical educator, teaching first herself and then pupils such as Cécile and Cavalier Danceny the skills of the "living theater." Her career is an exercise in self-creation according to principles intentionally laid down from "the fruit of profound reflection." This reflection her letters allow her to practice out loud. "I have created them," she says of those principles to Valmont: "I might say I have created myself" (Letter 81). As she transcribes actions and offers instruction and social analysis in a deft epistolary style, she converts the givens of a haphazard life into extemporaneous art. As the Prévan affair illustrates, her programs of ironic reversal and exposure are precisely planned and executed so that no victim fails to see the point when she has revealed his duplicity.

Letters offer the kind of world between reflection and action that Mme Merteuil handles best in incorporating her "principles" into fictions and intrigue. She is as sensitive in deciphering other styles as she is in enciphering her own designs and studying "character as it is displayed in physical features" and facial expressions. By controlling the web of communications, she also controls the rates of progress by which the various intrigues mature — the courtly games, all of whose stages she knows so well; the compiling of reputations (the fame of Valmont, the respectability of Rosemonde and Mme Volanges); and her own accumulation of documented credits in society. She understands thoroughly the discrepancies between the kind of private worlds that can be laid bare in a letter to a confidante and the formal argument one sends to Mme Volanges to implicate her in a particular plot. More important, having sharpened her own sensitivity to emotions by reading novels and attending the theater, she knows that a society is composed largely of make-believe images of oneself and others and that she can get people to play by cultivating the proper game instincts in them. She knows precisely how a world that is connected and makes sense can be put together in the enclosed circuit of a correspondence — which is obviously of some service to Laclos in assembling his own connected plot.

With so much under her command, in a world as controllable as her letter empire, we might expect to find her invulnerable. But Laclos entertains no illusions about the validity of that empire. Letters create only a very small and fragile enclosure. Outside the boundaries of the "play" a more massive viciousness awaits its chance in a world of multiplied connections, governed chiefly by money, position, and hazard. In pointing toward that world on several occasions (in letters from Cécile to Sophie and single letters from Father Anselme, the servant Azolan, and Gercourt, which provide glimpses of Paris and the affairs of business and church), Laclos carefully circumscribes Merteuil's intrigues. That she should be delivered up to law suits, disease, and wolfish scrambling is a fitting punishment for her indifference toward the victims of her own plots. What we suddenly realize in the final expansion of the novel's periphery is that the labyrinth of dangerous connections is many times larger than any that could be managed even by a consummate schemer.

Merteuil's ruin implies a criticism not only of her values, then, but also of the nature of the entire letter society and its exclusive, cultic self-interest. Lack of public confidence destroys intimacies and converts them into the kind of material that James's newspaper "reverberator" delights in exposing. Some of the games — dueling, for instance — can be deadly. Some kinds of publicity twist the truth too severely. Some bargains cannot be broken or rewritten at will even in the most artful correspondence. And some physical realities, too, crash through the defenses of the maskers and cannot be "lettered," any more than Barth's anonymous inventor of bottled epistles can transcend the physical limits of his endurance, or the size of a goat hide. For all the fictions one entrusts to them and for all the spirit encoded in them, Laclos suggests, letters allow none of the physical touch, dramatic immediacy, or expressive, unreflective emotion that social contact does.

The irony of Merteuil's and Valmont's ruin is a variation of an irony that Laclos generates throughout the novel by exposing, in surrounding letters, the comparative ignorance and narrow perspective of given correspondents, each of whom is enclosed in his own set of untested illusions. Everyone is vulnerable because everyone is ignorant of what is written and determined in letters unavailable to him. For example, the progress of Valmont's seduction of Mme Tourvel is forwarded by the ignorance of Rosemonde, Mme Tourvel's only confidante, who inadvertently assists Valmont's plans first by not seeing the danger he presents to Tourvel in her house and then by describing his distraught state to Tourvel after Tourvel has departed. This description (Letter 122) sets the stage for Valmont's clever pretence to despair in the melodramatic scene of his final victory over Mme Tourvel's scruples, following which, but before Rosemonde knows about it, Rosemonde writes to Mme Tourvel:

> I was very anxious to thank you for the good news you gave me of my nephew, and no less so to offer you my sincere felicitations on your own account. One is obliged to see this as truly the work of Providence which, in putting one to the test, has saved both. Yes, my dear, God, who wished only to try you, has saved you at the very moment when your strength was exhausted; and, in spite of your little complainings, you have, I think, some thanks to return Him. [P. 306]

Juxtaposed with Valmont's letter to Merteuil describing the seduction itself, Rosemonde's platitudes and philosophic consolations are exposed as fantasy from an entirely different game where virtue is still rewarded, providence still guides one through trials, and one writes goodhearted letters of advice and consolation to friends. This kind of intimacy and social agreement is decisively defeated by other kinds developed concurrently with it. It, too, is exposed as pure fiction from a narrow world of comforting self-deceit.

The timing of information that generates these special epistolary ironies and the segmentation of messages into isolated points of view have a marked effect not only on the reader's progress through a series of discrepant points of view but also on the novel's form. Given this kind of isolation among the characters and this brand of dangerous intimacy, Laclos is led to a special sense of the fictional enclosure and the reader's relationship to it. This sense can perhaps best be understood if we consider by contrast Pamela's happy progress and the tragedy of Clarissa. Both the main victim, Mme Tourvel, and the schemer Valmont deepen in character (somewhat unconvincingly) as the novel prepares for a change in tone after the seduction. However, none of the things eventuate that we might expect of comic or tragic melodrama in Richardson. Comic intrigue normally brings a new definition of identity in which tricksters are exposed and the sentimental favorites are happily married. Pamela's true character when it is finally understood justifies her high estate. Tragic intrigue on the other hand, as the death of Clarissa illustrates, brings traumatic knowledge and results in a cleansing by harrowing experience. Neither of these is precisely what the letter novel is prepared to deliver as Laclos conceives of it. The letter writer himself is too special a creature: because juxtaposed letters from different parties and the continual practice of rhetoric have constantly broken our entrancement with his point of view, we do not maintain a harrowing sympathy. Moreover, in *Liaisons* the sources of our most reliable knowledge are also the sources of greatest deception and evil who have nothing in reserve to rise above their immorality. Rather than arriving at a plateau of reflection and withdrawing from their playlike creations in some act of understanding occasioned by their setbacks, Valmont and Merteuil end appropriately by plunging blindly into their own contrivances. Indeed, in some respects, Merteuil's ignorance is the greatest of all the varieties that Laclos exposes despite her superior cunning. She lacks a saving moral sense that might cause her to accept guilt or remorse — those very useful emotions for the reingratiation of society's outcasts. Hence the letters deprive the reader of a comfortable moral center and of heroes and heroines.

And unfortunately, limited as Merteuil's analytic range is in moral matters, it yields ultimately to people still less capable of articulating anything like an acceptable public rite of purgation — namely, Danceny, Mme Volanges, and Mme Rosemonde, for whom we have had only limited sympathy from the beginning. The last few letters register the impact of the exposé and bind the survivors in an agreement — not to confront or to root out the sources of duplicity and willful blindness among them, but to limit the effects of the wreckage. The final letters illustrate what we might regard as a special kind of "documentary" ending, as, for instance, Rosemonde's letter to Chevalier Danceny:

> After what you have brought to my knowledge, Monsieur, there is nothing to do but weep and be silent. One is sorry to be still alive when one learns of such horrors; one is ashamed of being a woman when one hears of one capable of such excesses.
>
> I shall be very glad, Monsieur, to join with you, as far as I am able, in committing to silence and oblivion everything that may concern, and

everything that may ensue from, this lamentable affair. I even wish it may cause you no other distress than that which is inseparable from the unhappy triumph you were able to achieve at my nephew's expense. In spite of his misdeeds, which I am obliged to acknowledge, I feel that I shall never be consoled for his loss. But my inconsolable affliction shall be the only revenge I take upon you: it is for your heart to calculate its extent.

If you will allow me, at my age, a reflection that is scarcely ever made at yours, I must say that if one only knew where one's true happiness lay one would never look for it outside the limits prescribed by the law and by religion. [Pp. 384–85]

Such moralizing reveals clearly the letter's transformation of sentiments into the stuff of documents and epistolary ironies. Rosemonde's language is not the language of a tragic chorus wringing public assuagement out of harrowing experience; it is the language of an epistle confessing and lamenting in a manner that Dr. Johnson, with his instinct for "temptations to fallacy and sophistication," would have appreciated immensely. We respect Rosemonde's sincerity to be sure — probably no one in the novel has more of the right kind on other occasions — but it is after all a formal and somewhat calculated sincerity as the perspective of the novel closes down to the private intrigues of aged, pious aunts. Grief blends into the formal devices of the letter as smoothly as the message glides into the conventional close: "Were I afraid that you might deny me such a consolation, I should ask you to remember first that you have left me no other. I have the honour to be, etc." The death of her nephew and the exposure of Cécile's licentiousness trail off as weakly as "yours truly."[11]

With uncharacteristic soundness of judgment and sobriety, Danceny's reply to Rosemonde moralizes Cecile's fall and has the effect of further settling the events without understanding the issues — whereupon he too retreats to forget "this accumulation of horrors," leaving behind nicely turned epistolary phrases to cover his escape:

What young girl, just out of her convent, without experience and almost completely without ideas, taking with her into society, as nearly always happens, an equal ignorance of good and evil; what young girl, I say, could have offered a firmer resistance to such wicked designs? Ah, to be indulgent, it is enough to consider how many circumstances,

11. For a different reading of the ending, see Dorothy R. Thelander, *Laclos and the Epistolary Novel* (Geneva: Librarie Droz, 1963), p. 67. See also C. J. Greshoff, "The Moral Structure of 'Les Liaisons Dangereuses,' " *French Review* 2 (1964): 383–99.

quite independent of ourselves, maintain the terrifying balance between decency and corruption in our hearts. [P. 390]

The formality of the rhetoric and the repeated choral comments on
the sadness of the events tie up the loose ends in an obviously
epistolary way. Reminders of the documents are implicit in every
dated and signed exchange, shift in point of view, and change in
rhetorical tactics along the way.

But Laclos does not leave our sense of that special epistolary
succession to implicit leaps from letter to letter or to the oddities of
Danceny's and Rosemonde's concluding letters. Bound up in a single
package and presented as a set of historical records, the correspondence as a whole has a further dimension that is not immediately
evident in particular parts. The packaging says a great deal in itself,
as does the subtitle that Laclos appends to the bundle: *Letters
Collected in One Section of Society and Published for the Edification of Others.* The novel brings into the open a relatively intimate
group of connections and certifies its life and manners for the moral
improvement of outsiders, just as real documents do, as I suggested,
when they vouch for true gospel in a distant realm or for someone's
personal fidelity and passion. We are reminded by this that one of the
interests of the novel has always been news from somewhere else, a
taste for which runs concurrently with a taste for biography, journalism, travel literature, and other kinds of factual writing that "document" our curiosity. But we are reminded in reading the bundle of
letters that those foreign parts that are in one sense intrinsically
exciting when transcribed onto paper also collect some of the dust of
museums, just as Crusoe manages to reduce to inventory everything
his journal mentions. Laclos is more inclined to have it both ways
than his predecessors, to capitalize on the news-bearing function of
private letters laid open for a scandalized public, and at the same time
to expose the mediating artifice, both in the rhetoric of the letters and
in the presentation of the whole group. His personal delivery of the
collection, in the most epistolary part of most books, the prefatory
address to the reader, is announced as a certification (with tongue in
cheek, of course) of the authentic history he has discovered and
edited. Like the epistolary stylists he invents within, he thereby exposes himself as another fabricator of fictional games.

As perhaps the last of the worthwhile letter novels, *Liaisons* does what we might expect of a comparatively late product; it suggests the gulf between the real self and those licensed and stamped images that people mail abroad. The difficulty with letters is that they do not pull their audiences very far in. Each person that Merteuil has to deal with has inside him, as it turns out, dangerous inclinations that go undisciplined by the roles she has in mind for them. As stagy and thin as Valmont is, for instance, he is capable of abandoning her program and falling in love with his victim when they stand without a paper barrier between them. Thus if the novel exposes the smaller illusions and deceptions of its characters, as a whole package it also exposes the inadequacy of designs, coherent plots, and artifices of presentation when these approach mere play or mere documentary interest. Where reality may lie *except* in mannered expression, in masks and letters, in the news the mail brings, is difficult to say. Laclos does not offer a way of seeing through society's masks to any kind of effective self-expression, any more than Barth's archetypal storyteller can say finally what is real and what he has merely imagined — or even whether or not his letters have been received and answered or the sea has returned something he himself sent forth. We have only the record of the parchment and the letters to go on, and we see in that record only what it enables us to see. But of course the mannerist in Laclos implies that one of the things his bundle of letters reveals is the transforming, revealing distortion that fictions perform. We have the consolation of knowing more than the characters do, and we have the added pleasure of sensing the author's opinion as it is manipulated into the succession of letters as an overall arrangement of colliding points of view. That authorial presence is still godlike to the society it creates despite its indirection. It guides people toward just punishments and rewards as it guides us toward conclusions about "One Section of Society" we could not have seen as precisely this by any other means.

CHAPTER FIVE

Mixed Modes: Lyric and Cinematic Narrative

Letter fiction illustrates a peculiar and perhaps extreme influence of presentational method on an imagined flow of events, but every method has its oddities. An epic presenter enables the poet to say different things, invoke a different psychology of participation in the reader, and explore different subjects than a printed journal, a confession, or a history. It is true that the word *mode* usually means, and should mean, something more inclusive than these conventions of presentation or the author's posture toward his audience: it means such formal things as tragedy, expository writing, lyric, or narration; or it means such attitudinal things as humor, the grotesque, or the ironic. We encompass in these terms the broader matters of content, social implication, and complexities of historicity that make questions of form significant. But primarily structural aspects of modes must again claim our attention. They may do so legitimately because at their broadest they reveal at least a limited range of modal distinctions important in their own right. The movement proper to suasive rhetoric is that of speaker-audience relations and imparted or argued ideas and opinions; the movement proper to narrative is that of animated plots whose segments are linked as situational development, character change, and the psychology of linear experience; and so on with lyric, drama, cinema, history writing, biography. Not only given subject matters (if we can presume their independent existence), but ideas, attitudes, and conceptual devices such as dichotomy or polarity will obviously look different under these distinctions. To the rhetorician, for instance, a dichotomy is posed primarily on analytic grounds. Its elements are parts of a greater defining whole, as "anger" and "calm" are parts of "temperament"; or "good" and "evil" are aspects of "ethical categories." Thus the rhetorician "gets the best" of polarity (in Burke's terms) by applying rational controls to it, and he presumably uses that control to mold his audience to opinions similar to his own — assuming in the process that certain situations may be sized up better by polarity than by paradox or by irony, by elegiac feeling, by appeals for sympathy, etc. In melodic structure, to go as far in the opposite direction as possible, dichotomy is a nonanalytic, harmonious division, as in the "apartness" of two voices extending their measured distance in a temporal articulation of changing tones. In the lyric, dichotomy is likely to be rendered as a tensive *pathetic* division that complicates and disturbs a speaker's subjective equilibrium or meditative progress.

Where lyric renders dichotomies as internal complication, music as tonal opposition, and rhetoric as classifications within an analytic logic, narrative and dramatic modes give us personifications, or casts of characters, carrying out their polarity as phased actions and plotted collision — as progressive animate hostility. The passions of interested parties are exploited to move consequential actions, bring about crises, and eventually, in most cases, arrive at some kind of resolution.

As distinct as such modal principles seem when we take them at their broadest, almost no given literary text is pure, nor is a mode ever exactly the same from one writer or text to another. Therein lies our specific problem: to explore the new forms that emerge from the mixing of methods. The subject is not a new one. The entanglements of art and poetry in Lessing's *Laocoon* and in subsequent critics, for instance, suggest several repercussions of formal blends. But traditionally critics have been reluctant to consider the full implications of a *mélange des genres*.[1] The use of symbolic scenery in dramatic presentations, the union of verse and music in song and of song and drama in opera, and, more important from our perspective, the blending in the audience of experiences that overreach the boundaries of the work — these might conceivably have suggested even in Lessing's day a more encompassing theory of mixed forms. If, for instance, in foreshortened narration the reader fills in unrepresented gaps with certain inferences that join the unity of time, presumably a

1. See Gotthold Ephraim Lessing, *Laocoon*, ed. William S. Steel (London: J. M. Dent & Sons, 1930); Irving Babbitt, *The New Laokoon: An Essay on the Confusion of the Arts* (Boston and New York: Houghton Mifflin, 1910).

viewer may also cross from static portraiture to movement in "temporalizing" a painting. An audience may find pictures arranged in sequences calling upon an established sequential logic and suggesting animate illusions — if not strictly on the perceptual level at least at a conceptual level where images carry suggestions of foreshortened temporal spans. Or it may find sequential images evoking eventually partly fixed, spatial totalities. Thus extensions of pictorial meaning in the viewer, under the right conditions, may reach toward narrative beginnings, processes, and endings; and certain summary moments in linear arts may suggest the still design of visual composition. How exactly "process" in the first of these is embodied and imagined when it has no verbal phases is admittedly very problematic; but a storied painting does seemingly have a different impact than a picture whose dynamic stresses are totally governed by its spatial frame.

Though mixed modes find perhaps their most drastic contrast in the joining of pictorial and linear art, the critical problem of mixed modes extends in several directions. Not only may a story be told in still or moving pictures (comic strips, tapestries, cinema), it may also be accompanied by dramatic illustration, description, or melodic elements; or it may be cast into ballad form, epic, or opera. The narrator may put himself before an audience in analytic, histrionic, or historic garb. He may retreat entirely behind embodied or dramatic animations, as in the letter novel. He may ride beside the reader in the "carriage," chattering openly, as Fielding does. Or he may give voice to lyric outbreaks, as Milton does in *Paradise Lost*.

We cannot explore all these mixtures, but some of their implications are suggested by a couple of examples of cross-fertilization — the mixture of verse form and narration, and cinematic narration, one associating music and words, the other temporal and spatial structural principles.

MELODIC NARRATION

Using Jeremy Bentham's simple observation that poetic lines do not run to the right margin as prose lines do, Northrop Frye distinguishes between the formal recurrences of verse and the continuousness of prose works. Frye's point is that, lacking formal lineation, prose is read as though it were largely free of artificial segmentation despite the inwrought ornamentation of certain styles.[2] Grammar determines smaller units, sense the medium-sized ones (paragraphs mainly), and phases or segments of thought and action the larger ones (chapters, books). Thus the units of prose narration are more or less naturalized as segments of meaning, feeling, and action. Poetic measure, on the other hand, is highly microcosmic and artificial. Metrical feet, lines, and stanzas are complexes of repeatable accent and sound pattern much like music. In moving through them sequentially one is also returning formally to similar segments of presentation: each line is a little vehicle of forwarded meaning and action and yet a unit of musical repetition.

But criticism is seldom blessed with distinctions this simple, nor is this one particularly useful without the accompaniment of distinctions in subject matter. Prose narration has its own brands of recurrence, some of them dependent on formal devices, others on subject matters and the experience of readers. For instance, without glancing at the elaborately mannered prose styles of such works as Lyly's *Euphues* or Sidney's *Arcadia* or at other examples of ornamental decoration in prose narrative, we have already observed examples of redundancy in prose fiction (in *Robinson Crusoe* most specifically). Beyond that, every continuous narrative of any dimension finds ways to circle back upon itself in the rhythms of meditation, description, and narration. In the restatement of motifs it practices something akin to musical structure: it retrieves its own internal past and prepares for themes and images that lie ahead down the "crooked corridor" of its teased-out progress. Frye remarks with respect to James's later style, for instance:

> The long sentences . . . are *containing* sentences: all the qualifications and parentheses are fitted in to a pattern, and as one point after another is made, there emerges not a linear process of thought but a simultaneous comprehension. What is explained is turned around and viewed from all aspects, but it is completely there, so to speak, from the beginning. [P. 267]

Though a story is fully expressible only by the linear work of sentences clause upon clause (Frye's "so to speak" at least glances at that necessity), the Jamesian method is complex in its linearity. As J. A. Ward demonstrates in *The Search for Form*, James depends to some extent upon a spatial architecture and a sense of reiterated de-

2. Frye, *Anatomy of Criticism*, pp. 263ff.

sign.[3] Hence as Frye suggests, there emerges in the relative containment or retardation of a complex style not merely a linear process of thought but an overall view of its always combining patterns, "turned around and viewed from all aspects."

When a novelist includes lyric passages in extended stories, he makes use primarily of the lyric's stabilizing of mood or perception in a single dominant tone — elegiac, joyful, ironic. In a comparatively richly inwrought and highly rhythmic language, he establishes gathering points in what otherwise tends to be a discursive, extended, and circumstantial mode. Like the lyricist, he thereby lifts certain moments partly out of the unfinished movement of narrative and suggests a comprehensive attitude toward the work or part of it. Without the assistance of formal lineation, he keeps us "turning back." Thus if verse is always a braking of serial form by the halting edge of the broken margin, verselike or highly rhythmic prose accomplishes a similar effect by directing relatively more attention than average to preceding, parallel phrasal and imagistic units. It "wraps up" each moment more thoroughly in its formal reflexive system, in its contextual references and symbolic patterns, its cadence, and its sound system, all of which draw our attention away from the forwarding of events. From the opposite direction, though metrical feet, poetic lineation, and stanzas are highly recurrent in verse forms, these of course still move according to principles of connectedness and forward logic: a reader merely pauses, he does not stop, at the jagged margin. He returns to labyrinths of interwoven verbal pattern, but he does not circle aimlessly there without advancing in mood, meaning, and psychology.

Blends of melodic and story elements, from a structural viewpoint, may exploit in special ways this tension between the rhythm of formal recurrence and the psychology of narrative forwarding — between the inherent lingering of verse measure and the urge of expectations. A good many of the narrative classics of western literature might be cited as fruitful examples — *The Divine Comedy*; *The Faerie Queene*; romantic narratives such as "The Eve of St. Agnes," *Alastor*, *Prometheus Unbound*, and *The Prelude*; *Paradise Lost*; *Sir Gawain and the Green Knight*; a few of the *Canterbury Tales*; satiric poems such as *Hudibras* and "The Rape of the Lock"; and post-romantic narratives like *The Ring and the Book* and "The Comedian

3. Ward, *The Search for Form.*

as the Letter C." In these and other verse stories, a certain emphasis naturally falls on smaller verbal units and the demands of individual lines, stanzas, or verse paragraphs. This emphasis does not diminish the importance of the narrative stress system — the encounters of antagonistic parties, the principles of concealment and timely information, the witnessing and verifying of actions, the experiential psychology of the reader, and so forth — but the balance between purely formal factors and the flow of events is quite different from what it is in prose narration. Because each line unit of verse narration is composed of measured feet, it contains a little beginning and little ending of its own and a small discernible portion of thought, feeling, or action.[4] There are implications in this for a sociology of literary forms as well as for a psychology of forwarding actions, because by compacting the unit, verse puts its emphasis on those matters that can be so formalized and at one stroke excludes an empirical or observational approach to social realism. Though it is hospitable to wit and its habitual debunking of class pretentions, it is not likely to propose, for instance, a Marxist social epic in rhymed tetrameters or Spenserian stanzas.

The reasons are manifold and lie partly in the incessant small "measuring" of thought and feeling. When after a mock-epic invocation Pope begins the account of Belinda's stolen lock in a tautly compact couplet, for instance, we are implicitly admonished to proceed slowly and to turn back frequently to those associational elements conjured by the returns of rhyme and sound pattern. Each detail, by that reflective movement, generates a high potential for ironic crossfire and symbolic density, as in the couplet,

> Sol through white curtains shot a timorous ray,
> And oped those eyes that must eclipse the day.
>   [1.13–14]

4. Marvin Mudrick suggests in "Character and Event in Fiction," *Yale Review* 50 (1961): 202–18, that the basic unit of fiction is the event, and of verse, the word. But one might question that emphasis since the first organized whole in a poem is the metrical foot and the next, and more significant to a sense of poetic form, is the line: what one makes out of words is lines of poetry. Cf. David Lodge, *Language of Fiction: Essays in Criticism and Verbal Analysis of the English Novel* (London: Routledge and Kegan Paul, 1966), who argues convincingly that critics should pay more attention to the stylistic medium of the novel than they have. My emphasis on the comparative density of poetic language does not conflict with Lodge's axiom that the novelist's medium, too, is language. But it is nonetheless true that we pause less decisively on small units in the flow of prose fiction than we do on lines, images, and rhetorical units in poetry.

The intensification of language by rhythm, alternations of normal syntax, and poetic imagery is aptly served by the size of the units and the "punctuation" of rhyme. Much is happening in such a unit besides the beginning of a chronological chain of events.

As Pope's technique suggests, the condensation of images and the use of metaphor, symbol, and highly patterned parallels causes the complications of the narrative to filter into the individual parts more completely than we could expect in the always forwarding units of prose narration. At the same time, the suggestiveness of the individual verse unit is extended as it looks backward and forward in such a way as to linger over the doing — as the much ado about Belinda is retarded at every stage by the fine definition of the couplets. The "little pictures" of these are too rich to hurry past and too "precious" for a great deal of realistic, circumstantial social observation. In the example above, for instance, the rhythm pauses, and the rhyme sets up a return as well as a forwarding equation. The vowel and consonant patterns interweave a meaning entangled not merely in concrete images but in words as sound-objects. The several tentative stresses and balances ask for a reiterated reading. "Sol" and "shot," "eyes" and "eclipse," "ray" and "day," one entire line and the other, "eyes" and "Sol" together and the shooting and eclipsing together — these are pairings that by sound and rhythmic placement Pope makes us pause on.

The psychology of expectation and retrieval is altered by this dense localization of meaning in units. Revelations come not merely with turns of action and actual information but also with turns of phrase and choices of image. The difference between the novel and poetry in this respect is noted by Albert Cook in *The Meaning of Fiction*:

> Poetry, like philosophy, orders the world, mainly by analogical identification, into an order ideally both concrete and abstract. Fiction . . . is like history, and it combines its usually observational statements on the base of a narrative line. In fiction one statement is not a surprise or a revelation of another, as in poetry; it is merely in sequence; and of a long series of such unsurprising, rather repetitive, statements, each a flash of observation, is the novel composed . . . By this accretion of resembling insights a novel unfolds what Paul Goodman calls its "full expansion of slowly maturing sentences."[5]

On a larger scale, too, as we may see in many of the major works

5. Cook, *The Meaning of Fiction*, p. 91.

listed above, narrative development in verse carries along not merely an action but a framework of interwoven ideas, analogous types, and frequently allegorical levels. It leans toward fantasy, romance, or the supernatural rather than toward politics, property, manners, or household affairs. Belinda's guardian sylph, against the background of epic messengers, collects many echoes; every glittering detail of Pope's description counts for something. Other texts gain their density by being permeated with Platonic verities, a sense of teleology foreshadowed in the moment, elements of the typical and archetypical, the heroic as larger than life, or the representative in general. These things must continuously fill the smaller units and reward the attention they command if every pause at the jagged margin is to be justified. What Erich Auerbach describes as Dante's "figural realism" holds, with some alterations, for much verse narrative in this respect. The world beyond the limits of a given detail or narrative moment, adumbrated in that moment, is "God's design in active fulfillment." In relation to that design (which is not, of course, in every poet specifically God's), "earthly phenomena are on the whole . . . figural, potential, and requiring fulfillment," just as "all the dramas" of Dante's Florentines "are played over again in tremendously concentrated form . . . and in them, seemingly scattered and fragmented, yet actually always as parts within a general plan, the history of Florence, of Italy, and of the world, unfolds."[6] Similarly, in many verse narrations we discover embedded in surfaces, if not indications of the image of "paradise" or some providential control of history, at least a sense of the teleology of the work: we find hieroglyphs of the author's design. Or to put it negatively: the formality and symbolic density of *The Divine Comedy*, *The Faerie Queene*, or *Paradise Lost* would obviously be impossible to sustain in the prose life of a Don Quixote or a Lazarillo de Tormes, the realism of which casts satiric doubt over all devices of elevated style, artifice, or convention. As the reaction of prose realists to romance suggests in the early novel, when a narration risks verse speech or other aspects of the high manner, windmills had better in fact be symbolic giants and not merely corn-grinding machines.

As Pope's nicely compact and witty account of Belinda's eventful day illustrates, an ironic use of the extraordinary, in mock-heroic verse, combines prosaic reality and a sense of portentous design, gain-

6. Auerbach, *Mimesis*, pp. 171, 173.

ing thereby sufficient incongruities to allow each couplet to turn over new comic disproportions. Though Belinda's lock is destined eventually to ascend to the stars escorted by squadrons of supernatural beings, the more ordinary Belinda of the mundane world is less than the parallels with the *Iliad* might lead one to hope. A running comparison with epic figures both heightens and mocks her. Likewise, Chaucer's Sir Topas and Butler's Hudibras would not be so ludicrous if they did not ride forth to the accompaniment of rhythm and rhyme and constant incongruities that spring from a lame and halting verse. In a slightly different combination of formal tautness and linear development, the continuous comparison of dunce-filled London with the archetypes and traditional meanings of Eden in *The Dunciad* both judges the dunces and provides "poetic" substance for the poem. A sense of epic eras past and eschatological realities to come keeps the couplets reasonably charged and at the same time applies a very high ideal of verse revelation to a very low and drowsy subject. The apocalyptic conclusion to the poem comes both as the climax of comic debunking and as a grand view of shrunken ideals. It is prefigured by a tissue of allusions and images throughout that have used the heroic couplet as a deft weapon against pretenders to creative power.

These are instances not merely of the impact of verse units on the stage-by-stage progress of linear form but also of a special sort of narrative conditioned by Christian, Platonist, or chivalric views of things. Those views are in some respects inherently poetic in their love of highly articulate, cross-referenced, and ornamented structures, and while they prevail, most of the major narratives are in verse. They are also poetic in the sense that given instants in a narrative chain can be made the epitomes of a larger order. The intellectual habit of epitomizing is encouraged by a universe that is not only closed and sequentially logical but full of correspondences and parallels. Where the citation of one object or event may easily conjure others typologically related to it and where the historical process itself is rhymed and unitized, readers are conditioned to think in terms of symbolic condensations and constant returns to sources and archetypes. For no novelist, on the other hand, is Dante's figural realism, Milton's view of men's progress toward a restored paradise, Butler's devaluation of the questing knight, or Pope's apocalyptic satire an acceptable way of thinking about a story line.

In verse narration as well, however, the marriage of narrative and melodic elements is sweepingly reconceived between Milton's last great accomplishment in the serious heroic mode and the narratives of the romantics. In his version of the poet's growth in *The Prelude*, for instance, Wordsworth finds one of the difficulties of an auto-biographical mode to be the locating of "types and symbols of eternity" in scenes and incidents of the poet's past. Given the anecdotal nature of the past, how is the poet to justify a rhythmic medium of an intense and exalted kind? How can he transpose from an almost proselike style of personal narration to heightened moments of lyric intensity? Wordsworth's formal solution is not a highly lineated form but a variety of Miltonic paragraph that practices frequent enjambment:

> to the open fields I told
> A prophecy: poetic numbers came
> Spontaneously to clothe in priestly robe
> A renovated spirit singled out,
> Such hope was mine, for holy services.
> My own voice cheered me, and, far more, the mind's
> Internal echo of the imperfect sound;
> To both I listened, drawing from them both
> A cheerful confidence in things to come.
>
> [*The Prelude*, 1.50–58]

The rhythmic speech of Wordsworthian narrative answers to the high spirit of the poet's freedom and his embarkation on the long narrative. His words are not quite a perfect echo of the inner spirit, but they resound the truth of his feeling, rediscovered in the remembered circumstances of his youth. Certain incidents thus prove to be not merely parts of a linear biography of a prosaic kind but transcendent moments that stand apart from pure succession. Though they belong to time and place, they also mark a spiritual enlightenment that recurs and recurs.[7] Hence in their flexible answerability to the demands of meditation, description, narration, and lyric outbreak, Words-

---

7. Though narrative and lyric are combined throughout the history of each, as Christopher Salvesen points out in *The Landscape of Memory: A Study of Wordsworth's Poetry* (Lincoln: University of Nebraska Press, 1965) the rise of the novel contributed to the development of personal history as a literary subject in Wordsworth's manner. It embodied as a form the "flow of time—which one could almost say, was intented to contain it": "The detailed unfolding of a life, the gradual progress of a story which automatically creates a feeling of time, this was something new in the Eighteenth century

worth's blank verse units subordinate formal artifice to logical divisions and to paragraphs of meditation and description, yet are also capable of sufficient eloquence to respond when the poet "comes upon" the symbolic density of certain scenes and incidents. Narrative is placed in the service of a recurrent sublimity. Even when words fail him, as they sometimes do, the memory of an experience may nonetheless remain exalted:

> It was a splendid evening, and my soul
> Once more made trial of her strength, nor lacked
> Aeolian visitations; but the harp
> Was soon defrauded, and the banded host
> Of harmony dispersed in straggling sounds,
> And lastly utter silence! "Be it so;
> Why think of anything but present good?"
>
> [1.94–100]

In sum, a relatively loose account of the poet's growth is well served by a medium that can rise to the occasion, pass from scene to scene with easy transition, or descend to a recognition of prosaic and unfruitful days:

> Sometimes it suits me better to invent
> A tale from my own heart, more near akin
> To my own passions and habitual thoughts;
> Some variegated story, in the main
> Lofty, but the unsubstantial structure melts
> Before the very sun that brightens it,
> Mist into air dissolving! Then a wish,
> My last and favourite aspiration, mounts
> With yearning toward some philosophic song
> Of Truth that cherishes our daily life;
> With meditations passionate from deep
> Recesses in man's heart, immortal verse
> Thoughtfully fitted to the Orphean lyre.
>
> [1.221–33]

The way in which an observation disregards lineation and the poet's mind wanders freely among its wealth of memories and extemporaneous self-analyses indicates the compromise Wordsworth

.... A good deal of literary interest in time was evolved by way of the novel: the representation of time is one of the novel's tastes—just as is circumstantial description and the portrayal of ordinary people and the value of everyday events" (p. 23).

establishes between the loaded symbolic worth of measured lines and the continuousness of proselike observation. His verse is indeed "thoughtfully" fitted to the lyre, which responds to meditations from within and mounts with aspirations into longer units. That *The Prelude*'s overall form is somewhat baggy, however, will not be disputed by anyone who tries to locate a single rhythm in the work or to describe its direction and effect. Whatever else it may do, *The Prelude* obviously does not tell a well-turned, plotted story.

Less compromising to organic storytelling are Wordsworth's shorter narratives and their adjustments of the rival claims of realism and the extraordinary. These are perhaps more typical of romantic lyric narration in general. As Coleridge and Wordsworth insist, respectively, in *Biographia Literaria* and the preface to the *Lyrical Ballads*, the poet must labor at such an adjustment because the techniques of verse and the subjects of one's poems begin a certain distance apart. Wordsworth's task in their collaboration is "to excite a feeling analogous to the supernatural, by awakening the mind and directing it to the loveliness and wonders of the world before us."[8] The "world before us" refers to the strung-out matter of everyday life depressed by custom; it is a world really inhabited by men, who speak in their own language and should continue doing so even in verse. But since such subjects in Wordsworth's view are wonderful underneath, as well as commonplace on, the surface, one of the functions of meter and rhyme is to provide a twist away from custom, to discover what lies beyond our perceptual lethargy. Though a good many of the artifices of previous verse styles must be set aside to make room for a greater degree of realism, then, such things as meter, metaphor, and the native mysteries of the ballad form are indispensable to the reader's awakening to symbolically enriched perception.

My aim, however, is not to explore what happens under the impact of meter to the logic of stories like the Ancient Mariner's or Goody Blake's. (That would require a detailed reading of a number of

8. Samuel Taylor Coleridge, *Biographia Literaria*, in *Selected Poetry and Prose* (New York: Random House, 1951), p. 264. In Peacock's contrasting view, as civilization progresses, facts "become more interesting than fiction" and we mature beyond verse narrative, indeed, beyond verse of virtually any kind. See *Peacock's The Four Ages of Poetry; Shelley's Defence of Poetry*, ed. H. F. B. Brett-Smith (Oxford: Basil Blackwell, 1967).

individual cases.) It is merely to suggest that one way into the uniqueness of verse-narrative blends is to explore the collision between the different formative potentials of verse lineation and narrative's forward leaning. What happens, for instance, to the compromise between story and verse in Tennyson's idyls or Yeats's celtic myths? What modern twist is given to the contest between narrative realism and melodic techniques in extended verse narratives like Wallace Stevens's "The Comedian as the Letter C"?

To take the last instance, the inherent desire of the comedian to be heroic demands of him a highly exalted verse ballooned out with high diction, exotic description, and syntactical arrangements quite distinct from normal usage. But reality concedes much less to Crispin's verse than it does to Wordsworth's comparable autobiographical, anecdotal account of the making of a poet. For Stevens's less exalted poet figure, the only way a prosaic life can be made into poetry is to convert various regions into symbolic landscapes and then, by means of exaggeration and irony, to parody the high style of that translation. Crispin is obliged to say after all that the indisputable reality of one's life *does* mock poetry, and so he is obliged to seek a new way of "turning back" to reflect on what he has hoped and what he has said. If Wordsworthian returns are usually in the interests of a recalled spiritual magnificence and recaptured circumstances, Crispin's are more modest: he ends with a retrospective defense of prosaic circumstance that is so un-Wordsworthian as to turn the poem into a kind of antiprelude — a prelude not to a greater philosophic poem yet to come but, as it turned out for Stevens himself, to several years of virtual silence:

> The world, a turnip once so readily plucked,
> Sacked up and carried overseas, daubed out
> Of its ancient purple, pruned to the fertile main,
> And sown again by the stiffest realist,
> Came reproduced in purple, family font,
> The same insoluble lump. The fatalist
> Stepped in and dropped the chuckling down his craw,
> Without grace or grumble.[9]

As Crispin realizes, the difficulty in formulating a modern theory of poetic fictions is to find a way to treat reality as richly poetic but without adumbrations of ultimate things beautiful and rewarding in

9. Stevens, "The Comedian as the Letter C," *Collected Poems*, p. 45.

themselves — to treat reality without "grace or grumble" as an insoluble, unsymbolic turnip. Nothing lies beyond the moment to be "figured realistically" in it; figural realism is dead. Once past a named fact or an incident, Crispin has no reason to return to it. Yet the odyssey of a hero among sensuous guzzly fruits and "family font," if it is to sustain first one poetic line and then another over a lengthy period, must disclose ever new perceptions of reality, and it must do so in "Seraphic proclamations of the pure / Delivered with a deluging onwardness, muted, mused" (p. 45), a style "perfectly revolved" in "portentous accents" as of old. And so Crispin echoes the pregnantly delayed syntax and enjambment of Wordsworth's cumulative blank verse paragraphs but counterchecks their grandeur by sharp stylistic drops and works toward a "haphazard denouement." The "stiffest realist" becomes an observer not only of reality but of the frictional and explosive qualities of words and the summary debunking that the poet must crowd into the juxtaposition of two such incomparable words as the Latinate "insoluble" and the Scandinavian "lump." Mixing short and long sentences effectively and playing both against the frequently violated line, Stevens constantly shifts between disappointed expectation and resigned satisfaction. The verse thus denies all the higher ranges it seems to seek but offers ironic rewards nonetheless. It is rhythmic speech that moves relentlessly past its grand aspirations to recognition of Crispin's limits. As the audience of the man with the blue guitar insists, poetry

> Exceeding music must take the place
> Of empty heaven and its hymns,
>
> Ourselves in poetry must take their place
> Even in the chattering of your guitar.
> [P. 167]

The search for a melodic narrative free of myth and therefore without the reinforcement of symbolic or figural detail has been one of the continuing tasks of modern verse narrative. We see that search carried out with spectacular success in Yeats — not in the longer romantic poems of the early Yeats so much as in the later verse. Examples are worth dwelling on because we can observe in Yeats's case the distinct impact of song not only on narration but on theme and meaning. As a lyric narrator, Yeats typically searches for the most critical moments of the historical process and discards the rest, just as ballads compress incidents and bury most of the motives and details. As Yeats practices it, then, the art of balladic and songlike lyrics makes strategic use of a very few concrete details, sometimes converting them into general statements, more often making them concrete illustrations of larger mythic or symbolic patterns.

"Sailing to Byzantium" and "Two Songs from a Play" will illustrate the point. The two songs, which begin and end the one-act play *The Resurrection*, work a fine compression of dramatic ritual, mythic narrative, symbolic allusion, melodic form, and philosophic axiom:

I

I saw a staring virgin stand
Where holy Dionysus died,
And tear the heart out of his side,
And lay the heart upon her hand
And bear that beating heart away;
And then did all the Muses sing
Of Magnus Annus at the spring,
As though God's death were but a play.

Another Troy must rise and set,
Another lineage feed the crow,
Another Argo's painted prow
Drive to a flashier bauble yet.
The Roman Empire stood appalled:
It dropped the reigns of peace and war
When that fierce virgin and her Star
Out of the fabulous darkness called.

II

In pity for man's darkening thought
He walked that room and issued thence
In Galilean turbulence;
The Babylonian starlight brought
A fabulous, formless darkness in;
Odour of blood when Christ was slain
Made all Platonic tolerance vain
And vain all Doric discipline.

Everything that man esteems
Endures a moment or a day.
Love's pleasure drives his love away,
The painter's brush consumes his dreams;
The herald's cry, the soldier's tread

Exhaust his glory and his might:
Whatever flames upon the night
Man's own resinous heart has fed.[10]

As is well known, Yeats's view of history in *A Vision* and elsewhere
imposes a schematic theory of cycles upon it that in effect gives him
"metaphors for poetry." The two songs in their blend of lyric and
narrative obviously owe a good deal to this view, which enables Yeats
to think of the death of gods and human catastrophes not as extended narrative or linear sequences merely but as analogous, recurrent events possessed of symbolic dimensions appropriate to
melodic form. In Yeats's view, tragedies like that of Dionysus are enacted again and again in various historical equivalences and balances
and are readable as a system of organic correspondences, returns, and
echoes. As Athena takes the heart of the dying god to Zeus, her violence is converted into tragic ritual by that recurrence as well as by
the dignity of her bearing and the miracle of the still-beating heart.
While the grandeur of the vision is still fresh, the movement of history
itself seems invigorating, and the verbs receive dominant attention
("tear," "lay," and "bear"). The moment is infused with the high
drama of the gods and their perspective. As the word *play* suggests, if
one could read the incident solely in terms of the virgin's ritual it
would indeed be a grand, though tragic, spectacle; narrative matter
would be convertible completely to poetic, melodic, and dancelike art.

But the "as though" is cautionary and suggests that history perhaps only aspires to the condition of poetic ritual — as those who
would advise tragic resignation can only aspire to the condition of
dispassionate witnesses in "Lapis Lazuli." Unless the spectator has a
station safely above the cataclysm, he may be appalled by a history so
steeped in blood, so recurrently awful. Hence though the repetitions
of the next stanza are parallel to those of the first, the cycles it refers
to suggest a rather tired monotony: the old stories ultimately go nowhere. One needs a firmer sense of significant form than the same old
tragic tales afford in their dragged-out tests of endurance. Hence if in
the first song the events of history are found to be compressible to a
few symbolic moments suitable to melodic art — yet unable to
suggest an intelligible end toward which the historical process moves

10. W. B. Yeats, "Two Songs from a Play," *The Collected Poems* (New York:
Macmillan, 1954), p. 210.

— in the second song Yeats focuses on another subject, not the renewal of kindred cycles but time's costly passage. In life as opposed to song — whatever the grandeur of historical cycles may be — each instant flares and burns itself out. In place of the heart that Dionysus yields to the virgin, the poet finds the merely human heart; in place of the grand destruction of civilizations, he remembers the loss of "Everything that man esteems." The herald whom we might expect to announce the coming of something of great moment merely exhausts his meaning and his glory in the instant of his heralding; the soldier does not compile fame as a monument to his heroic endurance, he expends himself in action. Let Astrea, Athena, and Mary be as parallel as the great years decree, then, it makes little difference to mortal lovers, painters, or soldiers.

Yet this flaring, too, is eminently suitable to lyric narrative. We are prepared for the sinking rhythm and weariness of the last stanza by the boiling down of the narrative to the essence of monotonous consumings and to a reading of startling events as material for a "pathetic" elegy. A quieter tone is evident in the second stanza, in which all the past-tense narrative gives way to several generalizations. These encompass and freeze historical movement in typical images despite history's own essentially senseless movement. The energy of the verbs becomes self-canceling; or to put it differently, the verbs are so encompassed by abstract pattern and law that they portray a universally futile but impressive human effort. In the abstraction of "everything," all moments of all narratives are poised as though no longer moving, in an intransitive lyric attitude beyond historical outcome. Love's pleasure, as an act, drives love itself away; it consumes the essence of love. But it leaves behind an essence of lyric resignation. Men have a perpetually failing endurance, a perpetually consuming drive, and it is not surprising that the key verb — which occupies a position parallel to "tear," "lay," and "bear" — is "exhaust." The balance of energy and weariness in the final lines in effect repeats the structure of the poem and sums it up as expended energy. From this perspective Yeats is justified in converting a very long narrative into a very short song because historical cycles sweep the apparent individuations of history and a multitude of narrative careers into a single pattern. Without depending on older eschatological theories, Yeats discovers a fatality with which he can imbue any amount of illustrative details; the stuff of completion myths or supreme fictions is found in every common act. Merely to cite human activity is therefore to see its representative, symbolic density. If the lyric can devour the stories of dying gods, heralds, and lovers and reduce them to a single image, one has no need of the details of novels and epics. The resinous heart and the all-inclusive generality of "whatever" say it all: motion is summed up in the flaming heart consuming itself. All anecdotes are merely resin for a lyric flame.

Thus, paradoxically, if history is basically recurrent cataclysm, a lyric is its transfiguration into cathartic expression. Songs reconstitute history in their own verbal universes, and each has its principles of recurrence — word, rhythm, and image. Events are ordered in the poem not by history's own patterns finally but by meaningful axioms. Singing is itself the poet's consolation, as in "Lapis Lazuli" the accomplished fingers of the musician accompany the destruction spread out below the wise observer. Though we slight the acievement of that consolation somewhat in reducing it to technical terms, technique is clearly part of it — the modulation of clipped *t*s and surrounding vowel patterns, the assonance and rhyme, the blend of general statements and concrete illustrations, and the superb variation of rhythm in several balanced and symmetrical lines. Perhaps as important as any of these is the extraordinary associational complexity of Yeats's metaphors, and in this, technique and historical vision fuse. (One association, for instance, is that of men and gods, who understand one another's suffering and share one another's glory. Christ in pity for the human tragedy walks a room like any anxious leader in meditation and issues in a localized, historical action, in a "Galilean" turbulence.) But mainly, the general pattern is so embedded in incident, as the whole in its parts, that the burden of "everything" is felt in each historical detail. What anecdotes would string out, symbols gather together: times and places become fusions of the particular and the general, as "Babylonian" and "Galilean" designate not merely particular times and cultures but recurrent phases of the historical process. A finer balance of narrative incident, symbolic detail, and philosophic principle — and a finer blend of melodic and narrative elements — would be difficult to imagine.

In "Sailing to Byzantium" Yeats does something similar with the tension between a potentially protracted narrative and the rhythmic intensity and brevity of the lyric. In this case, however, the contrast between the extended processes of the narrator's sketched-in lifetime and the act of singing is a more explicit concern of the poem. It is also turned around by a paradox: while the life of the singer drags on but must soon end, the song itself is brief but will potentially last forever. The narrator's implicit "story" is told very briefly: he has sailed from a sensual country inhospitable to old men to Byzantium, the holy city of art. In the assumed present of the poem, on the verge of entering the city, he addresses the muses and asks them to rescue him from the linear world of breeding, growing, dying organisms and all their naturalistic stories. He asks to be drawn into the sphere of timeless artifice and fixed metallic art. By gathering him into that sphere, the sages who stand in God's holy fire, the masters of song, will liberate him from the mechanism of consequences and outcomes: they will liberate him from the condition of narrative and fix him in the condition of song. The song, and the singer who resides in it as its voice, would then stand outside ordinary bodily forms — as the poem "Sailing to Byzantium" in fact stands apart from those particular, successive times to which it sings. The subject of the poet's song would still be historical narrative and prophetic foresight — "what is past, or passing, or to come" — but the songs themselves would transcend their subjects as the melodic products of the soul.

It is by transformation into lyricists that old men in Yeats's view keep from becoming merely tattered coats upon sticks caught up in the rigorous logic of time. Where the two songs of the play find all human ideals consumed in their very enactment, then, "Sailing to Byzantium" would exempt at least the act of singing, and in a sense the singer. Lyrics are not consumed in the performance but are always renewable — tempered, not devoured, by "fire." Not accidental to this end, their materials are not prosaic or unique facts but recurrent images permeated with the rhythmic skill of the lyricist: form so dominates nature that nature — largely generalized and symbolic to begin with — ceases to be biological in the precincts of the poem and becomes hammered gold. The jagged right margin where rhymes gather and rhythms find their defining boundaries guarantees the shapeliness and durability of the song.

It would obviously not be wise to suggest from these somewhat special instances that lyrics always wish to "sail to Byzantium," into some mythic city that carries a historical name but none of the drawbacks of real temporality. When we think of larger and especially occasional lyric narratives, like Andrew Marvell's Cromwell poems and "Upon Appleton House" or Yeats's "Easter, 1916," it is clear that narrative songs and verse stories may also have discursive and rhetorical elements and can be committed to accounts of actual historical events, to the principles of the anecdote. As one part of Wallace Stevens insists,

> We keep coming back and coming back
> To the real: to the hotel instead of the hymns
> That fall upon it out of the wind. We seek
>
> The poem of pure reality, untouched
> By trope or deviation, straight to the word,
> Straight to the transfixing object, to the object
>
> At the exactest point at which it is itself,
> Transfixing by being purely what it is.
> [*Collected Poems*, p. 471]

A poem is after all surrounded with "the exquisite environment of fact. The final poem will be the poem of fact in the language of fact. But it will be the poem of fact not realized before" (*Opus Post-humous*, p. 164). It cannot always condense reality in a melodic nut-shell or seek a purity of form beyond the condition of prosaic anec-dote.

Yet by virtue of its rhythmic compression and commitment to poetic language, the lyric does inherently stress the microcosmic unit and does raise its linear details line by line into the relative perfection of melodic form. As Stevens remarks from the other side of his habitual ambivalence:

> Poetry is the subject of the poem,
> From this the poem issues and
>
> To this returns. Between the two,
> Between issue and return, there is
>
> An absence in reality,
> Things as they are.
> [*Collected Poems*, p. 176]

Thus despite its absence in reality, a poem seeks to remain relatively self-enclosed, a cosmos to itself; it is its own beginning and ending and points to the idea of a bounded universe:

The poem refreshes life so that we share,
For a moment, the first idea . . . . It satisfies
Belief in an immaculate beginning

And sends us, winged by an unconscious will,
To an immaculate end.
                              [*Collected Poems*, p. 382]

From another direction but with similar results, Robert Frost fully
appreciates the difference between the poet's and the novelist's
responsibility to historical reality:

> When in doubt there is always form for us to go on with. Anyone who
> has achieved the least form to be sure of it, is lost to the larger
> excruciations. ... The artist, the poet, might be expected to be the most
> aware of such assurance, but it is really everybody's sanity to feel it and
> live by it. ...
>   The background is hugeness and confusion shading away from where
> we stand into black and utter chaos; and against the background any
> small man-made figure of order and concentration. What pleasanter
> than that this should be so? Unless we are novelists or economists we
> don't worry about this confusion.[11]

This contrast in Stevens, Frost, and others between the necessary
confusions of realism and the concentration of small, formally excellent enterprises like an "idea, a picture, a poem," is largely a
modern contrast that has no doubt been fostered to some extent by
the modal differences between the documentary novel and poetry; but
faith in the special therapy of song and its capacity to transfigure
"larger excruciations" is by no means new. Milton illustrates that as
frequently and as well as anyone. For him, songlike celebrations often
coincide with the emergence of well-tested heroes from protracted
narrative-dramatic suffering into the harbored protection of divine
realities, the only appropriate response to which is melody or hymn.
The chief difference between Frost's modern assumption of a huge
and confusing background and Milton's view is that history itself for
Milton brings about the conditions of divine celebration. Eventually
it will fix those who deserve it in a state of constant poetry. A
visionary poem is not so much a self-contained order apart from
reality as a prefiguration of a state to come, a state of high intensity
conducive to those hymnal responses that angels and saints make
through eternity. Hence for Milton, the closer the poet approaches

11. Frost, *Selected Letters*, pp. 418–19.

divine realities the closer to lyric and hymn he comes; and this tendency to match vision and genre reinforces the impression we get from the verse narrative tradition that the melodic element of verse leans toward the self-sufficiency of moments, while the dynamics of narrative involve us always in an anxious movement through factual matter and realistic anecdote toward a distant denouement.

The contrast can be seen at several critical moments in Milton, not only in the initial generation of narrative drama and of history but also in the unfolding of creation, where a productive logos sets in narrative motion an answer to Satan's destructive narrative of chance and adventure. In observing the works of divine creativity, the angels and the recording scripture must move imaginatively backward against the flow of events to the source, which they celebrate in choral oratory. Angelic appreciation is thus devoted not merely to separate things unfolding punctually in history but also to the revelation which the creation collectively makes of its origins.[12] Even a narrative is therefore both a recitation of God's historical phases and a means of realizing, within them, a transcendent reality. Nearly all the narrator's lyric outbreaks and Adam's hymns of celebration come at moments of clarification (or appeals for it) when divine reality is discovered with special cogency in events of time and place.

But pure songs in the exalted sense of Milton's choral celebrations are not easily come by unless one is an angel. If song is responsive to transcendent stages of consciousness, narrative and dramatic presentation are responsive to segments of unforeshortened actions. The narrative-dramatic Milton, as opposed to the lyricist and hymnist, presents a flow of events not capable at every point of releasing the rhythmic fervor and enthusiasm of the beneficiary of epiphanies — though it may falsely stimulate Satan or Eve to unjustified flights of enthusiasm. At its best, dramatic narrative precedes a liberating discovery of some sort; at its worst it leads further and further into labyrinths, the archetype of which is the torturous landscape of Hell. The anxious debate in Pandaemonium over what to do next — how to construct a plot that will carry the fallen angels to a denouement they can live with — is obviously incompatible with celestial hymnody.

In the psychology of mixed verse narration, concentration and cathartic release from anxieties are typical products of melodic units.

12. See *Paradise Lost* 7.180ff., 252ff., 557-73.

In thematic matters, verse lineation has other repercussions. In this case the compression of verse transforms borrowings from the realm of expository reason and general statement into "pathetic" or melodic moods. Whereas in prose fiction a theme rides on the extended details of an articulate development and recurs at scattered intervals — often with explicit comment from the storyteller — a lyric theme, as Yeats's "Two Songs" illustrates, is likely to be more intensively registered as personal feeling. It is a way of giving the consciousness something to seize upon as the poem realizes "momentously" its single state or mood. In other respects, themes are singularly unaggressive in melodic handling: they look momentarily outward and carry a rhetorical or educational aspect, but they also direct us firmly back to the text in that same self-reflective complexity that metrical regularity and formal recurrence have. As Frost suggests, poets do not expect to wade into a social problem as the novelist does: "We are afraid it might prove too much for us and our blend of democratic-republican-socialist-communist-anarchist party" (*Selected Letters*, p. 419). Though themes in prose fiction may make the same round trip back to the text, they tend to go much further roundabout through mimetic detail; they thread their way into an outer world more exactly like the world in which the reader and author dwell. Hence realism's proximity to the details of experience suggests active theses and propositions for the conduct of life and manners.[13]

In brief, then, the poet who wishes melody to prevail over narrative formally blocks the discursive march of consciousness through the extension of the story and, more completely than the novelist, seals off approaches to extended experience. In the lyric moments of the novel, the narrator brakes that march to allow some of the mood and tonal dimensions of melody to register; in verse proper, most

13. From another direction, Northrop Frye suggests the following distinctions with respect to themes in drama, fiction, and lyric: "We said that the drama was an external and the lyric an internal mimesis of sound and imagery, both genres avoiding the mimesis of direct address. . . . Drama tends to be fictional and the lyric an internal mimesis of sound and imagery, both genres avoiding the mimesis of direct address. . . . Drama tends to be fictional and the lyric a thematic mode. . . . Purely narrative poems, being fictions, will, if episodic, correspond to the species of drama; if continuous, to the species of prose fiction to be examined later" (*Anatomy of Criticism*, p. 293). The difficulty with too neat a distinction, as Frye realizes, is that so many poems combine narrative, dramatic, lyric, and thematic elements. But in general, narrative is characterized by connectedness of action, and lyric by songlike technique and a consistent internal "I."

varieties of lyric, hymn, panegyric, the charm, and the elegy contain their own tonal bent and characteristic strategies, to which the narrative element is a subordinate, overlapping principle of connectedness. In prose lyricism, the pressure of the dramatic and narrative elements remains primary, but some of the effects of lyricism take form as stylistic parallels, formal units, thickened imagery, and the subjective movement of meditation or personal outcry; in verse, the extension of lyric feeling through details employs the progress of a story as a subject to arouse, sustain, and conclude an affective curve, as something to fix upon. The "story" in a lyric becomes thereby a correlative of a more central subject, the speaker's internal meditative and emotional career, as Wordsworth's Lucy and Matthew poems, for instance, use narrative details to generate a sense of lyric benediction. The details of the narrative are key symbolic objects and situations bold enough in outline and dense enough in significance to carry emotional weight.

CINEMATIC NARRATIVE

When we turn from verse or melodic narrative to narration by pictures, the theoretical implications of modal blends multiply. The principles of visual composition, as Lessing realized, are quite different from those of language or music, yet these three arts and more are combined in film-making. In fact, as is well recognized, the alliances that movies have with various arts include not only photography but costuming, scenery, architecture, and sculpture among the visual and spatial arts, and not only storytelling and music but stage drama, dance, and documentary history among principally temporal arts. Where the frame of a linear art is its beginning and ending and the frame of a pictorial art is its spatial edge, the frame of a movie is both a temporal limit and a bounded screen. The blending of these in the devices of film technology alters their usual components profoundly.

A slow-motion or frozen shot, for instance (as at the conclusions of François Truffaut's *The 400 Blows*, George Roy Hill's *Butch Cassidy and the Sundance Kid*, and Michelangelo Antonioni's *Zabriskie Point*), often calls special attention to the spatial framework at precisely the moment when great stress is also falling on the temporal crises of the story. A change of pace in projection draws us part way out of the psychology of moving or dramatic form and suggests the contemplative distance and detachment of a picture. We become aware simultaneously of the apparatus of scenery, actors, and color, and of composition, story, and plot. Movement itself becomes ballet-like; each phase is composed and each position comparatively portentous. Yet instant by instant the composition on the screen also continues to alter; the story goes on. Objects and changing poses and gestures are revealed not only in their visual artistry but in their functions, as the hinges of a plot.

The results of this mixing of linear and pictorial arts are paradoxical if we come to them from either art separately. In the slow-motion projection of high-impact scenes (like the ambushing of Clyde in *Bonnie and Clyde* and the gunplay of *Showdown at O.K. Corral* in the television "documentary" series "Appointment with Destiny"), altered pace intensifies realism. It registers more fiercely the violence of key events on audiences somewhat jaded with violence — for whom a mere bullet in the stomach and a gradual sinking to the ground is not sufficient to register a climax. (At normal pace a visual climax is quickly and inarticulately over; it lacks the verbal power of, say, Shakespearean tragedy, which memorializes the instant and weaves its significance into the fabric of the drama as a whole.) Yet the added exposure that slow motion gives to the raw facts of a crisis is also added time to translate event into meaning, impact into symbolic visual sensation. In the reiterated blowing up of the desert mansion in Antonioni's *Zabriskie Point*, for instance, item after item of an affluent civilization — wardrobes, food, parts of household appliances and equipment — float lazily past the camera. The repeated bright exposive colors and the dreamlike pace of the scene transform realism into a kind of visual ceremony or dance of objects; the violence is ritualized, cadenced, and cathartic. (Though the movie in some respects is an ineffective and uncritical portrayal of self-indulgent emotions, its effect even on sympathizers with its violence might be an expending, vicariously, of sadistic impulses.) The tone and impact of a rawness so obviously staged is quite different from the realism of pictures like *The Hospital*, Andrzej Wajda's *Ashes and Diamonds,* Robert Bresson's *Diary of a Country Priest*, Roberto Rosellini's *Rome, Open City,* or Louis Buñuel's *The Young and the Damned*, which offer no break in our entrancement in the narration and no obvious betrayals of technique.

A still or frozen frame is likewise odd enough as a device to call special attention to the cinematic balance of pictorial composition and movement. Though obviously not the kind of picture that Lessing and Babbitt have in mind in their discussions of *mélange des genres* and *transpositions d'art*, a still photograph in a movie is more than a fixed representation and more than a normal element of a progressing story. In the context of a movie's linear development, it suggests a memorializing of a segment of action as though it were being placed in an album or museum. Thus stop-motion both breaks and capitalizes upon the identification that viewers feel with characters within the stressful flow of a plot — where people are imperiled, learn, grow, and fail. A completely stalled action, as in the old-looking sepia photographs of *Butch Cassidy*, throws the entire incident into finished, distant history. In moving quickly from the present tense to the preterit, it puts the signature of the director or narrator on the photograph. It becomes something like documentary evidence which a viewer can seize as representative or symbolic, the director's decision to hold an image being in some ways a technological equivalent to the mind's act of abstracting from reality some imagistic fragment to pull into its special realm of cogitation. Something further happens as well, something akin to mannerism: as in the use of slow motion, as we are handed the albumlike evidence of a past event we are made more than ever aware of the illusion and the fiction. Though an event thus historicized seems true enough and we may lend it some of the credence we are willing to give old pictures, the sudden prominence of technique exposes the trick of making actors resemble legendary people. In *Butch Cassidy*, for instance, we see not simply two gunmen in their last stand but two actors fixed in their poses — resembling in fact the previews of coming attractions we may have seen in the showcase outside. They are thus caught in an ambiguous state that emphasizes both the story the film tells and the art with which it tells it — its name actors, its director, its musical accompaniment. A concluding frozen shot virtually ushers us back out of the theater to reminisce over the showcase, now, however, informed by plot sequences that put emotion and significance into isolatable scenes. The cooperation of fixed and momentous art, and the utter transformation of each in the blend, could not be more dramatically illustrated.

That the cinema's combination of pictorial techniques and linear storytelling (with all its devices of changed pace, juxtaposition, foreshortening, and scene changing) is unique to the mechanism of pro-

jected celluloid images is even clearer if we think of the impact of new
techniques in the history of cinema or of kinds of narrative pictures
that depend on other techniques of presentation. For example, events
like the introduction of color into a black and white medium and of
sound into a silent medium have at one point or another increased
the impact of cinema technology. Having grown used to one form of
film, the audience finds the introduction of another startling. Thus
when color was originally introduced in films, it heightened the shock
of reality and pointed up the usefulness of black and white for a kind
of silhouette show. (Without color the explosion of *Zabriskie Point*
would gain in simplicity and contrast but lose in tonal richness and
visual sensation.) Having grown used to normal speed in projection,
we are more likely to notice that a speeding up of motion suggests the
abstraction of pure comedy; a slowing down suggests idealized dignity — of elegiac, lyric, or honorific poses, for instance. The adding
of color and sound to these shifts in speed emphasizes the pluralistic,
adjectival, qualitative existence of objects and places, which in their
colored surfaces radiate their own tones, compose less easily around a
unity, and in general pull in the individualistic directions that a fuller
presentation of textures and sounds demands. (One thinks especially
of Federico Fellini's use of color in this regard.) Or to shift ground a
bit and think of other modes of picture narration: while celluloid
projection leaves very small gaps between pictures, Victorian narrative paintings leave very large ones. Whereas the eye alone (except
perhaps in overlaid images or in transitions from one sequence to
another) takes care of cinema gaps, which are flashed at sufficient
speed to give the illusion of simple movement, we require careful
inferential observation and imagination to bridge the gaps of tapestry or oil sequences. Here again we find a presentational method
governing the psychology of viewing. While in narrative pictures the
tempo of viewing is slow and is conditioned by a good deal of retreating and advancing, in movie watching the by-play of mind, the
regroupings, and the associating of one image with another is both
rapid and rigorously chained to forward advancement. (It would be
even if one had his hand on the projector and could stop it or rewind
at will, as is often done in television replays.) In still another method,
in hieroglyphs and pictures juxtaposed with commentary (as in em-
blem books), some of the inferential steps are filled in for us by explicit labels and verbal narration. Obviously, a different relation ob-

tains in such a mode between linear movement and aphoristic or philosophic matter, or between concrete movement and controlling idea.

Actually, behind the movement of any of these picture-narrative logics — movies, and pictures with or without commentary — we may find a single idea that happens merely to be broken into analytic or expressive stages. In that case, the final act of understanding, the true continuity, lies in the construction of a central, general thesis atop an inferential process. But in a mode whose narrative gaps are filled with inference or general statement, we come to that idea more quickly and entertain it more confidently than in a mode dominated by mimetic detail and drama. Where the continuity is that of a dramatic story, the formal principle of our movement lies in a psychology of crises and resolutions that cannot be abridged, that follows a mechanism of continuous action and reaction. In any event, the mode of thought and experience, to repeat, depends on the method of presentation.

Examples from other, nonvisual arts could also be cited. The moment we try to imagine the music of Bach or Mozart on the instruments of first-century Rome, or the poems of Wallace Stevens in the language of the Sioux, we realize that meaningful form depends on the instruments we have to deliver it. The vocal cords of an average singer cannot deliver the meaning or an aria from *La Bohème*. Of all the modes of presentation that one could explore, however, we are seldom so forcefully aware either of blended techniques or of the impact of presentation as we are in the movies, not only because of historically startling changes in film technology but also because we have grown used to seeing the components of picture narration separately; coming into a world already dominated by novels, plays, paintings, dance, and music, the cinema has grown up under their influence and taken advantage of, or suffered from, our awareness of its theft of old devices. Having been exposed to stage dialogue, for instance, we are keenly aware of how it is transformed by the technique of isolated focus and close-up under the camera's eye. The divisions and transitions, the exposition, rising actions, crises, and gradual unfoldings of information that are native to the stage and to fiction are also part of the cinema's linear form — along with such things as expectation, peripeteia, anagnorisis, resolution, and ironies generated by momentary ignorance. But music and still art alter these so completely in cinema that we are pressed to explain what the transformed blend signifies. Whereas melodic or verse narration qualifies its mixed elements by the special effects of measure — by the braking of dramatic continuity in the arbitrary device of metrical lines — movies qualify them by visual juxtaposition, curve and line, lighting, costuming, and foreground and background arrangements, all of which require a quite different structural language than we use to describe other kinds of linear narration. They require, for instance, a language of visual subordination and coordination — periphery and center, higher and lower, darker and brighter, line and color, downward and upward angles, medium- and close-range focus. In the matter of transitions alone, to take just one aspect of narrative jointure, the cinema's form of punctuation — straight cuts, dissolves, wipes, fades, turnovers, and the like — obviously makes for connectives quite different from the *then*s, *when*s, *however*s, and *yet*s of verbal narrative. Because pictures in themselves are mute, they make only implicit, undirected, and silent transferals of attention from broader to narrower subjects, from foreground to background, or from face to face. Without assistance from language, they would be devoid of abstract foreshortening, of verb tenses, and the logic of such constructions as "If X, then Y." Hence, visual art as such has nothing that could be called pace or verb complexes. Though the cinema may import these directly from language, it is difficult to find strictly visual equivalents for those layers of the past that in language are signaled automatically by pluperfect, past, and continuing past tenses, or by future systems such as *will be* or *will have been*. Nothing visual like sepia or soft focus quite takes the place of a verbal narrative's constantly interwoven degrees of pastness and variously dramatic and foreshortened perspectives on it. A picture in itself foreshortens space, not time; it speaks of an eternal now before us, not *then* or *as if* or *might have been*. (A cinematic equivalent to "To His Coy Mistress" would have to be cast in terms not of argument or philosophic statement, for instance, but of physical proximity, gesture, and express passion.) Going from one image to another or juxtaposing images simultaneously does not give us equivalents to prepositional phrases, subordinate clauses, adjectival modifiers, participles, periodic sentences, poetic rhythms, symbolic sounds — nor any syntax so precisely complex in its parallelism and placement of elements as, say, that of a John Donne meditation or an essay by Sir

Thomas Browne. And of course film juxtaposition as such has no punctuation quite so conventional as the comma, the semicolon, the colon, the dash, the parenthesis, or the period, though comparable effects are sometimes possible.

There are other contrasts as well. A strictly verbal story without the effects of camera and projector gives us characters, named identities, institutions, and places, upon which we fix a certain sympathy and judgment directed by the explicit guidance of the author and his summarizable generalizations. In novels, recognizable characters are set in motion at various rates of growth and change, accompanied by a constantly altering stream of psychological effects (fear, exhilaration, nostalgia, anxiety, hope, and so forth); yet, though things change, the names they bear remain the same. A verbal and intellectual control is exercised over reality that a camera does not inherently have. A word falls into place in the logic and grammar of sentences; by the very act of seizing upon something, it pulls what it names into that stable world of the dictionary where words are chained to contents — if not forever, at least with a certain show of tenacity. In that world, much of the movement and circumstantial, tactile uproar of a real lion is purged from the word *lion*, enthroned in its alphabetical place or its grammatical position.

These properties of words may not be entirely avoided in a moving picture of a lion, but the camera's view of things renders something less categorical and more unique. The typicality of textured and tangible objects is less able to dominate the flow of changing real presences. Films thus add to narration — or may add to narration — the impact of the unnamable and subtract some of the controls of grammar; they may add the mutely pictorial beauty or stark reality of objects and the inarticulate sensation of change as a camera reports it. A movie like *The Last Picture Show*, for instance, intentionally stresses the bare, the inarticulate, and the inexpressible as part of its emphasis on bleak loneliness and shabbiness; neither the poetry of Keats nor the romances of Hollywood, reported in fragments in the classroom and the local run-down theater of the movie, stand up by comparison to the plain unadulterated truth the camera shows us.

When we remember how much even the most realistic novelist stresses the typicality of his characters, as, say, James's Daisy Millers and Henrietta Stackpoles, and how well the verbal narrator is able to indicate in context that such people represent categories of manners

and moral deportment, we are struck with the particularity and muteness of certain screen images — Antonioni's Monica Vitti against the
backdrop of industry in *The Red Desert*, for instance. A series of pictures such as Antonioni's may suggest a kind of mute vertigo, or by
its control over the duration of an image give us a parade of fleeting,
partially misunderstood clues, people, and objects in dazzling abundance. It may present distorted views of mirrored and remirrored
things, half-glimpsed connections, the agitation of rapid motion
toward disaster — all of these legitimately where they might be in-
tolerable in printed equivalents. The uncertainties and doubts of mute
objects and silent actions may be further reinforced by the viewer's
placement almost within the pictorial world: a large screen envelops
its audience more completely than a book on the table before us, detached as it is from the reader and registering its signs and symbols
purely in the mind. The tactile matter of pictures thus comes to us
uninterpreted, as a simulated physical presence implemented by
sounds that seem to stem from the objects themselves. A novel could
tell us of Monica Vitti's helplessness in the face of loud machinery,
sharp whistles, oozing industrial waste, massive walls, and sulfurous
smoke, and it could add many things that visualization misses; but
neither it nor a stage play could allow these things to dominate the
audience quite as they do her: the verbal citation of a shrill noise does
not pierce the ears; the description of a color does not assault the eye.
If we have come to seek ever more violent sensations in the popular
arts, it is no doubt partly attributable to the differing strengths and
weaknesses of the media. Action pictures (from the comic strips to the
cinema) can exploit the drama of stories without care for the interpretive powers of language, and they can exploit the vividness of pictorial arts without care for composition.

At their best, however, movies combine the powers of language narration and the impact of visual and spatial arrangement. Even though it
cannot translate novels directly into films, this blend, when well
managed, has its advantages and leads us to ponder its special
resources.

What kind of connections do they permit between setting and
plotted action, for instance? On the stage, where the focus is steadily
on foreground actors, a visual component that does not move and
talk is very secondary. Only those props and scenic elements that are
handled and verbalized figure very prominently in the logic of the

dramatic progression. In prose narrative, as Thomas Hardy illustrates so often and so well, a setting can be brought into the causal chain of the narration in a constant interweaving of circumstantial surroundings and human motive. Thus when Hardy combines description and narration, he does not present merely one item after another, all of equal importance, but integrates each aspect of the heath or woodland with tone and thematic statement. Nature becomes part of the dramatic cast, part of the forces working with or against the courses that characters wish to take. To articulate that scenic field, Hardy subordinates some items and joins others coordinately, connects the present with the past, and offers interpretive views of the whole by drawing away in the perspective of abstract statement.

Sacrificing many of these explicit verbal controls and yet passing beyond the drama's use of scene, filmic description uses a combination of focus, sequence, language, and spatial relationships to interweave circumstance and action. The camera collects items as mute juxtapositions and sequences but not in the quiescent way the stage does. Its objects may intrude forcefully upon our attention by the simple fact that the camera fills the screen with them and for the moment gives us nothing else to see, or centralizes some object for an instant among a flow of other items that await their turn. Though particularizing and generalizing may be limited to what closeness or distance, narrow or broad scope can suggest, even a mute backdrop may assume momentary importance by these means. By comparison, the number of elements that a stage can compose is relatively limited: despite the advantage of its three dimensions, it cannot include large crowds, background panoramas, the great outdoors, or overlapping images and fade-outs (though in recent mixed-media presentations it has added cinema and slides to its devices). The matter of timing is also crucial. Novelistic scenes are always sketched in at the expense of foreground action, which must be delayed while scenic description is being presented; they affect tempo, attention span, and the progressive psychology of the reader. In contrast, in the film, scenes may be concurrent realities and exploit the advantages of spatial composition in making oblique timely comments, as one thing happens in the foreground and another in the background.

Quite apart from the way in which the film has been able to present the strong physical reality of cities, natural scenes, interiors of houses and apartments, visual displays of manners, color, line, and human presences, then, it has a number of quite special "scenic" advantages that derive from its *mélange*. A movie like *The Red Desert* or Ingmar Bergman's *The Virgin Spring* makes constant use of the interplay of scene and action. In the hands of a skilled composer like Sergei Eisenstein in *Ivan* and *Alexander Nevsky*, background is carefully integrated with foreground in ways inconceivable in either the novel or the theater. Whereas a viewer of still arts may look at a given picture scarcely a second or intermittently for several weeks and may shift his attention at will from foreground to background, Eisenstein's pictures in motion structure our attention and control the duration of a given "set." They give us memory connections, echoes, recurrences, the parallel movements of more than one continuum, and controlled passage from scene to actor, groups to individuals.

Because a version of reality and a way of thought are so bound up in presentational technology, a blended form like cinema has significance not only for aesthetics but also for hermeneutics and the reading of content. A visual art in motion establishes a different relationship between form and reality than another mode can. The balance between these is influenced by the use of a camera to record things set before it, which is of course a process of assembling quite unlike what happens when a painter takes up a brush or a poet a pen. If in verse narration conventions influence narrative movement and realistic observation in ways unique to the poet's search for an appropriate metrical language, in cinematic narration the reality before the camera may be handled less obtrusively, often without a tangible, stylized mediation, especially in documentaries. Interpretation is thus not constantly infused with an authorial presence, and we see quite literally what is there. Yet some mediation is always present in every art, even in the sequent recording of facts and actions on a news broadcast. We can see this once again in the tension between still composition — or the arrested composure of visual art — and the "decomposing" of plots, which present a constantly changing flow of events before a recording instrument. A director, too, manipulates, not words, but people and scenes; and he does so, no less than the poet, according to the dictates of a style, which amounts to a version of reality.

He does so within the boundaries of two extremes that we can call roughly the film poem (which emphasizes the aesthetics of photography) and the documentary film (which emphasizes an apparently true, unshaped unfolding of events).[14] An effective camera uses these as perspectives on each other: it makes the continuity or discontinuity of a story comment implicitly on the fixed poetry of well-arranged, stable scenes, with their landscape contours, their architecture, their focus on human countenances, their abiding natural shapes. It allows a reciprocal comment to pass the other way in registering shock, change, traumatic tensions, and denouement on the composition of scenes. One of the effects of a framed screen under the pressure of story movement, for instance, is that the fortuitous threatens to intrude into its field, as when objects suddenly crop up in the path of the Keystone Cops or when two people rush blindly into each other around a corner. Or working more obliquely, the screen can make the absurd a concurrent background, playing it off against a continuous action in the foreground and offering a silent commentary from the periphery. The film can also reassert control over these moving, decomposing objects and intrusions by fixing what lies before the camera in focus and stability. Narration by pictures has the same right as a painting by Botticelli to clarify mysteries and relieve anxious moments with all the certainty of light, form, and visual concreteness.

If at one extreme, then, the film's techniques include the rendering of moving, spinning masses, soft focus, surprise intrusions from outside, and distortion, at the other extreme it includes perfectly composed arrangements of formalized art, reinforced at times by the relative certainty of words. Many of the truly interesting formal moments in films are those in which these two tendencies are joined in an intelligent reciprocity. In *Alexander Nevsky*, for instance, Eisenstein makes use of the stable contours and beauty of the Russian landscape and the heavily timbered solidity of Nevsky's castle to suggest the hero's rock-ribbed Russian sturdiness and moral composure. He calls into play all the visual allies of a heroic, statuesque image and then places in opposition to that rugged strength the postures of invading Germans behind mysterious masks. The invaders by appear-

14. Siegfried Kracauer, *Theory of Film: The Redemption of Physical Reality* (New York: Oxford University Press, 1960), p. 158. See also Kracauer's treatment of story films and nonstory films, pp. 175ff. Allardyce Nicoll, in "Film Reality: The Cinema and the Theatre," in *Film: An Anthology*, ed. Daniel Talbot (New York: Simon and Schuster, 1959), pp. 33–50, likewise stresses the comparative realism of cinema.

ance alone suggest a wavering moral purpose and a sinister treachery suitable for being broken and scattered. In the climactic encounter of the two in the battle on the ice, Eisenstein ultimately clashes the "composition" of Russia and the "decomposition" of the intruders, balancing the confusion of mass movements against the poetic grace of the frozen landscape. After a choreographed battle of symbolic contrasts in black and white, he has the enemy sink silently beneath the ice and regroups Russia's beauty and strength over many a disappearing German head. As stillness triumphs over the invading turmoil, we discover as we suspected all along that Russia's supremacy gains as much from the beauty of her landscape as from the marble-like strength of her heroes.

In Truffaut's *The 400 Blows* a comparable tension between motion and arrested composition finds thematic reinforcement in an alternation of severe discipline and loosed impulse in the lives of Parisian children, who are squeezed in succession by home, school, and jail. Many of the scenes suggest a stagnant, confining rigidity; but at intervals the children break into unrestrained noise and truant escape. As the twelve-year-old protagonist Antoine Doinel progresses from one kind of "arrest" to another — from the tyrannical classroom of "Little Quiz" to the apartment of his parents, to a police cage, and finally to a reformatory — in none of these places can he find a satisfactory compromise between the normal growth and freedom of youth and the discipline he needs. He eventually escapes from the reformatory and is shown in a final sequence jogging in the dusk through a number of open countryside settings, each of which is composed briefly and fleetingly as the environment of a new freedom. The question still remains, however, where he will find a home and how he will compromise freedom and form. What new surrounding will frame his biographical portrait? These questions we discover to be parallel to the question, How will the story and the visual component of the film be adjusted? The movement of the child, as a linear action, seeks a locality suitable to it. Motive and act — the stuff of plots — require a place and an order. The answers come in a brief final sequence. As Antoine comes to the sea, he slows to a walk at the water's edge, where the sea laps around his shoes. He can obviously go no further in this direction; walls of one kind or another are everywhere. Hence as though caged by nature itself, he turns, and his biography concludes in a still shot that fixes his wondering countenance against waves stretched in placid horizontal bars behind him. In the context of the imprisonment theme and of so many attempted escapes, this final shot speaks eloquently, in its full arrest, of the stalemates of the youth in search of freedom. But having been boxed, wedged, and stifled by restricting routine and visual tight spots, Antoine is now stilled in a more pleasing and meaningful way, in the interpretive framework of art, in which he is fixed as a defined subject. Like the final rhyme of a sonnet which turns inward or backward to fellow sounds and images, the concluding shot collects several threads — the half-formed plans for the future; the tonal balance between hope, resiliency, and disappointment; and transition between day and night, between Antoine's escape and nature's recapturing of him. He is defined by "fixations," by imprisoning continuities; but where other cages seek to change him, Antoine's countenance against the waves suggests the organic harmony of a still fresh youth and the sea. With that composition, the film's statement is finished: as the biography (which is basically movement against resistance) passes into art (which is fixation against the flux), storied sequence and frozen art fuse. Stopped by the projector, Antoine holds still *for our comprehension.*

The tension between the film poem and the documentary is related to another tension in picture narration between the muteness of pictured objects and the explicitness of verbal art. As we have seen, without the linguistic controls of abstraction and authorial manipulations of verb tense, opinions, and explicit attitudes, the film tends to let objects and actions speak for themselves. For instance, by comparison with a written documentary, stories like Robert Flaherty's *Nanook of the North* and *Louisiana Story* mix little general commentary into the portrayal of a way of life. D. W. Griffith's *Orphans of the Storm* and epic romances in realistic historical settings like Akira Kurosawa's *Seven Samurai* likewise balance the mix in favor of direct visualizable representation. But this muteness does not necessarily mean a corresponding sacrifice of significant form or intelligibility, merely a shift in the way statements are made, a shift basically from grammatical to pictorial pattern. In the choreographed and charted movements of Charlie Chaplin's comic mechanism, for instance, what appears to be a chancy and near-disastrous uproar often turns out to be a kind of visual diagram, a discovered pattern on the move akin to dance. The typical plot of such sequences carries Charlie's frail, vulnerable body into the path of falling Murphy beds or swinging ladders and then out again in the nick of time. The danger is followed by a moment of comic appreciation and a letdown of anxiety as Charlie's frail form stands placidly framed in safe and neutral territory. Perhaps a more striking example of pictorial pattern emerging from peril is the walk of Chaplin's tramp along an icy ledge in *The Gold Rush*, in which a readily visible danger is combined with unstable movement in a way that would be impossible in print or on the stage. Tension is resolved simply by upright stability. Or again in the scene in the cabin teetering on the brink, the timing of comic routines and the visual perspective from inside and outside the cabin render a sequential dumb show of danger-and-escape that puts into graphic form the tension between narrative anxiety and pictorial stability. With each new tilt, reality threatens to assert itself and shatter the hero's progress; with each reprieve, ceremonial, comic dance wins out once again. Such a sequence is obviously possible only in moving visual narration, because a still portrayal of danger makes it merely statuesque, whereas a purely verbal narration would deprive it of kinesthetic anxiety and force. Sequential movement and visualization together make the danger both concrete and capable of a gripping psychological rhythm.

In its larger structure, Chaplinesque comedy also makes use of the temporal boundaries of arrivals and departures (which tend to emphasize the forming and dissolving of romantic attachments), and Charlie's trademark, the flickering walk that carries him into and out of comic escapades with the dance's special immunity from reality. This interspersed use of something like choreography is typical of comic mechanism in general in replacing verbal with visual pattern; stunt men fall off bridges only to land safely in passing automobiles, and thereby make us realize the cathartic value of visual composure. In the intersection of two timed routes, one of them unknown until the last instant, a pattern suddenly emerges: the destination of an uncertain narrative course is revealed, and the sequential psychology of surprise thereby drops expertly into quieted pictorial viewing. Sudden rescues of objects and people thrown about by an apparently dangerous and muscular chaos are perhaps more acceptable in the film than elsewhere because all reality flickers precariously, and the camera, by pulling back, creates ever new visual gestalts and timely intrusions of new logic.

The importance of timing to the balance of visual and linear aspects of film narration is evident not only in comic sequences but in any creation and dissolving of tensions. The filming of the Olympic high dive event in the thirties, for instance, to choose an example that fuses the film poem and the documentary extraordinarily, proved very compatible with the film's inherent liking for closely timed visual spectacle. Diving is itself a visual art for the spectator, performed in a limited space against the natural stopwatch of a short fall. On film, the diver's visual silhouette is pulled into a succession of precise forms before the temporal and spatial boundaries of "plot" meet at the water's surface. A drama of changing forms of this kind benefits from the two sorts of framework, the temporal duration of the individual dive and the edge of the screen in its framing of visual form. (Special devices such as slow motion and upward or downward angles emphasize the exactness of the form and its timed changes.) Yet documentary films often lack overall structure and continuity — for the same reason that an instant replay fails to create a fully logical narrative form. Entangled in history's own structureless flow, very few documentary subjects have a natural accumulation, pitch, or ending. And so in the diving sequences, though each unit is well shaped as a minimal sequence, the succession as a whole ultimately goes nowhere. Each segment remains a vignette, a glittering fragment, a caught segment of formal beauty having the drawback of lyric moments abstracted from continuous narrative.

The balance between composition and decomposition — which involves the balancing of a psychology of linear tension and the psychology of visual gestalts — is thus an important part of the film's construction of a reality. It demonstrates clearly that the technology of the camera is not neutral; it contains its own implicit epistemological, constitutive influences, which are both aesthetic and hermeneutic.

I want to turn now to some more strictly sequential elements of that technology and their influence on such things as point of view and implied authorial judgment.

One device of sequential movement that the film may use with exceptional effectiveness, for instance, is a quick shift of attention and focus, which is the film's main metaphoric device, or device of associativity. A film story may introduce insets and concealed strands without the more explicit devices of transition by which outside or hitherto unknown forces are brought into the coherent authorial web of verbal narration. A director's options in this aspect of focus and point of view are clearer when we consider the making of novels and plays into films. In Franco Zeffirelli's *Romeo and Juliet*, for instance, the camera's varieties of associativity stand in marked contrast to those of stage presentation. In the staging of the play, the spectator is partly responsible for creating his own focus, especially when a number of people are present on stage at once: by its nature, theatrical presentation is unlikely to cause him to see Romeo strictly through Juliet's eyes, for example, except where the speeches encourage it. In effect, the theatrical management of focus changes with every stage composition and presents both hero and heroine in situations that can be perceived broadly or selectively as the spectator chooses. In Zeffirelli's filming of the play, in contrast, the camera exercises its own selection of perspectives. By doing so it often suggests a lyric attachment to the lovers that is not necessarily inherent in the lines. Thus in the party scene, as Juliet singles out Romeo, the camera allows us to see him intermittently from her perspective and her from his. Amid the swirl of motions and emotions in the crowd — which forms a sensuous and potentially threatening periphery around their affair — the camera sorts out the path of their first encounter and "lyrically" charts the stages of a romantic plot of a certain kind. It changes the organization of the scene: becoming engrossed in what the lovers see and how they respond, we are less detached and critical of them than Shakespeare's play encourages. Assisted by music on the sound track and its concurrent mood selection, lyricism predominates over social panorama and ironic judgment.

Fixation in a point of view can be as much a novelistic as a cinematic technique, of course, given the novel's superior capacity to situate us inside the minds of characters. But we tend to forget more readily in films that a camera does not merely see, it sees from. It does so especially when it moves and places the viewer in a dynamic relationship with the action. Thus from the camera's platform, we compose, or experience the decomposing of, everything placed before us. Not even in James's carefully worked out points of view do we find anything quite comparable to the tempo of shifts that may result from the camera's taking up of successive positions. In looking into the witnessing of stories later we will explore some of the possibilities of our way of "knowing" fictive illusions; in the film we find a striking case of cinematic witnessing in Fellini's *I vitelloni* (*The Wastrels*), in which the satiric attitude of the film toward its aging young loafers is controlled by timely shifts of attention, primarily between those who follow lives of festivity and those who are absorbed in the bourgeois life of work and gain. Where Zeffirelli encourages a lyric indentification of the spectator's point of view and the lovers, Fellini encourages an ironic crossfire between these. Both do so by the camera's control over point of view. In a typical scene in a small shop, for instance, the viewer is exposed in rapid sequence to the perspective of the flirtatious wastrel Fausto, the archly moral wife of his employer, and the shopkeeper himself. Having seen the wife previously from Fausto's sensual eye during a festive occasion, we now glimpse similar enticing portions of her anatomy, presumably with Fausto's quickened pulse. Then in a reverse shot from her perspective we see him as a cocky, vain, and slightly threatening male. Finally, both parties to this byplay come under the critical scrutiny of the shopkeeper, who, before he fires Fausto, lets him know how he appears, in turn, from a husband's vantage point.

In such changes of camera angle and perspective, Fellini prevents us from becoming too entrenched in any continuous biography — though our having shared each perspective even briefly and intermittently keeps us moderately sympathetic with several people in turn. Perhaps more important, he constructs realities and continuities of existence so different in kind as almost to cancel each other. In this more serious crossfire, the film's view of social realities begins to take ironic and problematic shape. The effect is like that of shifting illusions in Pirandello or the ambiguities of stories like *The Sacred Fount* except that we are more completely at the mercy of a nontalking camera than we normally are of dramatic or novelistic presenters. Indeed, it is virtually impossible to struggle against the influence of the place from which reality is composed in films because the duration of our view, the selection of detail, and the context of juxtaposed shots are all we have to go on, and the camera does not openly declare its biases. It is *uncharacterized*. In Fellini's case, narrative structure hinges on the continuities it creates among the bourgeois order and the life of festivity: each way of life has its own daily rhythm and creates its own kind of progress. One accumulates honor, money, and respect in a continuity of established positions; the other passes each day and each season in a directionless alternation of ecstatic moments and boredom. Neither has a monopoly on truth; each holds the camera for allotted periods.

Fellini's ultimate imposing of order on these ironic shifts of attention depends on other narrative capacities that only cameras have, especially when equipped with moving tracks and the zoom lens. The final sequence finds Muraldo leaving town by train, and in a series of withdrawing shots Fellini pulls us out of the households of the various families in much the same way that Muraldo's eyes see the retreating platform. Our final point of view is thus constituted by a special kind of overlapping visual withdrawal from the contrasts of the story: as we retract from a close-up satiric-sympathetic judgment of the households one by one, we discover something like a generalizing statement about them. Whereas a concluding fixed picture may memorialize and define, as Truffaut's does, in a sequence like Fellini's the repetition of "rhymed" shots suggests that if the same motion is indeed repeatable in each household, there must be a kind of essence, a transferable quality either in the aspects of provincial life or in our way of regarding them. As we leave, we observe the things that both buffoons and workers, sons and father, share — their states of sleep, their monotonous daily cycles, their family situations, and their unpretentious houses. For both, life simply goes on — and on. Except for Muraldo (whom we might expect to turn up again in the Rome of *La dolce vita*, rescued from the provinces but dropped into another stale round of festivity and boredom), we therefore have no further curiosity about their conflict or their future. Our retreating seeing-station, our moving camera, is composed beyond reversals and further progress. It knows now, definitively, how to see.

NOVELS AND PICTORIAL MOTION

Few if any novels, or other narrative methods for that matter, make use of a tempo of shifts as rapid as that of *The Wastrels*. But it is instructive to note that since the development of film techniques with their special sense of continuity, "syntax," point of view, transition, and narrative animation, novels have also begun to use cinematic language, as the history of blends turns about. Harry Levin points out, for example, that in *For Whom the Bell Tolls* Hemingway presents a movielike flow of impressions at times. Certain passages have the camera's effect of reducing the gap between events and the reporting of events. As a given incident may find an observer first passively awaiting the approach of an event and then responding with a burst of excitement — drawn out of his passivity by an imminent threat to life perhaps — the reader is drawn into an unforeshortened sequence of almost tactile impressions. He adopts a point of view that shares the taut anxiety and released energy of characters as though he saw things from their eyes, as Hemingway tries not to screen our impressions for us through the complexities of commentary or interior meditation. Levin's choice of El Sordo's stand on the hilltop as an example will serve here as well:

> Look at him walking. Look what an animal. Look at him stride forward. This one is for me. This one I take with me on the trip. This one coming now makes the same voyage I do. Come on, Comrade Voyager. Come striding. Come right along. Come along to meet it. Come on. Keep on walking. Don't slow up. Come right along. Come as thou art coming. Don't stop and look at those. That's right. Don't even look down. Keep on coming with your eyes forward. Look, he has a moustache. What do you think of that? He runs to a moustache, the Comrade Voyager. He is a captain. Look at his sleeves. . . . Look. With a red face and blond hair and blue eyes. With no cap on and his moustache is yellow. With blue eyes. With pale blue eyes. With pale blue eyes with something wrong with them. With pale blue eyes that don't focus. Close enough. Too close. Yes, Comrade Voyager. Take it, Comrade Voyager.[15]

Whether or not Hemingway was actually thinking of the film in such a passage, the sequence reads much like a series of justaposed snapshots, each slightly different from the one before, repeated with variations that reveal an increasing particularity of detail as the doomed enemy comes within range.

Hemingway's technique is cinematic in other ways as well. It reduces dialogue to a minimum and implies moods and tones from a minimum of descriptive language. However, his use of cinematic methods is also very sparing in some respects. El Sordo does after all think and talk to himself as well as see and act; we know more than a camera could tell us about his mood and his reading of the enemy.

15. Ernest Hemingway, *For Whom the Bell Tolls* (New York: Sun Dial Press, 1940), p. 277. See Harry Levin, "Observations on the Style of Ernest Hemingway," in *Contexts of Criticism* (Cambridge, Mass.: Harvard University Press, 1958), pp. 144–67.

Nor does Hemingway make a spectacular disruption of normal novelistic points of view. In terms of focus, his fiction is much like that of
conventional hero-centered fiction of the tradition.

For more pronounced departures in the direction of cinematic form
we need to think of more recent experiments. Among the several that
might be suggested perhaps none is so singular as Ken Kesey's *Sometimes a Great Notion*. In returning from modal blends to the structure of verbal narration, our main concern, I want to pause upon it
long enough to suggest further implications of the theory of modal
combinations.

Especially movielike in Kesey's instance are the novel's tempo of
perspective shifts, its unusual style of serial juxtaposition — so largely
free of the continuity of an authorial logic and so hostile to straightforward storytelling — and its balance of composing and decomposing effects. As in Fellini's manipulation of points of view, much of the
impact of the novel can be seen in terms of the readers' taking up of
seeing-stations or composing centers in the midst of change. Indeed,
technique is more than ever content in this case. Each biographical
curve that the novel constructs is made crooked by interaction with
others, and each aspect of the reader's progress through them all is
rendered uncertain by the rapid pace of alternations — by highly segmented and dispersed blocks of time. Individualized versions of
reality are thus constantly forming and dissolving before us as no
single point of view is allowed to dominate for more than a few sentences or paragraphs at a time. Whereas Jamesian investigation unfolds a continuous dramatic sequence as the probing of a central
mystery, Kesey's brief units are purposely incongruous: the mysteries
are as multiple as the perspectives, and point of view is an instrument
of participatory, animate discontinuity. From any single perspective,
the difficulty is for each character to understand the logic of others
sufficiently to negotiate with them. The reader is required to link
nonchronological sequences much as Draeger, for instance, is required to put together a history from the pictures of a family album.
Though in a sense the concern of novels has always been the "reality"
that threatens to disappear among conflicting moral and social positions, for Draeger and Kesey's pursuing readers the problem is aggra-
vated by the need for gymnastic leaps where no national purpose,
economic grouping, or general cultural standards can be imposed on
the group. Kesey's Oregon coastal town is a microcosm of modern

confusion. (The movie made of the book is untrue to its source in all these respects, dominated as it is — ironically enough — by the story-line technique of conventional novels.)

However, individuals in the novel and the reader also benefit from coincidences of point of view. Kesey controls the discrepancies among individuals by having various people return to experiences that others have had and approach a common understanding of them. Much of the piecing together that the reader has to do is accomplished for him by people like Jonas Stamper, Leland's mother, and Vivian, who by their cyclical reduplication help explain each other. Their arrivals from the east and departures from the west, for instance, frame the novel and are akin to the reader's entry into and departure from the world of the Stampers. In a similar way we can count on the cycles of the years, the rise and fall of generations, and the perfect vengeance of Leland's plot (in doing to Hank exactly what Hank did to him) to help us interweave interior perspectives and individual episodes as a single action.

Communal life, too, is possible at least on rare occasions, and when it is, the result is a curious lyricism that the novel relishes nearly as much as its cinematic shifts in perspective. Such a lyricism is a way of imposing strong enough tonal control over our reactions that we have some guarantee of common ground and continuity. It often comes less from a community of explicit opinion among the characters, however, than from the mood of the landscape and the narrator — in a kind of scenic film poem that stands in marked contrast to the jumpiness of perspective in other passages:

> The first little washes flashing like thick rushing winds through sheep sorrel and clover, ghost fern and nettle, sheering, cutting . . . forming branches. Then, through bearberry and salmonberry, blueberry and blackberry, the branches crashing into creeks, into streams. Finally, in the foothills, through tamarack and sugar pine, shittim bark and silver spruce — and the green and blue mosaic of Douglas fir — the actual river falls five hundred feet . . . and look: opens out upon the fields.[16]

The movement here is that of a small picture expanding into a rendering of a broader geography. Throughout the novel, this sense of geography is conjured again and again to provide a relocation of our

16. Ken Kesey, *Sometimes a Great Notion* (New York: Viking Press, 1964), p. 1. Quotations are from the Bantam edition (New York, 1965).

position among the instabilities of action and character. For despite seasonal changes and a general fraying of nerves that it causes, Kesey's region, like Stegner's in *Wolf Willow*, remains steady and photographic, while people tend to give in, to arrive and depart, sicken and die. As the Wakonda Auga threads its way into strands of the action, it permeates them with the cyclical returns of daily and seasonal patterns, most of which evoke a rhythmic and poetic response.

The blend of modes does not end with the fusion of poetic description and cinematic perspectives. Kesey also makes use of documentary realism and comedy, including first-hand binocular views and directives from a prefatory commentator who reads and interprets signs for us. As in epistolary documentation, the evidence is often transcribed in letters, albums, and papers, with the assistance of which we probe the private worlds of isolated people. In more strictly visual matters, the "camera" cuts at will from one window-view of reality to another as we follow Joe Ben sitting outside the Grange Hall listening to the union meeting, discover Leland at the knothole in his youth and again when he returns, see Draeger and Evenwrite from Hank's perspective and Hank from theirs, and leaf through the album with Draeger. Beyond these rapid scannings of signs, we are exposed to more esoteric signals (as read by Indian Jenny and Joe) and to the signs of nature, accompanied as though on a sound track by almost intelligible calls of geese, the hush and stir of the wind, and the sounds and marks of the river in its rising and falling. When Hank at his critical moment on the other side of the knothole looks in upon Leland and Vivian, it is thus not a single act in a single jumpy continuity but a typical act in a multiple set of returns, reviews, and scannings of evidence, all dedicated to the untangling of the secret roots of familial and provincial "connections."

As I suggested, the society of the novel is consistent with these thematic and formal elements, the justification for which becomes clearer when we have suffered the effects of concealment and inquired into the chances a social agreement has to survive among so many angles of vision. How does one systematize the signs and make individual careers into a collective course?

For one thing, a strange elation and lyric expostulation comes from spying out secrets and assembling the pieces of someone else's puzzle. This elation is akin to the cinema's special moments when imperiled sequences suddenly arrive at a plateau of assurance; it is akin to the camera's spying into private worlds; and it is perhaps related further to the lyric, in that, unlike the film, the novel can pause to give full verbal expression to its discoveries, some of which are internal and personal. Though Draeger fails to achieve anything like elation — having placed too much confidence in the wisdom of his own axioms — Lee, in looking through the same album in the attic earlier, experiences as in a dream "that bright billowing medley of excitement and trepidation" that he first felt with his eye to the wall, like a camera, spying "breathlessly on a life" not his own. "For once again I spied," he remarks, "except that life before me now stood bared so much more" (p. 574). Presumably the reader as a vicarious onlooker is also rewarded with a sense of achievement in finding certain figures in the carpet: out of the decomposings of rapid movement and shifts in perspective, patterns do emerge.

Even so, moments of private elation provide no generally shared public experience of any scope and no communal point of view; and in a sense, despite the symmetry of its grand circle through the past and back to the present, the novel relies more on the lyric and pictorial occasions of local insight than upon the continuous movement of social institutions and their intrigues. In this respect the novel is the antibourgeois product of an avowed prankster who values special moments more than continuity. The Stampers work not out of duty and responsibility but out of joy, stubbornness, and sheer egotism; they take moments aside for practical jokes, assaults upon propriety, and romps through the brush. The entire plot, both the delivery of the logs and Lee's revenge, borders upon pranksterism; both sex and business are play. In some respects, this festivity carries us back to Fielding and the healthy plurality of Tom Jones's interests; but it is much more seriously conditioned by the desperateness of the struggle and the sense that the community is not finally well served by pranksters or ready to lament their reform and downfall. In any case, both the family and the town disintegrate. People become drunkards and commit suicide. Stronger people must dismiss or fight against a world of continual abrasion, wounds, and fatal accidents. Thus in making so much of its privileged moments, the novel sets aside the continuous logic of conventional narration and the sequential psychology and social stability upon which it depends. It stresses those fortuitous and indifferent forces of society and nature that tumble things together — and sometimes tumble them into the river. Nor can it do otherwise from Kesey's perspective: for an individual to join a community of the kind available to the Stampers is to sacrifice the local, personal acts of seeing that define him; it is to commit himself to a rigid social form out of keeping with a heroic response to the region's challenge.

Such a response the Stampers must make, and despite his ironic treatment of them Kesey obviously appreciates their effort. The rejection of collective and unionized answers to social problems throws one back upon the sanctity of the individual brain and stomach. Lives become more discontinuous, more romantically dependent upon the eye's momentary elations and a society's spontaneous fellowship. Once all the grounds for common views are disclosed to us, Vivian still continues to look on from a distance (clearing the fog away from her bus window); the townspeople remain constitutionally unable to understand Hank's point of view or he theirs; Draeger remains mystified; and the reader sees the two brothers distantly, dancing wildly on the logs as part of the scenic panorama of the river. This lack of intelligible cohesion and definite enclosure is reflected in the incurable jumpiness of the novel's camera work even at the end, where Kesey combines elation over the river journey with the sad finality of Viv's leaving and the frustration of the union men. The boundary of the work thus consists not of a completed action but — as in *The Wastrels* and *The 400 Blows* — of the formal device of a withdrawing series of views and fixed photos. Each of these is definitive in its own way, but no picture in the album renders a finished action.

Though the novel's synchronization of perspectives remains occasional and rare, the most singular cases are nonetheless revealing as a commentary on what society normally lacks. The logging incident in the state park, in which Hank, Joe, and Old Henry mesh as a work team (under the coercion of circumstances), is the most striking example:

> The three of them meshed, dovetailed . . . into one of the rare and beautiful units of effort sometimes seen when a jazz group is making it completely, swinging together completely, or when a home-town basketball squad, already playing over its head, begins to rally to overtake a superior opponent in a game's last minute . . . When this happens everyone watching *knows* . . . that, be it five guys playing

basketball, or four blowing jazz, or three cutting timber, that *this bunch — right now*, right *this moment* — is the best of its kind in the world! [P. 476]

The three of them find an answer, in the cooperation of work, to bickering unions, unheroic townsmen, and fighting families. It is not a political answer, and it presupposes no permanent social order. Others in the chain of production are left out, and though production is the goal of logging, it is the exaltation of the work itself and not its pragmatic value that inspires them. Theirs is a purely circumstantial and temporary fusion that comes about not under rules or repeatable controls but under favoring chances, the hazards of the hillside, and need. Their union is entirely devoid of those mediating moral principles and abstractions that normally provide the principles of a society and that fill Draeger's notebook. Like the busload of merrymakers Kesey piloted around the nation shooting yards of film, their bond depends upon the lucky find of something salvageable, something memorable, from the flow of events that passes before the camera.

But very little is memorable finally, either in an Oregon coastal town or on a bus tour of the United States, and as the logging unit breaks up, its synchronized points of view are quickly shattered. In a wild scattering of shots as though a camera were rolling loose, Kesey traces the path of a log that careers downhill and smashes old Henry's arm before pinning Joe Ben in the river. This startling decomposition not only disperses the fragile work unit but once again destroys the continuity of narration. Kesey recomposes the scene briefly, and Hank reads the signs more clearly. ("The message crystallized everything . . . before his eyes once more.") But each member of the work team is now fixed in his own dilemma and point of view; each is dominated by the hillside, chance, or the river. In the image of Joe overwhelmed gradually by the rising water, Kesey suggests the defeat of even the most intimate and familial cooperation. The pranks are over; one cannot laugh under water, and one's particular lungs cannot after all make use very long of borrowed air.

The difficulty posed by mixed methods of presentation such as Kesey's is in part that as the pace of the narrative progress is altered, the reader has differing opportunities to retrieve and associate

scattered segments of the work, and greater or lesser encouragement
to do so. The selection of what is salient is left more to him than it
normally is in novels of continuous logic depicting reasonably cohesive middle-class communities. But the problem of mixed modes is
by no means a new one, even though it is seldom staged in such a
strikingly fragmentary manner as it is in *Sometimes a Great Notion.*
Henry James, to take a more celebrated instance, stresses sometimes
visual portraiture and sometimes dramatic technique at the expense
of narration. We observed earlier Northrop Frye's opinion of James's
circular containment in which there "emerges not a linear process of
thought but a simultaneous comprehension." So much does James
talk about the pictorial and scenic aspects of his art and the "architecture" of narrative structure that it has seemed to many critics that
James intended a seriously mixed new mode. Thus J. A. Ward argues
in a chapter on "Picture and Action" that for James an action "becomes not a story, but a picture," and that the effect of its foreshortening is to convert narrative into fixed portraits. Moreover,
James's interest in characters is not in psychological development but
in "permanent psychological conditions." The development of an action "clarifies the central situation; it does not extend or alter it."[17]

Though quite justified as something that James himself insists
upon, the analogy between pictorial methods and verbal narrative will
seldom support "either . . . or" statements of this kind. The problem
of mixed modes more frequently demands a less extreme "both . . .
and," and a sense of what happens in compounds when their reacting
chemicals penetrate one another. If we observe these dynamics of
mixed forms without preconceived notions, we are obliged to concede that no narrative can avoid its linear nature for long: foreshortening has a multitude of temporal effects, none of which is precisely "simultaneity" or the rendering of instantaneous pictures; and
no psychology in narrative treatment can ever be quite "permanent"
— as though it could be freed from its occasions, events, and evolving

17. Ward, *The Search for Form*, pp. 33, 32, 40, 35. A number of James's critics have
made similar points with respect to his stress on encompassing situation or idea. See
Laurence Bedwell Holland, *The Expense of Vision: Essays on the Craft of Henry James*
(Princeton: Princeton University Press, 1964), pp. 49ff. Francis Fergusson, "James's Idea
of Dramatic Form," *Kenyon Review* 5 (1943): 495–507; Henry L. Terrie, Jr., "Pictorial
Method in the Novels of Henry James" (Ph.D. diss., Princeton University, 1955);
Wiesenfarth, *Henry James and the Dramatic Analogy*, pp. 1–43.

consciousness. The path that Jamesian consciousness takes is no less eventful finally than the perils of Pauline, only different in quality. It is difficult to conceive of any fruitful reading of James, in fact, that does not experience the finer excruciations of consciousness operating in ordeals of mystery, silence, and qualified revelation. Few novelists are more committed than James to the careful modulation of pace and control in the processes of dramatic discovery, from the placement of large constructional blocks down to the seating of adverbs in the movement of intricately suspended and explosive sentences. When paintings figure prominently in his work, as in *The Tragic Muse* and *The Sacred Fount*, far from rendering fixed icons in summary of the work they are themselves absorbed into an always probing, portentous searching out of the keys to social relationships through a reading of whatever gestures, signs, conversations, and events are available to the intelligence. To miss the fine balance between an implicit design and its unavailability to the probing consciousness at any given moment is to miss the essence of Jamesian narration.

However, though no novelist can replace linear art entirely with any other, he can supplement it with subtly conditional and complex ways of circling back and predicting. With this in mind, one can agree with Ward's remark that James scrapped plots of a certain kind in favor of a mode of narration whose basic center is states of consciousness:

> At times the design is revealed through action — events, movements, and gestures which objectify states of consciousness and moral and psychological relationships. In most cases the broad movements in James's fiction may be looked upon as initiations, aggressions, or searches, tracing the progress of a central character as he seeks access into (knowledge of) a social situation. [P. 46]

Or as James himself remarks in another connection, one notices "the odd inveteracy with which picture, at almost every turn, is jealous of drama, and drama . . . suspicious of picture. Between them, no doubt, they do much for the theme; yet each baffles insidiously the other's ideal and eats around the edges of its position; each is too ready to say 'I can take the thing for "done" only when done in *my* way' " (*The Art of the Novel*, p. 298).[18]

18. Cf. Friedman, *Stream of Consciousness*, p. 42. Friedman's main concern is with the mixture of musical techniques and fiction, especially the leitmotif, "music's most consistent contribution to fiction," but also the sonata, fugue, and contrapuntal technique.

In all cases of mixed modes, any altering of the ratio between forward inclination and the returns and interweavings of design is part of a narrative stress system that a poetics of narration is obligated to look into. This stress system includes the tension between sequent movement and comprehensive ideas and, as I have suggested, the vicarious sharing, in readers, of the characters' flow of psychic life and occasions. The "pace" of a work as we normally use the term is controlled by suspense, hurry, foreshortening, extension, or retardation. We experience these both through a hero and through the duration of the reading in our particular psychological time. The presentational technique the narrator superimposes on that vicarious psychological journey, the added complications of verse units, cinematic technique, descriptive pauses, static portraiture, and the logic of authorial essays — all of these take their cues from, and seek their justification in, animate plots, which ("alas!" as E. M. Forster says) are always central to stories.

Having suggested perhaps sufficient tentative and provisional influences of the mode of presentation on the reader's path through a procession of half-concealing, half-revealing moments, I want now to return to the central psychology of that linear form — the controlled and molded tautness of narration and its dramatic, descriptive, expository, foreshortened journeys of discovery. Whether mixed or as pure as the god Terminus could wish, narrative is basically a stress system of suffered experience different for characters and for readers, an indirect journey through symbols and successive representations. For participating characters, of course, the events of a story are never fully controllable, stylized, or designed, while for us, the readers, they are always the materials of art. Because words follow one another in the ways of grammar and image — not the ways of events or pictures or celluloid images — and because all design imposed upon them must acknowledge the flow of consciousness through them from sign to sign, the stress system of narration cannot be understood as a version of reality or a version of some other art. It is begun, phrased, sentenced, made into episodes, chaptered, and concluded as a string of verbal comments. Our awareness of its form is a safeguard against supposing that any mode of expression has a monopoly on the "real thing." It is also perhaps an encouragement in the long run to a sociology of literary analysis inasmuch as the shape of narrative is determined by the preconditions of the writer's and reader's reading of the signs. But that is another question, and before we can see very far into it — or look toward an integration of formalistic and sociological criticism — we need to isolate further and more specific principles of the psychology of narrative.

III. SUFFERED KNOWLEDGE

CHAPTER SIX

Narrative Stress Systems

In fictive systems facts are mirrored and remirrored, chopped up and segmented, and made into repetitive patterns and parallels. All the modes we have explored — myth and romance, documentary realism, epistolary fiction, melodic and cinematic narration — suggest by contrast to both life and history writing how thoroughly a system of fictive symbolization transforms any material surrendered to it. Actually, we can never be sure about what has gone into a work, only what lies on the page or what appears on the screen before us; but we do know, by contrast to any visitable past in our experience, that the presumed realities of fictions are highly organized and artificial. They foreshorten vaster realms and telescope them into a size and proportion appropriate for the design of the whole — or if the mode is satiric, perhaps into a size and *dis*proportion that reminds us even more readily of fiction's arbitrariness. (When Gulliver and the Lilliputians come together, for instance, their contrast in size constantly reminds us of the wit of their inventor.)

My aim in this concern with modes has been relatively simple: to explore ways in which narratives present not a world we can point to outside the work but codified systems and to suggest that one aspect of the narrative code is the special rhythm a reader follows on the presentational surface of the work — as distinct from the sequent order of the life imagined in the work. The distinction between these is complicated by the fact that every narration is both a method and a way of seeing something potentially real.

What we have not considered so far are the stresses and strains of narrative systems as drama. If all "as if" codes have in common a structuring of basic sensations, what separates fictions from other methods of formulation is in part their serial way of implicating an

221

audience psychologically in a process of interpretation — their way of presenting information in tensive, rhythmic form. The concreteness of visual arts gives to theories of them certain advantages in this regard; and though the materials of sound are somewhat less stable, music, too, presents aural configurations of some precision.[1] When a musical phrase is repeated, it is repeated physically; rhythms are established beyond reasonable doubt, and melody in its immediate presence to the ear makes unmistakable predictions, recurrences, parallels, and climaxes.[2] The minimal units out of which the artistic whole is composed are also distinct. Every sound produced in a sequence is held for just so long; and because it is exactly measured and determined in quality, place, and duration, its relationship with other units can be pinpointed. Thus, in Leonard Meyer's and Victor Zukerkandl's impressive analyses, musical structure, segmentation, and "syntax" prove to be knowable quantities that register exactly on the listener.

When we turn from either visual or musical structure to literature, we are struck by the disadvantages that a structural criticism of literature encounters and by its relatively imprecise language. For all that has been written about narrative, for instance, our critical resources remain somewhat thin and often depend upon questionable analogies with music and pictorial arts. We possess a few classifications of kinds of plots, some amplifications of Aristotle's structural theory in the *Poetics*, a number of essays on narrative modes, and now and then an ambitious system like Northrop Frye's or Claude Lévi-Strauss's.[3] These are notable, but among them we look in vain for (1)

1. See Rudolf Arnheim, *Art and Visual Perception: A Psychology of the Creative Eye* (Berkeley and Los Angeles: University of California Press, 1960); Anton Ehrenzweig, *The Hidden Order of Art: A Study in the Psychology of Artistic Imagination* (Berkeley and Los Angeles: University of California Press, 1967); E. H. Gombrich, *Art and Illusion: A Study in the Psychology of Pictorial Representation* (Princeton: Princeton University Press, 1960). See also Joseph M. Bobbit, "An Experimental Study of the Phenomenon of Closure as a Threshold Function," in *Readings in Perception*, ed. David C. Beardslee and Michael Wertheimer (Princeton: D. Van Nostrand Co., 1958), pp. 136–59; Hamlyn, *The Psychology of Perception*; Hirst, *The Problems of Perception*; Koffka, *Principles of Gestalt Psychology*.

2. See Gordon Epperson, *The Musical Symbol: A Study of the Philosophic Theory of Music* (Ames: Iowa State University Press, 1967); Leonard B. Meyer, *Music, the Arts and Ideas*; Victor Zukerkandl, *Sound and Symbol*, trans. Willard R. Trask (Princeton: Princeton University Press, 1956); Calvin S. Brown, *Music and Literature: A Comparison of the Arts* (Athens: University of Georgia Press, 1948).

3. See Lévi-Strauss, "The Structural Study of Myth," in *Myth: A Symposium*, ed. Sebeok, pp. 50–66, and in *Journal of American Folklore*. For a general discussion of

a convincing theory of minimal narrative units (phrasal or rhythmic units? sentences? paragraphs? topics? chapters? episodes? developed and believable characters? complete actions? plots and subplots?) or a sound idea of what might be done with them if we managed to isolate them; (2) any sure way of integrating matters of style and mood with kinds of action;[4] (3) any decisive treatment of differences between action and the duration and pace of reading;[5] (4) any integration of these narrative elements with problems of linguistic reference, symbolization, abstraction and concretion, the archetypical and the typical; (5) or finally, as we noticed in the last chapter, any adequate account of mixed modes — narrative, descriptive, dramatic, discursive or deliberative, stream of consciousness, musical, or "typographical" (that is, what printed books do that oral presenta-

---

structure in a number of disciplines including Lévi-Strauss's, see Jean Piaget, *Structuralism*, trans. Chaninah Maschler (New York: Basic Books, 1970). See also *Genre* 4 (1971) and *Twentieth Century Studies* 3 (1970); Frank, "Spatial Form in Modern Literature," in *The Widening Gyre*, pp. 3–62; Ralph Freedman, "The Possibility of a Theory of the Novel," in *The Disciplines of Criticism*, ed. Peter Demetz et al. (New Haven: Yale University Press, 1968), pp. 57–77. My emphasis falls closer to that of critics like Goodman, *The Structure of Literature*; Muir, *The Structure of the Novel*; Giorgio Melchiori, "The Moment as a Time Unit in Fiction," in *The Tightrope Walkers: Studies of Mannerism in Modern English Literature* (London: Routledge and Kegan Paul, 1956) pp. 175–87; Paul, "Time and the Novelist"; Scott, "Mimesis and Time in Modern Literature," in *The Broken Center*, pp. 25–76; Norman Friedman, "Forms of the Plot," *Journal of General Education* 8 (1955): 241–53; Margaret Church, *Time and Reality: Studies in Contemporary Fiction* (Chapel Hill: University of North Carolina Press, 1949); Beverly Gross, "Narrative Time and the Open-ended Novel," *Criticism* 8 (1966): 362–76; Graham Hough, "From: An Essay in Criticism," *Critical Quarterly* 8 (1966): 136–45; James G. Kennedy, "More General than Fiction: The Uses of History in the Criticism of Modern Novels," *College English* 28 (1966): 150–63; Kermode, "Novel, History and Type" and *The Sense of an Ending*; Miller, *The Form of Victorian Fiction*; Mudrick, "Character and Event in Fiction"; John Henry Raleigh, "The English Novel and the Three Kinds of Time," in *Perspectives in Contemporary Criticism*, ed. Grebstein, pp. 42–49; Brooks and Wimsatt, "Fiction and Drama: The Gross Structure," in *Literary Criticism*, pp. 681–98; Cook, "Plot as Discovery," in *The Meaning of Fiction*, pp. 202–41. See also Frye, *Anatomy of Criticism*, and Scholes and Kellogg, *The Nature of Narrative*.

4. For instance, David I. Grossvogel, *Limits of the Novel: Evolutions of a Form from Chaucer to Robbe-Grillet* (Ithaca, N.Y.: Cornell University Press, 1968); Watt, *The Rise of the Novel*; Friedman, *The Turn of the Novel*; W. J. Harvey, *Character and the Novel* (London: Chatto and Windus, 1966); Ralph Freedman, *The Lyrical Novel: Studies in Herman Hesse, Andre Gide, and Virginia Woolf* (Princeton: Princeton University Press, 1963). For stylistic matters, see Lodge's *Language of Fiction*; Auerbach's *Mimesis*; Leonard Lutwack's "Mixed and Uniform Prose Styles in the Novel," reprinted in *Perspectives on Fiction*, ed. Calderwood and Toliver, pp. 27–37.

5. See Harvey, "Time and Identity," in *Character and the Novel*, pp. 100–129.

tion does not, as in the oddities of *Tristram Shandy* or the intricate cross-referencing of Joyce's *Ulysses*).[6]

Even a brief glance at the problematic areas of a theory of fictions suggests several reasons for these deficiencies. Almost nothing about the reading of stories is proof against ambiguity and imprecision, and the materials of fiction are staggeringly varied and complex. The referential dimension of words and the masks of the *fictor*, or inventor; the *histor*, or knowledgeable truth-sayer; and the *hister* (the mimetic actor), to take merely a few areas of confusion, are so variable and interchangeable that we pass incessantly and often unconsciously back and forth from what is represented to the art of presentation. More basically, the structural segments of narrative — sentences, pieces of dialogue, episodes, images, chapters, flashbacks and other insets, essays, asides from the author, digressions, plots — are all variable and overlapping. In many instances a structural critic is forced to compose a sense of these himself out of raw materials — defining peripheries, concords or discords, image patterns, similarities among units, parallels and contrasts. He can never be sure when he has departed from what is actually perceivable in the work and what is the product of critical afterthought. The problem is not merely that one reader's *Ulysses* is not another's; after all, one listener's Beethoven may not be another's either. The problem is that two different *Ulysses* can be assembled on quite different structural principles from the same "score," put together from divergent points of emphasis, different thematic connections, and different senses of the work's shape. For instance, an image that is a subordinate part of a sentence and assumes a certain proportion and meaning as such may at the same time, through repetition or allusion, constitute an extragrammatical design of its own, a suborder apart from the logic of sentences laid end to end.

In its most basic aspect, the trouble is traceable to the writer's materials, words, which may idealize, arrange the past and future in different relationships, foreshorten, abstract, allude, or distinguish between hypothetical and real propositions. Most of these generalizing

6. The differences between oral and written presentation have been the subject of much discussion; the effects of print specifically have not been. See Kermode, "Novel, History and Type," and the discussion of *Ulysses* in Hugh Kenner's "James Joyce: Comedian of the Inventory" in *Flaubert, Joyce and Beckett: The Stoic Comedians* (London: W. H. Allen, 1964). See also Marshall McLuhan, *The Gutenberg Galaxy* (Toronto: University of Toronto Press, 1962) and *Understanding Media* (New York: Signet, 1964).

and time-defying leaps are inconceivable in painting or music. To put it in a slightly different way, whereas music focuses on self-generated repetitions within its own framework and avoids excessive wayward-ness, no writer can control completely the connotative actions and reactions of words in the animation of narratives: both words and conventions are hand-me-downs of a considerable history and as such come to the narrator entangled in a quantity of previous experience.

Another difficulty in settling upon a precise critical language in the theory of narrative is that all serial works, even those that turn out to be almost totally articulate and closed, are open until the end and re-quire a greater or lesser predictive genius. Narrative operates by anticipation and recall, and here again words are peculiar by com-parison to musical signals. Gestaltists, information theorists, and others who have experimented with randomness and probability have taught us a few of the basic principles of prediction; but not many of these principles prove to be self-evident in the reading of fictions. Even when a work is finished, a reader's reaction is based on mem-ory, and as Hillis Miller writes of the sense of an ending in longer works:

> The silence after the last word of a novel, like the silence after the last note of a piece of music, is by no means the silence of triumphantly perfected form. It is rather a stillness in which the reader experiences a poignant sense of loss, the vanishing of the formative energy of the work. This secret source of form was never reached while the novel continued, but was held open as a possibility toward which each page separately reached, as each note in a musical composition reaches out toward the whole. When the novel is over the sense of that possibility is lost, and this generates a feeling of nostalgia, a regret for having lost the last glimpse of a marvelous country which can be seen afar not when the music or the novel is over, but only while it is still going on in its continuous failure to be perfect or perfectable.[7]

Perhaps more than anywhere else the imperfectability of narrative forms and the difficulty of structural criticism is evident in this ambivalent view from the end. But from any other point as well, the echoes and repercussions generated by an extensive work are too

---

7. Miller, *The Form of Victorian Fiction*, p. 48. Miller's chapters "Time and Intersubjectivity" and "The Ontological Basis of Form," together with Muir's observations on time in the novel in *The Structure of the Novel*, make an excellent introduction to a theory of narrative linearity and a good corrective to conceptions of fiction that assign it "the closed perfection of spatialized form" (Miller, p. 15).

numerous and of too wide a variety and infinite an interaction to dictate reactions definitively.

Still another difficulty is that the experience of interpreting narrative clues shares too many qualities with the reading of events in living time. It shares with that reading, for instance, a distinction between backward and forward views that pictorial arts lack. It shares the relative certainty of the past despite its quick generalization into fading outlines; the uncertainty and anxiety of the future; the associational qualities of intuition and memory when these faculties work with half-certain evidence; and thus the excitement of imaginative guesswork in probing configurations. Since a story gives us one thing amidst the reminders and anticipations of many other things, our analysis is bound up in the complexities of a temporal foreground and background, manifest and concealed actions, explicit knowledge and surmise, and discursive and descriptive matter inserted at key points to interpret and to recapitulate.

It is also, as we saw earlier, bound up in a sense of rhythm that carries over from experience. As Dewey insists in linking art to experience, rhythm is one of the inherent linear structures that art and experience have in common. We will examine the principles of narrative retardation later, but in anticipation we note that narratives, like living organisms, are in part contained energy systems that depend upon resistance to their own forward motion. As such, as distinct from unorganized, sprawling or indefinite "wastes," they are divided and segmented *energetically* along the same lines of forward propulsion and friction that experience frequently is:

> A gas that evenly saturates a container, a torrential flood sweeping away all resistance, a stagnant pond, an unbroken waste of sand, and a monotonous roar are wholes without rhythm. A pond moving in ripples, forked lightning, the waving of branches in the wind, the beating of a bird's wing, the whorl of sepals and petals, changing shadows of clouds on a meadow, are simple natural rhythms. There must be energies resisting each other. Each gains intensity for a certain period, but thereby compresses some opposed energy until the latter can overcome the other which has been relaxing itself as it extends. Then the operation is reversed, not necessarily in equal periods of time but in some ratio that is felt as orderly. Resistance accumulates energy; it institutes conservation until release and expansion ensue.... The pause is a balance or symmetry of antagonistic forces. Such is the generic schema of rhythmic change.[8]

8. Dewey, *Art as Experience*, p. 155.

To some extent, a theory of linear modes and genres hinges on such a "balance or symmetry of antagonistic forces." Each literary mode draws upon the inherent rhythms of the human organism in which muscle opposes muscle, hope balances fear, attraction meets repulsion, and a dialectic of ideas operates in a constant near-symmetry of forces, imbalanced enough to make progress possible. Thus narrative art can be described in part in the terms we would apply to biological, biographical, social, and mental flows of time toward a consummation. We experience daily the rhythmic motions of opening and shutting, expansion and contraction, dance patterns, waving and undulation, and cyclical repetition (as in the recurrence of heart beats, sunsets, tides). Some of our rhythms derive from strictly mechanical movements, such as the rotation of the planet; others are the product of living organisms responding to an environment or are self-motivated. The mind as well as the hand and eye may open and shut; the emotions as well as the lungs may expand and contract; words and poetic lines as well as the feet may move in brief patterns. All of these are conceivable influences on the progress of a narration and aspects of mimetic as opposed to discursive "as if" constructions.

The upshot is that movement in a complex piece of verbal art is never straightforward — and like a point on a wheel, the pursuing mind of the reader, while going generally on, moves forward and down, stands, starts backward and up, and so on. Or to use a more common metaphor, the mind engaged in a narrative rhythm interweaves submerged and surfacing strands, bringing into manifest attention what has laid hidden, grasping again an old thread that has lain unused, all the while filling in a pattern that is never as dominantly *present* as the notes of a musical composition.

The distinction between the suffered rhythm of characters and the rhythm of reading must be doubly insisted upon in this regard, because, thanks to the art of foreshortening inherent in words, readers never gather information with anything like the "pathetic" or psychological states that a Robinson Crusoe experiences in his protracted trials. The difference is important not only in stories that are presented as past and over but also in present-tense, first-person, dramatic narration. In all forms of narrative, characters are deprived of the reader's distance and are continuously impassioned by and implicated in what are to them apparently random experiences whose episodes are conditioned by their incompleteness. As James suggests, life is "all inclusion and confusion" and experience "is never limited, and it is never complete; it is an immense sensibility, a kind of huge spider-web of the finest silken threads suspended in the chamber of consciousness, and catching every air-borne particle in its tissue."[9] Thus from inside the work, the view forward from given points has many alternative paths. Yet from the reader's privileged vantage point in the author's confidence, doubts about the future need scarcely be suffered at all. He may not guess what is coming, but he trusts implicitly in the consistency of the work. As he comes to expect only relevant attributes from people in fiction, for instance, he reads character in a way totally different from the way he interprets real people. The course of a character through a story is much more constricted by the functions of plot than the movement of people is by their habits and activities. As Melville suggests in *The Confidence-Man*, by comparison to the density of people whose parts are often as incongruous as the flying squirrel "and at different periods, as much at variance . . . as the caterpillar is with the butterfly into which it changes," characters are "mere phantoms which flit along a page, like shadows along a wall."[10]

The task of a theory of fictional dynamics, then, is in part to define the differing principles of continuity and rhythm in art and its subjects, and the differences between the suffering of an action by characters and the reader's vicarious gathering of information. What are the elements of anxiety on both these fronts? What effect does the distinction between the progress of characters and the vicarious course of readers have on various modes — comic, tragic, pathetic, sentimental?

FORESHORTENING, CONCEALMENT, HINDRANCE, ANTAGONISM, PROCESSION

The emphasis of the preceding chapters has fallen frequently on the timing of narrative information and formal periodicity. We must apply that interest further here to the operations of narrative rhythm, to the retrieving of the past and predicting of the future, to conceal-

---

9. James, *The Future of the Novel*, p. 12.

10. Herman Melville, *The Confidence-Man* (New York: Hendricks House, 1954), pp. 76-77.

ment, foreshortening, and chance, which contain many of the laws of narrative dynamics.

Ordinarily, for the reader chance, random events, and other uncertainties disappear bit by bit in narrative as aesthetic pattern and meaning replace surmise — as the work progresses from something unknown to something fully rendered. Thus whereas in life new enigmas appear as quickly as old ones are solved, in fiction an ending brings a comparatively thorough assimilation of all parts of an enclosed world. A portion of the reader's pleasure stems from the confirmation of hypotheses, from the discovery that what he has been presented — all the surface, procession of items, and profiles — are elements in a design. His rhythm is that of posed and solved riddles, anticipated and fulfilled desires, in which information and versimilitude serve not merely as glimpses of real people and events but as parts of a game. Hence if the pleasures of a hero are social, sexual, or whatever, the pleasure of a reader is that of resisted patterns of understanding.

Foreshortening

When we ponder more specifically how understanding is liberated from chance in narrative art, the nature of fictive foreshortening and of various techniques of extending and amplifying works appears in a special light. As James realized, narrative resists the intelligence almost successfully, with a fine elusiveness less prominent in realistic than in romantic narrative (which concerns "the things that can reach us only through the beautiful circuit and subterfuge of our thought and our desire"). A narrator need represent nothing directly if he chooses or he may represent nearly everything that happens in a given period, depending on how he wishes to tease out the judgments of taste and the fruits of perception and how much he wants plot to serve as a vehicle of manners, morals, and settings. Plot can be delayed by intensified inner probing, as in James; by the leaden weight of facts, as in Zola and Doris Lessing; or by intellectual deliberation, as in T. H. Huxley. But whatever his predispositions in this regard, a storyteller makes a choice: he decides that the material he has in mind is suitable for this rather than that kind of narrative rhythm and extension, that his interest and talent will lead him into this rather than that kind of logical development. If in drama we "agonize" hindrances and concealments more completely at the rate and from the perspective of the characters, in fiction we have the benefit of the author's intervention and all its options.

Consider, for instance, the matter of foreshortening in a brief fable of a kind that can be readily compiled out of common storytelling techniques:

> In former days, a cruel and ambitious stepmother, wife to a weak and compliant king, suggested to her woodcutter that he would be well-advised — and rewarded — if he quietly disposed of her stepdaughter, who as the king's favorite, was a threat to her son. The woodcutter, a man of principle, refused at first — until the queen reminded him of what frequently happens to those who oppose the royal will. He immediately saw the wisdom of her plan, and next day, on the pretext that he had discovered a patch of delicious wild strawberries, he enticed the king's daughter into the woods. As she bent over the grass in search of them, he was about to deal her a great blow with his ax when a bee caused her to raise her head and see him straining in the backswing. She fell to his feet and begged for her life. Man of principle that he still was, the woodcutter faltered in his purpose, remembering one moment his promise to the queen and the peril of his family, and remembering the next moment his fondness for the girl and his dislike of the queen. The resourceful young girl played skillfully upon his hesitation. When she suggested that with her stepmother out of the way she herself would someday be his employer, he saw her point as quickly as he had seen the queen's. Next day, inviting the stepmother to see the proof of his handiwork, the woodcutter executed against her the great stroke he withheld the day before.
>
> Despite occasional twinges of conscience, usually dispatched immediately by remembrance of the ironic justice they had rendered, neither the woodcutter nor the king's daughter had cause to regret what they had contrived. No investigation disclosed the fate of the unpopular queen, perhaps because no one investigated very thoroughly. Her son left court under cover of dark and never returned. For years after, the two conspirators passed almost daily in the courtyard, at first with some uneasiness in their complicity, then gradually with scarcely a nod of recognition.

In this barest of narrative skeletons, a minimal amount of detail and concrete imagery is used to represent the movement of the plot from inception to completion — or more accurately, from inception, to a faltering reversal, to the emergence of a "concealed force." Something like a logical statement could be extracted from it as a general discursive moral (concerning the biter-bitten, the unreliability of hired assassins, the unexpected benefits of bees, the shortness of memory). When a story is content with bare essentials in this way, it often is so because it exploits concrete animation for some such deliberative end. If the writer's interests were to extend to an imitation of manners and morals, however, he would obviously have to expand the skeleton by quoted drama and a much fuller representation of the interior states of his characters. By the addition of further circumstantial detail of that kind, he would be imagining a much larger world within which the plot, the counterplot, and pivotal characterizations could be augmented. The story might still be enlivened by the same narrative nerve system and connected by the same concept of reversed outcome; its primary unity of causal events and the imagined experience of its characters might be basically the same; but the reader's journey would be greatly protracted and the psychology of form altered accordingly. Most basically different would be the rhythm of expectation, forwarding and resisting information, and ultimate fulfillment.

Several narrative principles can be tentatively deduced from an elementary case like this. First, a slight framework that offers so little delay to the reader's progress does not force the intelligence to take the "beautiful circuit and subterfuge" that James mentions, but encourages him to skip potential complications in seeking a general intent. The writer's overview is made obvious by a severe truncating of events and his appeal to the reader over his characters' heads. This is not to say that a simple, rapid story lacks rhythmic implications; but it handles them basically as part of the relationship between author and audience. (That potential complications in expectation and movement are in fact often present in radically foreshortened fictions is illustrated by Christ's parables and the priest's elaboration of the parable of the law in Kafka's *Great Wall of China*.) The reader might well wonder how the woodcutter's choices weigh on him, how they are related to the social make-up of the court and its hierarchy under a weakened kingship, and what it is like to live in so close a proximity with a fellow conspirator over a period of years. Though such speculations come subsequent to the reading and exist to some extent outside the structure of "suffered knowing" built into the narrative sequence, they are implicit in the fable-as-riddle and vital to it.

In a radically foreshortened method, such things are merely hinted. Yet if very little is said directly about the woodcutter's interior conflict, the strain of his uplifted ax is nonetheless not all muscular. It can be said in his favor that his fear is not for himself alone but for his family and that he is quick to see that he escapes some of the moral stigma of murder by "executing" a would-be murderess. Armed with those two considerations, he is staunch enough to go through with a deed that will haunt him decreasingly as time goes on. In the girl's case as well, the fable is governed by its rhetorical posture, which appeals to the reader's sense of irony without detouring his imagination and feeling through mimetic complexities. If we are a little surprised to find an apparently helpless girl so devious and cunning, it may be because we expect Snow White types to be different from this, and that expectation can be used to reinforce the irony of the story. Indeed, the fable ends with a suggestion of unease and irresolution that acknowledges a kind of triumph of the indeterminate world over conventional fable patterns. Its point of view is stationed long after the event, in aloofness from the dramatic touch-and-go moments of the action, and its compression in effect insists that this is, after all, all one needs to know, since court politics give us very timeworn stories.

The key to the narrative stress system — as one plays with a typical case (not less typical, I hope, for being patently manufactured for the occasion) — is thus not to be located in the reader's vicarious, mimetic participation in real stresses only, but in the implicit ironic address of a storyteller to an assumed audience. The reader is assumed to share with the fabler a fund of knowledge that need not be referred to directly, and the fable's relationship to a presupposed real world depends upon the rules of a certain kind of game. The satiric thrust in this light is twofold: it aims at the compromises of politics and at the fairy tale's capacity to take a high tone with them. Where tales so often link "forever" to "happiness," a brief gradual fizzle might serve as a kind of retort. In any event, the fable seeks justification in the fact that even for accomplices in murder, other affairs are more pressing than their consciences: their pragmatism argues for an economy of moral expenditure that puts aside the burdens of the past in the interest of today's business.

Such observations of proportion, tone, and fictional logic will readily suggest that stories are sensitive mechanisms, and a small change from what we expect brings with it important alterations in narrative dynamics. As James realized in reviewing his work and assembling the prefaces gathered in *The Art of the Novel*, the working out of a story at any length requires tact and structural sense, especially with respect to the technique of foreshortening. He finds Balzac's skill in that regard especially noteworthy:

> No one begins, to my sense, to handle the time-element and produce the time-effect with the authority of Balzac in his amplest sweeps. . . . That study of the foreshortened image, of the neglect of which I suggest the ill consequence, is precisely the enemy of the tiresome procession of would-be narrative items, seen all in profile, like the rail-heads of a fence; a substitute for the baser device of accounting for the time-quantity by mere quantity of statement. Quality and manner of statement account for it in a finer way . . . The fashion of our day is to account for it almost exclusively by an inordinate abuse of the colloquial resource, of the report, from page to page, from chapter to chapter, from beginning to end of the talk . . . between the persons involved. Talk between persons is perhaps, of all the parts of the novelist's plan, the part that Balzac most scrupulously weighed and measured and kept in its place. [*The Future of the Novel*, pp. 121–22]

It is true that in his own middle period, James admonishes the novelist again and again to dramatize and in reviewing *Roderick Hudson* discovers that he has himself too radically compressed the material at a critical moment. A pace that moves too fast can be disastrous: "Roderick's disintegration, a gradual process, and of which the exhibitional interest is exactly that it *is* gradual and occasional, and thereby traceable and watchable, swallows two years in a mouthful, proceeds quite *not* by years, but by weeks and months, and thus renders the whole view the disservice of appearing to present him as a morbidly special case" (*The Art of the Novel*, p. 12). Yet despite this concession to the value of narrative extension and dramatization, James also realizes that "no action . . . was ever made historically vivid without a certain factitious compactness" (*The Art of the Novel*, p. 15). Apt foreshortening, as Balzac's method illustrates it, derives from the same sense of proportion and rhythmic effect as unfore-shortened dramatic speech: both, in James's eyes, should serve appropriate moments and an overall sense of organic form:

> To put all that is possible of one's idea into a form and compass that will contain and express it only by delicate adjustments and an

exquisite chemistry, so that there will at the end be neither a drop of
one's liquor left nor a hair's breadth of the rim of one's glass to spare
— every artist will remember how often that sort of necessity has
carried with it its particular inspiration. Therein lies the secret of the
appeal, to his mind, of the successfully *foreshortened* thing, where
representation is arrived at . . . not by the addition of items . . . but by
the art of figuring synthetically, a compactness into which the imagination may cut thick, as into the rich density of wedding-cake. [*The Art
of the Novel*, pp. 87–88]

James's comment on narrative tension and proportion are
especially authoritative because they come from one who articulated
so fully the adjustments that the writer must make between his own
real world and the crafted fiction he presents — who recognized so
frequently the shaping force of point of view and dramatic representation, largely by means of which the novelist constructs a story from a
fragile, unexpanded idea. They carry added weight for coming in the
period of James's highest interest in the drama, in the writing of *The
Tragic Muse*, when he called most often for full dramatization and
realized that in plays the dialogue alternation of points of view makes
for a tightness and a consistency "other than that of the novel at its
loosest." As he well knew, full dramatic representation has "the
charm of the scenic consistency, the consistency of multiplication of
aspects (*The Art of the Novel*, p. 90). By contrast, a novel like *The
Princess Casamassima* is "frankly panoramic and processional," and
novels like *War and Peace*, at the extreme of novelistic expansion, are
"large loose baggy monsters, with their queer elements of the accidental and the arbitrary." All the more reason, then, to value James's
acknowledgment of the artistry of apt foreshortening and dynamic
shortcuts to the reader's intelligence through abbreviated rhythms. It
is by that lopping of loose ends and the interweaving of what remains that art works its most marvelous transformations of life into
the rich density of symbol systems. As to loose forms of realistic
imitation:

We have heard it maintained, we will remember, that such things are
"superior to art"; but we understand least of all what *that* may mean,
and we look in vain for the artist, the divine explanatory genius, who
will come to our aid and tell us. There is life and life, and as waste is
only life sacrificed and thereby prevented from "counting," I delight in
a deep-breathing economy and an organic form. [*The Art of the Novel*,
p. 84]

Thus in retrospect on his dramatic period, James realized the short-comings of excessive extension. He realized that the question of what to show and what to tell is inseparable not only from the problem of making the reader follow the action at the right pace but also from the question of how the hero is to develop and master the hindrances of his course, since above all, *rhythm* to narrative is the sequent application of *fate*: it determines, if not what is to happen, how it is to feel when it happens, and that is inseparable from what it signifies.

Hindrance and Procession

If we set aside for a moment the author's explicit considerations of the audience and concentrate on characters, the movement of stories appears primarily a dance of forwarding and hindering elements centered in a protagonist and antagonist, or a hero and his situation. Such figures dominate the rhythms of plots and subplots and are to narrative dynamics approximately what melodies are to music. The dramatic psychology especially of longer works comes primarily from our vicarious participation in their actions as conceivable responses to precarious or uneasy situations.

Obviously, every period and mode reconceives the nature of the protagonist and his resistance. In fact, perhaps nothing reveals more clearly the strategic responsiveness of literary form to its social conditions than its mimetic handling of them. For instance, as Edward Alsworth Ross remarked near the turn of the century in *Sin and Society*, the "mutualism" of modern societies has created quite different sins and virtues than previous societies, thanks largely to the surrender of many of our vital interests to specialists:

> Nowadays the water main is my well, the trolley car my carriage, the banker's safe my old stocking, the policeman's billy my fist. My own eyes and nose and judgment defer to the inspector of food, or drugs, or gas, or factories, or tenements, or insurance companies. I rely upon others to look after my drains, invest my savings, nurse my sick, and teach my children.

With that surrender, we usher in "a multitude of new forms of wrong-doing":

> Most sin is preying, and every new social relation begets its cannibalism. No one will "make the ephah small" or "falsify the balances" until there is buying and selling, "withhold the pledge" until there is loan-

ing, "keep back the hire of the laborers" until there is a wage system, "justify the wicked for a reward" until men submit their disputes to a judge. The rise of the state makes possible counterfeiting, smuggling, speculation, and treason. Commerce tempts the pirate, the forger, and the embezzler. Every new fiduciary relation is a fresh opportunity for breach of trust.

The character types spawned by these fiduciary relations and their betrayal are obviously not at all like the chivalric hero and the ruffian: "How decent are the pale slayings of the quack, the adulterator, and the purveyor of polluted water, compared with the red slayings of the vulgar bandit or assassin!" Our "iniquity is wireless, and we know not whose withers are wrung by it. The hurt passes into that vague mass, the 'public,' and is there lost to view."[11] In such a society, the modern hero rides forth armed with expectations for a useful specialized job in his father's glass factory and encounters the attrition of social snobbery, the abrasion of a foreman, or the slickness of an advertiser. The power of his motives ebbs away or is syphoned off by this or that example of pettiness, and the whole affair is protracted by the strained relations he has with his mother, his wife, or his partner. Also, in the normal course of things, much of the battle turns inward as he has to adopt some of the attitudes that a complex, interwoven group of specialists requires, and these war with his initial character.

Yet, as mimetic or as realistic as characters may seem in this reflection of social structures, in the stresses of fiction they are still beholding to the special abbreviations of story form and authorial compression. Or to put it differently, centered in a hero, the stressful forces of even the most extended of narratives enact in pantomime a push forward and a resistance that are no less governed by the power of verbal abstraction than the rhythms of the parable. The structure of human relations is thus altered not merely by the evolution of new relations in real societies but also by the predispositions of given narrative forms. Unlike real-life counterparts, protagonists and antagonists may be and often are as well matched as Samuel Beckett's Watt and friend:

> I turned him round, until he faced me. Then I placed his hands, on my
> shoulders, his left hand on my right shoulder, and his right hand on

---

11. Edward Alsworth Ross, *Sin and Society* (Boston: Houghton Mifflin, 1907).

my left shoulder. Then I placed my hands, on his shoulders, on his left shoulder my right hand, and on his right shoulder my left hand. Then I took a single pace forward, with my left leg, and he a single pace back, with his right leg (he could scarcely do otherwise). Then I took a double pace forward with my right leg, and he of course with his left leg a double pace back. And so we paced together between the fences, I forwards, he backwards, until we came to where the fences diverged again. And then turning, I turning, and he turning, we paced back the way we had come, I forwards, and he of course backwards, with our hands on our shoulders, as before. And so pacing back the way we had come, we passed the holes and paced on, until we came to where the fences diverged again. And then turning, as one man, we paced back the way we had come, I looking whither we were going, and he looking whence we were coming. And so, up and down, up and down, we paced between the fences, together again after so long, and the sun shone bright upon us, and the wind blew wild about us.

To be together again, after so long, who love the sunny wind, the windy sun, in the sun, in the wind, that is perhaps something, perhaps something.[12]

Coming toward this dancelike model of the hero and his necessary double, Watt gets up as often as he falls or else he would not arrive; and one leg moves as the other does, or else they would not advance and retreat. The balancing elements of wind and sun, arms, shoulders, and legs renders them aesthetically right.

And so it sometimes is with the mechanical operations of the narrative spirit. Indeed, more characters than Beckett's behave as though they had been commissioned to make the novelist's formal task easier. No fictive hero is free of the need to live out his part in the fictive design while he moves in answer to the needs of aesthetic form: Tom Jones must encounter Tom Jones's kind of hurdles, and Emma Woodhouse another kind altogether. Defoe gives us an uneven but progressive dance of resourceful character and circumstance, James a dance of mutually inquiring and probing consciousnesses. Nor can we forget entirely the reader's silent part in this dance of formal elements. What characters are allowed to do is governed in part by what at a given point the audience is expected to experience. A protagonist acquires his opponents not only in proportion to his needs but also at proper moments, when they can contribute significantly to the reader's education. As mysterious and as self-willed as antagonists

12. Samuel Beckett, *Watt* (New York: Grove Press, 1959), p. 163.

may appear to be, they are thus created out of the hero's potential and out of the story's need as rhetoric. Not until the progress of Red Cross calls for Archimago will Archimago appear and proceed to fill in the system of pieties and impieties that Spenser canvasses under the heading of "Holiness."

Despite the frequent presence of well-matched antagonists in narrative dynamics, it is possible to overstate the importance of retardation in the timing of events, especially in forms like personification allegory that seek discursive and conceptual stability and the certainties of abstract form. Quite apart from the brief fable, any of the less mimetic modes makes the progress of our understanding somewhat distant from a vicarious involvement in the battles of characters. The fictionalist reserves the right to give us information openly and by essentially undramatic means — by authorial summaries, gnomic utterance, description, and internal monologue, all of which affect the rhythm of the "dance."

Even when he keeps out of the fiction as a characterized person himself, the author can minimize the suffering of knowledge by means of what we can call a processional unfolding, or a march through a plot that approaches pictorial, hymnal, or lyric design in the manner of masques or ritual dramas. For instance, the following declaration from Sophocles' *Antigone* sums up a view of mankind in a hymnlike way and stands sufficiently apart from the ordeals of characters to condense their suffering into a kind of verbal tableau — a little as Yeats condenses history in "Two Songs":

> nothing walks stranger than man.
> This thing crosses the sea in the winter's storm,
> making his path through the roaring waves.
> And she, the greatest of gods, the earth —
> imageless she is, and unwearied — he wears her away
> as ploughs go up and down from year to year
> and his mules turn up the soil.
>
> Gay nations of birds he snares and leads,
> wild beast tribes and the salty brood of the sea,
> with the twisted mesh of his nets, this clever man.
> He controls with craft the beasts of the open air,
> walkers on hills. The horse with his shaggy mane
> he holds and harnesses, yoked about the neck,
> and the strong bull of the mountain.
> Language, and thought like the wind

and feelings that make the town,
he has taught himself, and shelter against the fold,
refuge from the rain. He can always help himself.
He faces no future helpless. There's only death
that he cannot find an escape from.[13]

The images are of typical activities or recurrent universals; they foreshorten countless episodes from the panorama of mankind into a few
sentences. Such a catalogue not only suits the rising sense of strangeness that Sophocles wishes the audience to have at this point but also
prepares for the irony of man's helplessness before a tragic destiny so
broad that no one escapes its repercussions. The plot becomes
momentarily an illustration of a procession of great events, in display
of man's prowess and ultimate helplessness before death.

In fiction as well as in masque pageantry and drama, summaries
and processional images have a place in the control of the reader's
apprehensive course. By comparison to the technique of embattled
hindrance, in processional form nothing surprising emerges from unrepresented gaps that can cause an unexpected reversal. The stuff of
crises and ironies is missing. Thus if in undecided battles between
antagonists we have a highly unstable disarray of forces that have not
yet reached, or are unable to maintain, processional form and govern-
ment, in a procession we have matched, complementary, allied
parties, openly manifested and declared. For example, in *The Faerie
Queene*, Red Cross is educated not merely by timely encounters with
chivalric antagonists but also by various virtues and vices arranged as
pageantry. The sins on parade in the House of Pride are very orderly
and manifest in their unruliness; in ranking themselves from sins of
the senses to sins of the spirit, they march before him like chapters of
a book exemplifying in their iconographic way the categories of
"Pride." The reader in turn sees them over Red Cross's shoulder and
finds them iconic reinforcement of Spenser's didactic intent. Set apart
from the action, they are static illustration. (That they are clearer to
the reader than to Red Cross adds to our view of them an ironic attitude toward the hero, whose perceptions for some time run well behind the reader's.)

Most forms of epic and romance combine processions and battles

13. Sophocles, *Antigone*, from *The Complete Greek Tragedies*, ed. David Grene and
Richmond Lattimore, trans. Elizabeth Wyckoff (Chicago: University of Chicago Press,
1959), lines 332–59, pp. 170–71.

in establishing the rhythm of their opposing and complementary forces. *The Iliad, Chanson Roland,* and chivalric romances like Chaucer's *Knight's Tale* enumerate considerable masses in rank and order, as in the parades of knights in tournaments and forces lining up for impending battle. (The enumeration of a herd of sheep in *Don Quixote* is a mock example.) They emphasize usually the schematic order of the participants, successiveness, dress, manners, and visual signs of status, all of these set off stylistically by the repetition of phrases and the symmetry of clauses. Likewise, historical chronicles often arrange temporal events, dynastic succession, and kingdoms in processional display as a way of laying information before the reader in an undramatized fashion.

However, the processional element in given texts is ordinarily subordinate to an antagonistic plot in the long run, where it is used to alter narrative rhythm and enlarge focus. In *Paradise Lost,* for instance, Milton shifts frequently from battles to processions and back and suggests that each of these reflects something in reality itself. Processional displays mirror the orders of Heaven and Hell; on other occasions, they are useful in making timely revelations to Adam about the nature of the history he has set going. As in all revelation in Milton, the viewer is brought into the procession by the excitement of the new knowledge of reality that it contains. Adam's prefiguring vision of the Old Testament and the angels' view of creation, for instance, attune the beholder to the pace of revelation; and presumably, looking over their shoulders, the reader participates in their responsiveness. At the conclusion of the war in Heaven, after a relatively fast pace of explosive surprises in the largest of the epic's protagonist-antagonist scenes, war is converted into ritual procession as Christ enters the battle and makes surprise and hazard yield to clear divine manifestation: truth becomes settled and well witnessed for the angel warriors. In passages of more explicit enumeration and pageantry, the onlooker discovers an order analogous to the creation, in the six days' pageant of species and forms. Ultimately the poem itself presents a comprehensive pageantry of history and suggests that whatever happens anywhere exists in God's omniscience as a tableau: all highly suffered drama, from one point of view, is pure procession. Thus, the closer to the celestial perspective we move, the more narrative comes to resemble ritual ceremony — not, to be sure, quite in the comic mode of Beckett's two strange partners, but in a dance of symbolic encounters between God and Satan, who work out between them a panoramic destiny and a rhythm of response and counterresponse. The legions of angels, the entry of Christ into the war, the creation, the chronicles of the Old Testament, and, in *Paradise Regained*, the visions of Satan from the mountain expose us to large vistas, the parts of which are not merely coordinate and successive but members of a logical whole. In any naming or enumeration, from the listing of forms of life in Eden to the chronicles of kings and prophets, all names strive to realize a single purpose and move toward a predetermined conclusion. Whatever hard-won decisions the fallen angels arrive at and whatever momentary success they seem to have, their contribution to a greater good is already foreseen; no stage of the battle happens that has not already been "composed" into ceremony.

In some cases, however, as in the list of fallen angels in Book I (lines 374–521), the expectation of epic grandeur is purposely frustrated, and we are made to recognize, as in the parade of sins in Spenser's House of Pride, that processions can be ironically conceived as presentations of confusion. What we find in Satan's followers, for instance, is not a coordinated body but an antimasque rabblement. Milton's point is that the fallen angels prefigure the historical parade of false gods that will eventually obscure Christ's emergence into the Old Testament's procession of types and figures. Thus the themes of the catalogue of devils — so unified under Satan's tyranny in one way and so torn asunder in other ways — are abomination, blood sacrifice, and idolatry, all to be answered later by Michael's account of Christ's culminating sacrifice. The ranks are composed of types of Satan — Moloch, Thammuz, Dagon, Baalin, Ashtoroth, Astoreth, or Astarte, Osiris, Isis, and Orus. As these parade now in Hell they will later spread out in a temporal procession of "monstrous shapes," in the chronicles of "Fanatic Egypt," Greece, and Israel.

The balance of stressful and unstressful unfolding is obviously different in each narrative mode. If hindrances are often arranged schematically in romance, allegory, parables, and epic, in realism protagonists are characteristically exposed to what appear to them to be interventions and unexpected antagonisms following an irregular rhythm. The irregularity is perhaps partly due to the fact that — unlike the *Knight's Tale* or *The Faerie Queene* — the novel does not presuppose a ranked and orderly universe; both its societies and its events are relatively loosely connected but nearly always antagonistic, seldom processional. Whereas Adam's wilderness, as presented by Michael, is an allegorical pageant of types leading to a culmination in Christ, Crusoe's wilderness is a succession of apparent accidents — barley seeds that sprout unexpectedly after some years, grapes discovered in another part of the island, goats that just happen to be there, and unexpected visitations at irregular intervals from parties beyond the island's sphere. Both Adam and Crusoe manage to arrive at meaningful destinies, and Crusoe's progress in the long run is no less contrived by Defoe's sense of art than Adam's by Milton's. But moment by moment the connections among events seem to Crusoe and the reader to be hidden, largely unintelligible, and unrhythmic. Both pacing and cadence are uncertain, not only in the plot but also in the prose style. In the darkness of his unsymbolic world, Crusoe can only read the footprints of cannibals and guess: Why after all should they come to the island at such intervals? What are their motives and their means? How should one handle them? Crusoe expects their return imminently after the first discovery, but years pass as he continues to worry about them and alters his entire routine because of them. It tortures his assumption about a providential universe that people without the faith should exist to begin with and be such puzzling mixtures of barbarism and natural virtues. Given so much conflicting evidence and so little guidance beyond the phrases he hits upon in the Bible, Crusoe must become an opportunistic wilderness pioneer.

Even this degree of irregularity is slight, however, compared with the acknowledgment of untimely interventions that a fully developed naturalism makes. In Zola, for instance, as James suggests, "our sense of exhibition" is

> as little as possible an impression of parts and books, of particular "plots" and persons. It produces the effect of a mass of imagery in which shades are sacrificed .... The fullest, the most characteristic episodes affect us like a sounding chorus or procession, as with a hubbub of voices and a multitudinous tread of feet. ["Emile Zola," *The Future of the Novel*, p. 169]

Such a hubbub is the effect not only of naturalism but of all traditional forms of antilogical narrative such as Rabelaisian satire and picaresque, where antagonists and intervening forces are seldom expected or appropriate. Though they may suggest a procession at times, it is a hubbub, an epistemological puzzlement that, rather than resolving itself in declared identities as Crusoe's footprints eventually do (when Friday, for instance, is given a name and a function), remains a permanent part of men's nonsensical condition. Thus whereas in the teleology of Platonist and Christian world views and in the somewhat muddled but epistemologically confident world of the middle-class novel the hand of providence ultimately guarantees the hero's identity, the picaro inhabits a world whose rhythm is that of the prank, the empty stomach, and the exploded expectation. The difficulty for such disillusioned wanderers as Lazarillo de Tormes, the swindler, Quixote, and Candide lies in the culminating of identities, the finishing of an accumulative rhythm. They remain open to a multiplicity of values and a skepticism whose natural rhythm is that of scrapes, in which the hero falls into dire trouble, gets bruised, and escapes with something slightly less than a fatal injury.

In this respect, the main tradition of middle-class novels lies at the center of the spectrum of types somewhere between picaresque and traditional epic, romance, and allegory. In the former, interventions are unprovidential, unhistoric, and unhealthy; in the latter, episodes unfold with some regularity under the governing principles of the court, the church, ranks of knights, or the celestial host, whose typical representatives have easy access to the hero. The trick of middle-class realism is to acknowledge the waywardness and openness of a world that allows the Moll Flanderses and Pamelas of the world to rise against all expectations and yet illustrate a social logic that leads the protagonist to a suitable place. The rhythm of episodes is cumulative and revelatory even if irregular, and the value of a defined social position is unquestioned. Thus in Defoe, the old structure of picaresque is rearranged as the vagrant progress of deprived people toward the comfort of a hard-won prosperity. The hindrances that the hero faces are not those of the novel's earlier protagonists, even those of heroes he most resembles such as Lazarillo, Jack Wilton, Gil Glas, Guzman, or Don Pablos in *The Swindler*. (Neither Colonel Jack nor Moll Flanders encounters as many thieves, cheaters, and practical tricksters as the traditional picaro does.) They stem instead from nature, irregularities in the social system, and the hero's own propensity to stray from the straight and narrow. Progress is still definable

by the laws of accumulation, change in social class, the dynamics of
investment and return, sowing and reaping, or simply the mechanics
of labor and marketing. The main narrative gaps and intervals can be
described and predicted largely from what is already known, because
though not fully enumerated, reality is self-evident. If exotic things
like cannibals visit one's island, they prove to be controllable. (Unlike Crusoe, Candide or Lazarillo might well have ended up in a boiling pot, testing the principles of barbarism on their own reddening
skins.)

Thus though inexperience, sickness, providence, and human frailty
complicate the progress of the middle-class hero, in the long run anyone who lives in so fully a manifest universe as Defoe's, Richardson's, Fielding's, or Austen's can afford to be hopeful. Despite the
disconnectednesses of adjacent episodes, the perils of shipwreck, and
the attack of wolves, one who, like Crusoe, labors wisely and repents
of his waywardness is always rewarded. Likewise, when Oliver Twist
is exposed to the chaos of London and encounters first Fagin and
then Mr. Brownlow, though we assume momentarily that chance or
coincidence has placed these people in his path, the scurry and bustle
of the modern city eventually sorts itself out. Though the realistic surface of Dickens's method resists any open betrayal of a highly manipulated plot, manipulated it surely is. Its narrative formulas pay close
attention not merely to the periodical rhythm of peril and escape but
to symbolic appropriateness. Just as Crusoe encounters Friday when
Defoe wants him to, so Fagin and Brownlow come to Oliver almost
in allegorical procession.

In the realm of social realism, the subservience of episodes and
events to the reader's rhythm of puzzle-and-answer is nowhere more
evident than in the Jamesian novel, which of course is written by
more novelists than James. The trademark of Jamesian disclosure is a
retrospective sense of the rightness of everything that has happened
and its moral assimilation. With the exception of "The Turn of the
Screw" and *The Sacred Fount*, characters inside the fiction and
readers outside find apparent mysteries not only resolvable but
strongly registered on consciousness. As James remarks about the
sensibility of characters that interest him most,

> Their being finely aware — as Hamlet and Lear, say, are finely aware
> — *makes* absolutely the intensity of their adventure, gives the
> maximum sense to what befalls them. We care, our curiosity and sym-

pathy care, comparatively little for what happens to the stupid, the coarse and the blind; care for it, and the effects of it, at the most as helping to precipita'te what happens to the more deeply wondering, to the really sentient. [*The Art of the Novel*, p. 62]

Change in status is not often what the hero seeks in Jamesian novels, and economic difficulties are only part of what hinders his progress. Instead, he seeks a higher consciousness based on a discovery of the secrets of a select group.

In a different kind of concern with the "really sentient," the novel in the hands of Saul Bellow, William Faulkner, John Barth, Bernard Malamud, William Golding, D. H. Lawrence, James Joyce, and Marcel Proust explores less confidently the interior careers and the dynamics of memory, sex, particular occupations, and private identities. Its chief concealments are not the laws of a definable social order but personal relations, psychoses, and special situations (a death in the family, a divorce, the politics of the academy, or life in a prison camp). So interior, oblique, and unnamable are the forces that prevent the hero's instant realization of his preferences that neither the traditional antagonisms of "battle" nor the ranked alignments of an epic progression provide an adequate metaphor for the fictive stress system of such novelists, whose imbalance of narrative, descriptive, and propositional elements can only be encompassed by irony and dark humor. The old disillusioned wanderer finds his modern kinship in Louis-Ferdinand Céline, Barth, and Peter Matthiesson; the social novel finds its negative modern forms in Italo Svevo, William Styron, Norman Mailer, Wright Morris, and Katherine Anne Porter; the novel of interior consciousness pursues its disrupted rhythms in Conrad, Vladimir Nabakov, Flannery O'Connor, William Pynchon, Ralph Ellison, Carson McCullers, and preeminently Kafka. (Many of these forms join in *Ulysses*, whose narrative rhythms are perhaps the most entangled and complex in modern fiction.) Though remnants of a straightforward realist tradition are also prominent in novelists like Theodore Dreiser, Upton Sinclair, John Steinbeck, Ford Madox Ford, E. M. Forster, Edith Warton, Thomas Mann, Edward Wallant, and others, the tone of modern fiction is predicted much less by George Eliot or Thackeray than by the darker James, Dostoyevsky, and Chekhov — which is to say, by the broken rhythms of internal self-searching and the dissociation of events in the hero's life from the processes of meaningful discovery in the reader.

IRONIC DISCLOSURE

In these novels of discomfirmation and broken rhythm, we are unable to equate concealment and hindrance as we can when a hero confronts his antagonists openly and gets some idea about himself from their relative strength. The concealed strands of the plot are not always merely barriers to a decisive act.[14] As modern fiction often illustrates, the retarding of an action is not always identical with a postponement of knowledge, especially for the reader, nor is the completion of a plot equivalent to narrative enlightenment. In this separation we discover another basic reason for distinguishing between the progress of vicarious suffering and the progress of knowledge. It is true that in a great many narrative stress systems, they march side by side; but in others what a protagonist suffers is not enlightening for him, and perhaps not for the reader; and in return what he knows may not be put into action. Even in plots where suffering and knowledge are closely identified, the end of concealment may not be the end of action. In *The Faerie Queene*, for instance, Red Cross goes forth to further ordeals after his identity and his destiny have been fully explained to him. Though in Milton's epics Christ's knowledge and act are perfectly coordinated, for Satan all action is based on misinformation and false hope: without acting in error he could not act at all. He discovers his errors only after committing himself to an irreversible path, and by then suffering and eventual inaction are doomed to redouble upon him. For Malory's Lancelot, the vision of the grail should preclude his returning to the chivalric life, as a fuller but similar vision does for Galahad; but he acts in defiance of what he is given to know and makes vision and act ironically disproportionate. In the reverse of this, in Kafka's *The Castle* K's perplexities remain in abundance after the action is complete. In fact, the more Kafka's protagonists learn, the more impeded they become; the more an action of some kind is imposed on them, the less they understand it.

Self-knowledge and action tend to be noncoincident in most modern fiction, then. "Truth" to Kurtz in "Heart of Darkness" is too

14. Goodman, *The Structure of Literature*: "Discovery is the emergence of the hidden plot, to occupy the acted stage and to become part of the unity of time. Reversal is the destruction of the apparent plot and the succession of the hidden plot." Again, "The goodness of the protagonist is the seriousness of the apparent plot. Frailty is the possibility of emergence of the hidden plot" (p. 35).

destructive to issue in action; and in *The Secret Agent*, a consistently ironic novel, Winnie Verloc's first revelation leads to murder and its consequences push her toward suicide — an ultimate act to end action, the product of a final insight to put an end to knowing. A similar discrepancy between knowing and suffering is sensitively sustained in Patrick White's novel *The Tree of Man*, the central characters of which are consistently mute and inarticulate. In this case, the events of Stan and Amy Parker's long lifetime and the growth of a civilization around them give their careers the inherent logic of biological and social development. But beyond that logic they discover little by way of satisfying ends and purposes to guide them. Nature itself offers no readable signs and symbols; though men and nature correspond in a multitude of ways, none of these is fully verbalized. As a result of this muteness, each becomes an island to himself in a tangible, variable, richly physical environment. Each is deprived of the one action that might fulfill an inner potential for social communion. Even the mystery and the poetry that abound in "the extraordinary behind the ordinary," as White remarks, dries up eventually. Amy rids herself of lovely effigies because "poetry that has been used up must go out of the system."[15]

In greater extremes, as we think of more fully satiric narrative forms, a hero such as Gulliver, Candide, Quixote, Nathanael West's Lemuel Pitkin, or Barth's Giles Goat-Boy and Ebenezer Cooke marches blindly on, stumbling into this or that unforeseen shock. A bark on the shin heralds every small piece of unpleasant truth and reverses every innocent expectation. The fully disillusioned hero who eventually emerges so well marked by his progress finally has little left but to putter in his private garden; no universal piece of gnomic wisdom or hopeful humanitarianism survives empirical testing. One suffers a lot; one knows and does very little. One's progress is indeed marked by the *shrinking* of mysteries, the breaking of effigies, the expelling of "used" poetry from the system.

Such discrepancies between expectation and confirmation obviously widen the gap between the reader and the hero and affect seriously the relationship between author and reader. The reader's expectations march well ahead of the bruised hero's; or the defeat of innocence derails his sympathy en route. In the terms of Arthur Koestler's *Insight and Outlook* (a book much to our purpose at this

15. Patrick White, *The Tree of Man* (New York: Viking Press, 1955), p. 448.

point), a comic or satiric mechanism sets two lines of force on a collision course, and though the reader's mind leaps nimbly from one to another when they intersect, the feelings and passions, entangled in sympathy for a mimetic hero, are slower to adjust. Laughter signals the necessary realignment of mind and nervous system when "two independent and self-contained logical chains" cross.[16] It thus exposes the consequential movement of narrative at a perilous moment, when an unexpected complication threatens our entrancement in a single rhythm, when thought, feeling, and action become disconnected and the rhythm is broken or made complex. Such a change-about demands a new perspective and an accommodation of unlike things to each other, as when the flight of a pie contacts the immobility of a face. The briefest examples of disconfirmation are riddles and jokes; the most extended are the ironic reversal plots of the comic novel. Both illustrate vicarious derailings and point up the fact that, to react with laughter, the reader must have "shadowed" a figure or pattern of thought and risked stumbling himself. But of course readers fall very lightly and spring up very nimbly. The difference between a barked shin and a laugh gives a clear indication of the difference.

But vicarious participation and derailings are complicated affairs. The rhythms of buildup and laughter can be seriously qualified by a continuous plot, for instance. Though laughter is in some respects inimical to continuity and partial to episodic construction, in both anecdote and drama it often serves as punctuation for segments of a greater whole that is in no way totally disrupted by it. This is evident in writers like Barth, who uses laughter to relieve the pain of an ever increasing disillusionment, and again in Brecht and Gay. In the latter, the laughter that comes at such frequent intervals of *The Three Penny Opera* and *The Beggar's Opera* is qualified by turns in the action that it helps prepare for. Both plot and pieces of wit help to derail normal sympathy for respectable society and for the underdogs it creates. The ironic twists of humor and plot alike render consistent insights into the social scramble, and witty expressions of value find a ready illustration in action, as when Macheath laments (with some justice) in Brecht's version: "We bourgeois artisans, who work with honest himmies on the cash boxes of small shopkeepers, are being swallowed up by large concerns backed by banks. What is a picklock to a bank

16. Arthur Koestler, *Insight and Outlook* (New York: Macmillan, 1949), p. 20.

share? What is the burgling of a bank to the founding of a bank? What is the murder of a man to the employment of a man?"[17] (Under the circumstances, it is as logical to raise Macheath to the ranks of the nobility as to hang him.) Combining the comic spirit of Gay and Brecht with the metaphysical depths of Kafka, Barth deepens psychic wounds and embitters laughter but nonetheless releases the tension of continuous plots frequently with outlandish wit and verbal play. So qualified are the continuous plots of *The Sot-Weed Factor* and *Giles Goat-Boy* that we find it difficult to remember their outcomes. In the rhythm of expectations and hasty spills, we have come not to expect either an ultimate confirmation or an ultimate disillusionment, though Ebenezer Cooke at sixty-six finally succumbs "to a sort of quinsy," and Giles, too, realizes definitively that "late or soon, we lose. Sudden or slow, we lose. The bank exacts its charge for each redistribution of our funds. There is an entropy to time, a tax on change: four nickels for two dimes, but always less silver; our books stay reconciled, but who in modern terms can tell heads from tails?"[18] But the terms in which he puts it and the foreseeing of his own death in romantic terms lifts some of the burden, as does the comic apparatus of prefaces and posttapes that Barth puts between the reader and the fiction.

Comic discrepancies between what the hero knows and the action he is able to accomplish, or between what he and the audience know, are not what we always mean by an ironic plot, however. An ironic plot usually hinges upon reversals brought about when a concealed force overturns in its own erupting rhythm or counterrhythm what the protagonist has been led to regard as a controlling development. Thus, expecting to disclose the hidden figure who is responsible for the blight of his people, Oedipus discovers himself as criminal and must accordingly redirect the drive for justice against himself. The damage is too severe to be laughable, and the shadowing reader obviously seeks a different kind of catharsis. In "The Turn of the Screw," to take a less demonstrable case of ironic reversal, the governess in seeking to save the children under her care joins other schoolmasters in forcing them to acknowledge the evil of their associations and through her accusations thus overturns their de-

17. Bertolt Brecht, *The Threepenny Opera*, trans. Desmond Vesey and Eric Bentley (New York: Grove Press, 1949), 3.3.

18. John Barth, *Giles Goat-Boy* (New York: Fawcett Crest Books, 1967), p. 763.

velopment and her own expectations. The further her protective investigation proceeds, the more dangerous she becomes.

In some ways, ironic plots such as these are the most comprehensive of all fictional designs because their retardation, their mystifying predictions, and finally their forced review of misleading evidence, as provoked by the reversal, subdue both action and knowledge to a newly confirmed and more complex design. Even in plots of disillusionment, the strength of that design derives from the conviction of a solved puzzle. What has seemed an enigma, what has led to a false hypothesis, is redefined as a complex and unexpected sort of undeniable truth. In a similar way, Candide can acknowledge his naiveté; Agave (in Euripides' *The Bacchae*) can confess the cruelty and power of Dionysus and go sorrowfully into exile on the grounds that she has previously gone 180 degrees in the wrong direction and been forcefully turned about. If the worst proves to be true, merely to accept it is a comfort compared to beating one's head against a wall. For the audience, too, in terms of memory and recall, the previous moments of an ironic narrative or dramatic structure are summoned back by reversals in order to be re-formed, which tightens the recurrence of information into significant form and makes recall not merely repetition but dramatic reconstitution.

If, like Milton in *Paradise Regained*, the author wishes at that point to make a serious truth-claim for his fable, he can find no better time to enforce it than after a demonstration of a prideful investigation that has gone wrong and been purged of its mistakes. One of the functions of Satan in both *Paradise Lost* and *Paradise Regained* is to demonstrate the disaster of illusions, as for instance, the pursuit of forbidden knowledge, disbelief in God's manifest word, and misconceptions about the nature of freedom. The irony of the fallen universe is that only by exposure to Satan's way of interpreting things and to Eve's costly knowledge can the reader realize the complex truth of the course laid out for mankind. (Samson and the Philistines make a similar discovery in *Samson Agonistes* when Samson collapses the temple about them in demonstration of a superior power of his god, newly asserted after a long period of obscurity and doubt.) When by a forceful peripeteia an inadequate and single-minded hypothesis is replaced, the new command of knowledge over act usually either strengthens or destroys the protagonist. While perhaps no one would claim that Agave is better off for having mistakenly torn her son limb from limb under the influence of religious ecstasy — and then discovered what she has done — Eve is clearly better in some ways for her discovery of complex knowledge, and Adam is stronger for the preview of a sad, error-filled human history he is given. Rastignac's course is altered in *Old Goriot* when Collins (Vautrin) shatters the complacency of his view of how to get ahead and forces him to acknowledge the corruption around him. Though again Rastignac is not particularly strengthened by that knowledge, he can get nowhere without it, and his continued ignorance would soon close off our interest. Various underground or estranged figures such as Barth's Ebenezer Cooke, the traditional Spanish picaro, Dickens's Fagin, James Wright's Bigger Thomas, and Ralph Ellison's invisible man bring about or discover similar inversions of prevailing assumptions and replace them with strengthened, tested assumptions.

As these figures illustrate, the shock of reversal plots is not only to the process of knowing but also to our sympathy and the progress of feeling. Heroes who are cast down or out by reversals usually carry with them some of the sympathies that normally extend to victims. Like Lord Jim and like Winnie Verlock in *The Secret Agent*, the outcast has been "one of us," and if he can no longer be so, we must understand why. On the same principle, detective stories told from the criminal's point of view are frequently more taut than those seen from the perspective of society's detectives because they give us an oblique view of normal values and misleading assumptions about the public health. They uncover information with emotion and special cogency. However, they do so only if the criminal is not sentimentalized, only if he is in fact a criminal, like Macbeth, and not merely a misjudged man. For the reversal to register as dramatic shock, our shadowing course must be committed to someone sure to be overturned when legitimate powers come forward. The derailing of the criminal hero, whether in comic or tragic irony, presumably brings us back into a revised accord with a somewhat purged and corrected society. The rhythm of his expectations is crushed by the confirmation of society's continuity and renewable strength.

My stress on the rhythm of ironic plots has presupposed that the success of an ironic plot depends on sequence and timing. In linear art, irony is obviously a psychological matter that assumes a double progression of knowledge and feeling and works upon discrepancies between the audience's progress and the hero's. Only because the audience's realization races ahead of Satan's, Agave's, and Oedipus's do we take an ironic view of them and anticipate the peripeteia that strikes them down. As P. D. Q. Bach illustrates, such exploded expectations find a place in comedy and in music as well as in serious literature, but they are rare in discursive modes. Visual arts make only exceptional use of them because only the burying of clues and the establishing of a sequence of discoveries makes an ironic rhythm possible. The structural point is that if at its most mechanistic level, plot is a movement of enlivening attention across gaps between narrative units — held for a certain duration and intensity and proceeding at a governed, foreshortened pace and rhythm — in ironic variants the attention stumbles and rights itself; it undergoes changes of pace in reliving and resuffering what has happened, so that all events exist doubly. To Agave one and the same god is both wise and cunning, terrible and destructive. Since both his aspects are undeniable, she must learn to live with an ambiguous world in which what was all glory, clarity, and ecstatic triumph one moment turns to disaster the next.

None of these reconceptions and altered passions need be perfectly orderly. Sometimes characters react to new evidence like pinballs bouncing from one electrified bumper to another and running up a highly quirky score of revised views — like the course of Tristram Shandy through an association of ideas. But progressive realizations are nonetheless part of an always continuous record, whose moments are definable by relationship to "aspects" previously "rotated." To get closer to the fundamentals of that governing design, I want to turn now to the influence of privileged information, foreshortened and undramatized description, and, in general, authorial influences on the reader's vicarious course.

NARRATIVE UNITS AND THE AUTHOR'S PRESENCE

Some aspects of narrative rhythm properly fall under the special witnessing of fictions, which we will consider later, and the author's privileged information is one of them. But that information is also crucial to the guided course of the reader along the foreshortened surface of the telling, and hence is a matter of dramatic tensions and narrative stress as well as the verification of truths in the work. In fact, it is probably the single most important device in distinguishing fully enacted plots (on stage) from plots gathered up in authorial interpretation and summarized description.

For the sake of convenience, let us focus first on aspects of narrative art in which the author is visibly at work influencing the narrative rhythm. The segmentation of narrative units is one such aspect. Significant units — those that match up with meaningful episodes — are not merely incidents but pieces of a symbolic action charged with a certain energy and capable of unitizing our attention. In historical narration, all evidence assembled by the historian contributes supposedly to a view of finished events. The reader is not led through dramatic imitations or ironic reversals (though he may be told of things that could easily lend themselves to such treatment); hence the historian's smallest units are individual proofs strung together into argument, and his largest unit is a governing thesis. In contrast, most fictions do not present us with theses or assembled facts, and their details are often too plentiful to serve merely an illustrative function. Perhaps more importantly, their units are arrangeable in whatever way the author wishes, history having dictated none of them beyond what generic traditions, propriety, and rhetorical "conditions of appeal" may suggest. Hence they can be formally and psychologically right. Though Dickens could have chosen any of thousands of alternative details to render a sense of Barnaby Rudge's London and a historical view of the 1780 riots, he selects just those that are useful in carrying readers in certain directions at a certain pace. He presents them as the contingencies of a plot of a certain kind.

What are the segments and units out of which fictions are made? Clearly, characters are not, at least in themselves. They are understandable only as part of an elaborated system of meanings that prevails over their creation. Though as Paul Goodman demonstrates, novelistic characters frequently have traits, habits, sentiments, and complex interiors in excess of what a story (strictly as an action) requires,[19] in a fuller sense of relevance, even these complexities of full characterization make up a context in which a plot is interpreted.

---

19. Hindrances may come chiefly from inside the protagonist, from what Goodman calls "sentimental" complexes, which prevent him either from understanding himself completely or from committing himself to action. "The retardation (the hindrance) in a sentimental sequence is a persistent withdrawal from direct dramatic involvement: the essential action, the fixing of character, is occurring in a different time from the presented time" (*The Structure of Literature*, p. 161).

Plots or actual actions thus emerge from a set of possible but unrealized actions that define them. All the tributaries of a literary structure, whether settings, minor characters, social complications, objects, or other details, are linked not merely as causal agents but as a defining world of a certain symbolic density, truncated and compressed by the presenter as plots cannot be on stage. The difficulty they present to a concept of narrative segments is that unlike the historian, who arranges details as proof, the novelist presumably arranges them as animate forces at least partly like dramatic enactment. Thus on one hand, the novelist looks to the requirements of consequential logic to define the units of narration through generalization; on the other, he looks to historical documentation, portraits of a society, descriptive environment, and quoted drama as a filling out of his subject matter. To concede too much to mere facts in offering descriptions, mimetic scenes, or local actions, as Zola sometimes does, is to endanger the principle of narrative movement; to avoid such things is to empty that movement of all substance and dramatic interest.

Putting aside questionable compromises between documentation and foreshortened narrative, we can say that at their best, minimal narrative units are those segments of a cohesive stress system that bring forward new elements of conflict or new objects of perception and develop them. As parts of a psychology of form, they progress through partly unreadable clues to a clarification that in its dramatic shape is more than a deliberative interpretation of evidence or a presentation of facts. "Unquestionably the symbol-using animal experiences a certain kind of 'relief' in the mere act of converting any inarticulate muddle into the orderly terms of a symbol-system," Kenneth Burke suggests.[20] In narrative that relief depends upon a rhythm of confirmed attitudes that have been agonistically tested. The trademark of a truly functional formal segment is thus its capacity to present some aspect of a pretended reality in such a way as to build toward relief in a paced fusion of information, vicarious drama, and formal advancement.

A minimal unit of narrative rhythm is one that clarifies a portion of its own muddle and fulfills itself sufficiently to relax our vigilance momentarily and give pause to the forward urge of the work. It therefore makes necessary something of a new start, a new phase in the

20. Kenneth Burke, "On Catharsis, or Resolution," *Kenyon Review* 21 (1959): 363–65.

work's rhythm. It may either expand upon a former plot element or introduce new hindrances and disclosures. In this respect it is both like and unlike other units of statement: it has something of the integrity of the basic sentence, whose subject and action compose a single thought made up of subordinate parts; but its vehicle is also a mimetic action, some phase of which it leaves unfinished in order to generate new matters to be taken up later.

Since such units, as parts of a dramatic rhythm, are energized, they must also possess a certain intensity before we are able to consider them formal segments; they must have what we might call narrative salience, which is different from either dramatic climax or the controlling abstractions of expository prose. Moments that continue to stand out when the author needs to recall them are obviously more strongly serviceable as structural blocks than less noticeable moments. The smaller the unit the less complete it can be as a memorable affective unit, as part of the psychology of reading; anything smaller than an episode tends to get lost in the distances of a longer work. However, a minimal narrative unit can also be a scene, an anecdote or joke, a clever piece of exchange, a memorable image, any phase of a realized meaning set off by entrances and exits or shifts from dramatic to foreshortened presentation or perhaps marked by formal breaks such as chapters. It can even be a sentence if it is so precisely phrased, so ornamented, and so striking in itself as to be a small work of art. A sentence that by its syntax and wit raises a fine expectation and capitalizes on it both retards the unfolding of larger units and builds in its own way a special moment of feeling and thought. It may be so memorable in the insight it renders that it shifts the narrative balance, as verse does, from a unit of action to a unit of statement.

But even when a prose style abounds in such units, as John Lyly's, Sidney's, and Joyce's do, nothing prevents the author from putting them to use in larger segments, and thereby reinforcing natural curves and breaks in the subject with an increasingly fine rhythm. The comparatively distinguishable units of an extremely formalized work like *The Faerie Queene* suggests the many uses to which such a definite phasing can be put. Where episodes form distinct allegorical entities, for instance, a high degree of cross-referencing can be accomplished between ideas, images, levels of abstraction, and stages of the hero's career. Thus Red Cross's encounter with Fradubio takes up a definite posture across from Una's encounter with blind superstition — a posture that it could not have without the double plot of their separate courses, the interlocked system of comparisons and contrasts, and of course the boundaries of their episodes. The latter are marked not only by arrivals, encounters, and departures but also by formal units of presentation.

Tightest of all units with respect to consequential logic is a segment that, unlike an inset such as Raphael's in *Paradise Lost* or the individual stories of a collection like the *Canterbury Tales*, blends into a single causal chain, like the dinner at Lancaster Gate in *Wings of the Dove* or the various phases of the children's progressive deterioration in Golding's *Lord of the Flies*. The function of minimal units and episodes in such a system is of special interest because each rotation of an aspect defines alternatives for the hero, suggests renewed hindrances, and causes him gradually to commit himself to a line of development, as each decision of Golding's children guides them inevitably toward barbarism. Yet it is also true that episodes even in a strong unity of time such as this often represent back eddies, by-play, detours, short-term gratifications, or even distractions for both the hero and the reader. As discernible segments, they may operate on a different rhythm from the story as a whole or in competition with it. The temptation of Gawain by the lady of Bercilak's castle in *Sir Gawain and the Green Knight*, Aeneas's affair with Dido, and the separate adventures of Tom Jones displace, for a period, more distant and exalted consummations that are the hero's doom. In Milton's archetypal version of the "diversion" plot in *Paradise Regained*, the chief difference between Christ's view of the kingdom he is to found and the substitutions for it that Satan proposes is that the ultimate kingdom requires Christ to bypass all temporal offices and interim stages. He refuses to be a plot-maker because everything pertaining to secular power and learning is a detraction from his prophesied task. Thus where Eve mistakes the first offer of transcendent knowledge that comes her way as a chance to fulfill herself ultimately, Christ rejects all quick roads to the end and discovers that, ironically, that very rejection leads directly to the end.

It is not true that virtue lies always along the more arduous path. A protagonist may instead be required to forgo ultimate destinies on behalf of more immediate duties. For Malory's Lancelot the grail episodes, which are a kind of interlude in his main chivalric career, tempt him with not short-term but transcendent satisfactions. For Red Cross, the vision of the New Jerusalem tempts him with a deep beguilement of futurity — and therefore with the abandonment of his more immediate duties. However, most long nonsatiric works demand that the hero put aside diversions and momentary or episodic matters in dedication to a cause of some extent and duration. Aeneas must sacrifice Dido to found Rome; Adam should (apparently) reject Eve in order to maintain the continuity of Eden and its covenants. Calidore is clearly not meant to abandon his pursuit of the Blatant Beast for an extended interlude with Pastorella. (The pastoral world is quite often a diversionary paradise of immediate gratification within an epic or romance world of more heroic matters.) Either melodramatic or festive byways for the hero of this kind are hindrances to the realization of character-in-action and presumably to a more complete knowledge that can come only with a traversing of the entire spectrum of experience destined for him. When the hero accepts some transitory pleasure or rest as his end, he is in effect denying the teleology of his author's design in the interests of a more episodic structure. He is holding back one kind of rhythm on behalf of another. The "heroism" of Crusoe, for instance, consists to some extent of industrious, farsighted labor in building relatively permanent holdings. Like the capitalist who invests his money rather than spending it on festive occasions, he plans for next year's crops and saves powder for next year's hunt. This habit of accumulation and long-term accounting is what makes his career attractive to Defoe. By ruling himself according to the maturing of "investments" he binds daily life to schedules of increase and eventually to the development of those sophisticated arts that depend upon surplus and freedom from daily want. Only by looking forward to distant goals can he impose a continuous scheme on nature's shorter rhythms and abstract or "spiritualize" each item that comes under his control as part of a larger economy. Thus the units of the journal and the activities of days and weeks are subordinate to the evolution of a way of life over a quarter of a century and more, as circumstances are gathered one by one into the continuous logic of a developing estate. It is no wonder that Crusoe is not prepared to welcome even Friday with a paroxysm of friendship and uses the emotions of their meeting to form a long-term contract. "Storage" and postponed consumption make possible the steadying of his course.

The difference between works that evolve to a single rhythm and highly episodic plots that regroup their hindrances and forward impulses recurrently can be seen in the differences between growth figures like Rastignac in *Old Goriot* or Dorothea in *Middlemarch* and the picaro or the woman of pleasure. The picaro is a man of quick, small returns and "occasions," as he must be, because what he requires most is a roof over his head and a meal — not tomorrow but today. He cannot afford the luxury of long quests and slow returns, and he has no capital to invest. He knows nothing of divine far-off events slowly turning the cyclical wheels of history or of the beguilement of lost visions recovered through patient research. The ultimate significance of things is dwarfed by his immediate need to pick a pocket or steal an apple, to quiet a short-rhythm, uproarious stomach. When a nest egg sufficient to permit higher ambition falls to him (as it does to Gil Blas on occasion), he is foolish enough to lose it quickly, having acquired the habit of quick turnover. His perilous life has a special vicarious appeal to a reading public whose commitment to the continuities of social position does not allow it to spit, curse, steal openly, or pursue the quickened rhythms of escapades. In contrast, Balzac's Rastignac pursues a relatively continuous career. He encounters some of the same sharpies and unscrupulous connivers that a picaro might, but he maneuvers around them in compiling a connected social chronicle and in storing up a reputation. In *Old Goriot* he comes to Paris fresh from the provinces and by the end of the novel is poised at the edge of greater battles. In *Lost Illusions* he is subordinated to other parts of a larger chronicle, but the course of society itself remains continuous.

Likewise, Dorothea pursues the extensive rhythm of a single ambition through several phases, each causally related to the ones before and after. All subsidiary characters and plots are either analogous or directly relevant to her success. In contrast Cleland's woman of pleasure in *Fanny Hill* has no more long-range ambitions than a picaro. The rhythm of expectation and confirmation is governed entirely by the nature of her escapades, which exist primarily to give the reader vicarious excitement at frequent intervals. They deny her the privilege of growth, because, as Alan Friedman points out, in order to repeat so quickly the same anticipations, tensions, and resolutions with all their moral shocks and gratifications, she must return to virtually the same innocence after each of them.[21] Unlike Rastignac's or Dorothea's experience, then, hers does not accumulate, and where it may be headed in the long run is a matter of comparative indifference. In distinction from the picaro's experience, her escapades follow the rhythm of assault, token resistance, and voyeur satisfaction.

As Renaissance critics frequently point out, one of the differences between romance and epic is a similar distinction between the accumulative career of a single hero and the episodic fracturing of the narrative into smaller units, often scattered among multiple heroes. The epic hero by this distinction normally pursues a single plot that subordinates all episodes, whereas in romance, wizards like Archimago, having been defeated in one episode, spring to their feet in time for the next as a succession of heroes encounters a multitude of opponents. *The Faerie Queen* is a somewhat modified case, however. It offers a quantity of adventures, but unlike the nonaccumulative episodes of some romances and the rogue novel, Spenser's episodes are often arranged either in order of climax or as the unfolding of a comprehensive definition. A major victory is usually reserved for the end. Thus however fragmented into episodes it may be, Red Cross's quest has a main goal that sets firm temporal boundaries, and a continuous logic that depends on a central didactic aim.

Similarly, Tolkien, writing in the romance tradition in the trilogy, arranges his hero's hindrances along a scale that begins with a single threatening black rider, escalates into nine black riders, and then calls for increasing hordes of orcs ever closer to the hero. It finally renders whole panoramic battlefields of various good and evil combatants locked in a decisive struggle. Besides this quantitative crescendo, Tolkien offers an intensification of goods and evils, a heroic growth in Frodo and Sam, and a more malicious eye for Sauron, which sums up the evil of the universe as it probes ever nearer the hero. Each phase of the action thus gives the reader the momentary gratification that a reasonably complete episode should and at the same time points toward the completion of the ring quest, which leads the plot ever onward until it encompasses an entire epoch. Though Tolkien points to

21. See Alan Friedman, *The Turn of the Novel* (New York: Oxford University Press, 1966), pp. 5–10.

a succession of similar epochs before and after the story of the ring, the conclusion of the trilogy is decisive.

Expansive narrative rhythms depend not merely on the author's capacity to think of new episodes but on a conceptual sense of the real connectedness of the historic process they reflect. Tolkien's and Spenser's romances can continue only as long as the author finds still greater evils in the enemy, resources in the hero, or expanses of theme, society, or history to be filled. Given a sufficient sense of unity, the action becomes continuous meaning for the reader; but once a hero arrives at a perfect enemy and defeats him, he is no longer serviceable for the same argument. If the author wishes to continue, he must start over with a new set of characters and renewed difficulties to be overcome — which may be a little like following the apocalypse with more chronicles, or *Paradise Regained* with episodes in the life of Christ.

However, in less encompassing plots, battles can be renewed at a different level, as in the reduplicated structure of *Pilgrim's Progress* or Blake's always expandable struggles among always proliferating mythic figures. Even a highly schematic outline like Spenser's, once climaxed in a summing up of the twelve Aristotelian virtues in a perfect knight, could conceivably be filled in (given a very durable poet) by an expanded set of virtues and new ramifications of old ones. Much easier to imagine, however, is the development of social matter in a serial novel whose plot is less formal to begin with and more given to the accumulating of sheer social information. The separate works of Balzac's *Human Comedy*, though each is continuous in itself, could conceivably have become contributions to an almost infinitely expandable anatomy. Such saga epics as Galsworthy's Forsyte novels can turn to always new material because society itself evolves endlessly in its strata, its trades, the phases of its industrial development, and the character types of its historical epochs; new turns and hindrances are continually being generated in a rhythm of episodic starts and stops. The more continuous a history is as an aggregate, however, the less integrity it can give to individual careers and phases. The price a fictional presenter pays for pluralistic chronicles not very radically foreshortened by compressing commentary is a formlessness of larger rhythms and phases; or to turn that around, any strong continuum must dominate its segments or risk smothering its design and obscuring its greater rhythm in soap-opera crises, which are characterized in part by the absence of an ironic, judging, editorializing authorial presence.

I remarked earlier that for the reader an "action" is usually "meaning" and that the rhythm of episodes is therefore a rhythm of riddles, progressing toward comprehension. But the sources of rhythmic satisfaction in fiction are obviously more than these cerebral ones that the author offers. As Aeneas's affair with Dido and the always empty stomach of the picaro suggest, nature's own timetables are responsible for the inner shape of many of the episodic structures of fiction, and we may experience these vicariously in fiction with or without an attending argument. The phases of the biological organism — hunger and its satisfaction, life and death, the rhythm of courtship from first introductions to consummations, the cycles of days and years — suggest ready mimetic shapes and encompassing units for individual stories. Indeed, the most basic of all timing elements is the growth and decay of a single person in a natural time that both hinders progress and pushes forward at a certain rate: the same processes that prevent children from reaching the instant maturity they desire carry everyone through changes and toward conclusions that have nothing to do with merit, social complications, or intrigues — or anything to do with "meaning." Certain timely disclosures, anticipations, and recovered visions attend upon that irreversible career, and from awareness of it we take our perspectives on intenser dramas of a few hours' duration such as marriage arrangements or the shock of quick and untimely endings. Complex schemes, curves of psychological development, and even the progress of whole epochs take their measure from such basic careers as everyone experiences, as Tolkien realizes in gearing the movement of his vast ring plot to the events of a single generation from Bilbo to Frodo. The natural shape of the single life also accords well with the expanding circumference of social documentation, which a figure like Rastignac explores as the inevitable territory of a youth growing into manhood. Used as an inset or as a phase of a larger design, the biological curve forms a relatively discrete segment; made the central focus of the plot, it yields decisive beginnings and endings.

The dynamics of a broad social movement obviously follow another narrative schedule and create different kinds of episodes and phases. If an individual organism derives from the "spreading of pulsating pattern" through it,[22] a social order depends upon the laws of aggregate change. These, to be meaningful, require the stronger controls of theme and argument. As the education of Julien Sorel in *The Red and the Black*, Dorothea in *Middlemarch*, or Fabrice in *The Charterhouse of Parma* carries further into the secret powers that move the social order, the protagonist grows less able to control his own life, and the author rises further above them in the comprehensive interpretations of the aggregate. Knowing is inevitably qualified by suffering for the hero because no impulse to act can master the expansive scope of what the hero is given increasingly to see. An idea born in his mind must find convincing expression in words and actions before it can spread to others, and of course no social organism of any size permits the instantaneous spread of intelligence through its ranks. If Crusoe has no difficulty in this respect even when quantities of people find their way to his island, other novelistic figures become progressively less fortunate as the city becomes the medium of their relationships. The social order appears to them to be a confused, continuous infiltrating of ideas, manners, and codes into an indefinite corporate body.[23] Though classic realists such as Tolstoy, Stendhal, Balzac, and George Eliot are adept at synchronizing a broad social evolution and individual careers, a society has nothing like the natural shape of the single life.

The question of episodes and their function in overall plots takes on different dimensions when we consider the relationship of a hero's career to such group movements. Balzac again comes to mind as one of the first makers of integrated group and individual plots on a large, realistic social scale, thoroughly permeated by the presenter's explicit presence. It is not surprising to find him an enterprising editorialist. Georg Lukács is correct to consider him an "epic" plot-maker in his capacity to shape masses of social material into relatively unified actions:

> The power of Balzac's imagination manifests itself in his ability to select and manipulate his characters in such a way that the centre of the

22. Lancelot Law Whyte, *Accent on Form* (New York: Harper and Brothers, 1954), p. 104.

23. Cf. Michel Butor, "Thoughts on the Novel: The Individual and the Group," in *Perspectives on Fiction*, ed. Calderwood and Toliver, pp. 169–82; Raymond Williams, *The English Novel from Dickens to Lawrence* (New York: Oxford University Press, 1970).

stage is always occupied by the figure whose personal, individual qualities are the most suitable for the demonstration, as extensively as possible and in transparent connection with the whole, of some important
single aspect of the social process. ... Every incident is a step towards
the same end, although each single happening, while helping to reveal
the underlying necessity, is in itself accidental. The uncovering of deep-
seated social necessities is always effected by means of some action, by
the forceful concentration of events all moving towards the
catastrophe.[24]

But that control would be impossible were it not for the foreshortened method and the authorial essay. Central figures move at a pace
governed and usually frustrated by the aggregate, which, since it is
dynamic and fully historical — not composed of fixed institutions
and a stable order as in Defoe, Richardson, Fielding, and Austen —
requires an authorial interpretation of economic and cultural change.

However, Balzac's social rhythm is not always destined for such
positive conclusions as the one Lukács here describes in *Lost Illusions*. There lingers over the several phases and episodes of his plots
the suggestion of unresolved strands and chance events that even the
authorial perspective fails to dispel. The different rates of progress
that the family, money, and the conventions of romance follow in *Old
Goriot* are influenced by individual decisions, and they can be
imagined to continue endlessly, regardless of the fates of the Rastig-
nacs and Goriots who illustrate them. Even Rastignac's personal
career is not entirely finished in any one novel. The chief unresolved
question after the first one is, What precisely is Rastignac now that
society has worked its influences on him? Are there deciding rules of
the game to define how a young man should conduct himself and rise
to the prominence his character seems to argue? For all his revulsion
at the tactics of power, Rastignac never imagines anything that one
could consider public-oriented or humane values. He comes to no rest
in principles. And given his dependence on money, its continued flow
can only be imagined to create new liaisons and provoke further
changes in him, all of them relatively unguided by firm understanding on his part.

At the end of *Old Goriot*, however, Balzac does take advantage of
certain natural, realistic rhythms to suggest a conditional ending or

24. Georg Lukács, *Studies in European Realism*, trans. Edith Bone (London: Hillway,
1950), especially pp. 55–57.

decisive pause. In the course of gaining experience, Rastignac has put aside hesitation and learned to control his ambivalence toward society. He ends a long way from the openness of his plans and the irresolution of his first steps. Like the ending of *Paradise Lost*, the ending of *Old Goriot* is in a sense an expulsion of the hero from innocence and the forced beginning of a new, adult battle with the urban wilderness:

> Rastignac walked a few steps to the highest part of the cemetery, and saw Paris spread out below on both banks of the winding Seine. Lights were beginning to twinkle here and there. His gaze fixed almost avidly upon the space that lay between the column of the Palace Vendôme and the dome of the Invalides; there lay the splendid world that he had wished to gain. He eyed that humming hive with a look that foretold its despoliation, as if he already felt on his lips the sweetness of its honey, and said with superb defiance,
> "It's war between us now!"
> And by way of throwing down the gauntlet to Society, Rastignac went to dine with Madame de Nucingen.[25]

His master plan is decisive; there remain only the details. And though these may not match the splendor he seeks and may not satisfy his defiance (going to dine with Mme de Nucingen is scarcely a great beginning), he nonetheless sees the goal as worth the cost. The dying of Goriot has released an energy that he now directs toward the total of Paris spread out before him. Pulling back the camera to reveal that entire field while keeping the single hero in the foreground, Balzac gives us the sense of defined scope and arrested tension — here the resolved hero, there the field of his operation, here the specific bounded subject, there the general opportunity of an evolving society. Though he does not speak directly in his own voice, the presenter is clearly felt in the summary conclusiveness of Rastignac's action.

The tension between the normal progress of individuals and the laws of social change, so severe in social realism of Balzac's kind, reveals the difficulty of defining an action that is something like history itself — composed not of fixed elements like the shapes and configurations of a painting but of fluid, ever changing identities. As I have suggested in Balzac's case, our sense of these is controlled by a

25. Honoré de Balzac, *Old Goriot*, trans. Marion Crawford (Baltimore: Penguin Books, 1951), p. 304.

third rhythmic element, the author's explicit presence and his foreshortening of the material. By presenting the different aspects of Paris as typical and symbolic in authored explicits, Balzac makes Rastignac's life an illustration of similar things happening elsewhere. In this respect, the rhythm of the *Human Comedy* is ultimately neither the movement of individual biographies nor the historic process: it is the unfolding of a social blueprint, spread out between the ever present author and an assumed audience. The generalizing power both of Balzac's commentary and of his social symbolism does much to lift us out of realism's apparent randomness and our vicarious entrancement in particular sequences. The internal essay is a way of releasing information at times when it will qualify the reader's identification with the hero and clarify the broader issues his life raises. In the ironic mode that Balzac prefers, the reader is nearly always far ahead of the hero, for whom the dynamics of the social order constitute a large element of concealment. Thus, denied privileged access to the author's thought, Rastignac never sees the full social panorama that we do: he confronts at every turn an overwhelming mass of motives and powers ranged unpredictably around him.

Perhaps more important than lifting us out of his confusion, however, the narrator's commentary adjusts the focus constantly, not only officially and noticeably but also in unobtrusive and structural ways such as chaptering and juxtaposing episodes. These artificial units and matters of technique obviously affect the rhythm of the reading and control its affective curve. In some respects, they are the novelistic equivalents of verse segmentation. A storyteller who comes forth noticeably at certain junctures and who in the interim offers less obtrusive comments on the fable keeps tangible and intact the presentational surface or seeing-platform. Thus in Fielding, Spenser, Balzac, Chaucer, and a variety of narrative forms, we have inside evidence about the narrator's perspective. In *Paradise Lost*, to take a distinctive case, the poet maintains a certain distance from Eden, tells us about his favored but not all-comprehending intrusion in Heaven, and interjects his comment on the fall. In asking periodically for visitations from the spirit-presenter, he also takes a position with respect to the scriptural materials he uses: if divine light is an effluence from God and if the poet in turn expresses it, the poem is really the product of the same Logos that dictated scripture to Moses and other prophets. Engrossed in the fable at one moment, we are restored the next, by these reminders of the presentation, to the lyric rhythm of the poet's thought. In prompting awareness of the surface in this way, the narrator disengages the mimetic from the rhetorical matters of the poem, and disengages the reader's tempo from the fable.

We can see the profound effect of such prominent narrators on the reading of the work in texts as diverse as *Old Goriot*, *The Canterbury Tales*, *Tristram Shandy*, *Tom Jones*, and Conrad's Marlow stories. Where the chronology of events within the story and the special event of the telling remain distinct, the way is opened for a special intellectual and tonal control. Fielding's comic epic in prose and Sterne's *Tristram Shandy* add irony and humor to authorial intrusion — and numerous essays in support of the kind of digressions and history the narrator presents. In addition to the voice that interposes between us and the fable, Sterne makes the device of the printed book also part of the palpable surface — the chapters, the rearrangement and sequences of episodes, the addresses of the narrator to the reader, the typographical oddities and graphs with which the novel bristles — until the sheer matter of the presentation overwhelms the fictive chronology of dated events, and the chronicle of presenter-reader relations almost supersedes Tristram's story. Indeed, as Tristram discovers, unlike a foreshortened narration, the telling jogs along at an even slower pace than the events themselves:

> I am this month one whole year older than I was this time twelve-month, and having got, as you perceive, almost into the middle of my fourth volume — and no farther than to my first day's life — 'tis demonstrative that I have three hundred and sixty-four days more life to write just now, than when I first set out; so that instead of advancing, as a common writer . . . I am just thrown so many volumes back.[26]

Thus the reader is prodded and jerked forward or retarded as whim dictates, like the progress of Parson Yorick on his "meek-spirited jade of a broken-winded horse" (an apt image for the "ride" the novel offers).

However, in Sterne's case, as elusive as the past proves to be, the present narration is more or less of the same quality as the past it describes: it repeats the past in its assembling of opinions and odd connections, as both presentation and subject find a common ground

26. Laurence Sterne, *Tristram Shandy*, ed. Ian Watt (Boston: Houghton Mifflin, 1965), p. 214.

in associational habit. Thus as the mind is given ample opportunity to "ride out" sideways on associative excursions, we discover that these are to the chronology of presentation approximately what episodes are to the fable; that the intrusions of authorial information, though not precisely minimal narrative units, are units of rhetoric and dramatic exchange comparable structurally to events. It would not be quite accurate even so to say that the present-tense continuity of Tristram's rhetorical presence dictates the reader's course or is any way nonfictive. The author who addresses us in Milton, Balzac, and Sterne is no more the author than Hamlet in soliloquy is Shakespeare. The audience is merely pushed by the device of palpable narration to a second remove from an uncritical identification with the hero, realizing, for instance, that the narrator is as staged as his story. In effect, then, Sterne's reader pursues three sequences, the crenelated movement of Sterne's primary plot (Tristram's begetting and growing up), the palpable surface of Tristram's presentation in the present, and something much less demonstrable that amalgamates these with the reader's presence of mind. In Tristram's addresses to him, he catches glimpses of the trickster Sterne; he disbelieves, criticizes, evaluates, pauses and looks up, stops for dinner, thumbs forward and backward, or admires the binding of the book, all the while performing the work in his own way from the "score" in front of him. Sterne's attempt to control the divagations of that detachment by collaring him frequently merely offers tacit and humorous acknowledgment of that inevitable waywardness.

This distance between the reader and the story is of less importance in most cases of novelistic narration, and one can clearly overestimate the effect of a palpable mediation between reader and story. Even with a mode of representation as prominently divided, pasted together, and interrupted as it is in *Tristram Shandy*, the barriers between the pretended past and the galloping narration frequently break down as readers are drawn by a skillful narrative beguilement into the primary story and tend to forget everything else. Tristram's own reiterated desire to get the story told keeps him coming back to it as though to an indisputable truth: it is his hobbyhorse, and he must, by humor, continue with it, putting aside other interests, just as the narrator of *Paradise Lost* is seized by the overwhelming impressiveness of his material. Indeed, all first-person narrators live in two durations, the past and a train of ideas, images, and actions it arouses that serves as our window upon its events. Sterne, in displaying his devices with so much relish, calls into doubt not so much the past itself, then, as the possibility of converting one kind of reality into another — of transcribing events into the apparatus of chapters, styles, episodes, and words generally. Comments on the difficulty of verbalizing life are actually some guarantee that a life is there to be verbalized, in all the modes of argument, conversation, sermonizing, and narration that Toby, his father, Yorick, and Corporal Trim can muster. Indeed, as we see a narrow range of events translated into so vast a repertory of verbal effects, we come to understand that all the Shandys are symbolic translators of great energy, busily making various objects and situations into imitations and models. Their maps, their model fortifications, their verbal pictures, their substitute emblems, and even their strange laws of association are based on the analogies and epitomes of the symbolizing mind. All things have their parallels and mirrored reflections: the wooing of Widow Wadman is parallel in Toby's mind to wartime sieges (so is everything else). The sorrow of Yorick's dying is equivalent to blank, black pages. Digressions that are not digressions pull the main action into themselves as symbolic mirrors. The narrative bristles with metaphors, speeches, remembrances of similar things, and smaller figures of metaphysical wit by which relatively unlike things are yoked together with amusing ambiguity, as when Widow Wadman, expecting to see exactly where Toby is wounded, is shown the mapped anatomy of the battleground. The verbal world, the world of symbols, epitomizes a presumed reality the way Sterne's little homunculus carries the image of an extended life in its condensed model and its brief journey.

Like Sterne, other comedians of the novel such as Beckett and Barth stage the writing of the story decisively enough to make the events of the narrator's life almost secondary to the event of writing. In "Anonymiad," for instance, the pretended autobiography is only the beginning. With his bird's-feather pen and goat parchment, the narrator transcribes his past into scribbles, partitions it according to headpiece, body, and tailpiece, and puts it in bottles for transmission. A given idea is thus thoroughly processed and transformed by an assembly line and comes out no more like its original material than a finished automobile resembles iron ore and unharvested rubber. What really counts for Barth, as for Sterne, is the presenter's mind, hooking together its experiences like linked sausages.

It is evident from this that narrative rhythms so obviously tampered with by the narrator may be extremely multilayered at times. Besides the progress of individuals and groups in the subject itself, the reader follows the wayward movement of the narrator's ruminations and senses behind him the overall controls of the author, whose perspective is above or outside the story. The difficulty with a policy of obvious authorial intrusion is that we too readily discover that fate and necessity are merely masks for the author's will and that the proliferated world follows not from something in reality but from invention. It does so in Dickens and James as surely as it does in *The Faerie Queene*, the "Anonymiad," or *The Fellowship of the Ring*; but we are less disturbed by it in some texts than in others. We know that it is Tolkien who designs everyone's roles, legislates outcomes, manipulates episodes, and provides a perspective on his epoch's massively geared movements, just as it is Hardy who is the President of Immortals (who condemns Tess to execution), causes letters to go astray at timely moments, and arranges the setting of so appropriate a sacrificial scene as Stonehenge. From this viewpoint, it is also Milton rather than divine foreknowledge that determines the place and outcome of every man and angel in *Paradise Lost*, whatever historical materials the poet presumed he had. (The universe of the poem is obviously not the universe of Darwin, Marx, or Einstein; it is a universe of another kind of poetic myth, and it is uniquely Milton's in many respects.) The fact is that in any well-constructed fable, no one inside the story or stationed at the presentational surface discovers anything not purposely put there for him to discover at precisely the time scheduled for him to discover it. All rhythms are ultimately author-dominated, and the artist's hand is betrayed not only by the establishing of beginnings and endings and segmentation but also by every detail and logical turn of every sentence. But a highly visible presentation (like the pauses between pieces on a record or the ticks and scratches on its surface) reminds us more obviously of that. It makes us aware that what we are being exposed to is not an order of real events but an order of art. The author may disarm our skepticism by confronting that fact openly; or he may destroy entrancement in the rhythm of the subject without achieving commensurate gains, as John Fowles does in *The French Lieutenant's Woman*.

Even in the most effaced narrator, the act of presentation implies a perspective distinct from anything dramatized in the story. Jane

Austen's habitually ironic view of her characters, for instance, places them in a pronounced perspective and assumes a greater foresight than they themselves possess. We realize how pronounced it is when we remember the social realities it excludes. As Raymond Williams suggests, Austen's novels take for granted fortunes made from trade or colonial profit, as these are converted into houses, property, and social position, but they do not concern the making of the money itself. She makes settlements, in Williams's words, "like some supernatural lawyer," and these settlements exclude social recognition from those who cannot be "visited": "What she sees across the land is a network of propertied houses and families, and through this tightly drawn mesh most actual people are simply not seen. To be face-to-face in this world is already to belong to a class. No other community, in physical presence or in social reality, is . . . knowable. And it is not only most of the people who have disappeared. It is also most of the country, which becomes real only as it related to the houses, which are the real nodes. For the rest the country is weather or a place for a walk."[27] We are reminded again by this that every story is a version not of reality but of an author's *seeable* reality, within the foreshortening signs and symbols of his genre and mental set. The presenter-reader relationship and the artifices of style and unit segmentation are necessary aspects of the author's commitment to conventions and to points of view, since fictional works are governed not by the logic of evolving organisms and social epochs entirely but in part by a fatality of aesthetic form.

It may be helpful, before we move on, to recapitulate some of the general principles that have emerged so far. Because narrative stress systems are linear and dramatic, they are also essentially rhythmic. As the wind in a fir bough has its way, as Dewey suggests, until the compressed strength of the bough pushes it back, weakens, and is again compressed, so the forward propulsion of a story is resisted as protagonists encounter antagonists, gather strength, and push on. But unlike forms held fast, narratives also move relentlessly toward a goal. Certain subject matters possess inherent stages, goals, and paces: a biographical rhythm is set basically by birth, death, hunger, or an educational process in which a protagonist advances against

27. Williams, *The England Novel from Dickens to Lawrence*, p. 24.

difficulties; the rhythm of a social group derives from its tendency to preserve itself while changing, or from the complexity of interacting interests and individual wills and from the transmission of information from party to party until the collective will for a change comes about. Superimposed on such rhythms in symbolic systems are always a surface order of presentation and the author's short circuits to avoid full dramatic development. Hence on one level is a rhythm of life, or of societies, or of events; on another is the rhythm of symbolic, communicative act, of verbal art resounding in the mind of the audience. The latter deals freely with the former, mixing units of narration such as stanzas and chapters with phases of the subject and conducting readers through an interplay of normal experience and the special experience of significant form. Until these two sets of rhythmic principles are carefully distinguished, we cannot hope to understand imitation, the vicarious participation of audiences in art, or the psychology of storytelling. Yet try as we might to distinguish them, they are inextricably bound up in each other and in given cases may be easily confused, until the order of art and myth seems the order of nature and events — either in the fictions we take down from the shelf or in those social fictions by which in the *Realpolitik* is governed.

PARADISE LOST, SIR GAWAIN AND THE GREEN KNIGHT, THE WINGS OF THE DOVE

Once we recognize that some degree of arbitrariness resides in all narrative stress systems, we can begin to explain at least some of the hindrances, concealments, disclosures, episodic sequences, and cross-references as devices of presentation rather than relationships inherent in a subject matter. I want to test that general assumption by looking at a small variety of specific cases in more detail, entertaining in the process the suspicion that the *fictor*, or presenter, can be discovered in the dynamics of structure more often than a thoroughly "beguiled" reading might suggest. I assume that even in attempts at realism, the imagination seizes upon only those aspects of reality that it can make cohesive and meaningful. In any event, anything that finds its way into a fiction, however it may have wound up there, leads a quite different existence inside than it ever did outside; it is uprooted, systematized, and transplanted.

Milton's case is intriguing because Milton is frequently concerned with parallels between the poetic creator responsible for the poem and the Word that is responsible for a world of highly systematic and cohesive forms and events. Among Christ's many analogies, this one with the poet is one of the most important. We should note that each order — celestial, infernal, edenic, the wilderness — depends upon crucial exchanges between it and others through emissaries, and that the art of narration, description, and staging is thus everywhere vital to the functioning of Milton's universe. Satan's fate, for instance, hinges on his success in inculcating his view of things in man, after he has arranged the presentation of his plot before the fallen host in a well-manipulated public showing. His account to Eve of his tasting of the apple is accordingly magnificently narrated. Adam's role also hinges on Raphael's and Michael's narrative art.

The central results of such examples of effective tale-bearing register on Adam and Eve. The genres by which they are influenced are several. The information that comes to them before the fall is concordant with their state and is essentially nondramatic except where Satan is involved; it enriches and amplifies Eden by connecting them with analogous levels, in a hierarchy of nearly infinite richness. Until Raphael comes bearing news of the war in Heaven (their first exposure to such things), their ritual days are a sequence of vernal pleasures and untraumatic learning. Their lives are without the stress of normal narrative time: they lack antagonists, hidden strands, hindrances, reversals, chance, and — since they are to be without end — denouements. They live under the uniform rhythm of vernal days and nights. The information that comes to Adam and Eve after the fall is of another kind altogether. Michael's tale-bearing duty is to reconstruct out of the wreckage and confusion of the future a progressive alignment of God and historical events, which are chiefly the exile and alienation of man, the spread of evil, the concurrent faithfulness of the issue of Abraham, and, finally, the incarnation of Christ and the revelation therein of divine purpose and the restoration of paradise. At that the fullest rhythm imaginable will be complete.

From the perspective of Michael's narrative, which Milton stages in two books as a downward and then upward rhythm, Satan's experiment falls under the logic of redemption. Though Milton credits that redemption to God's word in action, the question raised by the poem's creation of its own consistent stress system is whether Milton's universe works out of a divine logic or a poetic design: is the order portrayed in poems not perhaps really the order of poems projected outward as a series of happenings? Might we not regard Satan, for instance, as not a real person in a literal story but a product of a narrative that demands his kind of antagonism? Just as definitions evolve through an opposition of terms that establish what is and what is not proper to a given category, so good requires evil, and a magnificent good that includes infinite mercy and grace requires a magnificent evil devoid of both. In any case, Satan emerges from Christ's original exaltation as spontaneously as the idea of dark from the idea of light, as though the creative Logos somehow summoned forth an opposite. Thereafter, open manifestation and epiphany are counterbalanced in the dance of narrative by concealment and intrigue; and everything that Heaven is, Hell defines by opposition. Clearly, no such epic narrative system would be possible without satanic rebellion.

From a skeptical point of view, it is to some extent this necessary symmetry of narrative actions and reactions, protagonists and antagonists — rather than an imitation of gods and devils in a certain kind of cosmos — that generates angelic battles, a wilderness to match Eden, a fallen Adam to match the unfallen, and the rest of Milton's magnificent narrative architecture. Given such elaborately balanced stresses, Milton assigns supreme importance to the exposure of one side to the other in the dramatic turns of suffered information and the shock of one innocent party exposed to another. (From this viewpoint, Satan is as innocent as anyone: his exposure to the sun, to Adam and Eve, and to Christ in *Paradise Regained* nearly turns him about and destroys his capacity to proceed.) Not only is each plane of Milton's hierarchy pervasively analogous to others, then, but each progresses from simplicity to division through the engagement of its opposites, and then, by way of resolution, to a restoration or a closed destiny, as all fates are sealed for an eternity and narration as such goes out of business. A review of Genesis indicates how highly organized and schematic Milton's story of the fall is by comparison. Nowhere in scripture are antagonists and protagonists so fully explicit. Milton perfects in countless details what is a bare skeletonal hint of balanced narrative forces in his sources. The great rhythms of his narrative are those of traumatic division and protracted mending under the healing power of repentence, patience, and renewed hope — until the entire universe is roughly back where it began.

In broad terms, to a theory of narrative as opposed to a theology, the movement of Milton's universe accords with the fatality of verbal systems and the definition of basic moral values extended in narrative demonstration. In more specifically structural matters, we see the poet's hand whenever the timing of presumably real episodes differs in some way from the order given to their presentation. Though in medias res technique is expected of epics, for instance, Milton does much more with nonchronological narration than rearrange the beginning, the climax, and the resolution in appropriate places: he leads the reader through a highly functional series of educational stages, exposing him to the separate orders of Heaven, Hell, and Eden. Whatever the sequences of events in his assumed universe, the sequence of fictional elements from the blocking out of the main segments of the plot to the syntax of individual sentences is very intricately patterned.[28] The rearranging is obviously designed in many cases to serve the timely exposure of one realm to another just when information will have the greatest dramatic impact, as when Satan and Beelzebub reserve mention of Adam and Eve in the debate in Pandaemonium until they can use it as a clincher, or when Michael delays mention of Christ in his narration to Adam until it can have a maximum psychological impact on Adam's view of the world to come and the reader's exit from the poem.

Perhaps more telling is Milton's use of timely overviews and nondramatic summaries to guide the reader's reception of phases of the plot. Omniscience at such points services both the fatality of aesthetic form and the psychology of reading. The function of the divine dialogues, for instance, is to render the logic of the plot and explain the roles of its agents in an unquestioned light — and especially, in Book III, to correct false views of the rebellion and man's potential fate

28. Gunnar Qvarnström speculates, for instance, that Milton's sense of structure carries down to the counting of lines and symmetrical balancing of passages throughout the epic, in reinforcement of a Christocentric universe where the Logos prevails in the minutest details. Both chronology in the calendar of events and the number of lines devoted to each phase are carefully measured out in an almost musical precision of intervals. See *The Enchanted Palace: Some Structural Aspects of Paradise Lost* (Stockholm: Almqvist and Wiksell, 1967). Stanley E. Fish, in *Surprised by Sin* (New York: St. Martin's Press, 1967), has detailed Milton's mastery of readers' psychology admirably, though one sometimes finds Fish expecting readers to register surprises that would require an incredible forgetfulness of passages they have just read.

proposed in the infernal dialogues. God moralizes the fable with a decisiveness that is very helpful to the rhythm of the work and in a way preferable to the poet's own open functioning in that role. Since God exercises an infallible power to make happen what he says will happen, Milton makes no concessions to chance and leaves nothing inarticulate or unfinished; God can make poetic justice come about and instrument the kind of doom that makes for enclosed form. He enables Milton to conceive of history as a contained field everywhere penetrated with significance.

Seen in the light of necessary or desirable narrative functions, Christ's role, too, is critical. The first phase of God's plan is Christ's elevation as the issuer of mandates. As God's expressive agent, he converts thought into historical reality and puts into arranged display what would otherwise remain invisible: he translates thought into narrative action and puts plots into motion. Thus as both the principle of illumination and the Word, he performs as a poet committed to organic form and complete intelligibility might wish, disseminating, in strict accord with a central intent, the materials of sacred truth and eventually rescuing by that publication the erring minds of those who have become lost in the wilderness. (*Paradise Regained*, as we will observe later, makes that publicity more explicit than *Paradise Lost*.) The first celestial dialogue, where his role as Expression turns toward human ends, is virtually a paradigm of authorial planning coming to bear upon events.

When we consider that paradigm more closely in the first divine conference, we find it encompassing the poem abstractly at a point when the reader needs to transcend the rhythm of unfolding events with a sense of the total cycle. That divine communication should have to be worked out in this way is an indication of Milton's bending of its presumed nature to fit narrative and dramatic form. To make the dialogue seem feasible, he must suppose a gap between Christ and God and a limitation in Christ's perspective that is akin to the ignorance, at any given phase, of the narration that is to follow. To be sure, Milton posits a similar limitation in Christ in *Christian Doctrine* where it is not prescribed by linear development. He defines the separation of the son and the father on the grounds that "unity and duality cannot consist of one and the same essence .... If two subsistences or two persons be assigned to one essence, it involves a contradiction in terms." He interprets phrases that may seem to suggest the oneness of father and son in scripture as an indication merely of "intimacy of communion, . . . in love, in communion, in agreement, in charity, in spirit, in glory."[29] However, even given this duality, the separation of divine parties in the poem has more interchange and plot exfoliation than we might expect to be possible. The dialogues in Heaven provide a pattern of "sweet interchange," root definitions of being and becoming, ideal marriages between intelligences, and gnomic theological and moral topics. To be understood at lower levels, these must then be translated into the educational speeches of Raphael and Michael and eventually into the agnostic trials of Adam and Eve. Obviously a word in Heaven goes a long way in history: the slightest qualifying clause in the divine dialogue may become a major era in the enacting or in the poetic realization of an adumbrated narrative plan: "Long the decress of Heav'n / Delay," Satan realizes in *Paradise Regained*, working on Christ's suffering of human time, "for longest time to him is short." The discord of opposing rhythms is very clear to one like Satan, whose sense of haste is a vital part of his violation of due place and procedure.

As it is made known to men, the perspective of the divine dialogues is far from irrelevant to the nature of temporal experience or to the reader's approach to the poem's outcome and central principles. In demonstrating that, Milton manages the final stage of the marriage between the poem's abstractions and the long narrative that encompasses the world of the narrator and the reader. The concluding focus of course is upon Adam and Eve as they enter the wilderness and initiate the chain of events that leads to the contemporary life of the poet and his audience. The first father and mother in whom are initiated those rhythmic cycles of human fallibility and redemption that all men share are encouraged by the eventual purposefulness of what they do. At the same time they are submitted to a world of wandering and apparent chance. The larger rhythm of their eventual salvation is challenged by the daily trials of the wilderness, but in the distant pageantry of the incarnation and eventual triumph at the end of their human period, they see the ironic indirection of a plot in which good is augmented by evil. In retrospect, every phase of that plot has fallen out on schedule: the messengers Raphael and Michael have prepared Adam and Eve for their critical roles at precisely the right time; the guardians of Eden, whose helplessness makes them seem stage

29. John Milton, *Complete Poems and Major Prose*, ed. Merritt Y. Hughes (New York: Odyssey Press, 1957), p. 928.

decorations, have marked a step in the unfolding and delayed Satan's plan — sharpening the timing of the plot until Adam and Eve are ready to be exposed to Satan (and as a bonus, sending a frustrated Satan several times around the world). And so at the end the rest of human bafflement and impatience, too, will no doubt work some purpose, disguised as yet in the unfinished course of affairs but predictable if by nothing else by the fatality of supreme fictions.

Almost as striking as *Paradise Lost* in the timely procession of episodes is the intricately symmetrical poem *Sir Gawain and the Green Knight*. The formal patterns of the poem are clearly intended to reflect the reality of historical epochs, but again one finds the close organization of materials remarkably suitable to narrative economy and structural cohesiveness. The extensive use of periodicity is a prominent example, in its repetitions of verbal phrasing, stanzaic form, and plot. The poem's cycles revolve on a number of levels. Commenting on two of these, the seasonal cycles and the turns of history generally, Morton Bloomfield suggests that

> *Sir Gawain* is soaked in time in all its aspects, and this rich chronological perspectivism is one of the strongest elements in the sense of solidity we get from reading the poem. ... These many dimensions of time are part of the bulwarks of life; they give security and strength. They are the framework of the human universe into which fantastic and puzzling irrationality penetrates and which it seems to wish to destroy.[30]

Actually, we can distinguish at least five kinds of periodic rhythms in the subject matter alone, each of which combines — ideally for dramatic interest and narrative masonry — the regularity of cycles and the wonder of new events: (1) the daily and yearly festivities of the two courts (Arthur's and Bercilak's); (2) seasonal growth and

30. Morton W. Bloomfield, "*Sir Gawain and the Green Knight*: An Appraisal," *PMLA* 76 (1961): 18. Cf. Dale Randall, "A Note on Structure in Sir Gawain and the Green Knight," *Modern Language Notes* 72 (1957): 161–63. See also Charles Moorman, "Myth and Medieval Literature: Sir Gawain and the Green Knight," *Mediaeval Studies* 18 (1956): 158–72; and William Goldhurst, "The Green and the Gold: The Major Theme of Gawain and the Green Knight," *College English* 20 (1958): 61–65. A number of articles applicable to our purpose is collected in *Critical Studies of Sir Gawain and the Green Knight*, ed. Donald R. Howard and Christian K. Zacher (Notre Dame: University of Notre Dame Press, 1968); others are collected in *Sir Gawain and Pearl: Critical Essays*, ed. Robert J. Blanch (Bloomington: Indiana University Press, 1966).

decay; (3) the life cycle and flourishing of individual heroes as they rise through ranks of honor and assume a place in the hierarchy accorded by public fame; (4) historical cycles of bliss and blunder that replace one civilization with another; and (5), more mysteriously, a recurrent interpenetration of divine and human events, measured in part by the yearly liturgical calendar and cycles of error and repentance. Some of the same problems of integrating secular and religious levels that we noticed in Malory's grail quests are present in the last of these, but the Gawain poet focuses comparatively more on the natural world. Moreover, whereas the grail quest draws Galahad and others permanently away from court, Gawain's quest is keyed to a cycle of departure and return which tests the court itself eventually. The natural seasons, the social order, and the church calendar are thus bound to a yearly rhythm, as is the exchange of ax strokes.

As a kind of microcosm of periodicity, the exchange of blows reflects more extensive cycles, including the founding and passing of civilizations, as the poet examines centuries in a single stanza initially, balancing bliss against blunder, "war and wrack" against "wonder," and situating Arthur's own reign within those cycles. As this panorama suggests, the key to each civilization has been the life of a single hero — the traitor who destroyed Troy, Aeneas, Romulus, Langobard, and Brutus, founder of Britain. And as this catalogue of heroes further implies, the shape of the typical story, in the long view, is a downward curve of war or an upward curve of heroic achievement — or both as a twofold movement. We infer from the list that Arthur's court, now at its youthful pinnacle and reveling in unhampered mirth, will not be immune to the general law. (The Gawain poet's fourteenth-century audience knew that it had not been.)

But initially, life sits lightly on the court, whose ceremonies are a recurrent arousing and satisfying of civilized appetites. The mirth of the court is apparently not meant to be reprehensible in a moral sense, and it does not lead to an expectation of cycles of licentiousness and poetic justice: Arthurian games are merely the product of an enclosed and harbored perspective as yet unaware of changes at work on history. Given that innocence, the Green Knight enters with a shock of incongruity already implicit for the reader in the cycles of bliss and blunder. (The strategies of alliterative verse, so many of whose pairs of words are exact opposites, suggest a similarly violent antagonism.)[31] If civilizations die as the opening panorama indicates, this figure with his murderous proposal and his ax is presumably an embodiment of some of the reasons. Though his entry is not specifically predictable, then, when he does appear he crystallizes a general tendency and advances it into open action and thematic statement.

With this intrusion, we find the first really convenient correspondence between the poet's narrative logic and his fictional matter. Gawain's antagonist is of course a purely mythic and invented creature imported into a relatively realistic setting as a catalyst. As a tester of the court's enclosed civilization, he issues a call to adventure of a kind that often characterizes new narrative forces — especially in those ideal forms of narrative, like the fairy tale, in which the logic of the story is not qualified or blocked by an overly literal version of reality. As a symbolic figure from the realm of the imagination, he tightens into stressed form the doings of the court and the reader's interpretive venture: he focuses the plot and directs us through an intriguing mystery toward an eventual clarification of the Arthurian "case," at the center of the historical survey.

The Green Knight is all the more appropriate for being not quite opposite to the court in all respects. He brings with him not only the dangers of nature's seasonal ax and the cycles of life and death but also certain kinds of courteous reciprocity in keeping with Arthur's love of ornamental manners. Though terrible in appearance, boisterous, and unrefined — his eyes like fire, his beard like a bush, and hung about with signs of nature — he is also slender of waist and richly decorated. The game he proposes is not merely murderous but governed by legality, decorum, and periodicity. The ax itself is finely wrought and adorned with tassels — not that these will soothe a severed neck. That he speaks in terms of purpose, covenant, and appointed times and places indicates that he understands rules, as indeed he must if the narrative is to pursue the aristocratic decorum, measured pace, and graceful manner its own ornate style suggests. Subject to the laws of logical outcome, he comes not to destroy Arthur's court but to explore its capacity to maintain its poise and

---

31. Larry D. Benson remarks that "the structure of the sentence, with its varied parallel constructions, its ellipses, its dependence on juxtaposition and analysis, is the model for the narrative as a whole" ("The Style of *Sir Gawain*," in *Critical Studies*, ed. Howard and Zacher, p. 115).

honor under antagonistic trial. He tests its more rigid decorum, where everything has a place and a time, by the raw power of fear and death, so basic to nature's cyclical order (as energetic force tests the alliterative, stanzaic form of the verse). He leads Gawain from the harbored circle of civilization to the edge of the grave — which the green chapel resembles more than it does a church — where the question is vividly and wonderfully poised: Is Arthurian civilization as represented in its hero capable of absorbing such a blow? Can its accustomed logic encompass an expansive and threatening wonderment of this kind? In all of this it is clear that the cooperation between form and content descends into minute aspects of structure and segmentation, which accord well with the poem's periodicity and the cylical movement of its central year. One effect of the beheading game, for instance, is to make seasons integral to the court's festivity in a more serious way — to make the court deeply conscious of the organic world and what it portends about the hero's personal life and death.

This seasonal awareness is well registered in stylistic and structural matters, as at the beginning of the second section, the first discernible hinge, which modulates carefully from the gaiety of the social year to an elegiac sense of the past. Like other descriptive passages, this transition is an interval between main episodes; but it is also more than a casual marking of time. It signals a coming forward of the poet and a more explicit guiding of the reader's course. It digests what has happened so far, offers a new perspective, generates new expectations for the future, and transcends the action enough to suggest a general link between the opening panorama and the year's cycle.

As a parenthesis, before looking more closely at it, we should note that the Gawain poet makes splendid use of such intervals, as he also uses the setting of the poem and the panorama to interweave several aspects of the poem's rhythm. At such moments, the poem reaches outward expansively to its wider contexts and suggests a meditative and moral dimension that belongs as much to transactions between author and reader as it does to the education of Gawain. At the same time, summary moments between phases of the action often prove to be episodes of a disguised sort, not merely authorial comments apart from the action but causal agents in disguise. When Gawain prepares for his second setting-forth, for instance, the poet employs a description of winter to link the middle of the plot to its last phase, as the first seasonal description has linked the beginning and the middle. The season is part of the trial. Indeed, Gawain must be most alert when apparently merely killing time: the moment before turns of the plot are quite due is the moment to beware, just as the moment of greatest festivity and preoccupation with civilized pleasures is precisely when the Green Knight makes his appearance. Hence the outcome of the beheading game, Gawain eventually discovers, has depended not merely on the rules of that particular game but on what he has done in the intervals — from which we may assume that the future of Arthur's court, too, may depend on its "incidental" reaction to the conclusion of the beheading game. The significance of these narrative intervals is in part that where all history is providential, as it seems to be to the Gawain poet, no moment is finally irrelevant. And here again the view of fictional time that the poem takes is ideal for its narrative system. Despite the poet's great love of ornament, decoration, and leisure in both plot and style, nothing proves to be merely decorative; everything, including apparent insets and asides, is symbolic and organic. Festivity, descriptive digressions, and moments of relaxation are thematically and formally instrumental.

The first passage on the seasons, to return to it, is just such an organic interval. It is rhythmic in itself, describes a rhythm, and marks the plot's overall pace. In accord with the cycles that it describes, it is a model of tightly woven form:

Gawayne was glad to beginne . those gommes in halle,
Bot thagh the ende be hevy, . haf ye no wonder;
For thagh men ben mery in minde . when thay han main drink,
A yere yernes ful yerne, . and yeldes never like,
The forme to the finishment . foldes ful selden.
Forthi this Yol overyede, . and the yere after,
And eche sesoun serlepes . sued after other:
After Cristenmasse . com the crabbed lentoun,
That fraistes flesh with the fishe . and fode more simple;
Bot thenne the weder of the worlde . with winter hit threpes,
Colde clenges adoun, . and cloudes upliften,
Sheer shedes the rain . in showres full warme,
Falles upon faire flat, . flowres there shewen,
Bothe groundes and the greves . grene ar her wedes,
Brides busken to bilde, . and bremlich singen
For solace of the softe somer . that sues thereafter
        by bonk;

And blossumes blone to blowe
Bi rawes rich and ronk,
Then notes noble innoghe
Ar herde in wod so wlonk.

After, the sesoun of somer . with the soft windes,
When Zeferus sifles himself . on sedes and erbes;
Wela winne is the wort . that waxes theroute,
When the donkande dewe . dropes of the leves,
To bide a blisful blusch . of the bright sunne.
Bot then highest hervest, . and hardenes him sone,
Warnes him for the winter . to wax ful ripe;
He drives with droght . the dust for to rise,
Fro the face of the folde . to flye ful highe;
Wrothe winde of the welkin . wrasteles with the sunne,
The leves lancen fro the linde . and lighten on the grounde,
And al grayes the gres . that grene was ere;
Thenne al ripes and rotes . that ros upon first,
And thus yirnes the yere . in yisterdayes mony,
And winter windes again . as the worlde askes,
              no fage,
      Til Megelmas mone
      Wats cumen with winter wage;
      Then thenkkes Gawayne ful sone
      Of his anious viage.

(Gawain was glad to begin those games in hall,
But if the end be harsher, hold it no wonder,
For though men are merry in mind after much drink,
A year passes apace, and proves ever new:
First things and final conform but seldom.
And so this Yule to the young year yielded a place,
And each season ensued at its set time;
After Christmas there came the cold cheer of Lent,
When with fish and plainer fare our flesh we reprove;
But then the world's weather with winter contends:
The keen cold lessens, the low clouds lift;
Fresh falls the rain in fostering showers
On the face of the fields; flowers appear.
The ground and the groves wear gowns of green;
Birds build their nests, and blithely sing
That solace of all sorrow with summer comes
              ere long.
      And blossoms day by day

Bloom rich and rife in throng;
Then every grove so gay
Of the greenwood rings with song.

And then the season of summer with the soft winds,
When Zephyr sighs low over seeds and shoots;
Glad is the green plant growing abroad,
When the dew at dawn drops from the leaves,
To get a gracious glance from the golden sun.
But harvest with harsher winds follows hard after,
Warns him to ripen well ere winter comes;
Drives forth the dust in the droughty season,
From the face of the fields to fly high in air.
Wroth winds in the welkin wrestle with the sun,
The leaves launch from the linden and light on the ground,
And the grass turns to gray, that once grew green.
Then all ripens and rots that rose up at first,
And so the year moves on in yesterdays many,
And winter once more, by the world's law,
         draws nigh.
  At Michaelmas the moon
  Hangs wintry pale in sky;
  Sir Gawain girds him soon
  For travails yet to try.)[32]

The balanced turning of stanzaic units and the alliterative lines — as of wheels weighted equally on each side — is nowhere more in keeping with the poem's parallelism than here. Patterned segments repeat themselves as they move forward; but at the same time they never come back to their beginnings, any more than an alliterated word repeats the one it echoes. The repeatability of events paradoxically makes us realize more poignantly than ever that time is irreversible and that in the long run all patterns point toward the end: unlike the Green Knight's reparable body, the hero's head, once severed, is not returnable; nor is a civilization, once dead, renewable. The year proceeds almost in haste, certainly with great force and energy; and nature in its downward course is full of animated powers, warning, driving, launching, ripening, and rotting according to the world's linear onrush.

A similar elaboration of formal regularity, in the context of the

---

32. The text is quoted from *The Age of Chaucer*, ed. Boris Ford (Baltimore: Penguin Books, 1954); the translation is Marie Borroff's (New York: Norton, 1967).

unique and the unreturnable, is visible also in the church calendar. Though the Gawain poet concentrates on the social matters of the court's daily and yearly doings, he sees these not only in the light of nature's wrath but also in the perspective of Christian historical thought. From that perspective, the order of creation and the events of Christ's life lie in the background of the sacred festivities of the court, and one's particular birth and death, though still reminders of nature's power, also recall an archetypal death and rebirth. Though creation comes from nothing and may return to nothing, God descends into nature's time and redeems it. At least he has done so and may do so again. It is appropriate therefore that the passage should remember Michael and that Gawain should think frequently of the providential hand in his affair.

When we follow his line of reasoning in this regard and look for a fatality of narrative logic to match it, certain aspects of his character appear doubly functional, especially his fidelity to promises and codes. He clearly helps the author keep his appointments, as nature and civilization keep theirs. The poem need only presume the codification of an assumed society to establish the best of narrative structures, so long as the hero is society's representative and plays its recurrent games. At the same time, Gawain's moments aside provide a chance to weave larger loyalties into those acts of the moment that generate the beheading game, as he associates the appointments he keeps with larger matters. (For instance, he remarks in refusing an offer to sidestep his trial that "the Lord is strong to save: / His servants trust in Him.") Mindful of the Virgin Mother and of his religious devotions, he recurrently searches for evidence of divine intervention in his quest. His observations along this line are something more than conventional expressions of piety: if he is to be saved from the ax, the doom forecast by the seasons must be broken not by general renewals but by some particular act of grace, and this grace amounts to a kind of poetic justice enacted by providence. It comes to focus in the deserving character of the hero and the poet's desire to construct an answerable moral system in which events and outcomes confirm what ought to be.

The laws by which societies are formed and perpetuate themselves are quite different from the laws of a single biological organism, and more different still from the perpetuity of a providential universe. Yet a single heroic action carries forward all of these, and decisions hinge upon the hero's success in reconciling them. From the first transitional passages, especially when we include the arming of Gawain in the icons of the Christian warrior, we know as surely as the hours and the stanzas turn that something highly purposeful and multilayered is forthcoming. But from Gawain's point of view both the Green Knight and providence operate inscrutably. Though prediction rests on reciprocity — in the answering of one event or season by another — the poem offers no clear idea of how coming events will answer what has gone before. The levels of interchange are too complex. The seasonal description does not indicate exactly how yearly cycles fit into the greater cycles of historical epochs except that they are generally analogic: all that grows also ripens and rots. But how exactly will Gawain's courtly love and fidelity be influenced by divine love? What does the continuity of Arthurian civilization have to do with Gawain's keeping of his appointment?

These questions and the discrepancies between cycles come to focus in the bargains of Bercilak's castle and the series of games that intervenes between the beginning and ending of the beheading game. In the bedchamber trial, Bercilak's lady must either be answered in kind, according to the practices of courtly love, or rebuffed because of some discrepancy between courtly love and the agreement between guest and host. Or perhaps because of some still greater duty of the kind Gawain remembers toward the Virgin Mother. Whenever two or three such levels of value clash, the hero is apparently expected to give preference to the higher one, but the grounds for doing so are not implicit in the rules of any of the games separately, nor are they explicable by any principle of cyclical recurrence. The "returns" of love dialogue, the petition and response of prayer, the beginning and ending of social bargains, all have their own procedures. Thus despite its highly elaborate structure, the poem has important elements of asymmetry that are as important to its conception of form as its wonders and surprises are. Beyond the notorious difficulty of fitting Morgan le Fay's motives into the poem, for instance, one is troubled by the elaborate parallelism of the three hunts and the lady's three visits. No matter how we allegorize the animals, what they do when pursued is quite different from what Gawain does or should do in the bedchamber. If we add together all the parallels between the social rules of the lady's approach; the scampering of boars, foxes, and deer; the shadow of the beheading game; and the other rituals of the three days — punctuated by visits to the castle chapel — the issues become anything but transparent.

Thus, incongruity is as prominent at times as the logic of rhythmic parallels. The shape-changing of Bercilak, the unmotivated interference of Morgan le Fay, the unreadable elements of the wilderness, and the grisly nature of the green chapel as it combines holiness and deviltry impinge upon the clarity of well-lighted courts, the lucid decorum of everything chivalric, and the periodic systems of challenge and response, action and reaction. Even the supposedly protective and benevolent hand of providence can be puzzling. When Gawain prays earnestly for a place to worship over Christmas, he is answered immediately with a vision of Bercilak's castle. Though this gift of a haven seems to indicate a clear reciprocity between human need and divine guidance — and thereby a kind of moral universe — the place that appears turns out to be the setting of Gawain's most dangerous trial. Is providence ironic? Does it make use of Bercilak's lady? Is Gawain's performance of religious duties later to be admitted as evidence on his behalf by the Green Knight? Indeed, what bearing does Gawain's entire complex of virtues and minor weaknesses have finally upon the wound the Green Knight gives him? Does the Green Knight administer a logic embedded in a moral universe, or merely a logic embedded in the poetic justice that a systematic narrative prefers? The mysterious and awesome elements of romance make for an effective combination of expectation and surprise, and perhaps it is in keeping with that generic tendency that the nick in the neck does not merely complete the beheading game but alters it. Anyhow, this alteration in pattern argues that the hero is not in the grip of perfectly regular cycles and that events are answerable, but only in mysterious ways, to moral performance. The Green Knight's stopping of the stroke at the inner layer of Gawain's skin reveals how slight a miracle is needed to reconceive the game and how difficult it is to account for events by any logic inherent in the material itself.

The poem suggests a connection between Gawain's story and cosmic cycles, then, but it also emphasizes the discrepancy between secular and religious heroes and leaves its various levels in a somewhat loose juxtaposition. In terms of characterization, Gawain as a pleasant man of chivalric manners and Gawain as a devout and penitent man chastened by his adventure remain somewhat apart. The poet in his easy tolerance refuses to sacrifice the worth and importance of any of the cycles of the poem — history, social festivity, nature, or the church calendar — to any other. The art of the poem is admirably attuned to each and to their coexistence — or is it that these are admirably attuned to the art of the poem as a narrative that values symmetry, ornament, and mystery?

Our third example of the cooperation that narrative systems exact from their materials is the banquet scene in chapter seven of *The Wings of the Dove*. Thanks to James's comments on the novel, it permits us to look into the author's express designs for the book. As the author's preface suggests, the preceding two blocks of material — one setting up the group at Lancaster Gate and the other preparing Milly for her introduction to it — make this particular block critical, "where all the offered life centres, to intensity, in the disclosure of Milly's single throbbing consciousness, but where, for a due rendering, everything has to be brought to a head" (*The Art of the Novel*, p. 300). The key is the requirements of a due rendering at this juncture, which apparently means an expressive efficiency appropriate both to the material and to a presumed audience. The rhythm of a Jamesian novel is that of intellectualized social discovery governed by deliberate dialogue, interspersed with extensive internal analysis and articulate guesses about what will be spoken and confirmed next.

At the table, Milly is more involved in scouting ahead than in taking in immediately what seems to be proffered to her. Her tentativeness is appropriate to the special arrangement of the table, where one or two people are near enough to talk intimately but others must be read from a distance: "Phenomena multiplied and words reached her from here and there like plashes of a slow, thick tide." More distinctly,

> the very air of the place, the pitch of the occasion, had for her so positive a taste and so deep an undertone [that she found herself completely involved]. The smallest things, the faces, the hands, the jewels of the women, the sound of words, especially of names, across the table, the shape of the forks, the arrangement of the flowers, the attitude of the servants, the walls of the room, were all touches in a picture and denotements in a play; and they marked for her, moreover, her alertness of vision. She had never, she might well believe, been in such a state of vibration.[33]

33. *The Wings of the Dove* (New York: Random House, 1930), pp. 177, 164–65.

Though her sensitivity is heightened by the urgent need to take in everything while she can, this is for James a not unusual case of intense awakening. It is also a clear sign of how completely *fictional* characters in novels are. In his desire for rigorous economy, James seldom gives them the leisure of digressions in which they can turn aside or disengage themselves from the due course of intellectual "vibrations" laid out for them. For instance, they possess no vulgarities or egocentric oddities that are not useful to the fiction. They are allowed to think and feel only what contributes to the rigorous course of social intelligence.

Though this typical Jamesian way of realizing a course of fictive events presupposes the imagination's absolute control over its materials, it also includes breakdowns in understanding and a residue of mystery that make for a continued discrepancy between merely intuited connections and explicit intelligence. At the dinner Milly sets for herself the idealistic and romantic task of following up extraordinary realities in finer discriminations, of discovering fashions, personalities, and manners, and seizing more fully upon what at the moment she merely senses. But she sets that task without the wisdom of the narrative system before her. Do others around the table, she wonders, duplicate "as intensifying by mutual intelligence, the relation into which [she] was sinking?" (p. 77). In any case, her particular reading of the signs must follow from the main device of the story — the exploration of the intense last months of a lady of limited experience. And at the same time the evidence is set up for her to read wrongly and for us to regard as enigmatic. As Kate sits at a distance, Milly's interim judgment of her is cast in falsely romantic colors that go uncorrected for some time — as they must, because it is by means of the portents hinted in the designs they have upon her but unseen by her that James "draws the occasion into tune," sounding ahead the deeps into which a fine sensibility will be enticed.

This sense of mystery demonstrates a fatality of aesthetic form appropriate to James's concept of the novel. A residue of mystery is inherent in any serial development, of course, but it is especially important to James's development of initial "ideas for stories," which so often turn on ironic, symmetrical relationships, gradually taking shape as surprises for the investigator. One is struck in the notebook sketches, for instance, by how often an idea hinges not upon self-explanatory situations or static portraits but upon a balance of doubles, matched pairs of characters, or ghost-story contrivances, the revelations of which reverse normal expectations. These devices are sometimes reminiscent of Guy de Maupassant, Poe, and Hawthorne, but James gives them added social twists and embeds their ironies in the processes of drawing room inquisition. Thus in "The Real Thing" he seeks to work out in plausible psychological and social detail the balancing of two pairs of models, one pair nothing in itself but excellent in assuming poses, the other, a man and wife (the Monarchs) exactly what they seem but of little use finally to the painter-narrator. The story consists of the exploring of the parallels between the two pairs and the implications for art of the copresence of reality and artifice. Though the device is intelligible enough, its inherent neatness promotes both a sense of oncoming surprises and a frequent turning over of ironies. Again, perhaps more notably, in *The Sense of the Past* James finds severe problems in the elucidation of an idea that calls for a young man who craves the past to exchange places with a double from 1820 who craves the future. In this case, the device proved too taxing and strained to allow James more than a fragmentary development, with a summary of the rest. Where an initial idea does not evoke fully illuminated and intelligible details like this, the growth of the characters may be stunted and the mysteries remain mysteries: the surprises may never quite yield to explained social phenomena. Perhaps for this reason a sense of unease and potential horror creeps into the relationship between the transplanted young man and his 1820 group, and the hero's odd situation emerges as a mystery for the author as well. Again in "The Beast in the Jungle," the great experience that John Marcher saves himself for proves to be merely the awareness that in waiting for a great experience he has failed to have one: the beast springs as the awareness that there is no beast.

In each of these cases and in others, the challenge that James sets for himself is the enlivening of a storytelling device, the turning around and around of an idea to discover its potential for development, and the anchoring of that development in an investigative intelligence in whom we can believe. The device of the condemned person with only a short time to live, though not a contrivance of the sort that proves so problematic in *The Sense of the Past* or of the kind that tempted James in stories of ghosts and uncanny doubles, also presents its difficulties in harmonizing forward-leaning mysteries and the rightness and completeness of understanding. How would Milly in fact respond to such a group as James provides around the table? How should such people as Kate Croy and Densher react in turn to her? How can the author hint just enough in the dinner situation to capitalize on the two blocks of material preceding and provide the impetus to Milly's curiosity, to guide her into the fatal course the original concept of the story demands? Due rendering involves all of these things, and in seeking it James obviously needs a combination of lucidity and halftones, glimpses, and unstated assumptions that will both test and reward the shadowing intelligence.

Actually, in exploring an idea possessed of as much potential as Milly's last months, James found himself changing it and discovering in it potentials that he did not foresee, so that mysteries were in the material for the author as well. Due rendering meant the discovery of a fictional logic that only the writing itself could fully produce. Milly's response to the dinner circle is set up by the creation of precisely the group that James needed for her development, but that group was not explicit in the original idea. The society is only gradually summoned from the shadows of unrealized expectation. It is summoned by the set of James's mind, by a given narrative mode, and by the preconceived character of Milly and her situation. Milly herself is transformed in the development of the story from the thin, insubstantial, and somewhat commonplace figure James first imagined: "She learns that she has but a short time to live, and she rebels, she is terrified, she cries out in her anguish, her tragic young despair. She is in love with life, her dreams of it have been immense, and she clings to it with passion, with supplication." That this hysterical young lady is not at all the Milly Theale of the novel is due to the flexibility with which James entertained an idea and the degree to which, in this case at least, he allowed intensely imagined social exchanges to work themselves out. Densher is filled out as a product of James's need for someone to bring Milly's passion into focus; and his entanglement with another woman is produced in turn by the need to make his commitment to the doomed girl very partial — as it must be if her relationship is to be tragically disappointed. (As James rightly insists, there would be something "pitifully obvious and vulgar" in presenting a remedy for her despair: " 'Oh, she's dying without having had it? Give it to her and let her die' — that strikes me as sufficiently second-rate." Far finer is the "delicacy of kindness" that results from its being already too late and Densher's being otherwise attached.)[34]

As one relationship unfolds from another in this manner, then, the courtship of the sick girl conjures the stalled engagement of Kate and Densher, the reasons for its delay in Kate's family situation, the full flowering of Kate's character as James's preface so well describes it, and thus piece by piece the entire situation at Lancaster Gate, most centrally, of course, the scheme to get Milly's money and provide her, at the same time, with the experience she craves. It is not until a second notebook entry several days after the first that James sees this far into Kate's scheme and conceives, with her, a line of action that will capitalize on all the circumstances of his initial situation. Kate "foresees that, under these circumstances, the girl will become capable of some act of immense generosity — of generosity by which her own life, her own prospect of marriage will profit — and without her really losing anything in the meanwhile" (p. 172). At this time James also sees — given the people and circumstances now unfolding so rigorously from the improved germ of the story — Milly's response and its return impact on Densher:

> The poor dying girl has an immense shock from her new knowledge — but her passion, after a little, is splendidly proof against it. She rallies to it — to her passion, her yearning just to taste, briefly, of life *that* way — and becomes capable of still clinging to her generosity. ... But the young man learns from her that she *knows* — knows of his existing tie. This enables him to measure her devotion, her beauty of soul — and it produces a tremendous effect upon him. He becomes ashamed of his tacit assent to his fiancée's idea, conceives a horror of it. In that horror he draws close to the dying girl. [P. 173]

Thus at the end of the causal chain, the altered relationship between Densher and Kate comes about as a result of Milly's crushed, futile, generous reaction to her discovery of their complicitly, which evokes a genuine love from Densher and guarantees that her shadow will interpose between him and Kate, as the last block returns the focus to them. That Milly's reaction changes further from the original sketch — she turns away from her knowledge and gives in under it but heroically does not retract her generosity — suggests again the kind of revision that promising material undergoes as the author discovers new and better things in it.

34. James, *The Notebooks*, pp. 169, 170.

A given scene like the banquet thus falls into place as part of a continuous, complex compromise between the fatal logic of an unfolding idea and the conceivable things that reality allows the author to do, given his commitment to social realism and to the novel. The narrative organism stems from a decided taste and bent in the author, but that bent is committed to a shaping form and to a sense of what might happen under given circumstances.

As Milly illustrates so poignantly, then, at least three shaping forces — the author's predisposition, the inherent logic of an aesthetic form, and the norms of reality — meet magnificently in the theme of renunciation. If ideas and themes can be said sometimes to have an inherent formal predisposition, James's version of sacrifice has. Its formal implications begin working immediately upon the germ and shape it consistently toward a kind of tragic catharsis and a death both generous and stoically disappointing. Densher, as we have seen, combines in a single ambiguous figure Milly's maximum promise and most effective countercheck, as someone who must be renounced *because he is prized.* The action is an "ideal" one for James precisely because it perfects and intensifies the act of reaching out *futilely*, the near-consummation of a relationship and a hard sacrifice that extracts the finest of moral qualities from the heroine. Indeed, renunciation as a principle of cathartic, aesthetic enclosure is often in the offing in this way when James is free to work his material as he prefers. Even in basically awkward ideas such as the one behind *The Sense of the Past*, a sense of heroic loss and leave-taking lurks behind its attraction for James and seeks for an excuse to express itself in social conduct and event. From that viewpoint, the inherent predisposition for a shaped action of a certain kind makes James himself "the beast in the jungle" waiting to spring at Marcher: his bent is the necessary source of tragic loss and missed opportunity, able so definitively to finish a story.

Such a finish also capitalizes on the mystery that leads us through the story, because renunciation depends upon a failure of trust and affection — upon a failure in the marriage of minds. This failure renders every exchange somewhat doubtful and portentous. Some dark area of moral disability or perhaps some concealed bond that will eventually bring a marriage of minds and yet prevent the consummation of a marriage plot hangs over the progress of the protagonist. It pulls both characters and readers in, as into a fatal mechanism. This helps explain why discrepancies in point of view are seldom resolved in James, because "truth" itself as, *The Sacred Fount,* "The Beast in the Jungle," *The Tragic Muse, The American, The Wings of the Dove,* and other major works demonstrate, lies in a pluralism of values, a social disjunction, and an individualism so basic as to drive everyone back upon his own lonely resources eventually. The very social negotiations that in thrust and recoil have moved the action must be broken off.

Milly's turning to the wall thus registers symbolically the failure of social communion even among people who have been close. One must finally live by his own light, as in *The Tragic Muse* Nick Dormer must follow his course and Julia Dallow hers, each passing out of the range of the other, or as Mrs. Briss must refute the narrator of *The Sacred Fount* rather than subscribe to his thesis, leaving him in absolute isolation and perhaps convinced of his own mad eccentricity. In other noteworthy cases, Hyacinth Robinson in *The Princess Casamassima* commits suicide and the hero of *Roderick Hudson* and Morgan Moreen in "The Pupil" die in demonstrations of frustrated will. Robinson's case speaks eloquently for them all because his is an "individual sensitive nature or fine mind, . . . a small obscure intelligent creature . . . capable of profiting by all the civilisation, all the assimulations [of London], yet condemned to see things only from outside — in mere quickened consideration, mere wistfulness and envy and despair" (*The Art of the Novel,* p. 60). And so the social exchanges initiated by the Lancaster dinner for Milly offer glimpses of a communion never to be sealed, of a knowledge never quite full or effective in binding its sharers in a society, of a romance of imagined relationships that will be crushed by James's sense of inevitable tragic closure.

It perhaps follows from these denials of social communion that the reader and the text, too, must have a wedge of ambiguity between them. No final recognition of the truth of any particular point of view or set of values can quite prevail or consummate the connections that characters have. The "ado about something" that a novel concerns is fated, but it is fated to remain ironic: neither the real world nor the predisposition of the author allows an absolutely perfect match between dream and objective action, between hinted mystery and revelation, or between desire and fulfillment. The renunciation that James habitually demands is thus several fold: characters are denied an accord of understandings even when full information is available to them; the author is denied the divine comedy of marriages of the kind that finish fables of a certain kind; and the reader is denied fully harmonized values and agreed-upon meanings — more so in *The Sacred Fount* and "The Turn of the Screw" than elsewhere but to some extent in all the major fiction. The "international light" and the "rotation of aspects" are often resolutely dubious, and endings are characterized by dispersals, realizations of error and betrayal, and defeats.

In sum, the process of creation from beginning to ending concedes for James a great deal to the mechanism of linear form as it seeks a fatal enclosure and the completion of a logical train of events. The stages by which possible stories develop seem to be these: key characters or situations come to mind and the rudiments of a story follow to exhibit their relationships. With James as with Turgenev the "origin of the fictive picture" began

> almost always with a vision of some person or persons, who hovered before him, soliciting him, as the active or passive figure, interesting him and appealing to him just as they were and by what they were. He saw them, in that fashion, as *disponibles*, saw them subject to the chances, the complications of existence, and saw them vividly, but then had to find for them the right relations, those that would most bring them out; to imagine, to invent and select and piece together the situations most useful and favourable to the sense of the creatures themselves, the complications they would be most likely to produce and to feel. [*The Art of the Novel*, pp. 42–43]

Similarly, as James remarks, the blest habit of his own imagination has "the trick of investing some conceived or encountered individual, some brace or group of individuals, with the germinal property and authority." He then sees his people in detailed motion, exercising moral preferences, as in *The Portrait of a Lady* he conceives of the central portrait "in transit." "I saw it as bent upon its fate," he remarks, upon "some fate or other; *which*, among the possibilities, being precisely the question" (*The Art of the Novel*, pp. 44, 47).

The next step is the most important to a poetics of narrative because it synchronizes all the elements of a narrative stress system, character, timing, techniques of presentation, antagonistic hindrances, theme, and the concept of an outcome attending upon a middle. If one begins with a sense of a main group and imagines its ado, one must sooner or later fill in the remainder of the personages as agents of the evolving structure, and the invention of these reveals the most intimate fusion of reality and art. As to secondary agents, "it is a familiar truth to the novelist . . . that, as certain elements in any work are of the essence, so others are only of the form" (*The Art of the Novel*, p. 53). Like Henrietta Stackpole, a "wheel to the coach" in *Portrait of a Lady*, certain figures in *The Wings of the Dove* fill out the design, not as a picture but as a working action, as its subsidiary agents. The invention of a group surrounding Kate Croy provides James with a number of such agents, and it is that fully concrete and extended circle that makes the novel what it is. Without them, the action would be the sketchy material of a short story. The society of the novel represents James's "absence in reality" as he searches for appropriate types and imitative substance; at the same time it reveals his commitment to the formal necessities that summon the group and weld it together as a moving picture of society and as a set of signs in a cognitive series.

Despite its systemization of life, every fictive work, even a fairy tale, tells us something about things as they are. In fantasies and romances, though the writer is free to make much shorter circuits through reality — to invent miracles, Green Knights, and beheading games — he submits fictive designs to the test of reality. The Green Knight must talk sense, and Gawain must react toward him in believable ways. But a narrative system organizes its realities as well as its fantasies according to a rhythm of expectations and confirmations worked out in collaboration with the author's foreshortened view of things, the predispositions of genre and material, and the controlling of a flow of information to readers.

Given the artful processes of illusion that we know fictions are and given the assumption that the artist conjures only what he needs, when he needs it, how are we convinced of the value and truth of illusions? If fictions do not *lie* because they do not *affirm*, as Sidney remarks, in what sense are their systems of progressive revelation also systems of useful knowledge? Do we really know anything about the world after reading *The Wings of the Dove* or *Sir Gawain* or *Paradise Lost* that we did not know before? Or does their aesthetic fatality preclude reference to a real world? How may we be certain that what we seem to know is "real"? When we ask such questions and ponder how processes of confirmation inside the work bear upon the reader's recognition of correspondence between the work and his habitual world, we are directed mainly to characters whose witnessing of what happens is akin to our own lines of inquiry or are in some way authoritative. We are also returned to certain structural matters because, as James illustrates, whatever we are induced to accept as somehow mimetically enlivening depends on the author's manipulation of the conditions of proof in an evolving plot. Hence we will concentrate next on examples of interior witnessing in order to suggest relationships between the internal coherence of stories and any conviction of reality that may carry across the gap between fictive illusions and the reader's world. Because witnesses register the impact of information, it is through them that we come closest to identifying the rhythm of presentation with the causal chain of events; in them, knowing in the reader and suffering in mimetic character close the gap.

CHAPTER SEVEN

Witnessing

The great chroniclers have clearly always been aware of this [that affairs matter *for* someone]; they have at least always either placed a mind of some sort — in the sense of a reflecting and colouring medium — in possession of the general adventure ... or else paid signally, as to the interest created, for their failure to do so.

Henry James, *The Art of the Novel*, p. 67

> When the blackbird flew out of sight,
> It marked the edge
> Of one of many circles.
>
> Wallace Stevens, "Thirteen Ways of
> Looking at a Blackbird"

When James brings Milly Theale into the Lancaster Gate Circle and has her begin exploring the surface and depths of that society, he is anxious to make "due rendering" of her singular consciousness. Such a rendering requires that the circle around the banquet table be implicated in her crisis: it requires a confirmation of her public effect as well as her own singular understanding. Each holds a light up to and certifies reality for others, not only for the society within the novel but also for the reader. "My registers or 'reflectors,' as I so conveniently name them (burnished indeed as they generally are by the intelligence, the curiosity, the passion, the force of the moment, whatever it will be, directing them), work, as we have seen, in arranged alternation," James remarks with respect to *The Wings of the Dove*: first Susan Stringham, then Kate Croy, "who is, 'for all she is worth,' turned on," and then the rest in order as they are required (*The Wings of the Dove*, p. xxii). Each is sufficiently possessed of a believable identity to serve as a registration of social facts; whenever what is obscure, unrealized, or portentous is brought forth to be grasped by them, it can also be grasped by us. Affirmations rise to consciousness with inevitable rightness, as though, in Stevens's words,

> twanging a wiry string that gives
> Sounds passing through sudden rightness, wholly
> Containing the mind, below which it cannot descend,
> Beyond which it has no will to rise.[1]

"Truth" is manifest action and thought confirmed by people who discover that they speak a common language in a "strong, large, important human episode" — who see a common reality in "something that marches like a drama."[2]

Proof and confirmation would mean little, however, were it not for the doubts that the author finds entertainable about a course of events. Verification and doubt are as inevitably twinned in narrative art as expectation and fulfillment. James provides not only many extraordinary examples of positive and close coordination between what happens and the intelligence seizing upon events but also many doubtful processes of investigation and unresolvable ambiguities. These yoke together with exceptional closeness the reader and the puzzled course of internal witnesses.

The implications of that identification are worth looking into as one of the bridges between the world of the fiction and the reader — between participants in a dramatic ordeal and outside onlookers. Yet the differences between internal witnessing and a reader's pursuit of meaning in a fiction are also remarkable. To begin with, fictive worlds are seldom ordinary; indeed, the study of fictive experience might well acknowledge at the outset the "adventure" that James mentions and the difference it makes both to participating characters and to external onlookers.

The fiction of Stephen Crane provides a more striking test of witnessing principles in this regard. Despite a respect for the commonplace, it insists upon new angles of vision, the bizarre, and the extraordinary, sometimes where we least expect them. A shipwreck strips men of their usual shields from nature, or some incident of war initiates the warp in perception that makes the "publishing" of eyewitness reports worthwhile. (The realistic novel and short fiction

1. Stevens, "Of Modern Poetry," *Collected Poems*, p. 239.
2. James, *The Notebooks*, p. 135.

originate partly in news that will reward reportorial accuracy and close attention.) In "A Mystery of Heroism," for instance, a man named Collins finds that through an uncontrollable sequence of taunts and assertions, he has somehow undertaken to bring water to the troops across a dangerous piece of open terrain. Cast "by quaint emotions" into that grotesque situation, he discovers ordinary perceptions suddenly being knocked askew. The value of witnessing lies in the new perceptions that follow, as little things are magnified, or settled and comfortable things (like the slow bubbling of water into a canteen) become infuriating. Every action in such a bizarre world awaits its opportunity to raise new anxieties about the stability of things. For both detached intelligences and suffering characters, witnessing becomes something quite special. Collins, for instance, cannot decide what category fits his action: if from one standpoint he meets the standards he has come to expect of conventional heroism, he also knows himself well enough to believe that the queer thing he does cannot be called dramatically great. In his dazed condition he realizes that "in this matter of the well, the canteens, the shells," he is "an intruder in the land of fine deeds."[3] In a similar way, Crane's witnesses to the ironic, the puzzling, and the absurd often feel themselves intruders in places where the ordinary has become displaced or cursed. They not only see things in a warped way themselves but are in turn strangely revealed. Battalions watch Collins's journey for water in wonderment at what he does: "In running with a filled bucket, a man can adopt but one kind of gait. So, through this terrible field over which screamed practical angels of death, Collins ran in the manner of a farmer chased out of a dairy by a bull" (p. 225).

To import the special into the ordinary in this way is one of the privileges of the working imagination in search of novelty and significant structure: vision by distortion is part of fiction's high incidence of excitement, accidents, and the bizarre. Though not every writer pays as much attention to internal witnesses as Crane and James do, we could multiply examples of departure from common perception and note in a variety of fictional modes the impact of the strange and marvelous on the processes of seeing and reporting. The terms at our disposal to describe the verifying of marvels — such terms as *confirmation, validation, authentication* — derive mostly from the

3. *The Complete Short Stories and Sketches of Stephen Crane*, ed. Thomas A. Gullason (New York: Doubleday, 1963), p. 223.

language of propositions and from legalistic and scientific means of establishing truth by testimony and accrued fact. They suggest that fictions, despite their concern with the unusual and the surprising, have something in common with ordinary discourse.[4] But whether or not such terms are appropriate to narrative or dramatic demonstration is problematic because unlike an onlooker at an experiment or a jury at a trial, a reader is not always safely above the ordeal of the events he observes. The puzzles that characters confront often draw the reader into the labyrinth of uncertain adventure; and though the ordeals of readers and characters differ in essentials, the reader's advantages in distance and perspective then tend to shrink noticeably.

The Sacred Fount provides an interesting case because skepticism can seemingly go no further than it does in an ambiguity that calls into question the reliability of our only source of information. I want to reopen the problem of witnessing in it as a way into the complications of a reader in the hands of a writer who tells him nothing directly or with personal vouchers — who draws him into the ordeal of discovery with only the most minimal guarantee of an outcome.[5]

As any perusal of the criticism of the story will suggest, the crystal palace of social theory that the narrator constructs, and even the creative process by which he assembles certain points of view and makes them public, are open to doubt. Though some of his information comes to him by direct observation and is confirmed by others, his feverish additions to it are guided by an active imagination and shaped by his instinct for intrigue. As several readers have remarked,[6] the collapse of his theory therefore has implications for the fictive processes generally: his view of the relationships among his

4. Cf. John Hospers, *Meaning and Truth in the Arts* (Chapel Hill: University of North Carolina Press, 1946), pp. 141–45. Hospers lists several meanings of *truth* in art—sincerity, acceptability, value for mankind, coherence of parts, consistency, greatness—and suggests with Hulme that significant form cannot be entirely unrelated to the rest of our experience, though neither does art give us knowledge of reality in a straightforward way.

5. For discussions of point of view and reliable narration, see Percy Lubbock, *The Craft of Fiction* (New York: Viking Press, 1957), and Wayne C. Booth, *The Rhetoric of Fiction* (Chicago: University of Chicago Press, 1961), pp. 169ff.

6. Criticism of *The Sacred Fount* is both voluminous and many-sided. A bibliography of it may be consulted in Jean Frantz Blackall's *Jamesian Ambiguity and The Sacred Fount* (Ithaca: Cornell University Press, 1965), pp. 176–83. See also Holland, *The Expense of Vision*, pp. 183–226; Leon Edel, "An Introductory Essay," *The Sacred Fount* (New York: Grove Press, 1953), pp. v–xxxii; F. W. Dupee, ed., *The Question of Henry*

friends and other people at Newmarch and its buttressing by close social analysis are too much like James's own building of artful structures to allow either them or the reader to escape unscathed. As Weinstein suggests, the narrator "in his ambiguous and suspect nature" embodies "a profound, if skeptical, version of the artist himself at work; and his theory — as unreliable as it may be — entails a process of verification and, more important, posits a view of experience that are essential elements in James's fictive world."[7]

The problem posed by a novel that identifies the reader's witnessing with the characters' so closely is not only how to see reality but how to report the findings and what to do about them. In this it is not unique among James's works. The telegraphist of "In the Cage," for instance, puts together a theory of Captain Everard out of cryptic messages, while her actual contact with Everard's society remains shadowy, poetic, romantic, and ultimately self-denying: neither the intellect nor the possessive social self is allowed the victory of "appropriation" or due rendering, at least of any blatantly factual or tangible kind. Thus the inevitable price of the sensitivity and privacy of the observer's social vision in both *The Sacred Fount* and "In the Cage" is the inability of the observer, for whom witnessing is all-important, to enter actively the doings of the world he oversees and constructs. The rules of seeing and telling occupy all his energies. Intimacies must somehow be puzzled out before they can be acted on; yet they must also be concealed or they will perish in the glaring light of explicitness and vulgar action. The most delicious triumph of Hugh Vereker in "The Figure in the Carpet" is the harboring of his lifelong secret from prying critics, who are so haunted by the notion of a master pattern in his work that they are willing to work and scheme endlessly to decipher it and make it public. The rapture of James's lovers,

---

James: A Collection of Critical Essays (New York: Henry Holt, 1945); Dorothea Krook, *The Ordeal of Consciousness in Henry James* (London: Cambridge University Press, 1962), pp. 167–94; Wiesenfarth, *Henry James and the Dramatic Analogy*, pp. 96–111; Tony Tanner, "Henry James's Subjective Adventurer: 'The Sacred Fount,' " *Essays and Studies* 16 (London, 1963): 37–55; Booth, *The Rhetoric of Fiction*, "The Uses of Authorial Silence," especially pp. 292–93; Sidney Finkelstein, "The 'Mystery' of Henry James's *The Sacred Fount*," *Massachusetts Review* 3 (1962): 753–76; Weinstein, "The Exploitative and Protective Imagination"; Maurice Beebe, *Ivory Towers and Sacred Founts: The Artist as Hero in Fiction from Goethe to Joyce* (New York: New York University Press, 1964), pp. 206–15.
7. Weinstein, "The Exploitative and Protective Imagination," p. 192.

too, is never grossly physical but always attuned to the shadows and subtleties of social exchange. The narrator of *The Sacred Fount* is accordingly urged on not so much by the evolving certainties of what he sees (until near the end) as by the receding edge of excitingly glimpsed relations. He is a voyeur of hints and intellectual shadows. He pursues discoveries not in order to be possessed of a ground for action but to savor the very occupation of discovery. "Like the artist," as Weinstein writes, "he is obsessed with the way things compose, with the figure in the carpet, with the latent story buried in the phenomena that, to the untrained eye or passive imagination, seem blankly innocent. He exaggerates in the interest of form; his deepest allegiance is to 'story,' an imputed pattern of human relationships, richer, more throbbing and intense than appearances may actually justify" (p. 193). He operates largely through flashes of insight gained from gestures, distant postures, unheard colloquies, silent glances, and the nuances of inarticulate signs and signals — all of which distance him from possible action and tighten his association with the reader.

The reader depends so completely upon the narrator, in fact, that except for the shakiness of the narrator's central hypothesis — that any marked improvement in bearing and wit in someone must be paid for by the deterioration of someone else — it is natural to find his compassionate and perceptive guidance and his firm tone both convincing and richly enlightening. His perceptions move forward with sure touches, poise, and a growing complexity that firmly engages us. His particular game, as he remarks to himself, is a "kind of high sport — the play of perception, expression, sociability." For all our reservations about his character and his accuracy, we have no solid reason to think that he is not on the track of *something*, though it may turn out to be a surprise. He possesses sufficient force of intellect to form a circle (a mystic circle as he thinks of it) of those working with the torch of the analogy he presents them, so that our identification with him is backed by other witnesses, most notably Ford Obert, the shrewdest and most disinterested of his confidants.

Moreover, there are clear advantages in our believing in his construction rather than Mrs. Brissenden's: his at least borders on the beautiful and the compassionate, whereas hers is less generous and derives its strength and brilliance from her "immense egotism." Though his theory eventually has to be abandoned in the face of her assault, it fills every instant of the main body of the story with a typically Jamesian compassion of discovery. Like the telegraphist, the narrator discovers largely what will draw him closer to people and trigger further discoveries. Even nature composes itself as though in a painting or a setting for the exquisite social drama he constructs. It grows more luminous and coherent with each turn the imagination gives it, as he compiles an ever growing poem of inferences, shades, and partial illuminations:

> Oh, it was quite sufficiently the castle of enchantment, and when I noticed four old stone seats, massive and mossy and symmetrically placed, I recognized not only the influence, in my adventure, of the grand style, but the familiar identity of this consecrated nook, which was so much of the type of all the bemused and remembered. We were in a beautiful old picture, we were in a beautiful old tale, and it wouldn't be the fault of Newmarch if some other green *carrefour*, not far off, didn't balance with this one and offer the alternative of niches, in the greenness, occupied by weather-stained statues on florid pedestals.[8]

Quite apart from nature, much of the narrator's discourse with others concerns the degrees of certainty and doubt they entertain concerning a given social sign in all its reverberations. Were his probing less disastrous to him, one could almost take it as a defense of poetry — as a demonstration of the spiritualizing of erotic, banal, and sometimes trivial social phenomena under the enlivening touch of the imagination.

But as he discovers, projecting highly subjective theories into social exchanges and coming into the marketplace with them is a very dangerous occupation; a good deal of ego is invested in their acceptance. The price of inexplicitness and of subtle, delicate shades of meaning that one prizes may well be rejection, isolation, and ultimately self-doubt. Unfortunately, the narrator cannot rigorously and candidly commit himself to the truth for its own sake. To protect others, especially May Server, he must dissemble, and though he does so for admirable reasons, he weakens his "palace" at vital points. He toys with people and teases them into false suppositions. Without candor and without what he calls "tone," he appears to his witnesses dangerous, meddlesome, and overly critical. Hence it is with some justification that Mrs. Briss demolishes his palace and replaces it with

8. Henry James, *Three Novels* (New York: Harper and Row, 1968), p. 388.

a less distinguished, partly borrowed version of it. It becomes clear as his confidence ebbs that indeed nothing is certain about his artful little world or his position in it. Nor is the act of witnessing by readers as safe as we have assumed. All is as fragile as "a beautiful old tale." "Truth" exists only in persuasion; it is carried only by personal force and conviction. It is entirely relative to the conditions of appeal in minds that catch it up and toss it back and forth like a social plaything.

As critics have pointed out, the narrator's theory proves correct in at least one element: one person does pay for the wit and imagination of another; and so he pays for Mrs. Briss's triumph, aging almost instantly as he believes "poor Briss" has aged. But unlike Briss and May Server, he is not a willing victim urged on by love: he serves Mrs. Briss by a painful surrender of his theory. Since he exists so much in and for his intelligence and feeling — in the shape and form it takes from the gathering — her triumph is a rending of his own finely woven consciousness. As his frail but "quite sublime structure" shrinks to the mere extravagance of a potential madman (or poet), the consequential logic into which he has projected his own career becomes "a mere heap of disfigured fragments." In the burnished mirror of the consciousness Mrs. Briss holds up to it, all things are transfigured: she redefines Gilbert Long not as a miracle of new wit but the same person he has always been; poor Briss has not after all been marvelously altered; Lady Long is not the partially depleted vessel of strained wit the narrator has described but a quite sufficient force to account for Long; Mrs. Server is not pitifully emptied and "idiotised" but just as she always has been. There have, in short, been no miracles; joyful flights of the imagination into elusive but finely shaded and colored realities are illegitimate. The narrator is not the center of a mystic circle formed around the wonder of his poetic perceptions or even a reliable social critic — merely a misled, almost dishonest outcast. Not merely a theory disintegrates under Mrs. Briss's touch, then, but a living organism, an intelligence, dwelling in its social relations, inhabiting the dramatic form of the very story the narrator has won by hard labor from difficult materials.

The question the reader must confront is whether or not the narrator deserves this severe disenchantment and how far he drags the reader down with him. Where so many readers have found the ultimate effect of the story puzzling and ambiguous, it would be rash to suggest that there are easy escapes from the trap the narrator falls into. However, we may narrow the confusion somewhat by a structural observation — and perhaps discover a piece of slightly less boggy ground to retreat to. The story has not a single but a double movement, a broken and resumed course of investigation as the initial set of intrigues lapses and the narrator desires to leave Newmarch. He feels, in fact, that he will be "in small haste to come back":

> For I should leave behind me my tangled theory, no loose thread of which need I ever again pick up, no stray mesh of which need my foot again trip. It was on my way to the place, in fine, that my obsession had met me, and it was by retracing those steps that I should be able to get rid of it. Only I must break off sharp, must escape all reminders by forswearing all returns. [P. 428]

The sight of Gilbert Long lounging and smoking to himself stirs a new interest, and an encounter with Ford Obert immediately afterwards fans the narrator's curiosity into full force again. However, in the renewed investigation his desire to protect May Server is noticeably missing: both his near-love of her and his willingness to complicate his relations with others in order to shield her — the strongest marks of his compassion and propriety — have disappeared. What follows is an increasingly prideful narrowing of the circle of those who are keen enough to follow him. First he drops Ford Obert aside and then in the first part of the last interviews with Mrs. Brissenden assumes an almost insufferable command over her and over the evidence that they mutually drag forth. My assumption is that he also forces the reader to step back; his assertion of the pride of knowing exposes new dimensions of distorting egoism. Having been more adequately checked in earlier phases of his curiosity, he begins now to draw away from the typical Jamesian fictive investigation of a protective and compassionate kind. He grows doubly convinced that Gilbert Long and Mrs. Brissenden have discovered each other and arrived at an implicit pact. As his exchanges with her become more than ever aggressive, and each displays information like trumps in a feverish card game, he remarks that his certainty has

> spread and spread to a distance greater than I could just then traverse under Mrs. Briss's eyes, but which, exactly for that reason perhaps, quickened my pride in the kingdom of thought I had won. I was really not to have felt more, in the whole business, than I felt at this moment that by my own right hand I had gained the kingdom. Long and she

were together, and I was alone thus in face of them, but there was none
the less not a single flower of the garden that my woven wreath should
lack. [Pp. 457–58]

The narrator's splendid theory collapses when he drives Mrs. Briss to
confess what are after all very common, even sordid, truths — truths
that an investigator no more advanced and subtle than poor Briss has
discovered: Gilbert Long and Lady John are lovers; May Server has
in fact been making love to her husband. If these are the facts, the
apparently beautiful stones of the narrator's edifice are not beautiful
at all: romance gives way on all fronts to a one-dimensional realism
that any gossip columnist might have anticipated.

For the reader at this point the two visions, his former one and
Mrs. Brissenden's, remain suspended; neither is quite sufficient to
account for all the evidence the story has presented, much of it verified by observers other than the narrator. Briss in his commonplaces
could be as mistaken as the narrator. Hence, though the narrator
himself abandons his perceptions, his inferences, and his knowing and
comes to speak merely of his imagination, his view of the group's
many intrigues has the virtue of explaining Mrs. Brissenden's startling youth and Briss's startling age; it explains the depths of May Server's unspoken communion with him in the garden; and it has the
support of Ford Obert in finding in Long a magnificent and entertaining wit (which Mrs. Briss merely denies without offering examples
or proof). Moreover, not all the symmetries, innuendoes, subtleties,
and secret-sharer relationships he has traced with such infinite patience and flights of imagination can be quite boiled down to commonplace flirtations.

What this lingering tension between the kind of observations he
and the Brisses represent amounts to is an antagonism in vision in
which neither party can be said to produce an indisputable version of
the truth. The reader's act of witnessing expands to include a collision of romance and realism articulated by no one, a collision that
suggests perhaps more than one layer to all social relations. Indeed,
as each layer offers us radically different kinds of intrigue, the one
clear principle that emerges is that the narrator must surrender, if not
his exciting tracing of relationships and his theories, at least the certainty with which he pursues his method. (That this may be all one is
expected to give up is suggested by his final remark, "I *should* certainly never again, on the spot, quite hang together, even though it

wasn't really that I hadn't three times her method. What I too fatally lacked was her tone" [p. 493].) Certainly the reader must surrender the immunity of one-track perceptions and is perhaps requried to combine both the delicacy and the coarseness of social relations — the splendor and poetry of one point of view and the sordid commonplaces entangled in them. Checked as violently in his theories as Mrs. Briss checks him, the narrator cannot so conveniently force every piece of evidence into line. He must accordingly surrender the "joy of [the] intellectual mastery of things unamenable, that joy of determining, almost of creating results" (p. 435).

To a certain extent the reader also shares the quandary of expressing what he perceives in those ambiguous materials and the difficulty of struggling in behalf of his theories against competing theories. He must shape the materials as best he can, the alternative being a passivity that renders him, too, toneless. Yet to marshal the "facts" aggressively and to overpower rival interpretations of so opaque a social material is to play Mrs. Brissenden with them (as criticism of the story has been known to do). If the novel confirms anything, then, it would seem to be the dilemma of intelligence trying to match communication and observation, and enter the public domain with an acceptable set of postulates. Every house of cards or palace of the imagination places others as subordinates in a self-centered fiction, because it is the nature of consciousness to shape its fictions around a personal center of observation, resisting absorption into the fictions and truths of others. Thus, too, the telegraphist in "In the Cage" is amazed to discover how much she does not know about Captain Everard, who coolly turns his back on her and leaves the grocery when she has finished her service to him, never to return. She has constructed a romantic fantasy that has only tangential bearings on her true place in the world she gleans from the telegrams. The exterior witness must learn to do better.

Unreliable testimony is not uncommon in fiction and is a very useful ironic device to conduct the reader, in the best roundabout way, to more complex realities than he might otherwise put together. But very few stories carry skepticism as far as *The Sacred Fount*, with such devastating implications for the nature of fictive verification and the potential solipsism of everything that issues from the dissolving, unifying imagination. In a sense, James was prepared for such a degree of skepticism by his habit of seeing moral problems so often in an "international light" that cancels one point of view with another, and in courting the mysteries of the ghost story — the first of these threatening to leave people suspended between social values of different establishments, the other relishing the unsolvable ambiguities of inhuman forces and vague sources of evil and misapprehension. Frequently in James, no single way of looking at things can be established, especially when two or more conflicting reflectors are equally respected or disrespected. Between Ransom and Olive in *The Bostonians*, for instance, who can choose finally, when both are so narrowly motivated and so obviously in error? Hyacinth in *The Princess Casamassima* cannot accept, finally, either the accomplishments of surplus wealth or social revolution.

What essentially James entertains in these conflicts of interest is the notion that society is composed of conflicting tones, styles, and manners whose worth is not intrinsic but assigned by its witnesses. Unfortunately, the best social conduct is the most oblique and sensitive, the least demonstrable and "seeable," and therefore the most dangerous as underpinning for a social standing. It is no wonder that James's heroes and heroines are required to turn to the wall, to walk out, to refuse to grasp or possess or even to protest. They "seize" finally only what is beyond actual possession; reality passes into the frame of the just-past and the unreachable in order to be apprehended and embraced by the mind. Unlike the novel in Defoe, then, Jamesian fiction does not probe indisputable truths and social contracts based on goods that can be bought and sold; it probes the psychological and cultural foundations of illusion and the styles by which testimony is offered on behalf of those illusions in society's tentative "as if" agreements. The difference between *The Wings of the Dove* and *The Sacred Fount* is not that one is epistemologically confident and the other ultimately ambiguous but that the generosity, courage, and grace of Milly Theale is so well enacted and so convincing that it registers beyond doubt on the people who surround her, who in their haste to appropriate her wealth have somehow missed the full implications she will have for them. A certain range of assumptions about society dissolves in the face of her superior reserve and her illustration of a superior style. Bearing witness to that style, Densher rewards it with the highest tribute James conceives of, a willingness to honor it on the altar of his own sacrifice. To know Milly fully and to render public acknowledgment, he must relinquish Kate at the very moment his relationship to her could have been publicly settled and witnessed.

The issue of testimony and truth-saying as James illustrates it is as critical to fiction in its way as it is to science, history writing, and to daily living. Certainly no theory of fictions could remain quite the same after James had entered the field (as the forerunner of Pirandello, Beckett, Barth, and a host of skeptical treatments of her unreliability and uncommunicableness). It is possible to view his influence as pernicious in this respect, inasmuch as he moves the novel away from one of its prime traditions, the clear observation of social orders and the urban, provincial, and rural facts of life. It is understandable, for instance, that Frank Colby writes with some exasperation in "In Darkest James":

> For years James did not create one shadow-casting character. His love affairs, illicit though they be, are so stripped to their motives that they seem no more enticing than a diagram. A wraith proves faithless to her marriage vow, elopes with a bogie in a cloud of words. Six phantoms meet and dine, three male, three female, with two thoughts apiece, and, after elaborate geometry of the heart, adultery follows like Q.E.D. . . . To be a sinner, even in the books you need some carnal attributes — lungs, liver, tastes, at least a pair of legs.[9]

But is also true, as Richard Bernheimer writes, that "the less a work of art fulfills the demands of a realistic aesthetic, the more it is prone to be credited with those miraculous activities which seem to be belied by its appearance."[10] It may be that the roots of artistic representation grow less out of a desire to imitate real things than out of a sense of indistinct phenomena that we get when explicit line, leg, lungs, and liver are subtracted and we are forced to witness primarily wraiths in a "cloud of words." If one of the functions of fiction is to present knowable communities, in Raymond Williams's phrase, not all of such communities are knowable in "carnal" signs. James believed that some communities are held together by the cryptic hints of telegrams, the turning of a back, the movement of a hand unaccom-

9. Frank Moore Colby, "In Darkest James," in *The Question of Henry James*, ed. Dupee, pp. 22–23.
10. Richard Bernheimer, *The Nature of Representation*, ed. H. W. Janson (New York: New York University Press, 1961), p. 12.

panied by words, the moments before and after a word is spoken. As Tony Tanner suggests, James's accomplishment is in part to transfer to the novel — always a factual mode preeminently — a dimension of legitimate wonder "introduced into the clotted complexities of society."[11]

It is also true that, although James marks a turning point in methods of fictional witnessing, a concern for witnesses is not unique to him or to modern fiction. I want to go in an entirely different direction for a moment and examine several older modes that are distinct and yet suggest similar structural complications. They will help us test further the assumption that fictions present us with an interplay of what to internal characters are linear ordeals but to readers are not only vicarious ordeals but systematic signals pursuing their own pace and rhythm.

INTERIOR WITNESSING: *PARADISE REGAINED* AND *THE MOONSTONE*

Neither *Paradise Regained* nor Wilkie Collins's *The Moonstone* is plagued with a skepticism as extreme as that of several of James's stories, but each presents symptomatic problems in the disclosing of assumed truths to internal and external audiences. Although reality is not permanently opaque to Milton (or to his epic presenter), it is problematic to key investigative witnesses, especially to Satan; and to some extent Milton assumes that it will be problematic to the reader. Collins settles upon a clear display of what has happened to the moonstone finally, but he, too, suggests enroute the fallibility of witnesses and the crossfire of perspectives. He has the less than reliable investigative methods of a number of internal detectives erect hypotheses inadequate to the material. Both make the reading of the text an investigative procedure concerned self-consciously with testimony, experimentation, and confirmation.

In *Paradise Lost* — to begin a step back from *Paradise Regained* — the intertwining of radically different levels of being is accomplished by several sorts of witnessing, some reliable and some not, as representatives of one sphere visit another and exchange information

11. Tony Tanner, *The Reign of Wonder*, p. 261.

and points of view. The moments of delivery are privileged moments in which the continuity of a given sphere is interrupted and made to incorporate perspectives from beyond it. Both *Paradise Lost* and *Paradise Regained* trace their main actions to the spoken authority of celestial beings. These can be divided into the perfectly reliable and all-encompassing witnesses God and Christ, for whom all time and space are a single tableau; reliable but limited witnesses such as Raphael and Michael, who accommodate their narratives to human intelligence; and at least one extremely dubious reporter, Satan, whose inaccuracy subjects him to constant irony and revision. As a bringer of gospel, Christ is of course the center of all revelations. Back of Milton's own reliable document, the poem, lies of course the testament that has Christ as its historical center. As Christ enters history in *Paradise Regained* expressly to reveal the Father's image in action, Milton's historical narrative pretends to reconstruct the means by which he does so.

Hence Milton can offer the poem as a document whose criterion for truthfulness is virtually the same as that of gospel. Just as the desert becomes paradise when Christ inhabits it, so the details of the poem discover their collective clarity when it publishes the image of Christ's divine identity. Or to put it differently, as Christ closes the distance between heaven and earth by publishing his father's purpose, the poem closes the gap between act and disseminated knowledge — between the event and its distant observers, whose view of what happens is through the telescope of the poet's re-creative imagination. As assumed history, the poem deals with what Milton considered true events; but as fiction, it also unfolds dimensions of those events in the images, dialogue, and actions of the imagination:

> Thou Spirit who led'st this glorious Eremite
> Into the Desert, his Victorious Field
> Against the Spiritual Foe, and brought'st him thence
> By proof th'undoubted Son of God, inspire,
> As thou art wont, my prompted Song, else mute,
> And bear through height or depth of nature's bounds
> With prosperous wing full summ'd to tell of deeds
> Above Heroic, though in secret done,
> And unrecorded left through many an Age,
> Worthy t' have not remain'd so long unsung.
>
> [1.8–17]

Because Christ's sojourn in the desert has gone unrecorded, the problem of distant onlookers (including the reader) is to bridge the outposts of history and the heroic pattern at its center.

What is the reality that the poem confirms? To some extent it is summed up in abstractions given flesh and in the paradigm of moral conduct disclosed ironically by Satan's probing and testing. One of these abstractions, for instance, is *glory*, a term used by both Satan and the hymning angels who bear witness to God's equipage and powers. Milton's task is to discover the kind of reality glory has in history. Its discovery there will then be a discovery of God's variable presence in events of greater or lesser magnitude, dispersed among human chronicles. As Christ's series of rejections makes clear, one either regains all of Paradise or none of it — sees the sum of God's design or understands no part of it — because whatever glory an event has is a distant reflection of that design. The difficulty with Satan's blueprint for his antagonist's earthly kingdom is that it arrogates, as Christ says of the philosophers, "all glory" to itself, "to God gives none." Other would-be heroes do the same by taking the initiative in action, by doing when they should be suffering; for "Who best / Can suffer best can do." To suffer is to endure the humiliation of suspended dignity and interim degradation in expectation of a fuller glory. Thus putting aside his own previous functions in Heaven as God's Word and executive or creative power, Christ believes that he must claim nothing himself; he must attribute everything to God as the single "publisher":

> his word all things produc'd,
> Though chiefly not for glory as prime end,
> But to show forth his goodness, and impart
> His good communicable to every soul
> Freely; of whom what could he less expect
> Than glory and benediction, that is thanks.
>
> [3.122–27]

Ironically, of course, that word is Christ himself, who here describes his own function — and describes by implication the imitative function of the poem in making "His good communicable to every soul," "Imparting" divine attributes in paradigmatic actions. In the final chorus — one of the key passages in Milton's system of proofs and witnessed demonstrations — the angels hymn a completed showing forth and at the same time complete the poem's own narrative-descriptive design. As Christ has put on human form, so the poem in its historical accuracy expresses a "godlike force":

> True Image of the Father, whether thron'd
> In the bosom of bliss, and light of light
> Conceiving, or remote from Heaven, enshrin'd
> In fleshly Tabernacle, and human form,
> Wand'ring the Wilderness, whatever place,
> Habit, or state, or motion, still expressing
> The Son of God, with Godlike force endu'd
> Against th' Attempter of thy Father's Throne
> And Thief of Paradise; him long of old
> Thou didst debel, and down from Heav'n cast
> With all his Army; now thou hast aveng'd
> Supplanted *Adam*, and by vanquishing
> Temptation, hast regain'd lost Paradise,
> And frustrated the conquest fraudulent:
> He never more henceforth will dare set foot
> In Paradise to tempt; his snares are broke:
> For though that seat of earthly bliss be fail'd,
> A fairer Paradise is founded now
> For *Adam* and his chosen Sons, whom thou
> A Savior art come down to reinstall.
> [4.596–615]

By recapitulating the entire plot in a few lines, Milton emphasizes its virtual simultaneity in God's mind ("him long of old . . . the conquest fraudulent"). With this "reinstalling" (reestablishment, validation, verification of intent), the wandering image recurrent in both *Paradise Lost* and *Paradise Regained* is redefined as a variable expression of God — in habits, states, motions, and temporal instants. Since Paradise is now present, both harbingers and historians may join as celebrants of a contemporary glory. Thus, too, prophet, king, and priest — the three historical roles of Christ — are unified in the act of refusing to act, or in strictly the publication of these roles.

The parallelism between the first exaltation of Christ in Heaven and this one in the desert tells us as much about the functions of the counterplot — as false hypothesis and error — as it does about Christ's own instrumentality in raising the image of Eden in the wilderness. Satan can see the truth about himself only when liberated from his own quest for "glory" — liberated painfully by the exposure of the satanic means of establishing kingdoms and welding alliances.

The plans that he proposes assist Christ's office indirectly, not as he intends but as a means of proving by negatives: "By contrary unweeting he fulfill'd / the purpos'd Council preordain'd" (1.126–27). This proof would be unnecessary were it not for the errors of perception Milton must presuppose in the reader. What turns out to be merely a ritual demonstration of the divine paradigm for Christ is for Satan and the reader (in varying degrees) cause for dramatic passion and agonizing. He is "inly rackt," "perplext," "desperate," "abasht" with fear, and sometimes "mute confounded . . . confused and convinc't / Of his weak arguing." If Christ deals in historical realities — or the historifying of realities — Satan deals in fictions, scenarios, and staged demonstrations. Desperate to gain knowledge and collect information that might confirm or disprove the rumors he has heard, he has not ceased to eye Christ suspiciously since Christ's birth. In order to read the prophecies, he turns out the full resources of his foreign intelligence and consults his dictionary of divine terms. The detective work he once performed in Eden was slight by comparison:

> I thought thee worth my nearer view
> And narrower Scrutiny, that I might learn
> In what degree or meaning thou art call'd
> The Son of God, which bears no single sense;
> The Son of God I also am, or was,
> And if I was, I am; relation stands;
> All men are Sons of God; yet thee I thought
> In some respect far higher so declar'd.
> Therefore I watch'd thy footsteps from that hour.
> [4.514–22]

In each of the temptations, Satan seeks to bring Christ to a means of display consistent with the kind of host Satan himself has gathered and controlled. The quick temptation to convert stone to bread is a preliminary index to them. Were he Christ, his way of offering proof would be to produce an instant miracle, a display such as magicians perform, which by way of a bonus would also do a notable public service. The trap is well designed because either in performing or in refusing to in the wrong way, Christ would abandon the role of the perfect man holding to the limited witnessing powers and demonstrations of the prophets. An answer must stay within their range and yet keep open the possibility of a higher feast, a subordinate part of glory. Proof of God's presence lies indeed, in a sense, in the eating of his substance:

> Man lives not by Bread only, but each Word
> Proceeding from the mouth of God, who fed
> Our Fathers here with Manna.
>
> [1.349-51]

The answer indicates that phenomenal nature may be useful as food, but "food," the most consumable of things, is also part of an entertainment that enters narrative time directly from the command of God and is transubstantiated into divine being. Meanwhile, for Satan, the "lying" of poetic fables is "sustenance," as Christ remarks: it is "thy food / Yet thou pretend'st to truth" (1.429-30). The difficulty both for the prophets and for Christ at this stage is to look forward to a revelation of full glory and yet not lay claim to it. Faith and patience are interim virtues between a first surmise and a final certainty.

Seeking to define in what "degree or meaning" Christ is the Son involves Satan also in the uncomfortable office of prophecy and therefore in the same predictions of design that the reader also engages in, except that Satan obviously gains less sustenance from scripture. To his past work as a pagan oracle, which Christ exposes immediately, he eventually adds a portentous storm to signify God's intent, which, as a reader of his own signs, he interprets for Christ:

> Whereof this ominous night that clos'd thee round,.
> So many terrors, voices, prodigies
> May warn thee, as a sure foregoing sign.
>
> [4.481-83]

Not to rely solely on the weather, he also invokes "the Starry Rubric" so useful in suggesting fearful anticipations. He finds no date "prefixt" for Christ's real or allegoric kingdom there — eternal sure, he remarks (thinking to cut a swath of ruin through God's terms by parody) if "without beginning" (4.389ff.). Thus he becomes a dispenser of "presages and signs, / And answers, oracles, portents and dreams" (1.294-95) and trades in marvels of a kind that only his vast storeroom of fireworks can bring to pass.

But to any clear view, the stars tell only the time of year and the elements only make one wet. In resisting each stage in the episodes of voluptuousness and wealth that Satan urges upon him, Christ forces Satan to become more and more aware that power is not self-predicated and programed, to be confirmed by military or political action or by staged miracles and signs. In particular, Christ's answers expose Satan's pretense to leadership as an exploitation of followers and a means of self-promotion:

> For what is [political] glory but the blaze of fame,
> The people's praise, if always praise unmixt?
> And what the people but a herd confus'd,
> A miscellaneous rabble, who extol
> Things vulgar, and well weigh'd, scarce worth the praise?
> . . . .
> This is true glory and renown, when God
> Looking on th' Earth, with approbation marks
> The just man, and divulges him through Heaven
> To all his Angels, who with true applause
> Recount his praises.
>
> [3.47–51, 60–64]

The archetype of parliamentary pretense and false acclaim is Pandaemonium, where all reality is lost in the tones and styles of assertion, where the best orators and most aggressive intellects prevail. In converting what had once been a celestial host into a colony, Satan deprives his followers of true divulgence, whereas the appropriate political branch of publication is the just applause of one's fellow creatures, for attributes accurately imparted. Fame among a confused group such as this submits glory to infinite segmentation and therefore to disconfirmation: the community of Hell can never be truly known to any of its members because the connective principle, their analogous likeness to a common creator, has been rooted out. As they confront each other, then, they discover a proliferation of fragmented substitutions for that absent being. As warriors, philosophers, musicians, parliamentary leaders, architects, Epicureans, and future deities of pagan cults, they become the plotters and enacters of a thousand future fictions that will invade history and make a promiscuous blending of appearances and reality — and thereby require the publication of corrective poems. The function of such poems is in part to reinstate the analogy between men and God as the basic ground of their mutual knowability, centered of course in the image of God descended into history — where it removes other apparent common bonds among men such as class, nationalities, philosophical schools, and the like. Men then have one central way of recognizing each other; they are variants of the creator, sons of God.

This is proved additionally by the Jameslike reflectors that Milton stations around the central revelation between the reader and the event. While Christ arrives ever closer to a definition of his role, the outer group of the poem keeps the ordinary world within range and suggests ways in which extraordinary actions and ordinary affairs may be interwoven in a Christian range of knowledge. Andrew and Simon retire in waiting to a pleasant place, filled with anxiety but prepared to see the promise that has been given to them verified by some further sign:

> on the bank of *Jordan*, by a Creek
> Where winds with Reeds and Osiers whisp'ring play,
> Plain Fishermen, (no greater men them call)
> Close in a Cottage low together got,
> Thir unexpected loss and plaints outbreath'd.
>
> [2.25–29]

As they lament the fall from "high hope" that their relapse has given them, we see in their domestic sphere a repetition of the test of patience and the loss of communion with high purposes. Like the Messiah, they know that the time is come and in choral prayer they attempt to make the future arrive ("arrive and vindicate / Thy Glory, free thy people from thir yoke!"). But at the same time, they must learn resigned obedience and faith, reinforced by acceptance of prophetic certainty and its relevance, despite all appearances, to the present: "he will not fail . . . / Soon we shall see our hope, our joy return" (2.54, 57). Though their way is less demanding than Christ's, for them, too, a redefinition of glory demands that they grasp the irony of verification-by-refusal, of heroic stature through humility and inaction, as Mary reasons her way to an equation of "afflictions high" and exaltation. (She finds that, paradoxically, the worst of conditions yields the highest of blessings if one has trust and bears witness correctly: "Afflicted I may be, it seems, and blest.") There remains, besides the witnessing, the living itself, since the real trials of the followers are just beginning. But all other trials have been set in focus by the trial set before them to be read, proved in the byways of

the desert. Though the exact application of Christ's triumph to family
and national interests is not the subject of the poem, we are to assume
that vatic utterance will now somehow transform these interests as
confirmation spreads outward to the periphery of all witnesses — as
evangelism transforms all households to the outermost edge of those
who read the right "publications."

The second fall of Satan in *Paradise Regained* confirms a number
of things — the consistency of his character; the recurrent form of
history, which turns ever back upon ritual demonstrations of God's
imprint; and of course, from man's viewpoint, the verities on which a
true knowledge of the universe can safely be based. Unlike the
unresolvable ambiguities of a social world whose hypotheses are
carried by style and tone, the ambiguities of Milton's universe are
resolvable. Much of what we witness in the poem is paradigmatic, so
that the universals usually attributed to fiction and the particulars of
history have no conflict. The entire problem of establishing truth is
solved by an inevitability of perspective: the story can be put together in only one way. An infallible intelligence bears witness to the
divine intent and guides us to its certainties. The abstractions of an
older mimesis — truth, glory, beauty, divine essence — are thus
established as the foundations of the Word itself.

From another direction, *Paradise Regained* has many of the traits
of a superior detective fiction — an archetypal story of crime, exposure, and punishment. (As W. H. Auden writes, detective fiction
has inherently much in common with the story of the fall and
redemption: "The fantasy . . . which the detective story addict in-
dulges is the fantasy of being restored to the Garden of Eden, to a
state of innocence.")[12] For Milton, no story of crime and punishment
is conceivable without reference to the detection of illusory glory and
exposure of the archcriminal Satan, whose amazed acknowledgment
of God's plan is the strongest endorsement it could have. The narra-
tive-historical universe is presided over by an all-seeing eye that scans
all corners of time and space and manages a solution for all dis-
turbances; ultimate justice depends upon perfect detection. As a form
of interrogation, the encounter between Satan and Christ in *Paradise
Regained* lays bare not what Satan hopes it will — the inherent

12. W. H. Auden, *The Dyer's Hand and Other Essays* (New York: Random House,
1948), p. 158.

weakness of all men in common with him — but his own disobedience repeated. Having spread to men through the original parents, it is now rooted out at its source, at least for a fit few. The central recognition of the poem is the discovery behind the two apparently human antagonists of their reiterated roles as celestial and infernal archetypes — discovery for them and for the reader. The crime that in one sense has been known so well all along from its repetition in everyman comes thereby to have new dimensions as open history linked to end things. Satan has no need to question further; he is presumably now or later to be cast out from further knowledge except for what concerns him directly, his own "port of worst."

The process of investigation, the validity of proofs, and the progress from crime to atonement that Milton models on so large a scale in *Paradise Lost* and *Paradise Regained* (and to some extent again in *Samson Agonistes*) we find on a smaller scale in many detection plots, which, because crimes are inevitably hidden, lead often into the innermost recesses of human motives. Normally in such plots, we are stationed close by a single investigative figure such as Oedipus, Hamlet, Satan, or James's telegraphist, who seeks to disclose what has gone awry and thus to solve, in some sense, the "riddle of man's curse," a curse that makes one person unknowable to others, or knowable but untouchable. Insofar as the detective is himself affected by the discovery, every new fact is an ordeal and leads toward the heart of a community of error and malice — assuming that the culprit, whether Adam and Eve, Oedipus, Satan, Hamlet's uncle, or Captain Everard, has the opportunity to disseminate corruption and destroy the bonds of trust that make a society cohesive. In Oedipus, Hamlet, and Christ, the detective himself — in restoring a semblance of health to the society — accepts the burden of the crime. In James, the detective loses his innocence by a turn of knowledge that casts him outside a community he had expected to join.

Wilkie Collins's novel *The Moonstone* is a convenient model of the investigative system of realistic fictions and the detective story proper; I select it to explore both for that reason and because it uses a variety of first-person views of an action to reconstruct a recent case history. It is simpler and less skeptical than James's probings of complicity and secret bonds, and it reveals novelistic investigation in a more blatant form. It is realistic in two senses, in the mimetic presentation

of fallible human views of a crime and in Collins's trust in the reality
of certain categories and truths upon which the novel depends. These
are not paradigmatic in Milton's sense, but Collins nonetheless takes
them to be broadly valid. Basically, in piecing together what has
happened from evidence contributed by a number of witnesses,
Collins discloses several layers in the events themselves, each of which
is susceptible only to particular lines of inquiry — the law,
psychology, or science. Eventually he points toward an encompassing
witness, Murthwaite, who approaches a story of considerable scope.
Indeed, in encroaching upon epic and romance and suggesting a
larger atonement for crime than the law or society normally asks, the
novel points toward some of the recurrent archetypes that older forms
of the crime-and-redemption myth embody.

Yet, all told, the novel concentrates mostly on drawing room
materials, and when we ask about such a work what it finally seeks to
prove, we are led to speculate primarily about social class, psychology, and the effects of a given crime on money, manners, and
family status. Though most detective fiction does not pretend to mirror life and manners with the breadth of Balzac or Tolstoy and is
likely to isolate a very small group in a hotel, household, ship, or
train, *The Moonstone* makes exceptional detours through Victorian
institutions. It regards proof and demonstration as part of a greater
problem in the transmission of beliefs through social strata. In fact,
one of the reasons that documents and manifest proofs matter so
much to the novel's method of investigation, narration, and process
of establishing guilt is that the bourgeois ethic itself depends upon
duly witnessed legal instruments — especially its property transfers
and inheritances. The source of the family difficulty in *The Moonstone* is appropriately a poisonous will that awards the moonstone to
Rachel. And the origin of crime lies in the impulse to violate legally
defined codes. Culprits prove to be those who are unable to resign
themselves to defined limits and the opportunities fate has delivered
to them. With the hubris of the tragic hero but without his stature,
they seize half-opportunities and cheat the system without challenging its essentials: like Mary Whittaker in Dorothy L. Sayers's *Un-
natural Death*, they hasten just a bit the death of an aunt to make
sure that the family fortune does not revert to the commonwealth or
pass out of reach. Or they overleap a true line of descendants to alter
positions on the family ladder — without questioning the ladder

itself. In the bourgeois order, these violations of legality are "intervening acts" equivalent to the fall that disturbs Eden, where Eve wishes to overleap the hierarchy and become as a goddess by stolen knowledge; they come from a rebel individualism that causes potential criminals to feel injured by recognitions of merit extended to others. Hence as Satan turns criminal the instant Christ is given a new position at his father's right hand, so the criminal of the bourgeois novel illegitimately puts himself at the center of a family order or business, capturing its financial resources and the power of a name. A restorative act of detection must then purge his malpractice and restore properties to their rightful, usually quiescent owners.

In Collins's variation of these themes in *The Moonstone*, Godfrey Ablewhite's theft of what is assumed to be a rightful family property hearkens back to a prior theft that casts suspicion on a broader, colonial robbing of India. As Betteredge illustrates, the family is everything; its privileges are sacred and the ranks of its households and their staffs are carefully measured. Yet an underlying bitterness and class feeling crop up prominently and suggest a deep suspicion of the English social institution despite a romantic hero and heroine who seem to sanction and perpetuate it. Since too many elements of the society are hidden initially to generate the best sort of trust, probing for the basis of social cohesion for Collins involves primarily the cross-examining of differing points of view and the settling of a widespread relativity in beliefs. Several kinds of society rub each other the wrong way, and prejudgments unsupported by any acknowledged criteria for evidence impede their approaches to each other. The novel's main detective, Sergeant Cuff (one of the first of his kind), is discredited in the first section by a wrong guess derived from too little evidence too seldom subjected to revision. In fact, all of the thoroughgoing empiricists and skeptics of the novel, Cuff, Betteredge, and Bruff, are resistant to what prove to be more fruitful lines of investigation. The mysteries of motive and act that lie beneath the surface are available only to another sort of delving.

The novel thus juxtaposes in its sequence of narrators a number of procedures for "The Discovery of the Truth," each of them inadequate by itself, but all of them necessary in the edition of truth laid bare by their combined perspectives. Unlike Oedipus' single line of investigation or Milton's reliance on an indisputable Testament script, Collins's information is collected by inference and induction from a multitude of eavesdroppings, dramatic reenactments, psychobiological experiments, traveler's journals and letters, mad ravings, dreams, and clairvoyance — from science, law, medicine, history, and religion, each possessed of its own methodology, each bearing upon the assumptions of the bourgeois social ethic.

The motives of the main thief, Godfrey Ablewhite, are explicable largely in social and financial terms without recourse to the deeper, motiveless aspects of evil. Consequently, the investigation of his part in the case carries into the London world of finance and "filthy lucre," presided over appropriately by Septimus Luker, and is governed by explicable rates and schedules of interest payment — that branch of bourgeois instruments whose key documents are wills, promissory notes, and deposit slips. For one who lives two distinct but related lives such as this, the most apt investigators are Bruff, Cuff, and the quick-eyed spy Goosebury, all of them quick to attribute to their objects of suspicion the divided life that a highly respectable and honorable surface seems to suggest. Being god-free and white, Godfrey requires no further plunge into those mysteries of India and eastern cults that occupy other methods of research. The scurrying, self-interested world of finance, which urges the cutting up of the diamond — a sacred idol in India — is only one segment of the novel's total society, however. Whatever the motives of the English thieves of the moonstone (Herncastle, Blake, Ablewhite), the mystery of the stone is clearly not solvable by an exposure of hypocrisy, greed, or financial difficulties.

Much more difficult to account for is the interior world of the subconscious, which fascinates Collins sufficiently to require its own central staging and eyewitnessing. It is the function of Ezra Jennings, an experimenter in esoteric medicine, to decipher two impenetrable phenomena, Dr. Candy's ravings and Blake's nightwalk trance. In Jennings's restaging of the latter, Collins obviously intends us to focus on the means of investigation itself since the experiment demonstrates what has already been explained. The varied crowd of witnesses that Jennings assembles, some of them quite skeptical, is calculated to make the verification palatable to the reader, who presumably will not withhold his assent if even Betteredge and Bruff swear in writing to what they have seen. Moreover, if Abelwhite's financial and social motives are meant to be realistic, Blake's are no less so. That Collins intends Jennings's findings to be plausible and not merely a confirmation of the novel's own system of clues is clear not only from the staging of the experiment itself but also from the 1868 preface: "Having first ascertained, not only from books, but from living authorities as well, what the result of that experiment would really have been, I have declined to avail myself of the novelist's privilege of supposing something which might have happened, and have so shaped the story as to make it grow out of what actually would have happened — which, I beg to inform my readers, is also what actually does happen, in these pages."[13] Thus through Jennings's delving, what has been private and esoteric becomes publicly acceptable and enters the domain of acknowledged motives.

Perhaps more important to the typicality and historical accuracy of what the novel demonstrates is the fact that Jennings is by no means an isolated phenomenon in the novel. Despite its predominant preference for social realism, *The Moonstone* is filled with references to dreams, experiments, and clairvoyance, and is concerned with outcasts who have access to these. Collins does not emphasize them merely to heighten the romance of the novel, whose pattern of guilt, punishment, and atonement hinges on Jennings's insight into the dark areas of knowledge where the secret alliances of society lie buried. What Jennings's trance demonstrates finally is the romance hero's participation in the underworld, and through him, the participation of respectable society in subterranean powers. As one who has himself been falsely accused of a crime and driven from society because of it, Jennings feels a strong kinship with Blake. Through Jennings, Blake is able to link the novel of manners, in which he is the central marriageable figure, to a romance whose society is chiefly Indian, outcast, or simply un-English. The detection of mysteries is thus a way to integrate invisible and visible worlds and locate the dynamics of their mutual influences across national and class lines.

For instance, in expanding the web of underground associations, Collins emphasizes at several points the secret sharing of outcast figures and members of acceptable society. (Rosanna Spearman and Rachel, the most prominent examples, might be said to compose the dark and light side of a single feminine figure, for instance.) To one society, the moonstone is a social ornament and piece of property, while to the other it is a visible token of mystical powers personified

13. Wilkie Collins, *The Moonstone* (Baltimore: Penguin Books, 1966), p. 27.

by the Regent of the Night. In one society, the stone sparkles in sunlight and social candlelight and rests in bank vaults; in the other it collects moonlight and the intangible powers of night and rests in the inner sanctum of temples. These differences and analogies point up again the inadequacy of any given system to sound the full range of governing rules — scientific, psychological, social, historical, esoteric, and chemical — that are required to explain either the course of the moonstone or social dynamics. From the standpoint of witnessing, the value of secret sharers and doubles in fiction is that they establish a corroborating pattern in two quite different spheres. By reiterating knowable patterns in linear events, they suggest the stability of types and archetypes and the veiled presence of myth in unexpected places.

The question that Collins's ambition as a novelist raises, however, is whether or not the vaster truths that his Indian myth suggests are indeed embedded in empirical realities within the scope of the novel. Several broadly cultural collisions are left unresolved and somewhat doubtful. Neither the fatal necessity that links fact to fact in the hypothesis of a Cuff nor the psychological laws that experimental medicine reveals to Jennings goes very far toward explaining the communal society that Murthwaite observes in India or the logic of the diamond's return to its original setting after eight centuries. As the novel passes beyond Western experience, in "sailing to India," it encompasses cycles of necessity that are increasingly large and difficult to witness in any methodology. Where Luker and Ablewhite return to repossess the moonstone according to the simple regularity of the bank's fiscal practices and where Blake returns to the scene of the theft by a demonstrable law of the subconscious, the moonstone returns to its ancient home by very mysterious and romantic powers. No detective approaches the secret of its eight-hundred-year course, any more than the daylight of Lady Verinder's household and the candlelight of Jennings's experiment unriddle the influence of Eastern gods. The normal romance-comedy ending given to Rachel and Blake consists mainly of a transfer of class prestige from the older to the younger generation in the bourgeois version of cyclical recurrence; although they carry the memory of emissaries from less open and visible worlds (Jennings and Rosanna Spearman), they have little to do with the spiritual inheritance or social cohesion of India. If the distant prospects that Murthwaite glimpses in the second society of the novel have a use, then, it is primarily to reinforce an ironic view of typical English insularity, pitiful in Miss Clack, smug in Betteredge, and almost curable in Blake.

With this emphasis upon the fissures between cultures and upon differences in witnessing procedures and logic, the final brief glimpse of India accordingly emphasizes the healing unity of the moonstone there and its opposite impact on English society. As Murthwaite reports the grandest spectacle of "nature and man, in combination" that he has seen, it is clear that the harmony of the East is analogous to, but far surpasses, the marriage harmony of the English plot:

> People this lovely scene with tens of thousands of human creatures, all dressed in white, stretching down the sides of the hill, overflowing into the plain, and fringing the nearer banks of the winding rivers. Light this halt of the pilgrims by the wild red flames of cressets and torches, streaming up at intervals from every part of the innumerable throng. Imagine the moonlight of the East, pouring in unclouded glory over all — and you will form some idea of the view that met me when I looked forth from the summit of the hill. [P. 525]

All other cycles, even the generations of priestly guardians, are swallowed up in the moonstone's greater periodicity: "So the years pass, and repeat each other; so the same events revolve in the cycles of time" (p. 526). Thus the novel points outward in its epilogue to those secrets of crime and atonement that cannot be confirmed in normal documents or the witnessed reports of realism. The difficulty is that at the very point at which Collins seems to represent actual history and glance beyond limited fictional witnesses, the novel strikes us as most romantic. The greater the scope of detection, the greater must be the testimonial power required to give it a stamp of approval.

THE AUTHORIAL WITNESS

We should not be surprised at Collins's difficulty in this regard because a feature of any number of fictions is that when the *fictor*, or presenter, rises above the internal logic of the material and seems to vouch for its place in some larger panorama — thus making a truth claim of large dimension for it — his credibility is placed under strain, especially if the authorial witnessing is not sufficiently borne out by the dramatic ordeal of the story or embedded in fully characterized internal witnesses. At the same time, as Wayne Booth has amply demonstrated, discursive insets from the author are sometimes necessary and beneficial. In their broader moments, they are comparable to the higher prospects of interior narrators and interpreters when, in drawing back from the immediate action, they put the entire plot in focus. So an author may, if he wishes, come forward to place the fictional world in perspective. Or he may perform constant smaller services in guiding our responses to people and places. In either case, his position is neither quite inside the fiction as a characterized witness nor outside as an avowed truth-sayer. For instance, when Balzac pauses to comment on the Maison Vauquer in *Old Goriot* and on the nature of the dramatic narrative he situates in it, his position raises the question, What kind of special privileges can be claimed for such an authorial posture that could not be claimed for a character? Would we be better off if James had exploited similar privileges in *The Sacred Fount* or "*The Turn of the Screw*"? Are Balzac's statements to be taken as propositions, the denial of which would necessitate our calling him a liar rather than a fictionalist? What of those generalizations that seem to include post-Revolution French society as well as the immediate fictional world and are thus knowable from history books as well as from the descriptive matter of the novel?

In some instances, Balzac compounds the problems of the authorial voice by insisting upon its veracity:

> And you will show the same insensibility, as you hold this book in your white hand, lying back in a softly-cushioned armchair, and saying to yourself, "Perhaps this one is amusing." When you have read of the secret sorrows of Old Goriot you will dine with unimpaired appetite, blaming the author for your callousness, taxing him with exaggeration, accusing him of having given wings to his imagination. But you may be certain that this drama is neither fiction nor romance. *All is true*, so true that everyone can recognize the elements of the tragedy in his own household, in his own heart perhaps.[14]

Despite the claim that Balzac makes here, what counts in such an intrusion is not literal factualness but the accuracy of the types and universals — the habits, economic laws, and manners — that the fiction presents, and for this kind of information we can accept the author's direct testimony as perhaps no more than a normal *fictor* implicitly vouches for. In any event, the reader is under no obligation to

14. Balzac, *Old Goriot*, p. 28.

accept what the author comes forward to say, though he may feel pressured by it. Nor is he to assume automatically that he is himself the insensitive owner of the hand holding the book, or that the "Balzac" who addresses the reader is really Balzac speaking to real readers: a hypothetical, dramatized reader could presumably be instructed by a hypothetical, dramatized author as part of the method of the fiction.

More important for our purposes than the question of how to take such authorial essays is the structural function of statements that transcend the normal witnessed narrative at given points. Is Balzac justified on these grounds in mentioning explicitly that his story is no romance, or that "nothing could be more depressing" than the sight of Madame Vauquer's living room? What would be lost or gained had he simply followed Rastignac into the house and reported his reaction?

Presumably, his essays solidify our concept of certain relationships, our view of the work's design, and eventually our belief in the mimetic accuracy of the fiction. Indeed, an authorial voice may be a unique part of the flow of *information* precisely because it is not part of the flow of *action*. It performs a structural function whenever, in shifting our attention from a sequence of events to a set of insights or propositions, it disengages us from one causal career to account for others. It gathers in typical, contrasting, or analogous matters that eventually help us interpret the whole of the fiction. Consequently, it should not bother us unduly that some of the matters that intrude may be purely fictional and others historical or that one kind of continuity follows a purely serial progression while another has the movement of discurisve commentary. At some point the reader has to negotiate between his world and the fiction, and the author may assist him directly. Thus Milton's introduction to *Paradise Lost* gives us an abstracted panorama from outside the unity of action, and from that privileged position we are led to ponder the nature of the entire plot — to construe its laws, to see it taking shape, and eventually to feel its impact on the presenter himself. Similarly, the author's essays in Austen, Balzac, and Fielding suggest a broader or at least different unity of action and a tone. Like prefatory material, footnotes, and epilogues, their essays are semiparticipating interpretations of suffered discoveries. Thus, too, when Balzac describes Rastignac as typically southern in countenance and having the "appearance,

manners and habitual bearing" of a son of a noble family (p. 39), he
draws back far enough to take in southern France and Rastignac's
past. The word *typical* gathers into the portrait a range of experience
that Balzac and the reader may presumably share but which does not
come from any information the work itself provides.

An authorial essay emphasizes the fact that no work is totally self-
constituted, that much of its information is "used" and derives from a
public collection, as the author weaves into the ongoing action
associative matters already a part of the public language. The design
of all the threads so interwoven is not necessarily perceptible in the
immediate action; the author-as-witness — not merely in explicit
intrusions but constantly — creates perspectives by every choice of
words and categorization of what happens.[15] In the long view, the
difference between dramatized (or fully interior witnessing) and discursive or authorial witnessing is further diminished when we remember the truism that nothing in the work is real in any literal sense, that
the designing author arranges every piece of information in exactly
the order he wishes and may arrange to speak for himself without
contradiction. If the effect of a serial method is to convert all events
at a controlled rate into significant form and statement — into
suffered, dramatic knowledge — we share the total design not with
characters but with the author, usually, but not always, through witnessing characters. Though James's restrained objectivity is admirable in its presentation of interior witnesses, the ultimate witness is
the reader and the ultimate thing to be witnessed is a developing idea
that has sprung from the actual, grown in the author's mind, and
taken shape as a distinct anecdote. Everything between author and
reader is a strategic, animate mediation, to be assessed in part for its

15. Percy Lubbock's point with respect to the superiority of James's method in *The
Wings of the Dove* is that when such a character does belong in the fiction, the information
we collect from him comes with a certain density and weight: "Not to walk straight up to
the fact and put it into phrases, but to *surround* the fact, and so to detach it inviolate—such
is Henry James's manner of dramatizing it" (*The Craft of Fiction*, pp. 176–77). But Wayne
Booth's reply in defense of certain authorial contributions provides a needed qualification;
one need only point at the presence of Fielding in *Tom Jones* and Chaucer in *The
Canterbury Tales* to demonstrate the case that can be made. All dramatic ironies depend
upon the differences between the perspectives of characters and the author's and reader's
perspectives. And yet one need not minimize James's innovation and skill in telling stories:
"No one has ever resisted with more intelligence and integrity the temptations to
unassimilated information that beset every novelist" (*The Rhetoric of Fiction*, pp. 173–
74). See also Scholes and Kellogg, *The Nature of Narrative*, pp. 240ff.

technical value as a transmission — though of course for much more than that.

The reader should realize, then, that the progress of a narrative is not a single investigative procedure but a severalfold movement — of events in a causal chain, of a tracing interior intelligence, and above all, of an author whose scope of observation includes all that is knowable in the work. Indeed, what we discover in the diversity of fictional methods at which we have glanced — in Crane's realism, in James's skeptical, psychologically oriented study of unreliable witnesses, in an epistemologically confident method such as Milton's in *Paradise Regained*, and in *The Moonstone*'s concern with various investigative procedures — is that the basic structure of the work is not dictated by a plot in itself but by several aspects of strategic form governed by a reader's rhythm of expectations and regulated by differing ratios of dramatic detail and abstraction. For readers the dramatic rhythm and learning process of a fiction is obviously not in any direct way equivalent to what a protagonist or interior society undergoes. Though inside the work in one respect, they remain supervening witnesses solidly on their own ground, reading an author at one or two removes.

The most tangible device for putting a reader in this inside-outside posture except for the author's direct address to him is the use of symbols. To interior witnesses, objects and events are usually phenomena of a single dimension; they are facts to be reported, or aspects of an action to be responded to. To the reader, however, as we have seen, they are not merely that but signs and symbols in an act of communication. Only insofar as the materials that the narrator of *The Sacred Fount* puts before him are seen in the greater context of a developing idea can they be ultimately meaningful; only insofar as we see beyond Murthwaite, Betteredge, and Blake into *The Moonstone*'s commentary on conflicting social strata can we resolve the tensions of the work with something like Collins's view of them. Hence in pursuing the principles of linear structure either as a cognitive series or as vicarious dramatic experience, we must turn eventually to the nature of symbols placed serially before us. We must consider the organization of the special kind of witnessing that symbols make possible in the freedom of fictions, where we are totally in the hands of the symbol maker.

IV. FICTIONAL SIGNS

CHAPTER EIGHT

Chronicle Time and Literary Symbols

Whether *homo fictus* is primarily a symbol-making or symbol-using creature, the symbols of his fictions are called forth by the mind's act of organization and perception. By means of the concrete, epitomizing representation that symbols make possible, the intelligence presents to itself and to others a formal view of experience. It might not be an exaggeration to say that consciousness becomes action only when it seizes upon symbols, because at that point it is no longer passively impressed by experience but makes a response to it. For the moment, however, I am less concerned with whether or not that response is strategic and practical than with the nature of anecdotal (as opposed, say, to discursive) symbolic arrangement. As an account of sequential events, a chronicle, for instance, organizes the record of past happenings very selectively, imposing, like a calendar or a map, a direction and a uniformity of symbolism on careers extrapolated from a mass of materials. Unlike more complex techniques of historiography and fiction, a chronicle does not explicitly specify causes, supply concrete descriptive detail, or conduct an argument. (Of Cicero's three kinds of narration, for instance, *fabula*, *historia*, and *argumentum*, only *historia* might conceivably make use of chronicle technique in unadulterated form.) Yet reduced to essentials, narration is always in part a product of the chronological imagination.

My aim in this chapter is thus to explore the impact of the densely compact significance of symbols on certain aspects of its serial animation as it proceeds, in chronicle fashion, "through many a perilous situation." That significance hinges on several qualities that symbols have — their concurrent reference to more than one thing at a time, the special way they have of directing our attention forward and backward in linear structures, their epitomizing capacity, and their flexibility in adjusting to particular modes.

By symbols I mean not merely those objects that are distinguishable from the texture of the whole, like plums in a pudding or tufts of grass that mark a swampy area on a map, but all those tangible means of presenting lively or moving pictures of things in which an image solidifies a meaning and presents it to the imagination.[1] Any detail that is not merely unassimilated information — that contributes to the forming of systematic connections in narrative — is in some sense symbolic; it seizes a particle of meaning and embeds it in a chronological sequence. Insofar as such a detail is chosen and positioned carefully, it is one of the writer's more pronounced instruments of intention; it implies associations and logical connections among scattered moments in the strung-out working of the chronological imagination. In James's phrase, it "sounds" the attention: it

> is addressed to the imagination, to the spiritual and the aesthetic vision, the mind led captive by a charm and a spell, an incalculable art. The essential property of such a form as that is to give out its finest and most numerous secrets, and give them out most gratefully, under the closest pressure — which is of course the pressure of the attention articulately sounded. [*The Art of the Novel*, pp. 346–47]

That symbols hold a special place in such a narrative beguilement is evident when we consider the doubleness of verbal art, the progress of which is both an aesthetic experience in itself and a pointing out of experience of another kind. Indeed, no attempt to make content coextensive with form can succeed so long as the verbal symbol remains different from what it cites.

Robbe-Grillet seems wide of the mark, for instance, when he insists concerning *Last Year at Marienbad* and the "new novel" that "the duration of the modern work is in no way a summary, a condensed

---

1. One of the interesting attempts to link images and knowledge is Jean-Paul Sartre's early work, *The Psychology of Imagination* (New York: Citadel Press, 1948), pp. 147ff. Cf. Richard Hertz, *Chance and Symbol: A Study in Aesthetic and Ethical Consistency* (Chicago: University of Chicago Press, 1968), and Eugene F. Kaelin, *An Existentialist Aesthetic: The Theories of Sartre and Merleau-Ponty* (Madison: University of Wisconsin Press, 1962).

version, of a more extended and more 'real' duration which would be that of the anecdote, of the narrated story."[2] The duration of symbolic sequences and the duration of the life we are to imagine through them must always be different, even in fully dramatic and unforeshortened presentation. Though it may be true that the entire story of *Marienbad* happens exactly "in one hour and a half" and not in two years or three days, it nonetheless implies periods of greater or lesser extent. If a movie screen refers to a spatial field much unlike its two-dimensional rectangle and if a map refers to airports, tunnels, and forests by means of compressed images, so a narration refers to aspects of an extended future and past — to realities not literally present in the image. These creep into the representation of Robbe-Grillet's characters no matter how mannequinlike and faceless he succeeds in making them. We infer, for instance, that older men were once younger and have not just now sprung into existence: their manners were learned in a social context; their clothes "bespeak" them; and so forth. No artist can prevent us from inferring such extensions of language because the chronological experience of the perceiver gives him the habit of seeing filled-out sequences. Any attempt to collapse content into form is as futile as, say, making the word *horse* somehow equivalent to the beast itself. Thus the representation of a tuft of grass on a map insists upon its artistry and its unreality as fiercely as a swamp insists that it is not a symbol but a real place.

The failure to observe the distinct course that the surface of the chronological imagination takes (apart from the things it represents) disregards not only the greater extension of unforeshortened realities, then, but also the special tangibility that images and media have in their celluloid, painterly, or verbal density. Indeed, the charmed imagination and incalculable art that James appreciates owe much to the freedom from reality that symbols have. Only because a tuft of grass is *not* a swamp may it have a pictorial distinction and at the same time, by the marvelous leverage of symbols, raise many times its intrinsic worth in real things. The interest of our reading of symbolic works derives from a constant filling in of the gap between the medium and the world it sounds — in the imagination's working of the silences and vacancies of representation. Narrative movement

2. Alain Robbe-Grillet, *For a New Novel: Essays on Fiction*, trans. Richard Howard (New York: Grove Press, 1965), pp. 152–53. Cf. Frank, *The Widening Gyre*, "Spatial Form in Modern Literature," pp. 3–62.

(from the reader's standpoint) consists of shifts from word movement to a represented world, each of which follows its own quite different pace and yet remains meshed in, and reciprocal with, the other.

The point here is that the order of represented things is transformed by the order of symbols. Even methods as simple as the chronicle project into an assumed historical world basic principles of likeness, foreground and background, and potential cause and effect; and these belong basically to the realm of images, grammars, and sequential logic. When we plot a course on a map, for instance, we arrange static symbols as a system of movements; we line up a given geography as a "story," creating potential chronicles out of visual signs. We make intersections out of static lines, and we project probabilities and foreseeable contingencies. We create an ever moving series of perspectives that look backward and forward, and thus we create hiddenness, arrivals, brows of hills to be seen over, and panoramas of ever partial views. In bridging isolated and discrete things by means of such an animate, temporal line, we chart a blueprint journey before venturing on the road; we choose one alignment of symbols and phenomena out of many possible alignments.

Thus in chronicles as well, by setting down sequences of dates and happenings we form chains of events out of scattered elements of time, laying down direction and outcome through a historical morass of namable things. As the plotting of a journey on a map realizes a continuous intent through a succession of localities, the phases of a chronicle mark a relative permanence of ideas through linear changes. The spine of the chronicle is some salient principle which, if it is to be symbolized, must keep one foot in some abiding principle never entirely visible or materialized at any one time. Such topics as the life of a monarch, a national event, or the course of a war lift a limited amount of material out of confusion and install it in history's pontoon bridge. In part, it is this element of the typical that gives symbols their leverage in rescuing chosen moments from oblivion: however unique and unrepeatable events may be in themselves, those that make it into a chronicle proclaim membership in a species, so that though the "thing itself" is singular in its location in space and time, the signs that designate it link it to other things under a common topic. In a more advanced form of historiography than the chronicle, its properties are absorbed into the contemporary intellectual world of the historian, with all its subsisting conditions, habits, and general social and natural laws.[3] Thus the kingship that Cromwell destroyed one time only under very special circumstances is associated with all similar institutions by the very title it bears. It becomes symbolic the instant it is named, and it becomes a narrative symbol the instant the chronological imagination seizes it. Similarly, when this year's most recent earthquake settles into the files under an appropriate heading, it is processed by an analytic system — by subclassifications and emotions that have previously transformed events of its family into symbolic categories and anecdotal systems.

This creation of chronicle symbols out of events is not without its inherent laws. The broader the generalizations by which chronicles make events into topics, for instance, the less detailed the account can be; the more generality we instill into chronicles, the less we can account for all the particular motives, anxieties, and circumstances that the raw materials once included. Whether fictional or historical, symbols must first "kill" the events they transcribe in order to resurrect them in the world of documents. Symbolic representation thus works much like the mind in Marvell's remarkable stanza in "The Garden":

> The Mind, that Ocean where each kind
> Does streight its own resemblance find;
> Yet it creates, transcending these,
> Far other Worlds, and other Seas;
> Annihiliating all that's made
> To a green Thought in a green Shade.

Chronicles reproduce the world, in a sense, but they also re-create,

---

3. On the balance, in history writing, between the unique record, or *res gestae*, and the foundations of science within which that record is enacted, see Frederick J. Teggart, *Theory and Processes of History* (Berkeley and Los Angeles: University of California Press, 1960). In "What Are Historians Trying to Do?" Henri Pirenne suggests that only when the billions of individual actions that make up history are related to collective movements do they become subject to historical study. See *The Philosophy of History in Our Time: An Anthology*, ed. Hans Meyerhoff (New York: Doubleday, 1959), p. 87. In the same volume see also Raymond Aron, "Relativism in History," p. 157 (the ultimate subject of history is a unique series of events; the aim of natural science is "a systematized complex of laws"), and Ernest Nagel, "The Logic of Historical Analysis." Like Pirenne, Nagel concludes that history cannot be a purely "ideographic" discipline concerned merely with concrete occurrences; historians may not establish general laws but they must make use of them (p. 205). Finally, see Louch, "History as Narrative"; Mandelbaum, "A Note on History as Narrative"; and Ely, Gruner, and Dray, "Mandelbaum on Historical Narrative."

transcend, and annihilate it. Their new worlds and seas are always far other than what common perception tells us exists outside our symbolic constructions. Again, no chronicle symbol is free from the pressure of its changing context. Unlike a purely abstract or dictionary kingship, the kingship of a chronicle of Henry VIII is constantly modified. Or again, in serial symbols, the end infiltrates previous moments, as the outcome of a journey reaches into the strategy of interim moments.

I want to single out a sufficient sampling of these and other principles to suggest the importance of symbols to a concept of narrative structure, beginning with one that most obviously derives from experienced time — the concurrent running of two or more serial chains and the necessary organization of that principle in plotted narration.

CONCURRENCY

All chronicles as a matter of course remake reality, fictional ones more than others, as we have seen, because of their structural freedom (though Aristotle, Sidney, and others suggest different reasons).[4] If the richness and cognitive complexity of symbols is ordinarily much greater in fiction, it is partly because fictional symbols may more easily dwell in more than one specific chronology and consequential action at a time. That is, the structural freedom of fictions does not consist merely of their arranging of events but also of their coding and cross-filing of events under imagistic, thematic, and associative patterns. As I suggested earlier, if most stories of any length are composed not of a single unity of time but of several interlocked scales, a symbol such as Red Cross's journey in *The Faerie Queene* may refer simultaneously to a number of related chronicles: to specific individual careers (Christ's and Saint George's), to recurrent human phenomena (the path of Holiness in everyman), to the movement of nations over an extended duration (English history and the Tudor dynasty). Symbols in the novel are just as capable of dwelling in two or more temporal logics, often on dissociated levels. Any given event for Crusoe, for instance, is likely to suggest one

4. Aristotle's and Sidney's distinction between philosophy, history, and fiction is based on an oversimplification of all three, especially of history, as the works by Teggart, Pirenne, Nagel, and others (note 3, above) demonstrate.

chronology based on moral cause and effect, another based on phases of psychological change, and a third illustrating an expanding economy.

We have no special critical name for this kind of cross-reference. It is not precisely "plurisignificance" or simple analogy because its primary characteristic is not multiple reference but multiple temporal chains in which continuity is foremost. Nor is it quite the same thing as double plotting, which may or may not give us symbolic cross-references. A symbol like the Maison Vauquer in *Old Goriot*, for instance, contains several parallel threads. In making an outward show of the people who live in the boarding house, Balzac registers the successive changes of several careers without changing the place itself greatly. Like a scenic prop in a play that remains constant during the unfolding of the action, the Maison Vauquer permits Balzac to place in one setting the pathetic downward course of Goriot, the struggling upward path of Rastignac, the criminal career of Vautrin, and other minor intersecting chronicles, marriage intrigues, murder plots, and the like. The setting comments obliquely on these, though we see it differently in its changing contexts even as it remains relatively constant in itself.

Perhaps more easily demonstrable is the concurrency in *Eugénie Grandet* of the two main courses, the ripening of Eugénie's love and old Grandet's amassing of still more fortune — in the sentimental and money plots respectively. In this case the concurrency is ironic, as it so often is in plots of discrepant progress: one course unfolds as a sterile denial of vitality and youth on behalf of capital growth, the other as a half-sympathetic, half-amusing chronicle of sentimental youth gradually hardening from contact with money and social intrigue. The eventual significance of the house as the central symbol of both lines of development hangs on the question, Will Eugénie soften her father and revivify the household as a continuous, renewed institution, or will he destroy her idealism and innocence and turn the household into a tomb? The household has the potential for either fate, and for a time it takes each course alternately. The natural rate of interest in capital accretion and the natural course of youthful love and sentiment prevent each other's unhindered realization. No adjustment between them can be conclusive; every intentional movement of Eugénie and her father is turned back by the next development of the plot, which introduces some new twist of love to torment the miser or some new embarrassment of wealth and greed to frustrate his daughter. Eventually, the perspective of the novel rises far enough above each plot that their movement appears cyclical: as one man dies, his heirs follow his pattern; fortunes continue to be amassed and transferred, and love continues to be born anew and crushed as each young man and woman matures. Such households continue on in their fatal ambiguity, barely tolerating the conflicting lives within them, each life making use of the same outward signs, each quite literally battling for the keys to the house, to take command of all that a household includes — a family name, property, perpetuity, and security.

Beyond the generalizing that symbols perform is another principle of concurrency, the transposing of levels. Above and beyond Eugénie's love and her father's money is a hint of a celestial economy in which Balzac ironically projects the conflict of the Grandet's beyond the confines of the house. Grandet's entrance into his heavenly abode, as he imagines it — in contrast to Mme Grandet's ("who spotless as a lamb . . . went to heaven")[5] — threatens to make heaven into his particular kind of place, controlled by a new set of keys and an old bourgeois accounting system. The transposition is easily accomplished (in his imagination) because, having been appealed to virtually as a god throughout his life, he sees no reason to alter the arrangement later. And so in that abode, too, he will write ledger entries in the doomsday book; and as he becomes eternity's chief accountant, with what relish he will hold Eugénie responsible for her expenditures! Appropriately, when he strains to kiss the crucifix, in dying, it is not a figure of Christ but a piece of gold gilding that he touches with his lips, applying a transposing Midas touch to every potential "high" symbol.

The transposition of symbolic realms is not his doing exclusively, however. As he transports materialism upward, Eugénie is engaged in bringing a certain angelic quality downward, into the realm of secular wealth that she inherits when he dies. As both the schedules of love and the schedules of interest-bearing continue through her middle and old age, her days in their eventless monotony in the house blend into the eternity for which she prepares — for which she has prepared her-

5. Honoré de Blazac, *Eugénie Grandet*, trans. Merloyd Lawrence (Boston: Houghton Mifflin Co., 1964), p. 150.

self in conceiving of love as a visible sign of the world to come, "an explanation of eternity" (p. 158). (In remembering both "her mother's death and her prophetic life," for instance, Eugénie has seen her "destiny before her at a glance. All that was left for her was to unfold her wings, stretch them toward heaven, and live in prayer until the day of her final deliverance" [p. 169].) But these levels are not well joined or stable even in her. Until she leaves the house permanently, she follows more and more the hard ways of her father. Though her acts of charity might be said to combine money and love and though she has "all the nobility of suffering, the saintliness of a person whose soul has never been contaminated by this world," she has also "the stiffness of an old maid and the mean habits which arise in the petty confines of provincial life" (p. 179).

PREDICTION AND RETRIEVAL

The generalizing that symbols perform on segments of reality is one of the transfigurations they work; and the making of concurrent plots and parallel actions is a second. But chronicle symbolization does not stop with these. It also includes a capacity to predict and recollect that the chronological imagination otherwise lacks. Here especially the complex interweaving that symbols make possible is clear the minute we imagine sequences devoid of them, as in musical progressions. In Husserl's view, for instance, our awareness of the similarity and difference between things as they are now and things as they have been is basic to a simple perception of both continuity and change. First, Husserl suggests, it is clear that if musical tones were to remain in our recollection as they were when originally sounded, we would be unable to string them together as melody:

> Instead of a melody we should have a chord of simultaneous notes or rather a disharmonious jumble of sounds such as we should obtain if we struck all the notes simultaneously that have already been sounded. Only in this way, namely, that that peculiar modification occurs, that every aural sensation, after the stimulus which begets it has disappeared, awakes from within itself a similar presentation provided with a temporal determination, and that this determination is continually varied, can we have the presentation of a melody in which the

individual notes have their definite place and their definite measure of time.[6]

In brief, "we arrive at the idea of succession only if the earlier sensation does not persist unaltered in consciousness but . . . is continuously modified from moment to moment" (p. 32). Second, the perception of a truly unified melody depends upon the unified system of parts, which must "run away" not in separate ways but in a like manner:

> That several successive tones yield a melody is possible only in this way, that the succession of psychical processes are united "forthwith" in a common structure. They are in consciousness one after the other, but they fall within one and the same common act. . . . the tones build up a successive unity with a common effect, the form of apprehension. Naturally, this form is perfected only with the last tone. [P. 41]

Both duration and change are therefore explained, at least psychologically, by the *system* formed from things now and things variously modified by their pastness. (As Friedrich Kümmel remarks concerning that continuity of present and past, "The unity of life as an inner form or entelechy, is the decisive trait of each form of duration presupposing always, as it does, that something remains the same even as it alters in time. . . . living form is a necessary presupposition of duration and . . . conversely, real duration itself makes possible the living form.")[7]

If Husserl's account of succession, interval, and duration in melodic form is basically accurate, these elements of serial form obviously do not include the main complications that arise in chronicle symbol-making, either in daily living or in literature. There the passage of events is not uniformly harmonious; nor is it untouched by symbolic action. Unlike music, for instance, our normal experience contains several superimposed chains of consequence, variously in and out of focal attention — a car driving off, a refrigerator running, a dinner digesting, a television news program passing from wars to heat waves to beauty contests. These run concurrently in our experimental com-

---

6. Edmund Husserl, *The Phenomenology of Internal Time-Consciousness*, ed. Martin Heidegger, trans. James S. Churchill (Bloomington: Indiana University Press, 1964), p. 30. Cf. Epperson, *The Musical Symbol*; Hirst, *The Problems of Perception*; Meyer, *Music, the Arts and Ideas*; Zukerkandl, *Sound and Symbol*.

7. Friedrich Kümmel, "Time as Succession and the Problem of Duration," in *The Voices of Time*, ed. J. T. Fraser (New York: George Braziller, 1966), pp. 35–36.

plexes, and we keep them from falling into confusion by a constant process of generalizing, selection, and saliency, which we can do only with the help of symbolization. Moreover, in memory they are joined to other sequences recent or distant, real or invented, and take their places among categories of like things represented to us by a very few emphatic, symbolic cases that stand for the rest. We thus give certain moments power of attorney over others.

If the chronology of experience is never a single cohesive "melodic" line — if it is omnidirectional and highly symbolic, in part intuitively and in part rationally — chronology in literary representations is similarly complex, though reduced to order and logical connection — reduced to plots. As any reader of representational narration realizes, prediction and retrieval in literature are quite unlike Husserl's musical model.[8] To account even minimally for them, we must take into account such things as associative complexes (some of them unconscious or preconscious), saliency, and frequency of repetition. These complicate considerably the reader's business of weaving a design out of the signs the author gives him.

They also overlap and reinforce each other frequently. For instance, associative complexes and saliency are closely related. Memory commonly lets some things escape and singles out others for retention on the grounds that the latter make up a complex, all the parts of which, when retrieved together, gain a mutual saliency. Actually, in music, too, a stressed phrase coming at a critical juncture in the composition may stand out sufficiently from more functionary or background phrases to be modified differently in its "running away." (One forgets the beginning of Beethoven's Fifth Symphony less easily than what follows it, for instance.) Whether or not such phrases are repeated, they will constitute a more vital and dynamic part of the composition in listening and remembering than minor flirtations of a flute or piccolo. Repetition performs a similar function in bringing recurrently to the foreground parts of a temporal gestalt and altering their successive modifications.

Similar principles of stylistic saliency hold true in literature, though no doubt more so in poetic than in prose narrative. Salient or privileged moments of high symbolic condensation and dramatic crescendo are usually signaled by stylistic devices, as when Adam in *Paradise Lost*, realizing that Eve has fallen, drops the garland he has

8. Cf. Lubbock, *The Craft of Fiction*, pp. 14–120.

prepared for her: "From his slack hand the Garland wreath'd for Eve / Down dropp'd, and all the faded Roses shed" (9.892–93). Milton carefully enriches the moment both by pointing toward it throughout and by presenting it as part of a tightly interwoven series of greetings, hand images, fading and immortal flowers, and falls. In their climaxing falls, the symbols stand forth enshrined in phrases stylistically noticeable and mimetically apt, as for instance in the repeated short *a* and long *e*, the inverted syntax and falling rhythm of the second line, and the imitation in sound of "dropp'd" of the garland's irrecoverable fall. Even novelists who do not attempt a great many stylistic experiments sometimes set aside special distilled moments, or set off plot crescendos, with epigrammatic statements of rare quality and thereby prepare for a memorializing of events through the style of the saying.

Whatever lodges in the mind in a narrative sequence usually does so for one of these two causes, then: the focusing of narrative on turning points in highly symbolic gestures and actions, and the memorability of particular phrases and images.[9]

Quite apart from the special effects of stylistic saliency, literary symbols are obviously capable of a highly selective retrieval, and by explicitly pointing toward specific past events, any present sign may incorporate them into the present — overleaping all intervals and changing what the event once was, in its unique place and sequence, in making it part of a larger configuration. At the end of Katherine Porter's compact story "The Grave," for instance, Miranda recaptures a very cleansed and crystallized image of her brother turning over in his hand a silver dove. Miss Porter recollects the main themes of the story at this point and gives both Miranda and the reader a recapitulated past: "Instantly upon this thought the dreadful vision faded, and she saw clearly her brother, whose childhood face she had forgotten, standing again in the blazing sunshine, again twelve years old, a pleased sober smile in his eyes, turning the silver dove over and over in his hands."[10] Like people outside the pages of fiction, char-

9. Discussions of style in the novel tend to neglect the interplay of narrative movement and style, though presumably the two could be better understood in the context of each other. See Lodge, *Language of Fiction*, especially pp. 17–18; Auerbach, *Mimesis*; Lutwack, "Mixed and Uniform Prose Styles in the Novel"; Karl Kroeber, *Styles in Fictional Structure: The Art of Jane Austen, Charlotte Bronte, George Eliot* (Princeton: Princeton University Press, 1971).

10. Katherine Anne Porter, "The Grave," from *The Leaning Tower and Other Stories* (New York: Harcourt Brace, 1944), p. 78.

acters have ways of retrieving parts of the past eccentrically or unexpectedly, as Miranda under the influence of a foreign scene reconstitutes events that originally looked somewhat different. And unlike the uniform modification of receding events in Husserl's model, the transformative effect of symbol systems in either life or art constantly alters what it retrieves. Nothing is inherently dead that can be symbolized anew and recaptured; and conversely, nothing passionately important one moment can be guaranteed survival in the future.

Still more disconcerting to Husserl's model of internal time consciousness is its omission of the epitomizing capacity of symbols. Because a melody as it recurs to us holds each note in proper sequence and interval, Husserl's past supposedly returns unforeshortened, its pieces locked together in exact retention. But actually, even when we reproduce a melody note by note, this is not always the way we do it. We do not, for instance, retain all the sensational aspects that once accompanied it, especially if it was played by a full orchestra.[11] Such things as the timbre and quality of a voice and the exact style of a performance are impossible to recall. What we retrieve is a melodic skeleton and a generalized impression of its instrumentation. And if this is true of remembered music, literary works in their greater complexity are still more subject to clarifying reduction. Symbolic epitomes and image patterns retrieve likenesses in a rescaled proportion, discarding many of the unsystematic, individuating attributes of time, weight, place, and manner. Even so brief a story as "The Grave" surrounds its earlier episodes with a quantity of detail that cannot be re-presented in Miranda's final symbolic return. Insofar as her past is revivified in memory in the Indian marketplace, it must be cleansed and purified. In long narratives, especially novels, masses of detail are much more severely truncated, sometimes according to keys that the novelist offers even before he presents particulars. Thus at the outset of *Eugénie Grandet*, Balzac suggests a generalized framework, under the overall caption "Bourgeois Faces," that will govern much of what follows:

> In certain provincial towns there are houses which inspire a feeling of melancholy equal to that aroused by the gloomiest cloister, the

---

11. However, Mozart claimed to be able to survey an entire composition in his mind even before he had scored it, "like a fine picture or a beautiful statue." He did not hear the parts successively but "gleich alles zusammen." See Brewster Ghiselin, ed., *The Creative Process* (New York: Mentor, 1955), pp. 44–55.

dreariest moor, or the most dismal ruins. Perhaps these houses combine the silence of a cloister, the bleakness of moors, and the sepul-
chral atmosphere of ruins; there is so little life and activity within them
that a stranger would think them deserted, did he not suddenly notice
the wan, cold gaze of a motionless figure whose faintly monastic face
appears above a window sill, at the sound of unfamiliar footsteps.[P. 5]

By means of interspersed asides and essays thereafter, Balzac continues to summarize the meaning he discovers in the face of reality,
thus encouraging us to recall not a quantity of particular items but
their general significance.

We are more familiar with the processes of epitomizing in poetry,
where images and symbols are naturally more conspicuous. When
Donne and Marvell mirror greater worlds in lesser, for instance, they
emphasize the distilled essence of the microcosm. To Marvell, any
visible object such as the drop of dew may conceivably compress a
great deal into itself. Such a reduction to essences is both
memorializing and transforming. For Donne's canonized lovers, the
strung-out story of their troubled career and its worldly setting will be
reduced after their death to a single memorable pattern, from which
others will draw new life:

> And thus invoke us; You whom reverend love
>   Made one anothers hermitage;
> You, to whom love was peace, that now is rage,
>   Who did the whole worlds soule extract, and drove
>   Into the glasses of your eyes,
>   So made such mirrors, and such spies,
> That they did all to you epitomize,
>   Countries, Townes, Courts: Beg from above
>   A patterne of your love!
>
> ["The Canonization"]

The value of a mode of thought and expression that can capture in a
condensed image the essence of the lovers' lives has an obvious value
in a less shapely world of transactions. Likewise, when Milton has
Christ reject the multitudinous world of active power, learning, and
wealth in *Paradise Regained*, he finds in the kingdom concentrated in
Christ's image all that is of value in the world and much that transcends it. Marvell follows a similar procedure of epitomizing, moral
selectivity, and transcendence in "Upon Appleton House," but with a

significant difference: the tension between the world's distractions and the ideal form of Maria Fairfax's small enclosed estate cannot be fully resolved. The poem reminds us at every turn of the fictiveness and artistry of its verbal strategies, which include informal sectioning, the framed period of the poet's wandering, symbolic actions, archetypes and models, analogies and classifications, polarity, and — primarily — the way one thing stands in loose analogy with others. If "Beasts are by their Denns exprest" (line 11), so are poets by their poems and Fairfaxes by their estate. Indeed, in all the symbolic epitomes of poetry "things greater are in less contain'd." But they are not merely contained; they are also improved upon, reordered, and reduced to the verbal world, just as Appleton House composes its constituent parts in a perfect but very modest and exclusive symmetry. "These holy Mathematicks can / In ev'ry Figure equal Man" (lines 47–48); but figures remain figures, and men, men.

In keeping with the inevitable shrinkage of things into the symbols that represent them and the further shrinkage, within the work, of previously amplified particulars into a simplified recall, chronicle predictions of the future are also generalized, simplified, and condensed by prefiguration. True to its name, foreshadowing gives us only the spectral outline of a future without its full-bodied animation. The opening description of Eugénie's house foreshadows merely an outline of the future in the wasting away of Eugénie in her melancholy old age. We know by the way in which the contents of a package from the Russian empress are anticipated by the prisoners of Jean Renoir's *La Grande Illusion* that the package will not contain the caviar they are almost tasting in expectation; but we can recognize only after the fact the ironic appropriateness of Renoir's specific choice of dusty books on geometry, grammar, and history. Giving the contents a name and a full visual existence fills out a reality we are unable to grasp until it arrives. In this respect as well, the forward pointing of literary plots and symbols is probably somewhat less sure than the anticipations of music: whereas a composer may work against a definite sense of musical expectancy for surprises and variations (once motives have been established), in most varieties of complex narrative the future may gather up or recapitulate so vast a multitude of past details — some of them not particularly noteworthy in passing — that we can predict only very uncertainly.

NARRATIVE MODES AND SYMBOLIC CITIES

In all these functions — in their saliency, their epitomizing, and in presentiment and retrieval — symbols adjudicate a tension between mimetic detail and clear structural outlines and stand between the world of real objects and the presentational surface of art. The more detail a work includes, the less symbolic each detail becomes and the less retainable. The same is true of symbols in nonfictional chronicles: the historian who confronts his "mess of facts" armed with topics must select what will be representative, and the larger his design, the less detail he can afford. The choices are somewhat more open in fiction, where the narrator is not obliged to represent "what actually happened." E. M. Forster's well-rehearsed complaint against James suggests that in exercising a rigorous structural control some novelists value pattern too much over the mimetic presentation of people in all their attributes:

> The longer James worked, the more convinced he grew that a novel should . . . accrete round a single topic, situation, gesture, which should occupy the characters and provide a plot, and should also fasten up the novel on the outside — catch its scattered statements in a net, make them cohere like a planet, and swing through the skies of memory. A pattern must emerge, and anything that emerged from the pattern must be pruned off as wanton distraction. Who so wanton as human beings? Put Tom Jones or Emma or even Mr. Casaubon into a Henry James book, and the book will burn to ashes, whereas we could put them into one another's books and only cause local inflammation.[12]

The tension between pattern and mimetic detail is inevitable no matter how a narrator chooses to handle it. The conversion of apparently wanton and random details into symbols allows the novelist to have it both ways in his happier moments, but he does so only according to the prevailing laws of given modes. Each narrative method strikes its own compromise and makes its own use of the epitomizing power of symbols. (Indeed, it is never truer than it is with respect to symbols that "kinds are the very life of literature," as James insists [*The Art of the Novel*, p. 111].)

The city figure is a convenient index of those modal differences and the capacity of symbols to reach into the multiplicity of objects that

---

12. E. M. Forster, *Aspects of the Novel* (New York: Harcourt, Brace, 1927), p. 161.

realism demands. In the documentary novel, for instance, the city is clearly not the illustrative, simplified, and well-organized kingdom or celestial place of romance and epic; nor is it the model commonwealth of utopian works. It is a loose aggregate within which a good many threads are likely to be interwoven and some left unwoven. As we would expect, the continuity and prosperity of the novel's cities does not depend upon the well-being of heroes: it depends normally upon a complex exchange of goods and ideas, clashes of ideologies and social levels, and more intangible moneyed and political forces. Balzac's Paris, Dickens's London, Bellow's Chicago, and Frank Norris's San Francisco suggest that what the novel explicitly portrays, multitudinous as it may be, is but a sample of a vaster totality outside the range of explicit representation. Though as Raymond Williams points out, the novels of Dickens by comparison to earlier novels make the throng "knowable" in the sense that it enters the plot, the plenty of street life is not symbolizable in its full detail without confusion. Even to represent it typically is to offer "a hurrying seemingly random passing of men and women, each heard in some fixed phrase, seen in some fixed expression." Hence, though the city is "shown as at once a social fact and a human landscape" and the novelist "can respond warmly to the miscellaneous bustle and colour of a mobile commercial life," it cannot be revealed to the extent that the life of provincial communities and courts can be.[13]

Chicago in Norris's *The Pit* (part of "The Epic of the Wheat") is a case in point — or more precisely, the pit itself is. It is through the Exchange that the capitalist Curtis Jadwin attempts to control an immense human aggregate (by cornering the world's wheat supply). As he seeks a lever that will move the mass, the novel seeks an image or set of images that will epitomize the social aggregate and bring it under the control of plot and character. From both angles, the pit is the center of a raging battle of individuals and their paper impedimenta. After each day's fracas, its floor is covered with the remains of the very products the combatants have been fighting over in their abstract paper listings:

> Swept clean in the morning, the floor itself, seen now through the thinning groups, was littered from end to end with scattered grain — oats, wheat, corn, and barley, with wisps of hay, peanut shells, apple

13. Williams, *The English Novel from Dickens to Lawrence*, pp. 32, 37.

parings, and orange peel, with torn newspapers, odds and ends of memoranda, crushed paper darts, and above all with a countless multitude of yellow telegraph forms, thousands upon thousands, crumpled and muddied under the trampling of innumerable feet. It was the débris of the battle-field, the abandoned impedimenta and broken weapons of contending armies, the detritus of conflict, torn, broken, and rent, that at the end of each day's combat encumbered the field.[14]

The clerk Landry Court finds himself in danger of being devoured by the herd that rampages through the pit in a crisis:

Hands clutched and tore at him, his own tore and clutched in turn. The Pit was mad, was drunk and frenzied; not a man of all those who fought and scrambled and shouted who knew what he or his neighbour did. They only knew that a support long thought to be secure was giving way, not gradually, not evenly, but by horrible collapses, and equally horrible upward leaps. Now it held, now it broke, now it reformed again, rose again, then again in hideous cataclysms fell from beneath their feet to lower depths than before. [P. 388]

Everyone is caught up in the same train of disasters eventually, including Jadwin, who remarks, "The wheat cornered me, not I the wheat" (p. 419).

The debris is not only an appropriate symbol of the disintegration of a certain society into a scarcely governable mob, but also a good example of the uncoordinated, arbitrary "retrieval" of realistic symbolism. Norris could have listed any number of alternate items in the inventory of goods. He chooses these not because they hang together well or tell a particular story but because a certain number of them in disarray suggests a collective image; they epitomize the day's events of a very large, uncoordinated world. Indeed, the pit is the representative center not merely of Chicago and surrounding farmlands but of much of the world in its productive and commercial aspects — the Argentine republic, the Russian steppes, India, the San Joaquin Valley, Burma (p. 189). In its paper exchanges, it gathers titles, properties, farm mortgages, bills of currency, and contractual agreements from a vast legalistic empire, governed by a tight schedule of payments. People are supposedly known through their currency; the products of their labor are surrendered to the world of paper just as their national histories and figures are reduced to pictured icons on the faces of bills of exchange.

In this respect money and other paper impedimenta are substitu-

14. Frank Norris, *The Pit: A Story of Chicago* (New York: Grove Press, 1956), p. 105.

tions rather than signs, to follow a distinction that Bernheimer makes:[15] they replace the realities to which they draw attention and remain separate from them rather than actually pointing toward them. And this withdrawal into a separate world detached and alienated from the realities of soil, seed, weather, harvest, and hungry nations tells much of the story of Jadwin's failure, the failure of the financier divorced from the materials and labor of his culture — and indeed from its arts and learning as well. In pursuing the idolatry of moneyed power, which depends upon a kind of effigy that puts real products at a great remove and leaves the effigy in hands of brokers and exchangers, the financier tries to seize a ghost of power without the body. The goods behind the bills of exchange sooner or later reassert themselves. The manipulation of figures and prices comes crashing into accord with the truth of manufacture and distribution, tied by a tether that makes the market react to economic fact even in the feverish isolation of the pit: all the illusionist tricks of all the agents cannot free them permanently from the basic categories, types, and quantities of goods they and their rows of figures represent. Certificates, stocks and bonds, and dollars are phony symbols until they point as accurate signs to grains of actual wheat and grams of actual gold. In any case, as the marketplace of stocks and bonds reduces the world to heaps of trash, Norris tabulates the wreckage in a manner more appropriate symbolically than the alphabetical lists of prices that appear in the morning papers — more appropriate because less orderly and more answerable to the transient and quickly useless instruments of the financial world.

Other typical market and city symbols of realism suggest a similar confusion but ordinarily with the goods and services themselves visibly present rather than abstracted in bills of exchange. Dickens's London, for instance, often speaks forcefully of the difficulty of establishing a single chronology for large masses, except as a collective random movement. Like Nicholas Nickleby, Barnaby Rudge, and others who are introduced to the total "field" of London, Oliver Twist is filled with justified amazement by the dazzling tumult he finds in an early morning journey across town:

> The ground was covered, nearly ankle-deep, with filth and mire; a thick steam, perpetually rising from the reeking bodies of the cattle, and mingling with the fog, which seemed to rest upon the chimney-tops,

15. Bernheimer, *The Nature of Representation*, pp. 38ff.

hung heavily above. . . . Countrymen, butchers, drovers, hawkers, boys, thieves, idlers, and vagabonds of every low grade, were mingled together in a mass; the whistling of drovers, the barking of dogs, the bellowing and plunging of oxen, the bleating of sheep, the grunting and squeaking of pigs, the cries of hawkers, the shouts, oaths, and quarrelling on all sides; the ringing of bells and roar of voices, that issued from every public-house; the crowding, pushing, driving, beating, whooping and yelling; the hideous and discordant din that resounded from every corner of the market; and the unwashed, unshaven, squalid, and dirty figures constantly running to and fro, and bursting in and out of the throng; rendered it a stunning and bewildering scene, which quite confounded the senses.[16]

This is a prime example of the throng that in Raymond Williams's view becomes so prominent in Dickens: the trades, merchant classes, manufacturers, criminal outcasts, bourgeois householders, the rich, and the poor confronting each other as social types capable of entering the active business of the novel.

Indeed, if a plotted story is to be made of the city, people of all sorts must become knowable to one another in rather special and sometimes chancy exchanges of information and collisions of purpose. Perhaps even more typical in this respect than Oliver's encounter with the whooping and yelling din is the kind of meeting that Mr. Nadgett, the spy, and Tom Pinch, the most open and honest of men, have in *Martin Chuzzlewit*. If Dickens is to make a connection between them, and between the realms they stand for, he must cause them to "meet and pass" in the streets in some sense. This he does adroitly in a transitional passage:

As there are a vast number of people in the huge metropolis of England who rise up every morning not knowing where their heads will rest at night, so there are a multitude who shooting arrows over houses as their daily business, never know on whom they fall. Mr. Nadgett might have passed Tom Pinch ten thousand times; might even have been quite familiar with his face, his name, pursuits, and character; yet never once have dreamed that Tom had any interest in any act or mystery of his. Tom might have done the like by him, of course. But the same private man out of all the men alive, was in the mind of each at the same moment; was prominently connected, though in a different manner, with the day's adventures of both; and formed, when they

16. Charles Dickens, *Oliver Twist* (New York: Holt, Rinehart and Winston, 1962), p. 153.

passed each other in the street, the one absorbing topic of their thoughts.[17]

Their object of common thought is Jonas Chuzzlewit, who, like Pecksniff, keeps a foot in two quite different worlds and is thus exposed to the thoughts of shady characters and honest men alike. The passing of Nadgett and Pinch in the street enables Dickens to cut from the affairs of one world to the affairs of another as though shooting plot arrows over houses and letting them land where they will; of such transitions and shifts of attention are plots made in the urban conglomeration.

What is true of people in this respect is also true of objects, which encounter each other by apparent happenstance, flying off on tangents that are ostensibly uncontrolled but ultimately in service to the novel. The animation of Dickens's plots extends to hats that fly from heads unaccountably, wooden legs that walk into wine cellars, dragging their owners with them, and sneezes that take it upon themselves to rattle out at untimely moments. Such things are under the command, not merely of a taste for eccentricity, but of timed revelations, of a flow of plot information. They are evidence less for an absurd misrule inherent in matter itself finally than for quixotic coincidences necessary to the prodding along of organic stories. All umbrellas jab and leap to the tune their inventor calls for the entertainment of readers — who, it is assumed, will be dissatisfied with a mere normative realism.

Even so, nothing in what Oliver sees in the market scene is more memorable than anything else to him, nothing is salient, nothing subordinate. All objects in a swarm that is treated as circumstance and background are more or less equal; they are appropriately rendered by serial listing and recapitulated abstractly as merely a group of "dirty figures" "constantly running to and fro." But of course therein lies one of the virtues of a literary symbol: by going part way toward the confusion of the world it portrays, it gathers *symptomatic* aspects of reality into an enclosed field. It places local confusion within an encompassing design that can tolerate a miscellany precisely as background or circumstance. It is also true, as we noted earlier, that no totality of urban realities and social institutions

17. Charles Dickens, *Martin Chuzzlewit* (London: Oxford University Press, 1951), p. 589.

is included in even the most naturalistic and ambitious of novels —
only a representative slice of the poorhouse, the opera, the middle-
class household, the underworld, or the town. Though Oliver is
understandably dazed by the jumble before his eyes, the novel is by
no means thereby thrown into confusion, any more than the plot of
Martin Chuzzlewit is endangered by the description of the view from
Todgers or the long detour to Eden. The chronicle of Oliver's journey prevails over potential careers scurrying in the background as instances of what he must be saved from. Oliver maintains his destined
history by escaping the obscurity of a city that so eagerly reaches out
to seize people and cancel their distinction in a constant seething activity — or prepare them for the hanging that respectable society is
quick to believe they deserve. It is thus possible in the image of a city
to suggest a proliferation of potential chronologies, careers, and
crossing paths, yet to reduce these to a set of scenic inventories,
commentaries on a foreground action, or timely devices of transition,
as in Pinch's almost-encounter of the slinky Nadgett.

James does these things as well as Dickens in his way, as he sets up
Boston, New York, London, Paris, Venice, Florence, and Rome as
contrasts in national culture or as a periphery of confusion
surrounding a more contained sphere of gradually enlightened moral
behavior. Of Paris in *The American*, for instance, he writes:

> I saw from one day to another my particular cluster of circumstances,
> with the life of the splendid city playing up in it like a flashing foun-
> tain in a marble basin. The very splendour seemed somehow to witness
> and intervene; it was important for the effect of my friend's discom-
> fiture that it should take place on a high and lighted stage, and that his
> original ambition, the project exposing him, should have sprung from
> beautiful and noble suggestions — those that, at certain hours and
> under certain impressions, we feel the many-tinted medium by the
> Seine irresistibly to communicate. [*The Art of the Novel*, p. 23]

As F. O. Matthiessen remarks of another Parisian novel:

> The very air of Strether's Paris has the taste of "something mixed with
> art, something that presented nature as white-capped master-chef." But
> James was not ignorant of what he called "the huge collective life"
> going beyond his charmed circle; and at the end, when Strether is
> meditating on Madame de Vionnet's suffering, he thinks too of the
> vast suffering Paris has witnessed, and senses in the streets their long

ineradicable "smell of revolution, the smell of the public temper — or perhaps simply the smell of blood."[18]

More explicitly, James writes with respect to the London of *The Princess Casamassima:*

> It is a fact that, as I look back, the attentive exploration of London, the assault directly made by the great city upon an imagination quick to react, fully explains a large part of it [i.e., the birth of the book] . . . . One walked of course with one's eyes greatly open, and I hasten to declare that such a practice, carried on for a long time and over a considerable space, positively provokes, all round, a mystic solicitation, the urgent appeal, on the part of everything, to be interpreted and, so far as may be, reproduced. "Subjects" and situations, character and history, the tragedy and comedy of life, are things of which the common air, in such conditions, seems pungently to taste. . . . Possible stories, presentable figures, rise from the thick jungle as the observer moves, fluttering up like startled game, and before he knows it indeed he has fairly to guard himself against the brush of importunate wings. He goes on as with his head in a cloud of humming presences. [*The Art of the Novel*, pp. 59–60]

To move from Dickens to James in this fashion is to move backward with respect to the range and variety of types who meet and pass; but those who do meet in James obviously take fuller cognizance of each other than people in modes dominated by anatomy or picaresque. Oliver's innocence in observing the training of Fagan's boys and in carrying out missions assigned to him is inviolable: he is among them but not of them. And generally, as their circumstances change, sometimes radically, Dickens's people do not themselves grow intellectually or change in inner ways under the influence of the throng. With James's urban people quite the opposite is the case: they plunge in.

One of the most fortunate symbols James discovered for the urban encounter as a socially problematic affair is the telegraphist center in a story we glanced at earlier, "In the Cage," in which the heroine is exposed to a multitude of signs and cryptic messages from a number of social spheres. The social mix exists for her not as in Dickens's streets — in the miscellaneous observations of the passing eye — but

---

18. F. O. Matthiessen, *Henry James: The Major Phase* (New York: Oxford University Press, 1944), pp. 34–35.

in the imagination working at the center of a vast human concourse. Her wire enclosure is located in the darkest corner of a grocery, on the fringe of a rich social district of London, so that she stands in one element but singles out another for rapt attention. The social types she meets offer maximum opportunity for contrast, as does James's strategy of making her a nearly destitute and highly impressionable young woman. Thus, seated amidst the poisonous fumes of a gas heater and surrounded constantly with the smells of food, she is the intelligent center of a constant stream of messages of all kinds, sensory, social, personal. More significantly, perhaps, like a sifting journalist-novelist she takes in the shorthand communications handed to her for transmission and applies to them a connective and structuring gift of inventive imagination.

The glimpses the telegraphist gets of all phases of the urban society are necessarily hurried and passing, as befits impressions from the midst of an ever changing throng; and except for a feverishly working brain, she is herself inactive in that throng: she causes nothing to happen and passes no messages of her own. (Telegrams are not answered through her post.) But she is "moved," and what moves her is the realization of all shades of fortune, high and low, as marked chiefly by the clink of coin, the leisure activities and appointments made through the brief epistolary medium, by the social set whose comings and goings are her central investigation:

> *They* never had to give change — they only had to get it. They ranged through every suggestion, every shade of fortune, which evidently included indeed lots of bad luck as well as of good, declining even toward Mr. Mudge and his bland firm thrift, and ascending, in wild signals and rocket-flights, almost to within hail of her highest standard. So from month to month she went on with them all, through a thousand ups and downs and a thousand pangs and indifferences. What virtually happened was that in the shuffling herd that passed before her by far the greater part only passed — a proportion but just appreciable stayed. Most of the elements swam straight away, lost themselves in the bottomless common, and by so doing really kept the page clear. On the clearness therefore what she did retain stood sharply out; she nipped and caught it, turned it over and interwove it.[19]

19. *In the Cage and Other Tales*, ed. Morton Dauwen Zabel (London: Rupert Hart-Davis, 1958), pp. 189–90. See Zabel's introduction, pp. 1–28; L. C. Knights, *Explorations* (New York: New York University Press, 1964), pp. 182–85.

Unlike a Dickens character, then, she is feverishly employed in synthesizing: her "doing" is basically "understanding" and the forming of organic plots amid the circumstances the city places before her. She sorts out and reconceives the missing words and the coded obscurities of the telegrams until they form a web of communications in an interwoven society.

The telegraphist, like the narrator of *The Sacred Fount*, thus resembles James as he expands clues for a story into a full account of manners and conduct and a full view of a social condition. Her imagination is also subject to dangers inherent in the divisiveness of social levels and interests. James's city resembles Dickens's enough to suggest the unknowability, finally, of the actual place one holds in social circles. The telegraphist badly misjudges the cohesiveness of the web she weaves. Turning toward the most entrancing sphere, she repulses the rest, reaching out to collect from her experience what she requires in shaping the romance she prefers: "She pressed the romance closer by reason of the very quantity of imagination it demanded and consumed" (p. 185). Though she knows all the smells of cheeses, fish, soap, and varnish from the grocery, "without consenting to know them by their names," she relegates them to subliminal consciousness beyond articulation and turns her eyes to a group among whom she can forget her fiancé, plain Mr. Mudge, and the dreariness of her class.

In this story and again in *The Princess Casamassima* and other urban settings in *The Bostonians* and the Paris novels, James gathers, snips, and interweaves more of the city totality than he is commonly given credit for. Like the caged telegraphist, he lets the greater part of the shuffling throng pass and sink into the unknowable commonality. But that throng provides a peripheral, contrastive setting for those he does single out, who because they are thus placed on the verge of the crowd stand out the more sharply. The throng is never far from James's awareness — when he writes plays to please it, sends news from Paris for New York papers, or considers the pernicious effects of damaged privacy on the novelist. He clearly condemns and resents the urban mass as such, in its unintelligent, blind crisscrossing in the streets, in its sniffing after broad and scandalous "signs" from spheres it does not know first-hand, and most of all in its obtuseness to fine discriminations in conduct and in art. But he, no less than Dickens, realizes its influence in the fictional work as an all-encompassing symbol; it must be known and named to be repulsed; it must be reduced to messages and signs and reassembled in the organic social intelligence of the caged telegraphist. Even in the most secure households, behind doors that quiet the hubbub of the streets, one is often aware that the encounters taking place inside have required the closing of the door before they begin: James's people talk in a just-then created social enclosure.

Such graphic portraits of the city as Norris's, Dickens's, and James's are symbols of collective lives that the modern city throws in the path of novelistic heroes as a kind of collective hindrance. They contain a potentially unending concealment that a protagonist cannot penetrate because he cannot know or manipulate such large masses. Only some process of epitomizing will allow the novelist to reflect the flow of broad circumstances and at the same time allow the hero to issue from the labyrinths in which he finds himself. Even then, reduced to symbolic representation, urban scenes are related to the hero and his course very problematically, the novel having no equivalent to the conclusively epitomized symbols of romance and fairy tale such as the Ultimate Boon. The novel, that is, offers no treasure or trophy to the hero as a symbol of conclusive achievement as decisive as those gifts that certify the accord of the hero with gods and goddesses in heroic modes. If the goal of many myth and fairy-tale plots (such as those charted by Joseph Campbell and Vladimir Propp) is the expression and curing of psychological and social unease through custodians of some elixir of being, such a cure is inconceivable in the cities of realistic fiction, where the hero is not tested in isolation, found worthy, and returned to society after an exposure to archetypes, temptresses, guardians of the threshold, mandalas, crosses, and the like — all functional symbols in the standard plots of myth.

Actually, the household, the city, the realm, and the universe all serve as enlarging spheres of a heroic education in whatever mode they appear, and each has its own symbolic centers and rewards consistent with its hierarchy. But the difficulty with the novel's seeking of aesthetic conclusions through some symbol comparable to the high treasures of myth is that a realistic urban setting cannot be saved from the dispersal of its goods by epitomizing. For Henry James, for instance, the spoils of Poynton, the golden bowl, the Aspern papers that lie at the end of a protagonist's ordeals are finally burned, cracked, or placed beyond reach. In Balzac, neither Rastignac's mistress nor his funds will lay all Paris at his feet. Whereas a writer of romance like the Gawain poet may place a hero in a central position in his society and whereas Spenser's Cleopolis, Aeneas' Troy, Milton's Eden, and Bunyan's celestial city assign to lesser courts and cities a meaningful and subordinate place, Norris's Chicago or Dickens's London does not point toward archetypes or legitimate powers of attorney. Their directions are not laid down by abstractions comparable to such highly schematic symbols as the cardinal virtues, the deadly sins, or typological revelations; nor are they defined by some contrasting utopian model stuck away in the corner of the visionary imagination. Instead, they are moved from within by the dynamics of throngs and elite cliques, or from without by largely unnamable forces. So many fundamental values are brought into question by a sympathetic portrayal of people like Moll Flanders, Pamela, and Joseph Andrews that the novel from its beginnings registers a severe problem in symbolism. As James says of novels by Guy de Maupassant and Flaubert (*Une Vie* and *L'Education sentimentale*, respectively), the necessity of a plot "has in no way imposed itself" on the materials, and de Maupassant's effort especially "has been to give the uncomposed, unrounded look of life, with its accidents, its broken rhythm, its queer resemblance to the famous description of 'Bradshaw' — a compound of trains that start but don't arrive, and trains that arrive but don't start" (*The Future of the Novel*, p. 219).

It follows from this looseness that though no object in an intelligible structure can be totally mute and indefinable, the thingness of the novel's objects often overwhelms their signification. In Zola in particular, "the sense of crowds and processions," in James's view, results in a disproportion between "scheme" and "material." Even Balzac gives us difficulties in tracking the author's intent through a labyrinth of details:

> The figures he sees begin immediately to bristle with all their characteristics. Every mark and sign, outward and inward, that they possess; every virtue and every vice, every strength and every weakness, every passion and every habit, the sound of their voices, the expression of their eyes, the tricks of feature and limb, the buttons on their clothes, the food on their plates, the money in their pockets, the furniture in

their houses, the secrets in their breasts, are all things that interest, that concern, that command him, and that have, for the picture, significance, relation and value. It is a prodigious multiplication of values, and thereby a prodigious entertainment of the vision — on the condition the vision can bear it. [*The Future of the Novel*, p. 112]

But at least Balzac chose what has "significance, relation and value," whereas the novel in other hands does not always do so. The absurdity of objects and circumstances that makes Antoine Roquentin, Sartre's hero in *Nausea*, physically ill, and the unreadable, pure objectivity of things in the "new novel" of Robbe-Grillet both testify to the existentialist's insistence upon a meaningless social and natural environment. Indeed, as Roquentin realizes, one's own story is essentially meaningless:

> I marvel at these young people: drinking their coffee, they tell clear, plausible stories. If they are asked what they did yesterday, they aren't embarrassed: they bring you up to date in a few words. If I were in their place, I'd fall over myself. It's true that no one has bothered about how I spend my time for a long while. When you live alone you no longer know what it is to tell something: the plausible disappears at the same time as the friends.
>
> You let events flow past; suddenly you see people pop up who speak and who go away, you plunge into stories without beginning or end: you'd make a terrible witness. But in compensation, one misses nothing, no improbability or story too tall to be believed in cafes . . . .[20]

Though Roquentin selects scenes, objects, and people to represent absurdity and thus makes them "stand for" it, he cannot force them to yield meanings foreign to them. By intent, the existentialist is anti-philosophic, and his fictions tend to be anti-novels and anti-plays, the "recognitions" of which are basically realizations of the unsymbolic opaqueness of objects and events.

TYPES OF SYMBOLIC REPRESENTATION

As I remarked earlier, variations of the tension between symbolic pattern and detail occur in all modes and in figures other than the city (which I've explored merely as an example). Three quite different modes, the detective story or riddle plot, the anatomy, and typological narration, will serve to suggest the impact of genre on the

20. Jean-Paul Sartre, *Nausea*, trans. Lloyd Alexander (New York: New Directions, 1959), p. 15.

chronological imagination and the influence of symbolism and linear anecdote on each other.

When we consider a typical crime story such as Margery Allingham's classic *The Fashion in Shrouds*, it is clear that details are used mainly to push along the detection of an intrigue. In this respect, symbols are unusually instrumental to witnessing, and clues are readable as symbols arranged by basic analogy: the reader and internal detectives are expected to guess the nature and identity of the criminal from similarities between his handling of certain crimes and his less concealed behavior on other occasions. In *The Fashion in Shrouds*, thematic concerns govern those analogies. Until the reader sees the integration of the fashion theme, the pattern of the crimes, and the style of the culprit's habitual manipulations of people, he is not prepared to distinguish salient facts — and therefore symbols — from merely background materials. It is the function of theme to convert details constantly into symbols and make meaning dominate mere information. Once a pattern has emerged from the investigation — which Allingham causes to happen relatively early — the reader can predict the necessary countermoves of the detective and in broad form the outcome of the plot.

Some such process is typical of most detection or riddle plots, where the linear unfolding of details both advances a present action and fills out a historical crime or already completed pattern under thematic controls. As to the solution of the riddle — the object of our search — it is complicated by other interpretive and predictive patterns that offer alternative paths for the reader and the internal detectives. These all prove to be dead ends, but they momentarily play upon us as though they were true: pending definitive proof, they must be entertained as potentially significant, raising all the hopes, sorrows, or anger in internal characters that the truth does. The storyteller is thus able to suggest a gamut of imagined social relations, emotions, and possibilities before settling upon one that is most comprehensive and meaningful: everyone has the opportunity to suspect everyone else for a variety of reasons, sometimes with lasting effects, before all but one person proves innocent. Misleading clues are as necessary to the figure in the carpet as misleading passages to a maze: only if wrong choices are possible for the witness can the intelligence learn to reject its errors and reaffirm its accurate perceptions.

Such affirmation is characteristic of all resolvable riddle plots, which, unlike, say, the plot of *Nausea*, do not force us to abandon coherence and meaning. Even when the worst turns out to be true, a tragic investigator such as Oedipus, whose "right road" leads to self-destruction, adds to the normal discoveries of one's prophetic soul the irony of an inescapable fate and a pattern predictable if not by mortals at least by the gods. Hence of all modes of investigation, the kind that eventuates in the detection of a definite crime committed by a clearly condemnable criminal allows perhaps the clearest dominance of detail by significant clues and patterns. The riddle construction not only aligns rigorously all immediate facts but in probing motives reaches backward to assess the history of social relations that lead to the act and forward to the consequences. Thus beginning and ending are bound tightly to two basic climaxes, the crime and its detection.

The accomplishment of *Oedipus Rex* and *Paradise Regained* is to apply the tight structure of investigation plots to societies of tragic and epic dimension in justifying the righteousness of the gods and their oracles. Most detective fiction proper leaves the reader so completely detached from its thinly sketched characters that the assembling of the pieces of the puzzle is a purely cerebral affair; the dramatic present is secondary. But where everything about a given world, including the present, hinges on the details as they turn up, as in *Oedipus*, *Hamlet*, *Paradise Regained*, Ibsen's *Ghosts*, or several of Dickens's novels, the reader finds his reaction to each disclosure brought into proximity with the ordeal of internal investigators. Each detail, because it counts in a tightening net, reverberates as it enters the manifest plot and causes a sensation that is not merely momentary but a gathering of the accumulated knowledge and feelings of the entire work. Rather than working episodically, every new stage recalls all previous stages.

At the opposite extreme from the detection plot in this regard is the anatomy, which imposes only the loosest structure on its materials. This is not to say that the anatomist's interests coincide with those of the realist or naturalist: his domain is much more the domain of ideas and ironic attitudes. As Northrop Frye suggests, whereas "the novelist shows his exuberance either by an exhaustive analysis of human relationships, as in Henry James, or of social phenomena, as in Tolstoy," the satirist or anatomist, in dealing largely with intellectual themes, "shows his exhuberance in intellectual ways, by piling up an enormous mass of erudition about his theme or in overwhelming his pedantic targets with an avalanche of their own jargon."[21] Details dominate the work, and in place of a narrative thread to conduct a normal hero along a meaningful course, the anatomist offers a set of attitudes and ideas ripe for deflation. In their tolerance of erudition and encyclopedic matter, anatomies are therefore much like treatises rearranged as illustrative episodes. Works like *Gulliver's Travels*, *Candide*, and *Erehwon* attack an extensive quantity of fixed ideas and institutions in a large variety of contrasting situations and styles. They digress freely and discourage psychological continuity in their protagonists. Rather than seeking a single culprit for a single crime, the protagonist finds culprits and crimes everywhere, obvious enough to require little detective fervor in him, most of them successful in separating him from his inherited ideals and his cash. From the standpoint of narrative rhythm, the environment bristles so greatly with hindrances (the clues to which are as subtle as a kick in the shins) that we are forced to stop and start again at many irregular intervals. Where Oedipus pursues a course of well-timed symbolic clues to a central discovery, the protagonists of anatomy turn the pages of their encyclopedias of experience more or less at random. Some entries are short and some long; their juxtaposition is arbitrary; and they lead nowhere.

However, they have a uniform style, and we can be assured of at least some linear patterns and a rudimentary symbolism. If nothing else, misfortune offers its recurrent formats. Jack Wilton's narrative in Nashe's *The Unfortunate Traveler*, to take a typical case, pursues certain "stratagemical acts and monuments" that his "winnowing wits" rehearse for us, and though the lack of plotted continuity makes it difficult to recall either the events of Jack's life or the order in which they occur, we can make predictions of a general sort. Wil-

---

21. Frye, *Anatomy of Criticism*, p. 311. Cf. Philip Stevick, "Novel and Anatomy: Notes toward an Amplification of Frye," *Criticism* 10 (1968): 153–65. A number of critics have argued that the term *picaresque* should be more limited in use than it has sometimes been. See W. M. Frohock, "The Failing Center: Recent Fiction and the Picaresque Tradition," *Novel* 3 (1969): 62–69, and "The Idea of the Picaresque," *Yearbook of Comparative Literature* 16 (1967): 43–52; Philip L. Gerber and Robert J. Gemmett, "Picaresque and Modern Literature: A Conversation with W. M. Frohock," *Genre* 3 (1970): 187–97; Frank J. Kearful, "Spanish Rogues and English Foundlings: On the Disintegration of Picaresque," *Genre* 4 (1971): 376–91; Freedman, "The Possibility of a Theory of the Novel."

ton's social attitudes are consistently irreverent no matter what he encounters; each episode presents renewed revels, tumbling disorder,
fervency, oath-swearing, and violence. If we could boil these patterns
down to a single aspect, violence would be its key. The world directs
its blows not only against the protagonist but against any fixed idea
or institution that attempts to remain continuous and rigidly established. Anabaptism, for instance, suffers grievously in Jack Wilton's
well-armed world:

> When Christ said the kingdom of heaven must suffer violence, he
> meant not the violence of long babbling prayers to no purpose, nor the
> violence of tedious invective sermons without wit, but the violence of
> faith, the violence of good works, the violence of patient suffering. The
> ignorant arise and snatch the kingdom of heaven to themselves with
> greediness, when we with all our learning sink down into hell.

Thus in Jack's eyes the followers of Jan of Leyden, the Anabaptist,
betray themselves as devout asses for whom "inspiration was their
ordinary familiar, and buzzed in their ears like a bee in a box every
hour — what news from heaven, hell, and the land of Whipper-
ginny?"[22] In retaliation, his own violence is directed verbally against
the "unspeakable vehemence" of the Leyden fraternity and the fixed
ideas of their dogmatic sect.

On a less murderous plane, the matching of wits among those
accustomed to living by wits is also a part of normal picaresque violence. The sects and schisms of religion are merely another example
of society's splintering warfare in which each man's path carries him
vehemently across the paths of others, in a form that celebrates
individualism and its violation of communal norms. The cagiest person keeps to the road; the rest find themselves in the ditch. Even
when the parties and the localities of the action change frequently,
such repeated patterns have the epitomizing and retrieving functions
of more solid and continuous symbols. They are reinforced, in
matters of style, by the local effects of repetition. Such a sentence as
the following, for instance, suggests both the quick, rough rhythm of
the many untamed objects and the recurrences of form and symbolic
or typical acts:

> Yet drums and trumpets, sounding nothing but stern revenge in their
> ears, made them so eager that their hands had no leisure to ask coun-

22. Thomas Nashe, *The Unfortunate Traveler*, in *Elizabethan Prose Fiction*, ed.
Merritt Lawlis (New York: Odyssey Press, 1967), p. 468, 467.

sel of their effeminate eyes. Their swords, their pikes, their bills, their bows, their calivers slew, empierced, knocked down, shot through, and overthrew as many men every minute of the battle as there falls ears of corn before the scythe at one blow. Yet all their weapons so slaying, empiercing, knocking down, shooting through, overthrowing, dis(soul)joined not half so many as the hailing thunder of their great ordnance. So ordinary at every footstep was the inbruement of iron in blood that one could hardly discern heads from bullets, or clottered hair from mangled flesh hung with gore. [P. 473]

The collisions are merely more severe and the forward progress more boldly kinked and twisted than they are in normative realism; the linear functions of the symbols are not radically different.

Combined with confessional elements in picaresque narrative, the anatomy also draws upon the cohesion of a single personality. Chance governs the life of the picaro and prevents his establishing of milestones along a vagrant path; he marks no significant dates or achievements on a personal calendar. But again the prominence of discontinuity in his story does not mean that it lacks symbols or symbolic gathering points, merely that what is symbolized is often the discrepancy between logic and experience. Such standard tropes and symbols as the journey, the city, and the household become in picaresque and anatomy not enduring and continuous institutions but sets of rules and decorums to be violated, remnants of an order teeming with conniving and rule-breaking. The picaro knows his society largely from the hostility it manifests on the open road or from outside the shuttered households of more fortunate people. He sees social spheres not as desirable things to join but as things to penetrate, exploit, and leave.

Picaresque should not be confused with foundling fiction in this regard. For one thing, the foundling novel is more sentimental: in picaresque, feelings are never wounded, though bodies are, and no evil short of murder is taken to be more psychologically damaging than a prank. Criminality is bad only if one is caught or victimized by retaliation. Also, picaresque, in *Lazarillo*, for instance, is unburdened with the accumulated property of the bourgeois novel, the problem of reputations, or enduring social contracts that must be upheld; nor is it weighed down with meticulous realism. (The circumstances selected for narration bear direct anecdotal value even where they carry no symbolic import.) The foundling novel, on the other hand, has many of the qualities of romance in linking its adventurous wanderings to

the establishing eventually of heroic standards, decorum, and households. The hero is subjected to the street view of the throng and is
well battered by it, but he is not beyond adding up clues to an
announced identity.

It is true that anatomy and picaresque also employ basic elements
of sequential logic in framing the untidiness of their protagonists'
adventures, usually at the beginning and ending: a young man or
woman is cast loose from the confines of a family (Gil Blas, Guzman,
Lazarillo, Moll Flanders, Colonel Jack, Lemuel Pitkin, Ebenezer
Cooke), progresses through a series of trials, and eventually achieves
some stability beyond the hazards of the road. But these stabilities are
obviously somewhat different from those of more continuous modes,
even the urban novel, because symbolic acts in such works are not
firmly anchored in a single overall chronology. Except for the internal structure of anecdotes and the beginning and ending of the entire
sequence, the serial order in which things happen is largely a matter
of indifference. Where chronology fails to dominate like this, rich
opportunities for radical juxtaposition, temporal gaps, broken logic,
encyclopedic plentitude, digressions, subconscious patterns of association, and satiric dissections of types, ideas, and attitudes open up. In
contrast, where symbolic patterns are pinned to a strict consequential
development, we have a consistent growth work in which each facet
of the hero's character that comes forward for expression finds a social or other matching situation collaborating with it to form
characteristic actions. Because the reader identifies to some extent
with a developing protagonist, each new fact produces a stronger
dramatic reaction than it does in our response to figures in anatomy.
(To see that, we need only recall how effective the recognitions and
rescues of sentimental romance are, even when we recognize their
stagy and contrived nature.)

Typology as Milton employs it in the concluding books of *Paradise
Lost*, carries that kind of growth to an extreme and at the same time
suggests some of the potentials of anatomy — which Adam and Eve
make possible by their error. For a world controlled by Satan as Milton conceives of it would be a world of random and incoherent
chance, gross insult, exploded expectations, pranks, vicious ironies,
and ultimate destruction. The strategy of Michael's narration is to
point out that, given the fall, if one removed the redemption from
Adam's wilderness Adam would be dismantled (as surely as a Lemuel

Pitkin or a Candide). As it is, however, every event of Adam's future presents to him some new aspect of a single unfolding archetype, and every manifestation of crime leads eventually to a fuller understanding of the original fall and its cure. Thus, if at first Michael's approach to typology suggests the plenty of anatomy and if the initial phases of Adam's education expose him to apparent chaos, each stage also places a distinct piece in the puzzle. Michael's symbolism has for its ultimate reference not the normal restored society of a crime detection plot but a community of beings raised to a new eminence around the revealed identity of the Savior, who in Milton's version undergoes historical incarnation precisely to restore in human hearts an inherent analogical likeness to their creator. All personal and historical episodes are thus governed not by sequences run amuck but by a rigorous logic operating behind the obscurity of providence and moving toward a single predestined end.

In this respect Michael's typology presupposes a quite different relationship between men and gods than is ordinary in epic. Frequently in traditional epics, as Northrop Frye observes, "the gods affect the action from a continuous present: Athene and Venus appear epiphanically, on definite occasions, to illuminate or cheer the hero at that moment." Somewhat closer to Milton's practice, Eliot in *Burnt Norton* makes the time of the human action "a horizontal line, and God's timeless presence a vertical one crossing it at right angles, the crossing point being the Incarnation" (*Anatomy of Criticism*, p. 321). The visitations of the angels and of God himself in the garden have been roughly of this vertical sort in the Eden books of *Paradise Lost*, in which, at given points, direct divine influence is inserted into the continuous foreground, human action. In Michael's Christocentric typology as well, divine intervention is intermittently renewed if not quite continuous and immediate: presumably, no point of Adam's exile will be untouched by the program of redemption and its symbolic manifestations. God is present in all signs; and lesser epiphanies can come at any time and place — though the most important unriddling in Milton's version, as we have seen, is reserved for Christ's emergence in the desert in *Paradise Regained*. All doubts about signs and clues are therefore removed for Adam by Michael's explicitness, as he makes use of Milton's editorial powers and of future scripture to incorporate into the text a pervasive allegorical commentary. Despite ample opportunities for a satiric anatomy of human error, then, Michael renders for Adam not the miscellaneous episodes and types of evil of a loosely symbolic chronicle but the enactment of a consistent, programmatic manifestation of divine will.

Indeed, one of Michael's functions is to teach a system of communications appropriate to a new discrepancy between symbolic surfaces and veiled meanings, and thereby to provide an answer to Satan's experiments in scrambling the sign system. In preparation for this symbolic rendering of what are to be Old Testament events, Michael's own arrival is heralded by a startling allegorical tableau, as nature yields several newly expressive symbols:

> Nature first gave Signs, imprest
> On Bird, Beast, Air, Air suddenly eclips'd
> After short blush of Morn; nigh in her sight
> The Bird of Jove, stoopt from his aery pow'r,
> Two Birds of gayest plume before him drove:
> Down from a Hill the Beast that reigns in Woods,
> First hunter then, pursu'd a gentle brace,
> Goodliest of all the Forest, Hart and Hind.
>   [11.182–89]

Nature's book of types is partly fearful (Adam and Eve are obviously the victims of the hunt), yet partly hopeful as well, since the bird of Jove foretells not merely nature's hostile mood but also the coming annunciation. Nature's impresses, icons, and types will hereafter become the fragments of the redeeming Word.

The second part of Michael's narration from the symbolic hill of "Visions of God" unfolds as a discovery of "supernal Grace contending / With sinfulness of men." It forecasts covenants and laws that will be delivered from a similar hill later:

> God from the Mount of Sinai, whose gray top
> Shall tremble, he descending, will himself
> In Thunder, lightning and loud Trumpet's sound
> Ordain them Laws; part such as appertain
> To civil Justice, part religious Rites
> Of sacrifice, informing them, by types
> And shadows, of that destin'd Seed to bruise
> The Serpent.
>   [12.227–34]

The office of Moses is to bear in figure the mediator without whom one finds no access to God (12.240). This news marks for Adam the beginning of the high point of Michael's dialogue:

> O sent from Heav'n
> Enlight'ner of my darkness, gracious things
> Thou has reveal'd.
>
> [12.270–72]

As the Word comes into the language of temporal events, the Spirit dwells in it as well, "the law of Faith / Working through love" (12.288–90). The name *Jesus* completes the unfolding of the metaphor of the seed "disciplin'd / From shadowy types to Truth, from Flesh to Spirit" and thus may indeed now become the "copious matter" of the narrator's song — only in historical form rather than celestial revelation, in man's native realm rather than the angels'. As the allegorical seed of the new covenant, Christ completes the new terms of man's ordination from "strict laws, to free / Acceptance of large Grace," and after receiving this addition to his vision, Adam is prepared to descend from the hill and undergo exile, assured of the symbolic nature of Old Testament and New Testament chronicles. The final position of Adam and Eve as they leave Paradise is that of wanderers in the apparently hazardous and chance-filled wilderness of the picaro, but guided by providence and by a concept of an overall human progress that will carry them eventually to the confines of the celestial city. The chronological imagination discovers in symbols of the moment an epitomized recollection of all the past and a foreshadowing of all the future.

As unlike as typology and anatomy are in their use of symbols, we find suggestions of a middle ground not only in Michael's Old Testament "encyclopedia" of evils but also in the novel — in Bunyan, Defoe, and Dickens, for instance. There they represent the extremes of the novel's tendency to combine a throng of ideas and people with social types, fateful courses, and surviving hints of a providential hand in history (more than hints in Crusoe's case). Bunyan combines types of vice and virtue with enlivening anatomistic contexts by several means, perhaps most notably by nomenclature, which so effectively carries the combination at times that it removes the need for descriptive amplitude. Situated in middle earth between an archetypal

Heaven and Hell, such places as the City of Destruction, the Slough of Despond, the Valley of Humiliation, Carnal Policy, Hill Difficulty, and By-path Meadow frame a typological structure into which realistic incidents and dialogue can be meaningfully fitted. Together with Bunyan's touches of colloquial flavor, they suggest both the programmatic aspects of an allegorical journey and the miscellaneous adventures of anatomy. Bunyan's acts of naming thus contain at once barbed satire, fabulist simplicity, and typology.

Although each of these lends assistance to confession and moral instruction (which are close to the center of Bunyan's genre), however, some tension nonetheless exists between Christian's rigorous spiritual development and his reduplicative, back-tracking, echoic adventures, so characteristic of anatomy. The people he encounters — Worldly Wiseman, Legality, Presumption, Lord Time-server, Fair Speech, Mr. Facing-both-ways, Mr. Anything, Two Tongues, Money-love, Talkative (son of Say-well from Prating Row) and Lord Hate-good — speak to him as their types dictate and are clearly meant to deliver his wayfaring fable piece by plotted piece by their symbolic presence. Yet, all told, they are very plentiful; and the scattering diversions of evil that they represent are much more memorable than the stages of virtue through which Christian proceeds. Consequently, more of the satiric anatomy creeps into Christian's backsliding journey than is good for the immediate easing of his burden.

The dispatching of Faithful is typical of Bunyan's more effective combinations of typology and anatomy:

> First among themselves, Mr. Blind-man the Foreman, said, I see clearly that this man is an heretic. Then said Mr. No-good, Away with such a fellow from the earth. Ay, said Mr. Malice, for I hate the very looks of him. Then said Mr. Love-lust, I could never endure him. Nor I, said Mr. Live-loose, for he would always be condemning my way. Hang him, hang him, said Mr. Heady. A sorry Scrub, said Mr. High-mind. My heart riseth against him, said Mr. Enmity. He is a rogue, said Mr. Liar. Hanging is too good for him, said Mr. Cruelty. Let us dispatch him out of the way, said Mr. Hate-light. Then said Mr. Implacable, Might I have all the world given me, I could not be reconciled to him; therefore let us forthwith bring him in guilty of death. And so they did; therefore he was presently condemned to be had from the place where he was, to the place from whence he came, and there to be put to the most cruel death that could be invented.

They therefore brought him out, to do with him according to their law; and first they scourged him, then they buffeted him, then they lanced his flesh with knives; after that they stoned him with stones, then pricked him with their swords; and last of all they burned him to ashes at the stake. Thus came Faithful to his end.[23]

In pure anatomy, such a group would be summoned by other names and would speak with less symptomatic brevity. But the blunt pointedness of Bunyan's prose and the sharp irony of the author are nonetheless reminiscent of Voltaire and Swift; and the outraged moralistic energy of the passage Bunyan has in common with all those who combine utopian hankerings with an unclouded eye for human failings.

Dickens brings together anatomy and typology in still another way. He does so intriguingly — in a couple of senses of that word. As we have seen, everything that happens to Oliver Twist for instance, is ultimately predestined, no matter how crooked the corridor Oliver takes. The function of Dickens's symbols is to look ahead darkly and intriguingly to the working out of a preconceived design. Again in *Barnaby Rudge*, the hero's course suggests an older typology doing battle with a social plenitude and irrevelancy reminiscent of anatomy. Dickens makes use of the Gordon Riots of 1780 to combine a fateful, almost providential event with an outbreak of urban violence that would stun a seasoned Gil Blas. He also joins a good many fictional types with some literal, historical cases, which suggests that imagination supplies the coherence, the types and universals, and the governing fate, while real history supplies the materials of the anatomy and calls for the reporter and the historian to render them. The riots, which climax the novel's several movements, bring together a number of individual strands otherwise somewhat random. They give outward expression to an analogous interior wildness that many of the characters share, and at the same time they test the stability of stronger men, especially representatives of English middle-class institutions and households, the mainstays of Dickens's society. In a sense, in melting individualism into a violent mélange, they release a common animalism as the uniting force of the rabblement — a central type of riot inherent in everyone. They thus "represent"

23. John Bunyan, *The Pilgrim's Progress* (New York: P. F. Collier and Son, 1909), p. 102. Spelling modernized.

tendencies that otherwise lie inexpressive and mute — tendencies at the heart of a social aggregate that normally feels little call to unified action. Paradoxically perhaps, the greatest opportunity to discover the general laws of human nature and their underlying typology is a period of greatest disorder.

Barnaby Rudge is unlike most novels of manners in honoring individual eccentricities in this way. Though religious ideology and class feeling are paraded as the motives of the rioters, each of the individuals we follow into the riots — Hugh, Simon Tappertit, Barnaby, Ned Dennis, Gashford — is moved by much baser impulses, animal exuberance, envy, insanity, the exercise of unrestrained power and revenge. These suggest a commonality of basic emotional drives rather than a commonality of economic motives or ideologies. They are the divisive motives of the social anatomy; and many of the figures themselves are rogues capable of unleashing a collective quantity of tricks and devilment beyond anything picaresque normally envisions. If in the pre- and post-riot phases of the story's many strands people remain comically eccentric and relatively inconsequential, in their public collaboration they contribute to a unified rabblement held together by the excitement of destruction. Thus whereas a true revolution takes place under the influence of common ideals strong enough (presumably) to guide and sometimes to survive the bloodshed, the Gordon Riots in Dickens's view have only the fury and none of the intelligence or national spirit that produces permanent social changes.

The fact is that Dickens does not imagine anything like a national character or a unified social concourse of the kind that might produce a revolutionary novel or a set of positive symbolic types, all analogous in their ideologies. Unlike Milton or Bunyan, he does not work with a concept of everyman. *Barnaby Rudge* is composed of too many careers to suggest a common cause or a gathering in some central heroic course. The career of Barnaby, his raven, and his mother; the murder plot involving his father and Haredale; his two courtships, Edward Chester's of Emma and Joe Willet's of Dolly Varden; Simon Tappertit and the apprentices; the riots themselves and the subsequent (very brief) lives of their leaders; the course of the Varden household; the course of the Maypole Tavern group; Hugh's career between the hanging of his mother and his own hanging; and the private affair of Sir John Chester and Haredale — all of these pursue their own logic. Nor are Dickens's people changed in like ways by the riots or forced to mold themselves into a tighter society by class line or some other generalizing principle. After the temporary, heated fusion of the mobs, they remain as individualistic as ever and meet only in their special corners, as in the reunited Solomon Daisy, Phil Parkes, Tom Cobb, and John Willet, or in reconstituted households like Gabriel Varden's. Each is destined to dance to his own music. As the lengthy unraveling of the novel reveals, the components of society disperse. Thus the convulsed, foreshortened, hurried time of the riots brings to an immediate head fates that have been taking years to unfold, but these then continue to finish at their own distinct rates, as some people proceed toward the grave, others live abroad, and still others return to home places where they merely grow old.

CONCLUSIONS

Some of the structural implications of chronologically arranged symbols are evident from such modes as detective fiction, the anatomy, typology, and their combinations. By means of recurrent and parallel themes and images, the types of narrative lift their details from the realm of represented phenomena to a world of controlled signs, converting them into catalysts of the reader's dramatic reaction. When each moment takes up its place in the rhythm of foreshadowed and confirmed events, in the pattern of concurrent and parallel segments of an organic whole, it obviously conditions the reader's perception of all other moments and qualifies his special kind of ordeal. At the same time, to return to a truism, no system of intentional signs, of which symbols are such key elements, can ever correspond to, or represent, a world beyond. Indeed, it is never more evident than in reading typological narratives such as Michael's in *Paradise Lost* or the fated courses of figures like Oliver Twist, Nicholas Nickleby, or Barnaby that fictional symbolism is radically unlike the signs we discover in the open fields of experience, which histories, too, reshape as more or less continuous plots. The anchoring of fictive design in concrete symbols and types is a device of intelligibility denied to our interpretation of most phenomena. The icons, symbols, figures, effigies, agents, and types placed along the reader's route are instruments by which the uncertainty of his adventure is transformed into knowledge of a definite linear kind. Addressed to "the imagination, to the spiritual and aesthetic vision," each narrative kind leads the mind "captive by a charm and a spell, an incalculable art" of its own. Yet it also insists — to the unease of the truism — that art render "things as they are." As Stevens realized so frequently in creating his poetic fragments of the supreme fiction, it is paradoxically in the presence of fictions that we learn to see two such contradictory worlds as the imagination's and reality's in light of each other; and we perhaps never see them more distinctly than in those concrete symbols in which something palpable is lifted from its environment of fact, turned by a governing purpose, and seated in a design that guarantees its significance. The animate life that various narrative kinds create and the illumination that characteristic symbols cast develop under a chronological spell that progressively absorbs reality into a transformed world.

The value of symbols in that absorption has not been lost on those who, like Blake, wish ultimately to roll the extensions of anecdote into compressed, single views of reality. As one of the most ambitious creators of verse narratives, in fact, Blake offers a cogent commentary on the tension between fictions as imitations of protracted actions and fictions as modes of symbolic rendering and vision, capable of transcending a pluralistic and scattered world. Blake insists that what seem successive stages in our experience are really coexisting states of mind and that a narrative thread, too, however labyrinthian and extended it may seem, winds ultimately into a ball. Time is then demonstrated to be not linear, cyclical, or spiral at all but ensphered, self-contained, and instantly seeable. It is seeable precisely in symbols rescued from a world of hazard and made luminous as instruments of a complete ending:

> I give you the end of a golden string,
> Only wind it into a ball,
> It will lead you in at Heaven's gate
> Built in Jerusalem's wall.
> [*Jerusalem*, end of chap. 3]

Thus we may begin, in a prophetic narration, by thinking that we are located in historical times and places; and certainly from a normal perspective the entry into Blake's heaven is through some local "wall" standing in time. But the act of transfiguration that occurs at the gate, for Blake at least, negates the serial process that leads to it.

Once through Blake's barrier and safely arrived in the inner city, the former pilgrim-reader has presumably transcended the condition of anecdote; and to some extent, as we noted with respect to condensed lyric narration, the attempt of all temporal art is to impose a central vision or mood on extended materials *despite* the chronological nature of syntax and dispersed understanding. Its only conceivable means of doing so is a symbol that can gather everything into itself and enable the reader, as Blake tells him,

> To see a World in a Grain of Sand
> And a Heaven in a Wild Flower,
> Hold Infinity in the palm of your hand
> And Eternity in an hour.
> ["Auguries of Innocence"]

Such at least is the aspiration of a prophetic artist who would take the stuff of the organic world (flowers) and the very essence of scattered and insignificant multiplicity (grains of sand) and liberate them in some artifice of eternity.

But of course narrative art, as I have insisted throughout (against a recurrent critical tendency to spatialize it), also insists on the rolling up of the ball — on the dramatic ordeal of an approach to the gate in imitation of chronological experience. The necessary extension of narrative belies the compression that Blake seeks, belies it more obviously than most other literary forms. The psychology of rhythmic, serial experience is of the essence in it. Symbols capable of rendering worlds in a grain of sand belong to a realm of ideas altogether different from that of the chronological imagination. The goals of all narrations, finally, can be reached only through accounts of numbers of things, points of view, witnessed social and psychological divisiveness in a state of dramatic evolution, and all the tangible properties of a time-ridden mode.

Theories of Fiction
and History

As a footnote to the last section of the introductory chapter, two areas in fiction and historiography should be cited, both important to a sketch of the influences on Vaihinger and subsequent theorists. These are the theory of imagination and linear progress in the romantics (especially the transition evident in them from the traditional world calendar to modern concepts of secular progress and cyclical renewal), and the revision of thought about historiography after the romantics.

The first of these areas has been treated at length and impressively by M. H. Abrams, which makes unnecessary more than a reminder of a few points here. As Abrams points out, behind the development of a view of history in the romantics lies an awareness of those decisive beginnings and endings that the Christian tradition envisions.[1] To some extent, a new appreciation of the positive, secularized values of the imagination in both the German idealists and the romantics replaced the older world narrative — or measured it against the personal experience of individuals and their times — but this does not mean that they abandoned entirely belief in a divinely guided historical movement. In his essay "Idea of a Universal History from a Cosmopolitan Point of View," for instance, Kant argues that "the history of the human race, viewed as a whole, may be regarded as the realization of a hidden plan of nature to bring about a political constitution, internally . . . as the only state in which all the capacities implanted by her in mankind can be fully developed." So in accord are outcome and historical processes in Kant's view that "all

1. M. H. Abrams, *Natural Supernaturalism: Tradition and Revolution in Romantic Literature* (New York: W. W. Norton, 1971), pp. 21–70, 201–17, 225–37, 313–24.

capacities implanted in a creature by nature are destined to unfold themselves, completely and conformably to their end, in the course of time."[2] Hegel's contribution to a concept of general world movement and futurity is the notion of a World Spirit realizing itself through stages, often through violent revolutions and dynamic heroes such as Caesar. Myth and sociology are combined in such concepts of a culture hero; though some men and some epochs are more obviously agents of the Spirit than others, history is pervaded by teleology, and the way is cleared for a moving Spirit to escape tabernacles and temples and enter directly into new social incarnations.

More immediately important to romantic fictions is the secularizing of concepts of an ending, which helped to free the imagination to invent its own means of progress. The imagination becomes both an instrument of fictive invention and a mode of perception; and like the historian, the poet seizes upon the inner life of events and things and links men to a creative power. He repeats in himself the "eternal act of creation," in Coleridge's words:

> The primary imagination I hold to be the living Power and prime Agent of all human perception, and as a repetition in the finite mind of the eternal act of creation in the infinite I Am. The secondary Imagination I consider as an echo of the former, co-existing with the conscious will, yet still as identical with the primary in the kind of its agency, and differing only in degree, and in the mode of operation. It dissolves, diffuses, dissipates, in order to re-create; or where this process is rendered impossible, yet still at all events it struggles to idealize and to unify. It is essentially vital, even as all objects (as objects) are essentially fixed and dead.[3]

Despite its notorious difficulties, Coleridge's definition of the imagination clearly assigns it two distinct powers, the power of perception, in which physical things are re-created in the mind, and the power of reconstitution, by which the objective world is dissolved, diffused, and dissipated. From the perspective of linear development myths, rather than waiting for a World Spirit to realize itself in a far-off historical culmination, the poet discovers spirit and intelligence in nature immediately before him. As "The Eolian Harp" suggests, the

---

2. Immanuel Kant, "Idea of a Universal History from a Cosmopolitan Point of View," in *Theories of History*, ed. Patrick Gardiner (New York: Free Press, 1959), p. 23. G. W. F. Hegel, *The Philosophy of History*, trans. J. Sibree (New York: Dover Publications, 1956).

3. Coleridge, *Selected Poetry and Prose*, p. 263.

images the poet forges reflect "the one Life within us and abroad"; the tangible forms of that life are like the "organic Harps" of "animated nature": "O'er them sweeps, / Plastic and vast, one intellectual breeze."

These powers of the imagination — the perception of animating powers of nature and the re-creation of life in idealized and unified poetic symbols that assist our perfectibilitarian urge — resemble the creative act that Sidney describes in *An Apology for Poetry*, and it hearkens back in another way to Marvell's celebration of the imagination in "The Garden":

> The Mind, that ocean where each kind
> Does straight its own resemblance find;
> Yet it creates, transcending these,
> Far other worlds, and other seas;
> Annihilating all that's made
> To a green thought in a green shade.

To other Renaissance poets as well, the many kinds of the original creation are repeated in the mind, whose oceanic population teems with a diversity of forms.[4] Despite the resemblance between Coleridge's concept of the fictive imagination and the re-creative power of the Renaissance poet, however, thought for Marvell works within an already exclusive green world: no social progress or perfectabilitarian spirit is involved in the imagination's activity, which is withdrawn from historicity at the outset. And the poet's inventions, to Coleridge, are not so firmly tied to the myth of Eden or paradise restored.

Similar differences hold for Wordsworth, too, for whom the individual imagination is concerned less with comprehensive myths than with personal history. When Wordsworth speaks of "the modifying colors of imagination," he thinks mainly of poetry's twofold mimetic and re-creative function: it is first of all a means "whereby ordinary things" may be "presented to the mind in an unusual aspect," with stress on presentment as opposed to the act of making. He thinks also of course of poetry's effect on common men.[5] To this Coleridge

---

4. M. H. Abrams in "The Poem as Heterocosm," in *The Mirror and the Lamp: Romantic Theory and the Critical Tradition* (New York: W. W. Norton, 1958) traces the line of Platonist theory on the imagination from Plotinus to Coleridge.

5. William Wordsworth, Preface to *Lyrical Ballads*, 2d ed., in *The Poems* (Boston: Houghton Mifflin, 1932), p. 791.

adds that he and Wordsworth have sought out known and familiar places and thrown over them the "sudden charm, which accidents of light and shade, which moon-light or sun-set," diffuse. (Coleridge's particular task in the ballads is to "transfer from our inward nature a human interest and a semblance of truth sufficient to procure" for "shadows of imagination that willing suspension of disbelief for the moment, which constitutes poetic faith," while Wordsworth's is to awaken the mind's attention from "the lethargy of custom" and direct it to "the loveliness and the wonders of the world before us" [Preface to *Lyrical Ballads*, p. 781]). This presentation can and often does follow striking narrative turns in which the "unusual aspect" of things derives from a revealing action and suggests something about the teleological direction if not of cultures at least of individuals. However, both the narrative and the descriptive talents of the poet are placed under some strain by their twofold commitment to the ordinary and the extraordinary. In his concern with common reality, the poet chooses "incidents and situations" not from heroic or mythic life — moving toward visionary ends — but from events that can be described "in a selection of language really used by men." What the poet creates resembles always "the passions produced by real events." As an image of common man and common nature, poetry may become more factually historical than even previous mimetic theories encouraged. Thus Wordsworth is led to date and place the occasions of some poems and to reconceive epic not as a return to first things or end things (in Milton's sense) but as a form of narrative auto-biography — an account of the poet's particular growth. His direction is thus not toward a traditional paradise but toward the writing of a philosophic poem; his end is realized virtually in his own universe of words and imaginative acts.

The effect of the romantic concept of linear growth is to move the end toward the personal present and find it embodied in self-sustaining "types and symbols of eternity" both in poetry and in nature. Not surprisingly, romantic narratives such as *The Prelude*, *Alastor*, *Endymion*, "The Eve of St. Agnes," and "The Rime of the Ancient Mariner" tend to trace the progression of heroes to epiphanic moments in which what might well have been transcendent and distant in the tradition become momentary and immanent. The hero's progress is not sustainable, and since it carries to no final conclusions, the hero must return to time and normal society, sometimes painfully. He remains vulnerable to the charge that he has merely escaped into a private and isolated world where intellectual and imaginative faculties remain unchallenged by historical fact.

The difficulty in making powers of imagination convincing is evident in Shelley, in his response to the charges of Thomas Peacock's *The Four Ages of Poetry* against the poet. Both Peacock and Shelley are symptomatic and crucial to an understanding of the romantic reaction to fictions. Peacock crystallizes in a small witty treatise the growing preference of certain men of letters for factual writing and the condescension they feel toward the entire tribe of poets. In Peacock's view, poetry in its first age, despite a predisposition for falsity, tumid hyperbole, and self-intoxication, was at least useful to those who wished to be memorialized: it was a form of inaccurate history. In fact, poets were then the only historians and "chroniclers of their times," as yet "the sole depositories of all the knowledge of their age." But since that knowledge was merely a "crude congeries of traditional phantasies" and not a "collection of useful truths,"[6] it predicted the future of poetry. In the present age, when science, history, and philosophy are in pursuit of truth, poets insist upon chasing fictions; worst among them are the romantics, with their fictionalizing of past cultures and their incessant mysticism:

> Mr. Scott digs up the poachers and cattle-stealers of the ancient border. Lord Byron cruizes for thieves and pirates on the shores of the Morea and among the Greek Islands. Mr. Southey wades through ponderous volumes of travel and old chronicles, from which he carefully selects all that is false, useless, and absurd, as being essentially poetical; and when he has a commonplace book full of monstrosities, strings them into an epic. Mr. Wordsworth picks up village legends from old women and sextons; and Mr. Coleridge, to the valuable information acquired from similar sources, superadds the dreams of crazy theologians and the mysticisms of German metaphysics, and favours the world with visions in verse. [Pp. 15–16]

Peacock's skepticism would be more amusing than serious were it not that it finds an answering spirit in the ambivalence of the romantics themselves — in Wordsworth's self-doubts, in Coleridge's moments of dejection, and in Keats's progressive disillusionment with the imagination.

That Peacock's indictment is cast as a historical consideration of

6. *Peacock's Four Ages of Poetry*, p. 5.

poetry's four stages of development may have influenced Shelley's own developmental theory of poetry and forced him to consider more closely the function of narrative chronology in the functions of poetry. In any case, Shelley's defense is hardy and resourceful in discovering legitimate functions for fictions. Regardless of the techniques it uses, Shelley insists, "essential" poetry is an instrument of knowledge and therefore of spiritual completion. Indeed, Plato himself "was essentially a poet — the truth and splendour of his imagery and the melody of his language, are the most intense that it is possible to conceive. He rejected the measure of the epic, dramatic, and lyrical forms, because he sought to kindle a harmony in thoughts divested of shape and action."[7] The rhythm of a true poem is an echo not of "temporal movement" but "of the eternal music."

The *Defence* is resolute on this point, and in one of its key passages (with respect to linear structure), Shelley recasts the distinction between true poems and narrative stories in a revealing way:

> A poem is the very image of life expressed in its eternal truth. There is this difference between a story and a poem, that a story is a catalogue of detached facts, which have no other connexion than time, place, circumstance, cause, and effect; the other is the creation of actions according to the unchangeable forms of human nature, as existing in the mind of the Creator, which is itself the image of all other minds. The one is partial, and applies only to a definite period of time, and a certain combination of events which can never again recur; the other is universal, and contains within itself the germ of a relation to whatever motives or actions have place in the possible varieties of human nature. Time, which destroys the beauty and the use of the story of particular facts, stripped of the poetry which should invest them, augments that of poetry, and for ever develops new and wonderful applications of the eternal truth which it contains. [P. 30]

If the action of a philosophic, poetic narrative or drama is not to be merely a catalogue of facts, it must be answerable to some process of discovery; the substance of true poetry is not the times, places, or circumstances that occupy secular history and its novelistic echoes. If a poem seizes upon the facts of time and place, it does so only to make beautiful what is otherwise distorted in them; as a form of symbolic action it *applies* eternal forms to them. Only then does narrative become serviceable; only then does temporal unfolding become a

7. Ibid., p. 29.

revelation of "new and wonderful *applications* of eternal truth."

As Earl Schulze remarks, Shelley's definition of such truth is broader than Plato's in some respects. The general causes that Plato assigns "to an abstract world of Forms" Shelley assigns "to the psychological and culture-seeking processes of human intellect and feeling." He argues that the superior delights which the imagination derives from "eternal truths" are "charactered" by the poet. But he does not press very far toward the applicability of those charactered truths to historical realities finally. Though the "calculating faculty" of statesmen and politicians fails to solve social ills and though poetry might gain an advantage over that faculty if it succeeded in registering its deeper truths on the age, Shelley is reluctant to claim infallibility for the social blueprints that poets create. Poetry's power is of another kind ultimately: it is psychological before it is social or historical. Poetry "creates new materials of knowledge, and power, and pleasure," and "it engenders in the mind a desire to reproduce and arrange them according to a certain rhythm and order, which may be called the beautiful and the good."[8] Shelley insists that poetry "is at once the centre and circumference of knowledge; it is that which comprehends all science, and that to which all science must be referred" (*A Defence of Poetry*, p. 53). But a gap nonetheless remains between the psychological pleasures of aesthetic fictions and their reformative, didactic functions. Given this gap, it proves difficult to argue the immediate practical effect of any particular fiction or to point toward specific legislative powers that poetry has over the utilitarian world. Poets remain after all the *unacknowledged* legislators of mankind.

In the long run, then, Shelley does not succeed in distinguishing potentially realizable prophecies from the fantasies that Peacock accuses poets of entertaining. To minds of skeptical, pragmatic bent, the truth claim of poets remains as intangible as Hegel's World Spirit. The progress of most romantic narratives remains spiritual or psychological; it realizes internal powers in momentary spots of time, when landscapes and events crystallize as symbolic manifestations of a fleeting, animate power operating in something other than historical or plotted ways. The career of the individual spirit toward such

8. Earl J. Schulze, *Shelley's Theory of Poetry* (The Hague: Mouton, 1966), pp. 195, 50, 52; cf. the discussion of narrative form, pp. 191–207; see also Brooks and Wimsatt, *Literary Criticism*, pp. 412–31.

moments of enlightenment, though it may be itself a narrative affair, has no demonstrable relationship to the course of social matters generally, especially in their institutionalized and economic facets.

If romantic narratives of spiritual progress maintain some contact with social history, most contemporary and subsequent historical theory makes no corresponding attempt to keep in touch with the contributions of the imagination in charting the movements of societies. Indeed, that theory scrupulously tries not to keep a foot in myth or poetic creation. We need not explore extensively the logic of the new historiographical forms that Turgot, Condorcet, Lamarck, Saint-Simon, Proudhon, Darwin, and others illustrate, however, to see the impact of the separation of "true" and "mythic" chronicles on narrative consequence and ending.

The most dominant influence among the revisionists of the traditional world calendar is the theory of biological and cultural progress, which informs nearly all revised general chronologies and eventually binds social anthropological history, as Comte and his fellow sociologists sought to do.[9] However, in even the most optimistic of linear calendars, biological change and cultural progress are not often construed as teleological,[10] and in that change from the Christian-Hebraic view and from the perfectabilitarian element of romanticism and German idealism lies much of the difference between older and modern concepts of progress toward an end. All variations of the old calendar provided at least some point at which spiritual forms and their permanence transcend the record of merely human events, while in the new kinds of reckoning cultures advance, flower, and die without the benefit of final culminations. As the positivists insisted, therefore, historiography had to be liberated from those formal structures of the imagination that lean toward aesthetic enclosure and concepts of culmination.

9. See Auguste Comte, *System of Positive Polity*, vol. 3, *Social Dynamics; or, The General Theory of Human Progress* (New York: Burt Franklin, 1966). See also Teggart, *Theory and Process of History*, p. 104; J. B. Bury, *The Idea of Progress: An Inquiry into Its Origin and Growth* (New York: Dover, 1955); Antoine-Nicolas Condorcet, *Sketch for a Historical Picture of the Progress of the Human Mind*, trans. June Barraclough (London: Weidenfeld and Nicolson, 1955); Karl Jaspers, *The Origin and Goal of History* (New Haven: Yale University Press, 1953).

10. Linear theories of progress continue to be challenged by cyclical, rhythmical, and trendless histories. See Grace E. Cairns, *Philosophies of History* (New York: Philosophical Library, 1962).

What might take the place of those structures remained problematic. F. H. Bradley's solution to the evident lack of purpose in
historical events was to replace a teleology built into nature with a
satisfaction located in the historical method itself: that is, history may
or may not evolve toward a definite end, but historiography arrives at
a definitive understanding of what the historian himself has done with
it. The historian's goal is thus the discovery of the contemporaneity of
old events operating under ever valid laws.[11] He constructs an order
of words out of and around a body of evidence, so that however open
to chaos he may find himself outside that circle, inside it he has the
protection of a self-defined meaningful purpose.

As both practicing historians and theorists began to realize more
clearly after Bradley's generation, such a relocation of history's true
presence in the mind of the historian — once he is truly liberated
from world calendars — results in a pluralistic appreciation of a great
many methods. The historian is free to choose among quite different
kinds of history that accord with particular areas and his own
preferences: histories of art; music (opera, instruments, performers,
etc.); institutions (armies, bureaus, governments); peoples and cultures; individuals; transactions; wars; religions, philosophies, and
ideas; history itself; science; literary forms, styles, and movements;
voyages and explorations; popular phenomena, fads, customs; sports;
media; words; natural phenomena such as droughts, floods, storms,
earthquakes, oceans; the world; the solar system; the galaxy. When
such topics are considered in their own right, it becomes obvious that
each has its special problems and establishes contact with others in a
mutual culture in a number of ways. If a culture is an organic growth
pursuing its own variable laws of associativity, in pursuit of those
laws one kind of historiography might legitimately overleap centuries
while another kind might demand a minute chronology of facts. The
history of words, images, and figures, for instance, like the history of
ideas, can trace the career of its subject from one book to another
(sometimes from index to index) without risking exposure to the light
of common day. For others, a narrative, a diary, a description, an
analysis, an introspection, or an attested documentation might be
appropriate. Some events and historical topics are relivable in the
present, like performed music or plays; others are pursuable only as

11. Francis H. Bradley, *The Presuppositions of Critical History*, ed. Lionel Rubinoff
(Chicago: Quadrangle Books, 1968; originally published 1874), p. 89.

distant facts. Imagination may figure prominently in some; facts may dominate others.

The upshot of this pluralism of topics and methods is that to some historians it became clearer than it had been to classical and Renaissance historians that, beginning with the very naming of a subject, the historian constitutes his own reality. Every layer of facts he exposes or makes use of bears the mark of his method; his chronicle is tainted with method even before he commits the first word to paper. Despite an initial separation of fiction and truth in theory, the two in practice turn out to be less separable than one might have hoped, especially since the turn inward that Bradley takes in locating the form of history in the historian's method is matched by the novel's turn outward in locating the matter of the fabler in real societies. (Journalism and scholarly documentation come together in the historical novel, for instance; and the techniques of the novel find their way into accounts of real events.) Thus the scenic embellishment and narrative forms of a Bernard DeVoto resemble too exactly the techniques of a Sir Walter Scott or Thomas Hardy in situating fictional events in real places and times. Each kind implies not only a working program and a schedule by which one thing is added to another but a way of seeing reality — of selecting, abridging, arranging, and interpreting.

Both historians and novelists of the nineteenth century, in practice and in theory, thus frustrated the positivist's desire to separate science and myth. Indeed, as Haskell Fain acknowledges, the modern historian finds no place among those who expect to construct unquestionable laws of events such as the social scientist. From a skeptical point of view, a historian can never achieve an epistemological consummation among his heaps of corroded coins, locks of hair, and shards; in most forms of historiography, in fact, he hears and reports merely snatches of conversation from the other side of a nearly impenetrable wall.[12]

Together with the historian who insists upon an absolute distinction between fact and hypothesis, myth and verifiable record, there developed another kind of historian who insisted that historical

---

12. Haskell Fain, *Between Philosophy and History* (Princeton: Princeton University Press, 1970), p. 117. Cf. Fleishman, *The English Historical Novel*, pp. 3–15; W. B. Gallie, *Philosophy and the Historical Understanding* (New York: Schocken Books, 1964), pp. 22–71; Levin, *In Defense of Historical Literature*, pp. 1–33.

narrative is after all akin to fictions — fictions of the kind that Bentham and Vaihinger find where one least expects them. Such a historian condemns, as Croce does, a spiritless and dead history that relishes mere facts.[13] Whereas reality, as the film critic Jean Epstein remarks, has no stories ("There have never been stories. There are only situations without tail or head"), the historian in this view falls into confusion unless he invents chains of cause and effect that begin and end somewhere. Merely by putting one sentence behind another, he creates meanings where circumstances give him only facts; he

13. Croce, "History and Chronicle," in *History: Its Theory and Practice*, pp. 11–26. Collingwood also insists that true history is the history of thought, not something appended to science: if a natural process is a process of factual events suitable to disciplines like geology and archeology, "an historical process is a process of thoughts." The historian must reenact in his own mind the thoughts of past men; a mere chronicle is nonhistorical. See *The Idea of History* (New York: Oxford University Press, 1956), "History as Reenactment of Past Experience."

To suggest a random sampling of opinion on the dispute between analytic or sociological history and narrative history: Frederick J. Teggart remarks that if we are to have a science of man, historical investigation must be freed from its subordination to the art of history writing, because "the unity of any history is the creation of an artist." But in freeing investigation from narrative we also unfortunately separate the study of events (history) from the study of progressive change (anthropology and ethnology), and the two must be combined. The natural laws of change and the influence of unique events must be investigated together. Narrative should therefore be given a subordinate place in historiography. See *Theory and Process of History*, p. 34. Frederick J. E. Woodbridge argues in *The Purpose of History* (Port Washington, N.Y.: Kennikat Press, 1916) that storylike history can be written without distortion because there are genuine careers to be written about; as seeds in a garden follow a natural course to fulfillment, so the "garden" of history contains many interacting careers. The end that the historian explains is a termination of the logic of one career among a pluralistic set (pp. 47–49). See also Erich Kahler, *The Meaning of History* (New York: George Braziller, 1964); W. B. Gallie, *Philosophy and the Historical Understanding*; Heinrich Gomperz, *Interpretation: Logical Analysis of a Method of Historical Research* (Chicago: University of Chicago Press, 1939); Karl Löwith, *Meaning in History* (Chicago: University of Chicago Press, 1949); Karl R. Popper, *The Poverty of Historicism* (New York: Basic Books, 1957); John Herman Randall, Jr., *Nature and Historical Experience* (New York: Columbia University Press, 1958); Robert Stover, *The Nature of Historical Thinking* (Chapel Hill: University of North Carolina Press, 1967); Arthur C. Danto, *Analytical Philosophy of History* (Cambridge: Cambridge University Press, 1965); Morton White, *Foundations of Historical Knowledge* (New York: Harper and Row, 1965); Ernst Cassirer, *The Problem of Knowledge: Philosophy, Science, and History since Hegel*, trans. Wm. H. Woglom and Charles W. Hendel (New Haven: Yale University Press, 1950); Siegfried Kracauer, *History: The Last Things before the Last* (New York: Oxford University Press, 1969), pp. 29ff. For an anthology of opinion, see *Theories of History*, ed. Patrick Gardiner (New York: The Free Press, 1959). See also note 4, chap. 2.

creates epochs, periodicity, and synchronization where nature and human confusion provide only sedimentary deposits, birth registers, and material for statistical tables. Grumbling impatiently over the dead literalness of much history, Nietzsche rejoices in the desire of men to create such fictions, even if they have to dispose of the past and all its records to do so: "If there is no constructive impulse behind the historical one, if the clearance of rubbish is not merely to leave the ground free for the hopeful living future to build its house, if justice alone be supreme, the creative instinct is sapped and discouraged." Next to the fictive imagination, science and the historical instinct appear not merely dull but hostile to the "pious illusions" by which men live: "Art has the opposite effect to history; and only, perhaps, if history suffers transformation into a pure work of art, can it preserve instincts or arouse them. Such history would be quite against the analytical and inartistic tendencies of our time, and even be considered false."[14]

Nietzsche is colorfully and uniquely Nietzsche, and one hesitates to make him typical of anything. But equally bold endorsements of the historian's necessary transformations of fact have been formulated since Bradley by a great many respectable spokesmen, some of them reacting explicitly to the same separation of science and humanistic needs. Michael Oakeshott and R. G. Collingwood are two examples. To Oakeshott — perhaps the most extreme of the antipositivists — human experience itself is a single, undivided whole that demands from the historian a reliving of events and a narrative method answerable to their re-creation: "What is achieved in experience is an absolutely coherent world of ideas, not in the sense that it is ever actually achieved, but in the more important sense that it is the criterion of whatever satisfaction is achieved." Such a statement gives clear priority to human evaluation and intellectual satisfaction over what is literally in the record. By definition, in Oakeshott's terms, to have been fully "experience," what is now "history" must once have been coherent and intelligible. It was not then and should not be now merely a tissue of conjunctions, coordination without subordination,

14. Friedrich Nietzsche, *The Use and Abuse of History*, trans. Adrian Collins (New York: Liberal Arts Press, 1949), p. 42. Nietzsche adds, "I call the power 'super-historical' which turns the eyes from the process of becoming to that which gives existence an external and stable character—to art and religion" (p. 69).

or enumeration without integration.[15] As it is also for Croce and Collingwood, history must therefore be fully present, in somewhat the way a work of art is: as we speak of the doings of a Shakespearean play in the present tense (because they exist more or less as they always have), so we may speak of the past as an always contemporary reality insofar as it consists of thought. The logic of historical narration is the progress of our own understanding — the progress of a revived past transformed into the order of words.

The task of a history, so conceived, resembles what novels do with the germs of stories lifted from actual events. Henry James, for instance, frequently suggests that the fictionalist is even more pleased by the past then he is by the present because he can grasp the whole of something as an idea only when its actual historical course is run. Thus in compensation for the loss of his cousin Minny, he has a new possession of her in her dying that translates her from "this changing realm of fact to the steady realm of thought." Such a translation is parallel to what art accomplishes when the novelist seizes upon the germ of a real situation and incorporates it into an intelligible framework of his own invention. There, enshrined in a narrative order, its potential is displayed piece by piece in a "sacred mastery of structure." (Minny herself turns up in James's fiction fully "possessed" and transformed as the world of animate fictions demands, where expression answers to the novelist's encircling of a subject — where the art of composition is an act of seeing through.)

Such similarities as these between factual and fictional narration should not of course be stretched too far; but a line of theorists in historiography from F. H. Bradley to Croce, Collingwood, and W. B. Gallie clearly suggests a less than absolute separation of the structuring imagination and the literal record. And the common ground is broader than merely the common use of narrative form. In Oakeshott and Collingwood, the organic logic of a written history is always more than a causal sequence; it possesses the attributes of a renewed life and a structure pervaded with a living idea. In fact, mere causality in Oakeshott's view brings historiography to the brink of chaos, because, forcing history's past dimension upon us, it explains nothing.

15. Michael Oakeshott, *Experience and Its Modes* (Cambridge: Cambridge University Press, 1933), pp. 27, 89. Cf. Jack W. Meiland, *Scepticism and Historical Knowledge* (New York: Random House, 1965), pp. 41–62.

Serial causes by definition disappear ever backward until one runs out of evidence and plunges into an abyss of time; or they scatter into innumerable ramifying byways. And when the historian has failed, as he must, to produce a sufficient final cause, he is forced to settle for unexplainable incidents and random events. Hence to Oakeshott "everyone of these so-called rigidly causal sequences is, in fact, merely an unrecognized conflux of coincidences" (*Experience and Its Modes*, p. 138). For instance, the "causes" of the fall of the Roman Empire that historians locate in migrating Eastern hordes (that drove barbarians southward into Roman provinces) and in a coincidental internal weakness in the empire itself prove on further examination to require further and finer breakdown. They are in turn the "result" of other coincidental chains of influence, and these are the product of still finer and more scattered influences. Thus outside the closed fields that characterize narration, every causational chain that tries to remain rigorously true to the complexity of reality becomes a meaningless tissue of accidents. History writing must therefore seek the tighter coherence that we find in logical constructions such as fictions. It must encircle the past or a segment of it in the way, perhaps, that James seeks in his materials a "clear order and expressed sequence," entirely intelligible to rational thought, entirely governed by the wholeness of its "little mosaic."

Unfortunately for a theory of fictions, neither Collingwood nor Oakeshott is willing to distinguish exactly what contribution to intelligibility and organic wholeness the historian's own talent makes. Nor do we find even in James's several accounts of the novelist's transforming of germinal situations an adequate account of the changes the imagination has wrought. If true historicism is the rethinking of past thoughts, how can we distinguish actual rethinking from creative invention? (As Montesquieu remarks — wisely, at least from the standpoint of lovers of literal accuracy — "To transfer into far-off centuries all the ideas of the century in which one is living is the most fecund of all sources of error.")[16] Abandoning entirely the concept of cause and effect and divorcing the historian from the

16. Quoted from Charles W. Hende's introduction to Cassirer's *The Philosophy of Symbolic Forms*, 1:38. Critiques of Collingwood's position and Croce's have been both numerous and effective; see *The Philosophy of History in Our Time*, ed. Meyerhoff, passim; Kracauer, *History*, pp. 62–79; White, *Foundations of Historical Knowledge*, p. 147ff.; Patrick Gardiner, *The Nature of Historical Explanation* (London: Oxford

sciences might well seem a high price to pay for narrative coherence. If the lack of an all-inclusive calendar means that no segment of temporality is meaningful in its backward pursuit of causes, surely not only professional historians but storytellers in general are reduced to inscrutable silence.

Certainly most practicing narrators are quite willing to leave to chance if they must the coincidence that brings a foot to a slippery peel or a Roman Empire to its barbarians: they are willing to assume the normal apparatus of gravity, surface tensions, and fallible human eyesight, and to explain events pragmatically. It seems useful if not cosmically definitive to do so — to answer some particular inquiry with statements like, "You ask how Joe broke his arm? By slipping and falling. A banana peel did it to him." Or, "Droughts in the east forced a shift of populations first into northern Europe and then into the empire, which for a variety of reasons found itself unable to fend off its invaders." These are obviously quite different positions from those we normally find novelists taking; the historian and the novelist tend to answer different questions and put the art of narration to different uses. Both may dispute the positivist's monopoly on "truth," but they must ultimately do so for different purposes and by different means.

The parties to the debate over the logic of presented history stick on many of the same problems: how to discover what is real, how to preserve and transcribe it, and how to disentangle what events are, in themselves, from what our perceiving mechanism attributes to them. What hinders both idealist historians such as Croce and Collingwood and the positivists in their reactions against myths and fictions is the failure held in common by the tradition to isolate clearly the transformative effects of different modes of imaginative structure. It is left for postromantic theorists of the pragmatic imagination and the mind's inherent structuring — theorists such as William James, Dewey, Vaihinger, Burke, Cassirer, and Stevens — to pursue the subject in more productive directions.

University Press, 1952), pp. 49ff. White argues sensibly that a number of kinds of explanation are required by social behavior and its contributory causes; when thought is not *the* cause of an action, history cannot be a history of thought merely. Different interests in historians lead them to ask different questions (p. 125).

Secondary Bibliography

Abrams, M. H. *The Mirror and the Lamp: Romantic Theory and the Critical Tradition*. New York: W. W. Norton, 1958.

――――. *Natural Supernaturalism: Tradition and Revolution in Romantic Literature*. New York: W. W. Norton, 1971.

Alexander, Samuel. *Space, Time and Deity*. London: Macmillan and Co., 1934.

Alter, Robert. *Rogue's Progress: Studies in the Picaresque Novel*. Cambridge, Mass.: Harvard University Press, 1964.

Anton, John P., ed. *Naturalism and Historical Understanding: Essays in the Philosophy of John Herman Randall, Jr*. Albany: State University of New York Press, 1967.

Arnheim, Rudolf. *Art and Visual Perception: A Psychology of the Creative Eye*. Berkeley and Los Angeles: University of California Press, 1960.

Auerbach, Erich. "Figura." *Archivum Romanicum* 22 (1938): 436–89.

――――. *Mimesis: The Representation of Reality in Western Literature*. New York: Doubleday, 1957.

――――. "Typological Symbolism in Medieval Literature." *Yale French Studies* 9 (1952): 3–80.

Babbitt, Irvine. *The New Laokoon: An Essay on the Confusion of the Arts*. Boston: Houghton Mifflin, 1910.

Barnes, Harry Elmer. *A History of Historical Writing*. New York: Dover Publications, 1962.

Barr, James. *Old and New in Interpretation: A Study of the Two Testaments*. New York: Harper and Row, 1966.

Beebe, Maurice. *Ivory Towers and Sacred Founts: The Artist as Hero in Fiction from Goethe to Joyce*. New York: New York University Press, 1964.

Berdyaev, Nicholas. *The Meaning of History*. Cleveland and New York: World Publishing Company, 1962.

Berger, Harry, Jr. "The Renaissance Imagination: Second World and Green World." *Centennial Review* 9 (1965): 36–78.

Berry, Francis. *The Shakespeare Inset: Word and Picture*. New York: Theatre Arts Books, 1965.

Black, Frank Gees. *The Epistolary Novel in the Late Eighteenth Century: A Descriptive and Bibliographical Study*. Eugene: University of Oregon Press, 1940.

Black, Max. *The Labyrinth of Language*. New York: Frederick A. Praeger, 1968.

———. *Language and Philosophy: Studies in Method.* Ithaca, N.Y.: Cornell University Press, 1949.

———. *Models and Metaphors: Studies in Language and Philosophy.* Ithaca, N.Y.: Cornell University Press, 1962.

———. *Problems of Analysis: Philosophical Essays.* Ithaca, N.Y.: Cornell University Press, 1954.

Blackall, Jean Frantz. *Jamesian Ambiguity and The Sacred Fount.* Ithaca, N.Y.: Cornell University Press, 1965.

Bloomfield, Morton W., ed. *The Interpretation of Narrative: Theory and Practice.* Cambridge, Mass.: Harvard University Press, 1970.

Bobbitt, Joseph M. "An Experimental Study of the Phenomenon of Closure as a Threshold Function." In *Readings in Perception,* edited by David C. Beardslee and Michael Wertheimer. Princeton: D. Van Nostrand Co., 1958.

Bodin, J. E. "Fictions in Science and Philosophy" *Journal of Philosophy* 49 (1943): 673–82, 701–16.

Booth, Wayne C. *The Rhetoric of Fiction.* Chicago: University of Chicago Press, 1961.

Bradley, Francis H. *The Presuppositions of Critical History,* ed. Lionell Rubinoff. Chicago: Quadrangle Books, 1968. Originally published 1874.

Braudy, Leo. *Narrative Form in History and Fiction: Hume, Fielding and Gibbon.* Princeton: Princeton University Press, 1970.

Bronson, Bertrand. "Literature and Music." In *Relations of Literary Study,* edited by James Thorpe. New York: Modern Language Association, 1967.

Brooks, Cleanth, and Wimsatt, William K., Jr. *Literary Criticism: A Short History.* New York: Vintage Books, 1957.

Brown, Calvin S. *Music and Literature: A Comparison of the Arts.* Athens: University of Georgia Press, 1948.

Brown, E. K. *Rhythm in the Novel.* Toronto: University of Toronto Press, 1950.

Brown, Huntington. *Prose Styles: Five Primary Types.* Minneapolis: University of Minnesota Press, 1966.

Buchanan, George Richard. "Rhythm and Experience: The Art of Rhythm in the Novel and Film." Ph.D. dissertation. University of Chicago, 1973.

Burke, Kenneth. *Attitudes toward History.* Boston: Beacon Press, 1961.

———. *Counter-statement.* Los Altos, Calif.: Hermes Publications, 1931.

———. *Language as Symbolic Action.* Berkeley and Los Angeles: University of California Press, 1966.

———. *The Philosophy of Literary Form: Studies in Symbolic Action.* New York: Vintage Books, 1957.

———. *The Rhetoric of Religion: Studies in Logology.* Boston: Beacon Press, 1961.

Burke, Peter. *The Renaissance Sense of the Past.* New York: St. Martin's Press, 1969.

Bury, J. B. *The Idea of Progress: An Inquiry into Its Origin and Growth.* New York: Dover, 1955.

Cairns, Grace E. *Philosophies of History.* New York: Philosophical Library, 1962.

Calderwood, James, and Toliver, Harold E., eds. *Perspectives on Fiction.* New York: Oxford University Press, 1968.

———. *Perspectives on Poetry.* New York: Oxford University Press, 1968.

Calvino, Italo. "Notes toward a Definition of the Narrative Form as a Combinative Process." *Twentieth-Century Studies* 3 (1970): 93–101.

Campbell, Joseph. *The Hero with a Thousand Faces.* New York: Meridian Books, 1956.

Carnap, Rudolf. *The Logical Structure of the World: Pseudoproblems in Philosophy.* Translated by Rolf A. George. Berkeley and Los Angeles: University of California Press, 1967.

Cassirer, Ernst. *The Philosophy of Symbolic Forms.* 2 vols. New Haven: Yale University Press, 1953.

———. *The Problem of Knowledge: Philosophy, Science, and History since Hegel.* Translated by Wm. H. Woglom and Charles W. Hendel. New Haven: Yale University Press, 1950.

Cebik, L. B. "Narratives and Arguments." *Clio* 1 (1971): 7–25.

Chandler, Frank Wadleigh. *The Literature of Roguery.* New York: Burt Franklin, 1958.

———. *Romances of Roguery: The Picaresque Novel in Spain.* New York: Burt Franklin, 1961.

Cherry, Colin, ed. *Information Theory: Papers Read at a Symposium.* London: Butterworths Scientific Publications, 1956.

Church, Margaret. *Time and Reality: Studies in Contemporary Fiction.* Chapel Hill: University of North Carolina Press, 1949.

Collingwood, R. H. *The Idea of History.* New York: Oxford University Press, 1956.

Collins, R. G., ed. *The Novel and Its Changing Form.* Winnipeg: University of Manitoba Press, 1972.

Comte, Auguste. *System of Positive Polity.* Vol. 3, *Social Dynamics; or, The General Theory of Human Progress.* New York: Burt Franklin, 1966.

Condorcet, Antoine-Nicolas. *Sketch for a Historical Picture of the Progress of the Human Mind.* Translated by June Barraclough. London: Weidenfeld and Nicolson, 1955.

Cooke, Albert. *The Meaning of Fiction.* Detroit: Wayne State University Press, 1960.

Croce, Benedetto. *History: Its Theory and Practice.* Translated by Douglas Ainslie. New York: Russell and Russell, 1960.

Cullman, Oscar. *Christ and Time: The Primitive Christian Conception of Time and History.* Translated by Floyd V. Filson. Philadelphia: Westminster Press, 1964.

Danielou, Jean, S.J. *From Shadows to Reality: Studies in the Biblical Typology of the Fathers.* Westminster, Md.: Newman Press, 1960.

Danto, Arthur C. *Analytical Philosophy of History.* Cambridge: Cambridge University Press, 1965.

D'Arcy, M. C., S.J. *The Meaning and Matter of History: A Christian View.* New York: Farrar, Straus and Cudahy, 1959.

Davis, Walter R. *Idea and Act in Elizabethan Fiction.* Princeton: Princeton University Press, 1969.

Day, Angel. *The English Secretary; or, Methods of Writing Epistles.* Ed. Robert O. Evans. Gainesville, Fl.: Scholars' Facsimilies and Reprints, 1967.

Day, Robert Adams. *Told in Letters: Epistolary Fiction before Richardson.* Ann Arbor: University of Michigan Press, 1966.

Dewey, John. *Art as Experience.* New York: G. P. Putnam's Sons, 1958.

——— *Experience and Nature.* La Salle, Ill.: Open Court Publishing Co., 1959.

Dupee, F. W., ed. *The Question of Henry James: A Collection of Critical Essays.* New York: Henry Holt, 1945.

Ehrenzweig, Anton. *The Hidden Order of Art: A Study in the Psychology of Artistic Imagination.* Berkeley and Los Angeles: University of California Press, 1967.

Epperson, Gordon. *The Musical Symbol: A Study of the Philosophic Theory of Music.* Ames: Iowa State University Press, 1967.

Fain, Haskell. *Between Philosophy and History.* Princeton: Princeton University Press, 1970.

Fleishman, Avrom. *The English Historical Novel: Walter Scott to Virginia Woolf.* Baltimore: Johns Hopkins Press, 1971.

Fletcher, Angus. *Allegory: The Theory of a Symbolic Mode.* Ithaca, N.Y.: Cornell University Press, 1964.

Forster, E. M. *Aspects of the Novel.* New York: Harcourt, Brace, 1927.

Fraisse, Paul. *The Psychology of Time.* Translated by Jennifer Leith. New York: Harper and Row, 1963.

Frank, Joseph. *The Widening Gyre: Crisis and Mastery in Modern Literature.* New Brunswick, N.J.: Rutgers University Press, 1963.

Fraser, J. T. *The Voices of Time: A Cooperative Survey of Man's Views of Time as Expressed by the Sciences and by the Humanities.* New York: George Braziller, 1966.

Freedman, Ralph. *The Lyrical Novel: Studies in Hermann Hesse, Andre Gide, and Virginia Woolf.* Princeton: Princeton University Press, 1963.

——— "The Possibility of a Theory of the Novel." In *The Disciplines of Criticism,* edited by Peter Demetz, et al. New Haven: Yale University Press, 1968.

Friedman, Alan. *The Turn of the Novel.* New York: Oxford University Press, 1966.

Friedman, Melvin. *Stream of Consciousness: A Study in Literary Method.* New Haven: Yale University Press, 1955.

Friedman, Norman. "Forms of the Plot." *Journal of General Education* 8 (1955): 241–53.

Frohock, W. M. "The Failing Center: Recent Fiction and the Picaresque Tradition." *Novel* 3 (1969): 62–69.

Frye, Northrop. *Anatomy of Criticism.* Princeton: Princeton University Press, 1957.

Gallie, W. B. *Philosophy and the Historical Understanding.* New York: Schocken Books, 1964.

Gardiner, Patrick. *The Nature of Historical Explanation.* London: Oxford University Press, 1952.

_____, ed. *Theories of History.* New York: Free Press, 1959.

Gerard, R. W. "The Biological Basis of Imagination." In *The Creative Process: A Symposium,* edited by Brewster Ghiselin. New York: Mentor, 1955.

Gerber, Philip L., and Gemmett, Robert J. "Picaresque and Modern Literature: A Conversation with W. M. Frohock." *Genre* 3 (1970): 187–97.

Glacken, Clarence J. *Traces on the Rhodian Shore: Nature and Culture in Western Thought from Ancient Times to the End of the Eighteenth Century.* Berkeley and Los Angeles: University of California Press, 1967.

Goldmann, Lucien. *Pour une sociologie du roman.* Paris: Gallimard, 1965.

Gombrich, E. H. *Art and Illusion: A Study in the Psychology of Pictorial Representation.* Princeton: Princeton University Press, 1960.

Gomperz, Heinrich. *Interpretation: Logical Analysis of a Method of Historical Research.* Chicago: University of Chicago Press, 1939.

Goodman, Paul. *The Structure of Literature.* Chicago: University of Chicago Press, 1954.

Grebstein, Sheldon Norman, ed. *Perspectives in Contemporary Criticism.* New York: Harper and Row, 1968.

Gross, Beverly. "Narrative Time and the Open-Ended Novel." *Criticism* 8 (1966): 362–76.

Grossvogel, David I. *Limits of the Novel: Evolutions of a Form from Chaucer to Robbe-Grillet.* Ithaca, N. Y.: Cornell University Press, 1968.

Hamlyn, D. W. *The Psychology of Perception: A Philosophical Examination of Gestalt Theory and Derivative Theories of Perception.* London: Routledge and Kegan Paul, 1957.

Harvey, W. J. *Character and the Novel.* London: Chatto and Windus, 1966.

Hegel, G. W. F. *The Philosophy of History.* Translated by J. Sibree. New York: Dover, 1956.

Henn, T. R. *The Bible as Literature.* New York: Oxford University Press, 1970.

Hertz, Richard. *Chance and Symbol: A Study in Aesthetic and Ethical Consistency.* Chicago: University of Chicago Press, 1968.

Hirst, R. J. *The Problems of Perception*. London: George Allen and Unwin, 1959.

Holland, Laurence Bedwell. *The Expense of Vision: Essays on the Craft of Henry James*. Princeton: Princeton University Press, 1964.

Honig, Edwin. *Dark Concert: The Making of Allegory*. Evanston, Ill.: Northwestern University Press, 1959.

Hook, Sidney, ed. *Philosophy and History: A Symposium*. New York: New York University Press, 1963.

Hospers, John. *Meaning and Truth in the Arts*. Chapel Hill: University of North Carolina Press, 1946.

Hough, Graham. "From: An Essay in Criticism." *Critical Quarterly* 8 (1966): 136–45.

Howe, Irving. *Politics and the Novel*. Greenwich: Fawcett Publications, 1967.

Husserl, Edmund. *The Phenomenology of Internal Time-Consciousness*. Edited by Martin Heidegger. Translated by James S. Churchill. Bloomington: Indiana University Press, 1964.

James, Henry. *The Art of the Novel*. New York: Charles Scribner's Sons, 1934.

———. *The Future of the Novel*, ed. Leon Edel. New York: Random House, 1956.

———. *The Notebooks*. Edited by F. O. Matthiessen and Kenneth B. Murdock. New York: Oxford University Press, 1961.

James, William. *Pragmatism and Four Essays from The Meaning of Truth*. Cleveland and New York: Meridian Books, 1955.

Jaspers, Karl. *The Origin and Goal of History*. New Haven: Yale University Press, 1953.

Kahler, Erich. *The Meaning of History*. New York: George Braziller, 1964.

Kany, Charles E. *The Beginnings of the Epistolary Novel in France, Italy, and Spain*. Berkeley: University of California Press, 1937.

Kennedy, James G. "More General than Fiction: The Uses of History in the Criticism of Modern Novels." *College English* 28 (1966): 150–63.

Kermode, Frank. *The Sense of an Ending: Studies in the Theory of Fiction*. New York: Oxford University Press, 1967.

———. "Novel, History and Type." *Novel* 1 (1968): 231–38.

Klibansky, Raymond, and Paton, H. J., eds. *Philosophy and History*. New York: Harper and Row, 1963.

Knight, Everett. *A Theory of the Classical Novel*. New York: Barnes and Noble, 1970.

Koestler, Arthur. *The Act of Creation*. London: Hutchinson, 1964.

Koffka, K. *Principles of Gestalt Psychology*. New York: Harcourt, Brace and Co., 1935.

Kracauer, Siegfried. *History: The Last Things before the Last*. New York: Oxford University Press, 1969.

———. *Theory of Film: The Redemption of Physical Reality*. New York: Oxford University Press, 1960.

Kroeber, Karl. *Styles in Fictional Structure: The Art of Jane Austen, Charlotte Bronte, George Eliot.* Princeton: Princeton University Press, 1971.

Krook, Dorothea. *The Ordeal of Consciousness in Henry James.* London: Cambridge University Press, 1967.

Kubler, George. *The Shape of Time: Remarks on the History of Things.* New Haven: Yale University Press, 1962.

Lawson, Lewis A. "Wilkie Collins and *The Moonstone.*" *American Imago* 5 (1963): 61–79.

Lessing, Gotthold Ephraim. *Laocoon.* London: J. M. Dent and Sons, 1930.

Levin, David. *In Defense of Historical Literature.* New York: Hill and Wang, 1967.

Levin, Harry. *The Gates of Horn: A Study of Five French Realists.* New York: Oxford University Press, 1963.

———. *The Myth of the Golden Age in the Renaissance.* Bloomington: Indiana University Press, 1969.

———. "Toward a Sociology of the Novel." *Journal of the History of Ideas* 26 (1965): 148–54.

Lévi-Strauss, Claude. "The Structural Study of Myth." *Journal of American Folklore* 68 (1955): 428–44.

Levy, F. J. *Tudor Historical Thought.* San Marino, Calif.: Huntington Library, 1967.

Lodge, David. *Language of Fiction: Essays in Criticism and Verbal Analysis of the English Novel.* London: Routledge and Kegan Paul, 1966.

Lord, Albert B. *The Singer of Tales.* Cambridge, Mass.: Harvard University Press, 1960.

Louch, A. R. "History as Narrative." *History and Theory* 8 (1969): 54–70.

Löwith, Karl. *Meaning in History.* Chicago: University of Chicago Press, 1949.

Lubbock, Percy. *The Craft of Fiction.* New York: Viking Press, 1957.

Lukács, Georg. *The Historical Novel.* Translated by Hannah and Stanley Mitchell. London: Merlin Press, 1962.

———. *Realism in Our Time: Literature and the Class Struggle.* New York: Harper and Row, 1962.

———. *Studies in European Realism.* Translated by Edith Bone. London: Hillway, 1950.

McCarthy, Mary. "The Fact in Fiction." *Partisan Review* 27 (1960): 438–58.

McCormick, John. *Catastrophe and Imagination.* London: Longmans, Green and Co., 1957.

Mandelbaum, Maurice. "A Note on History as Narrative." *History and Theory* 6 (1967): 413–19.

Mazzeo, Joseph. *Structure and Thought in the Paradiso.* Ithaca, N.Y.: Cornell University Press, 1958.

Meiland, Jack W. *Skepticism and Historical Knowledge.* New York: Random House, 1965.

Melchiori, Giorgio. *The Tightrope Walkers: Studies of Mannerism in Modern English Literature*. London: Routledge and Kegan Paul, 1956.

Meyer, Leonard B. *Music, the Arts and Ideas: Patterns and Predictions in Twentieth-Century Culture*. Chicago: University of Chicago Press, 1967.

Meyerhoff, Hans, ed. *The Philosophy of History in Our Time: An Anthology*. New York: Doubleday, 1959.

Middleton, John, ed. *Myth and Cosmos: Readings in Mythology and Symbolism*. Garden City, N.Y.: Natural History Press, 1967.

Miller, J. Hillis. *The Form of Victorian Fiction*. Notre Dame: University of Notre Dame Press, 1968.

Miller, Stuart. *The Picaresque Novel*. Cleveland: Case Western Reserve University Press, 1967.

Mink, Louis O. *Mind, History, and Dialectic: The Philosophy of R. G. Collingwood*. Bloomington: Indiana University Press, 1969.

Mish, Charles C., ed. *Restoration Prose Fiction, 1660-1700*. Lincoln: University of Nebraska Press, 1970.

Moles, Abraham. *Information Theory and Esthetic Perception*. Translated by Joel E. Cohen. Urbana: University of Illinois Press, 1966.

Mudrick, Marvin. "Character and Event in Fiction." *Yale Review* 50 (1961): 202-18.

Muir, Edwin. *The Structure of the Novel*. London: Hogarth Press, 1967.

Murch, A. E. *The Development of the Detective Novel*. London: Peter Owen, 1958.

Negley, Glenn, and Patrick, J. Max, eds. *The Quest for Utopia: An Anthology of Imaginary Societies*. New York: Henry Schuman, 1952.

Nietzsche, Friedrich. *The Use and Abuse of History*. Translated by Adrian Collins. New York: Liberal Arts Press, 1949.

Nye, Russel B. "History and Literature: Branches of the Same Tree." In *Essays on History and Literature*, edited by Robert H. Bremner. Columbus: Ohio State University Press, 1966.

Oakeshott, Michael. *Experience and Its Modes*. Cambridge: Cambridge University Press, 1933.

Ogden, C. K. *Bentham's Theory of Fictions*. London: Kegan Paul, 1932.

O'Hare, Charles Bernard. "Myth or Plot?: A Study in Ways of Ordering Narrative." *Arizona Quarterly* 8 (1957): 238-50.

Ortega Y. Gasset, José. *History as a System and Other Essays toward a Philosophy of History*. New York: Norton, 1961.

Pascal, Roy. *Design and Truth in Autobiography*. Cambridge, Mass.: Harvard University Press, 1960.

Patrides, C. A. *Milton and the Christian Tradition*. New York: Oxford University Press, 1966.

————. *The Phoenix and the Ladder: The Rise and Decline of the Christian View of History*. Berkeley and Los Angeles: University of California Press, 1964.

Paul, David. "Time and the Novelist." *Partisan Review* 21 (1954): 636–49.

Paulson, Ronald. *The Fictions of Satire*. Baltimore: Johns Hopkins University Press, 1967.

———. *Satire and the Novel in Eighteenth-Century England*. New Haven: Yale University Press, 1967.

Piaget, Jean. *Structuralism*. Translated by Chaninah Maschler. New York: Basic Books, 1970.

Popper, Karl R. *The Poverty of Historicism*. New York: Basic Books, 1957.

Preston, Thomas R. "Historiography as Art in Eighteenth-Century England." *Texas Studies in Language and Literature* 11 (1969): 1209–21.

Propp, Vladimir. *Morphology of the Folktale*. Austin: University of Texas Press, 1968.

Quigley, Carroll. *The Evolution of Civilizations: An Introduction to Historical Analysis*. New York: Macmillan, 1961.

Raglan, FitzRoy R. S. *The Hero: A Study in Tradition, Myth, and Drama*. London: Methuen, 1936.

Randall, John Herman, Jr. *Nature and Historical Experience*. New York: Columbia University Press, 1958.

Robbe-Grillet, Alain. *For a New Novel: Essays on Fiction*. Translated by Richard Howard. New York: Grove Press, 1965.

Rorty, Richard, ed. *The Linguistic Turn: Recent Essays in Philosophical Method*. Chicago: University of Chicago Press, 1967.

Rubin, Louis D., Jr. *The Teller in the Tale*. Seattle: University of Washington Press, 1967.

Sacks, Sheldon. *Fiction and the Shape of Belief*. Berkeley and Los Angeles: University of California Press, 1967.

Salvesen, Christopher. *The Landscape of Memory: A Study of Wordsworth's Poetry*. Lincoln: University of Nebraska Press, 1965.

Scholes, Robert, and Kellogg, Robert. *The Nature of Narrative*. New York: Oxford University Press, 1966.

Scott, Nathan A., Jr. *The Broken Center: Studies in the Theological Horizon of Modern Literature*. New Haven: Yale University Press, 1966.

Sebeok, Thomas A., ed. *Myth: A Symposium*. Bloomington: Indiana University Press, 1958.

Singer, Godfrey Frank. *The Epistolary Novel: Its Origin, Development, Decline, and Residuary Influence*. New York: Russell and Russell, 1953. Originally published 1933.

Spearman, Diana. *The Novel and Society*. New York: Barnes and Noble, 1966.

Stanzel, Franz. *Narrative Situations in the Novel: Tom Jones, Moby-Dick, The Ambassadors, Ulysses*. Translated by James P. Pusack. Bloomington: Indiana University Press, 1971.

Stevenson, W. Taylor. *History as Myth: The Import for Contemporary Theology*. New York: Seabury Press, 1969.

Stevick, Philip. *The Chapter in Fiction: Theories of Narrative Division.* Syracuse: Syracuse University Press, 1970.

———— "Fielding and the Meaning of History." *PMLA* 79 (1964): 561–68.

———— "Novel and Anatomy: Notes toward an Amplification of Frye." *Criticism* 10 (1968): 153–65.

———— "The Theory of Fictional Chapters." *Western Humanities Review* 20 (1966): 231–41.

Stover, Robert. *The Nature of Historical Thinking.* Chapel Hill: University of North Carolina Press, 1967.

Struever, Nancy. *The Language of History in the Renaissance.* Princeton: Princeton University Press, 1970.

Talbot, Daniel, ed. *Film: An Anthology.* New York: Simon and Schuster, 1959.

Tanner, Tony. *The Reign of Wonder: Naivety and Reality in American Literature.* London: Cambridge University Press, 1965.

Tate, Allen. "Techniques of Fiction." *Sewanee Review* 52 (1954): 210–25.

Teggart, Frederick J. *Theory and Process of History.* Berkeley and Los Angeles: University of California Press, 1960.

Thelander, Dorothy R. *Laclos and the Epistolary Novel.* Geneva: Librarie Droz, 1963.

Tillyard, E. M. W. *The English Epic and Its Background.* London: Chatto and Windus, 1954.

Vaihinger, Hans. *The Philosophy of "As If": A System of Theoretical, Practical and Religious Fictions of Mankind.* Translated by C. K. Ogden. London: Routledge and Kegan Paul, 1935.

Vico, Giambattista. *The New Science.* Translated by Thomas Goddard Bergin and Max Harold Fisch. Ithaca, N.Y.: Cornell University Press, 1968.

Ward, J. A. *The Search for Form: Studies in the Structure of James's Fiction.* Chapel Hill: University of North Carolina Press, 1967.

Watt, Ian. *The Rise of the Novel.* Berkeley and Los Angeles: University of California Press, 1957.

————, ed. *The Victorian Novel: Modern Essays in Criticism.* New York: Oxford University Press, 1971.

White, Morton. *Foundations of Historical Knowledge.* New York: Harper and Row, 1965.

Whyte, Lancelot Law. *Accent on Form.* New York: Harper and Brothers, 1954.

Wiesenfarth, Joseph. *Henry James and the Dramatic Analogy.* New York: Fordham University Press, 1963.

Williams, Raymond. *The English Novel from Dickens to Lawrence.* New York: Oxford University Press, 1970.

Woodbridge, Frederick J. E. *The Purpose of History.* Port Washington, N.Y.: Kennikat Press, 1916.

Acknowledgments

Grateful acknowledgment is made to the following publishers and persons for permission to use copyrighted material:

Alfred A. Knopf, Inc., for quotations from *The Collected Poems of Wallace Stevens*, copyright 1923, 1931, 1935–37, 1942–52, 1954 by Wallace Stevens, and from *Opus Posthumous* by Wallace Stevens, copyright © 1957 by Elsie Stevens and Holly Stevens. Reprinted by permission of Alfred A. Knopf, Inc.

Doubleday and Company, Inc., for lines of poetry from "The Far Field," copyright © 1962 by Beatrice Roethke, Administratrix of the Estate of Theodore Roethke, from the book *Collected Poems of Theodore Roethke.* Reprinted by permission of Doubleday and Company, Inc.

Faber and Faber, Ltd., for quotations from *The Collected Poems of Wallace Stevens* and "The Far Field" by Theodore Roethke. Reprinted by permission of Faber and Faber, Ltd.

The Macmillan Publishing Company, Inc., for "Two Songs from a Play" from *The Collected Poems of W. B. Yeats,* copyright 1919 by The Macmillan Company, renewed 1947 by Bertha Georgie Yeats. Reprinted with permission of Macmillan Publishing Company, Inc.

Mr. M. B. Yeats, the Macmillan Company of London and Basingstoke, and the Macmillan Company of Canada for "Two Songs from a Play" from *The Collected Poems of W. B. Yeats.* Reprinted by permission of Mr. M. B. Yeats, the Macmillan Company of London and Basingstoke, and the Macmillan Company of Canada.

Harcourt Brace Jovanovich, Inc., for eight lines from "Junk" by Richard Wilbur, from *The Poems of Richard Wilbur.*

Penguin Books, Ltd., for the extract from *Sir Gawain and the Green Knight,* edited by Francis Berry in Ford, B. (ed.): *The Pelican Guide to English Literature 1.* Reprinted by permission of Penguin Books, Ltd.

W. W. Norton and Company, Inc., and the Longman Group, Ltd., for the quotation from Marie Boroff's translation of *Sir Gawain and the Green Knight.*

Index